D1081178

BRAZILIAN COOKERY

Margarette de Andrade

BRAZILIAN COOKERY

4ª EDIÇÃO

EDITORA RECORD
RIO DE JANEIRO • SÃO PAULO
2005

CIP-Brasil. Catalogação-na-fonte
Sindicato Nacional dos Editores de Livros, RJ.

A568b
4ª ed.
Andrade, Margarette Sheehan de
    Brazilian cookery / Margarette de Andrade. — 4ª
ed. — Rio de Janeiro: Record, 2005.
    592p.

    ISBN 85-01-06054-2

    1. Culinária brasileira. I. Título.

01-1640
CDD — 641.5981
CDU — 641.568(81)

Cover photograph: Felipe Goifman
Production: Bar do Arnaudo
Graphic design: Glenda Rubinstein

All rights for Brazilian publishing:
DISTRIBUIDORA RECORD DE SERVIÇOS DE IMPRENSA S.A.
Rua Argentina 171 — Rio de Janeiro, RJ — 20921-380 — Tel.: 2585-2000

Printed in Brazil

ISBN 85-01-06054-2

PEDIDOS PELO REEMBOLSO POSTAL
Caixa Postal 23.052
Rio de Janeiro, RJ — 20922-970

EDITORA AFILIADA

Affectionately dedicated

to the memory of my mother
JANE WILLIAMS SHEEHAN
from whom I learned the rudiments of cookery

to fond recollections of my father
JEREMIAH JOSEPH SHEEHAN
who instilled in me an appreciation of fine cookery

and to my husband
GABRIEL DE ANDRADE
who introduced me to the vast realm of Brazilian cookery

Contents

FOREWORD

*Taking food and drink is a great enjoyment for healthy
people, and those who do not enjoy eating seldom have
much capacity for enjoyment or usefulness of any sort.*

CHARLES W. ELIOT, "THE HAPPY LIFE".

The heritage of a people is manifested in many expressions of its culture. This is as true in the culinary art as in any other form of art. Thus, in Brazil, where the ethnological background is Luso-Afro-Indian, we find that the traditional Brazilian recipes still in use today are derived from these three sources. The Indian supplied uses for the meals and flours native to his environment and for the fish found in the rivers and in the ocean. The Portuguese contributed codfish *(Bacalhau)* dishes and their stews *(Cozidos)* and they also brought with them the use of wine in cookery. It was from the Portuguese, too, that the Brazilians inherited the habit of using many eggs, cinnamon and sugar; a fondness which was introduced into Portuguese culture by the Moors. The African slaves were responsible for palm oil, condiments, spices and coconut milk, which they incorporated into such well-known Brazilian dishes as *Vatapá, Caruru, Moqueca*[1] and the fabulous desserts that call for pure coconut milk.

Add to these three strong roots the lush vegetation that produces practically all fruits and vegetables known to North Americans, as well as numerous others with which North Americans are not familiar, and you will have unlimited possibilities of preparing a variety of tasty and exotic dishes!

---

[1] *"Moqueca"* is sometimes spelled "muqueca."

9

The Brazilian cuisine is based, therefore, not only on a great wealth of raw material, but also on the diversity of skills and cultures applied in preparing what a bountiful Nature has provided.[2]

As the science of cookery evolved in Brazil, with new recipes devised along the way, the three main origins of native cookery became more or less blended into a distinctive type of cuisine. This does not mean, however, that regional food habits lost their identity through absorption into a common style of cookery. Certain areas of the country still serve predominantly regional dishes as an everyday item of the menu, as, for instance, *Vatapá*, which is available in all restaurants of Bahia as a daily part of the menu, while in Rio de Janeiro, the dish is only served occasionally in some restaurants.

At the same time, through the influx of large numbers of immigrants who settled in Brazil, such as the Germans in Santa Catarina and Rio Grande do Sul, and the Italians and Japanese in São Paulo and Paraná, new food habits were introduced. Coupled with this was the impact of the French cuisine, which was felt in Brazil, as in the rest of the civilized world, leaving a person to wonder how any of the original roots of Brazilian cookery have survived.

But survive they did! While the urban inhabitants, who travelled and were exposed to the cultures of other countries, were quick to accept new dishes, people who lived in the backlands and in smaller communities, separated from cities by hazardous and long journeys, were content to subsist on the same fare as their forefathers. This was fortunate for the Brazilians because it preserved many dishes which might otherwise have disappeared. The traditional recipes, that were copied in long hand and passed on from one generation to another, are part of the folklore of Brazil. Many of these notebooks were used by the distinguished Brazilian sociologist, Gilberto Freyre, in the preparation of his book, *Assucar*.

Although the number of recipes from which to choose is very large, it was decided to include in this book only those that would find acceptance by the American taste and, at the same time, be representative of an orthodox Brazilian cuisine. Sometimes it was difficult to adhere to this principle, as many popular dishes in

---

[2] This does not apply to the arid Northeast where periodic droughts wreak their toll in the destruction of livestock and vegetation.

Brazil, such as stuffed peppers or cabbage, several creamed and au gratin dishes, omelets, and others are quite well-known outside Brazil. Recipes in this category were omitted. Foreign recipes were also excluded, except, of course, those of Portuguese origin, which, in a final analysis, cannot really be considered foreign.

In many instances, due to increasing convenience in packaging, freezing and canning foodstuffs, it was found expedient to make use of prepared products. Consequently, the recipes offered have been modified to take advantage of this convenience. This expedient was not resorted to, however, if it interfered with an exact preparation of the Brazilian dish.

A few dessert recipes that originated in the kitchens of the Big Houses[3] of the sugar plantations were too sweet and rich, some calling for as many as 36 eggs. In a few such instances, the compiler has taken the liberty of adapting them to the modern economy and taste by diminishing the quantities of sugar and eggs, without any appreciable loss to the original recipe. Enough harm has already been done to foreign recipes through substituting ingredients and by so-called simplification to warrant exposing these excellent Brazilian recipes to such a fate. We have tried to avoid this pitfall of substitutive and short-cut cookery into which many a good recipe has been precipitated.

For the most part, the majority of recipes remain as they were received. Only the measurements have been converted from the metric system. All recipes have been tested and subjected to oven temperature control, which was introduced into Brazil a few years ago. The yield of each recipe in portions is purposely omitted as

---

[3] This was the name given to the great sugar and coffee plantations that flourished in Brazil until the last century. The master's house was erected in a courtyard and was surrounded by several smaller buildings used as slave quarters, infirmary, storage, barns, kitchens, etc. The Big House, in addition to living quarters, had its own chapel, library, playrooms and dining halls. Often it was furnished with rare antiques and works of art. Many times the master took care of his charges' money and the education of their children. In these surroundings, the master lived, and ruled and when he departed this life he was buried under the floor of the chapel. Thus the Big House represented a complete economic, political and social system, for it served as fortress, bank, hospital, school, church and cemetery. For a complete description of this phase of Brazilian living, see Gilberto Freyre's book, *The Masters and the Slaves* published by Alfred A. Knopf, Incl, New York, 1945.

we feel this is an arbitrary measurement, since a serving to one person may not be the same to another. However, when standard-size baking tins or molds have been used, the yield is included in the recipe.

It should be remembered that using equal measurements each time does not necessarily guarantee that the resulting product will be exactly the same. Two cooks may use the same cake recipe, but due to differences in beating, in the type and size of baking pans or the quality of the sugar, flour or size of eggs, or even the insulation of the oven, the texture of the cakes will vary.

Attention is also called to the Conversion Charts for weights and temperatures included at the end of the book for the convenience of those who use the metric system, and to the list of Egg Yolk, Egg White Recipes to facilitate the use of leftover portions.

Sample menus are given for informal and formal meals so that the reader will have some idea as to how menus are planned in Brazil.

Original Brazilian names have been preserved not only because of their interesting descriptive connotation, like "Dreams", "Mother-in-Law's Eyes", "Mother Benta", "Little Couples", "I Want More", "Old Clothes" etc., but also because these recipes are traditional and are known throughout Brazil by these names.

As a final word, may we express the hope that this modest work, inspired by a keen appreciation for the Brazilian people and all the good things of their great and wonderful country, will not only serve to bring many delicious Brazilian dishes to North American tables, but will also, through the fine art of culinary skill which speaks a universal language, enable us to know, to value and to understand our Southern friends better.

ACKNOWLEDGMENTS

I am indebted to many people for their help in making this book possible, especially to those kind Brazilians who were so willing to share their treasured family recipes with me. I started collecting and translating Brazilian recipes for my own use and enjoyment as far back as 1927. Whenever possible, I have indicated the name of the donor of the recipe and his/her place of birth. However, through the many transitions and vicissitudes with which passing years can be fraught, a few recipes were separated from the names of their gracious donors. These anonymous contributors merit a special word of grateful appreciaton together with an apology for the circumstances producing their anonymity.

However, many whose names do not appear with recipes participated in the organization of this work. I am very thankful to two of my dear friends who passed away before this book went into print: the late Dr. Gustavo de Sa Lessa, for his cooperation in collecting old family recipes from Brazilian gourmet cooks and for the precious time allotted me from his own busy schedule; and to the late Ambassador João Carlos Muniz, Brazilian statesman and man of letters, who furnished excellent suggestions for the format.

Several recipes are translations I made and adapted to standard measurements and oven temperature control. These recipes, all of which are accompanied by a notation of their source, were used with the permission of the following authors and publishers: Maria Tereza Senise, *A Cozinha Deliciosa e Moderna,* published by Editora Minerva, Ltda., Rio de Janeiro; Myrthes Paranhos, *Receitas Culinárias,* published by Editora Letras e Artes, Rio de Janeiro. Tecnoprint Gráfica, Rio de Janeiro allowed me to use recipes of I. Lund and Lígia Junqueira from *A Arte de Fazer Doces, 150 Receitas de Aves* and *150 Receitas de Docinhos.* Recipes are also included from *Noções de Arte Culinária,* by Maria Tereza A. Costa, São Paulo by permission of her daughter, Alice Abreu Costa. This was published by the Instituto D. Anna Rosa, São Paulo.

13

Livraria José Olympio Editora, of Rio de Janeiro and São Paulo, allowed me to translate and publish some recipes from *As Receitas para Você da Tia Evelina*, 4th edition. The Livraria São José, from Rio de Janeiro, permitted me to translate and publish several recipes from *A Arte de Comer Bem* by Rosa Maria, as they now own the rights to this book written by Mme. H. Leonardos.

Mr. Bolivar Figueiredo, from Decorações Old & New, in Rio de Janeiro, was instrumental in obtaining the recipe for "Sopa Leão Velloso," Ambassador Leão Velloso's famous fish soup, from Mr. João Machado, owner of the noted A Cabaça Grande restaurant in Rio de Janeiro, where this soup is featured. I also appreciate the kindness of Dr. Gilberto Freyre in allowing me to include his Recipe "Quindins de Yayá" from his book *Assucar*. I should mention too that Dr. Freyre's monumental work, *The Masters and the Slaves* was a very valuable source of reference.

A kind word of thanks is due to my old friend, Mrs. Beulah Kilduff, who tested five of the recipes for me, and to my Brazilian friends, Mme. Ignez Barros Barreto Correia d'Araujo for her recipes and for acting as a sort of liaison contact with some Brazilian authors and publishers, and to Mr. Victor da Silva, who rendered the same service.

I also wish to express my appreciation to Mme. Paulo Cirne, the daughter of Mme. Gudesteu Pires (Laurita Pires) who made her mother's recipe notebook available to me, and, when time prevented copying all the fine recipes I had selected, Mme. Cirne herself kindly typed them and brought them to me the day I was leaving Brazil. I was also fortunate in having at my disposal the notebook of Mme. Hilda Leite Queiroga, which her daughter, Mme. Elza Queiroga, allowed me to use. My old friend, Mme. Eder Jansen de Mello, gave me many of her favorite recipes, and, in some instances, when distance made research difficult, my queries to her brought prompt replies.

The New York Times Cookbook gave me permission to reprint the recipe they published for "*Feijoada*" and *The Washington Post* and *Gourmet Magazine* allowed me to use some of my material which appeared in their publications. The data on "Testing Candies", taken from Meta Clivens *Modern Encyclopedia of Cooking*, is reprinted by permission of the J. C. Ferguson Publishing Company. The nostalgic account of Easter in Victoria was translated from a short article written by the Brazilian journalist, Dr. Newton de Freitas. As he was out of Brazil, in Victoria, where Easter is celebrated in a pituresque manner, Mme. de Freitas very kindly informed me she was sure her husband would not object.

14

Acknowledgements

The beautiful "Butterfly Cake" is the creation of Miss Cybele Simões Magro who baked and decorated it. This cake and a running commentary on it also appeared in *The Washington Post*. Mr. Luiz Flávio de Faro lent his skill as a photographer in capturing the beauty of Miss Magro's workmanship and artistry.

The distinguished Brazilian artist, Carybé, has brilliantly transcribed the spirit of the book by his outstanding and excellent illustrations. His lovely designs not only enhance this modest work on Brazilian cookery, but they convey that particular and special sense of local color emanated by Brazil, which is distinctive to Brazil alone.

To the Charles E. Tuttle Company, Inc. and their wonderful staff in Rutland, Vermont and Tokyo, Japan, I offer very special thanks! They were exceedingly patient, courteous and friendly in coping with the many improvements made to the original manuscript. Their suggestions to make the book more attractive were of great value. They considered *Brazilian Cookery: Traditional and Modern* a challenge to their best ability and achievement and for this approach, and for the reasons mentioned above, I take pleasure in letting all you readers know how very much I am indebted to the Charles E. Tuttle Company, and especially to Mr. Roland A. Mulhauser, Production Section Chief, who painstakingly supervised the book's production and to Mr. Kaoru Ogimi, who was responsible for the basic design.

It can readily be seen from this formidable list of distinguished personages, in which the publisher is included, that whatever merit this book has stems from the collective assistance and good will derived from many sources as well as my own desire to present the best of Brazilian cookery to the English-speaking public.

However, in addition to the many people who were so willing to cooperate and to share in what has been a most happy and rewarding adventure to me, I must add a special word of thanks to my colleagues on the staff of the Brazilian Embassy in Washington, where the idea for this book took root nearly four years ago. Their continued interest and enthusiasm in the project, which has never waned during this time, was more than an inspiration! It was like that extra prod the experienced jockey uses to spur his mount past the flag. Their eagerness and their encouragement to see or possess this work in its finality furnished me a goal. And now the goal has been attained!

CHAPTER 1

THE BRAZILIAN HOUSEWIFE
PLANS A MENU

Although middle class and wealthy Brazilian families adhere to the French manner of menu-planning and serving, this does not necessarily mean that they restrict themselves to French cuisine. On the contrary, taking into consideration the rich background of Brazilian cookery, the development of regional dishes and the diversity of raw materials, especially fruits and vegetables, menu-making in Brazil can be a very interesting chore and can result in an infinite variety of combinations, without having to resort to foreign dishes.

Beverages, while not indicated in the following menus, accompany the meal and may precede it as an appetizer or apéritif. This applies to both alcoholic and non-alcoholic beverages as well as liqueurs which are part of all formal meals. Hors d'oeuvres, or tidbits which the hostess serves before the guests are seated at the table, may be found in the chapter on "Appetizers and Sandwich Fillings," are also omitted from these menus.

Formal meals are served in courses and often informal lunches and dinners are also brought to the table in courses. Fruits, of which there is a great variety in Brazil, are always a course of all formal meals and are frequently a part of informal lunches and dinners as well. Cheese usually comes to the table with the dessert course, especially when the meal is not ceremonious. Meals are always concluded with the ever-present Brazilian demitasse. While not shown in some of the following menus, it goes without saying that the staples — beans, rice and manioc meal (*Farinha*) — are always available for lunch. These foodstuffs, incidentally, form the basic fare of the great laboring classes of Brazilians and are the mainstay of their subsistence.

Soup comes into its own in Brazil! It is served extensively for both lunch and dinner. The standard breakfast in most parts of the country, and in all urban areas, consists of coffee with milk, bread and butter and possibly fruit. Therefore, when lunch time arrives a hearty meal, often beginning with soup, is quite in order.

Holiday fare differs from everyday menus in that special dishes are traditionally served. Christmas, Easter and St. John's Day are the principal festive days, each characterized by certain foods: turkey for Christmas, or possibly roast suckling pig; codfish for Easter, with *Rabanadas* for dessert. *Rabanada*, which is a glorified French toast, appears again at Christmas. Foods prepared with pumpkin or corn are served at St. John's Day parties. In Bahia State, this day brings forth *Mungunzá*, a sweet pudding made of hominy and cinnamon.

Feijoada is also a festive meal and one which the Brazilian takes pride in introducing to foreign visitors, as well he might, for properly prepared, a *Feijoada Completa* is actually gourmet fare. *Cuscuz* and *Vatapá* are also special dishes which could be served as a whole meal. The Brazilian hostess, however, prefers to have them highlight a meal.

Informal Luncheons
Almoços Informais

Bean Purée with Coconut Milk *(Feijão de Coco)*
Baked Stuffed Fish *(Peixe Recheado)*
Vegetable Cake *(Bolo de Legumes)*
Mango Sherbet *(Sorvete de Manga)*

Chopped Beef, Brazilian Style *(Carne Picadinha)* with
Butter with Manioc Meal *(Farofa de Manteiga)* and
Mashed Potatoes *(Purê de Batatas)* or
Brazilian Rice *(Arroz Brasileiro)*
String Beans *(Vagens)*
Milk Sweet, with Cheese *(Doce de Leite com Queijo)*

Codfish with Chick-peas *(Bacalhau com Grão-de-Bico)*
Stewed Lamb Kidneys *(Rins de Carneiro Ensopado)*
Brazilian Rice *(Arroz Brasileiro)*
Velvet Pudding *(Pudim de Veludo)*

Farmer's Soup *(Sopa Camponesa)*
Chicken and Bacon *(Frango com Toucinho)* with
Fried Potatoes *(Batatas Fritas)*
Cassava Cake with Cheese *(Bolo de Mandioca com Queijo)*

Edward Salad *(Salada Eduardo)*
Old Clothes *(Roupa-velha)* with
Black Bean Tutú No. 2 *(Tutu de Feijão No. 2)* with
Kale or Collards Mineira *(Couve à Mineira)*
Orange Foam *(Espuma de Laranja)*

Formal Luncheons
Almoços de Cerimônia

Baked Fish with Beer *(Peixe Assado com Cerveja)* with
Corn "Pirão" *(Pirão de Milho)*
Chicken with Fruit Sauce *(Galinha com Molho de Frutas)*
Plain Lettuce Salad *(Salada de Alface)*
Chestnut and Sponge Cake Pudding *(Pudim de Pão-de-ló e Castanhas)*

Chicken Soup with Rice (*Canja*) with
Cornstarch Rusks (*Roscas de Maisena*)
Steak, Portuguese Style *(Bife à Portuguesa)* with
French Fried Palm Hearts *(Palmito)* and
Pineapple Salad *(Salada de Abacaxi)*
Coconut Blancmange *(Manjar Branco de Coco)*

Avocado Mousse *(Musse de Abacate)* garnished with
Ham Cigars *(Charutos de Presunto)*
Hot Stuffed Pork Loin *(Lombo de Porco Recheado)* with
Carrot "Farofa" *(Farofa de Cenouras)*
Broccoli Pudding *(Pudim de Brócolis)*
Prune Soufflé *(Soufflé de Ameixas)*

Palm Heart Salad No. 1 *(Salada de Palmito Nº 1)* with
Algerian Biscuits *(Biscoitos Algerianos)*
Veal Cutlets No. 1 *(Costeletas de Vitela Nº 1)* with
Multicolored Pudding *(Pudim Multicolor)*
Heavenly Cream *(Creme de Céu)*

Corn and Shrimp Casserole *(Caçarola de Milho com Camarão)* with
Brazilian Rice *(Arroz Brasileiro)*
Beef cooked with Beer No. 2 *(Bife com Cerveja Nº 2)* with
Potato Roly-poly *(Rocambole de Batatas)*
Apple Pudding *(Pudim de Maçã)*

Informal Dinners
Jantares Informais

Black Bean Soup *(Sopa de Feijão Preto)*
Codfish Soufflé *(Soufflée de Bacalhau)* with
Brazilian Rice *(Arroz Brasileiro)*
Meat Balls No. 1 *(Almôndegas Nº 1)* with
Chayote Grapes *(Chuchu como Uvas)*[1]
Brazilian Pudding *(Pudim Brasileiro)*

Eggplant with Shrimp *(Berinjela com Camarão)*
Chicken with Dark Brown Gravy *(Frango ao Molho Pardo)* with
Brazilian Rice *(Arroz Brasileiro)*
Spinach Salad *(Salada de Espinafre)*
Cheese *(Queijão)*

Pumpkin Soup No. 1 *(Sopa de Abóbora Nº 1)*
Fish Pudding *(Pudim de Peixe)*
Liver No. 2 *(Fígado Nº 2)* with
Cabbage and Wine *(Repolho com Vinho)*
Baked Bananas with Cheese *(Bananas Assadas com Queijo)*

---

[1] The chayote *(chuchu)* is imported from Puerto Rico and is usually available in Latin American grocery stores of the larger American cities. As a good substitute the flat, green round squash can be used. (See chapter on vegetables.)

Cheese Pie *(Empada de Queijo)* with
Green Peas *(Ervilhas)*
Meat Loaf *(Bolo de Carne)* with
Florida Rice *(Arroz Flórida)*
Walnut Cake *(Bolo de Nozes)*

Cold Codfish Salad *(Salada de Bacalhau)*
Steaks in Milk Sauce *(Bifes com Molho de Leite)* with
Stuffed Sweet Potatoes *(Batata-doce Recheada)*
Orange "Bom Bocados" *(Bom-bocados de Laranja)*

Formal Dinners
Jantares de Cerimônia

Peanut Soup *(Sopa de Amendoim)*
Crab Meat Scramble *(Fritada de Caranguejos)* with
Beer Twists or Rusks *(Rosquinhas de Cerveja)*
Stuffed Veal *(Vitela Recheada)* with
Golden Baby Turnips *(Nabos Dourados)* and
Buttered Green Peas *(Ervilhas com Manteiga)*
White Short Cake *(Bolo de Claras com Morangos)*

Turtle Soup No. 1 *(Sopa de Tartaruga Nº 1)* with
Crackers *(Biscoitos)*
"Prato Fino"
Fresh Roast Pork *(Pernil de Porco)* with
Golden "Farofa" *(Farofa de Ouro)* and
Stuffed Carrots *(Cenouras Recheadas)*
Wafer Cake *(Torta em Camadas)*

Palm Heart Soup *(Sopa de Palmito)*
Stuffed Avocados No. 1 *(Abacates Nº 1)* with
"Cuca"
Shrimp in Cognac *(Camarão em Cognac)* garnished with
Wedges of Buttered Toast *(Torradas)*
Chicken in Peanut Sauce *(Galinha com Molho de Amendoim)*
with Shoe String Potatoes
Leticia's Cream *(Creme Letícia)*

Cream of Cucumber Soup *(Sopa de Creme de Pepinos)*
Fish Steaks with Rose "Pirão" *(Costeletas de Peixe com Batatas Rosadas)*
Stuffed Rolled Beef *(Bifes Recheados)* with
Bean Scramble *(Fritada de Vagens)*
Coconut Pudding No. 1 *(Pudim de Coco Nº 1)*

Shrimp Bisque *(Sopa de Camarão)* with
Croutons
Veal Loaf No. 1 *(Bolo de Vitela Nº 1)* with
Beetroot and Potato Salad *(Salada de Beterrabas e Batatas)*
Tropical Duck *(Pato Tropical)* with
Cauliflower with Ham *(Couve-flor com Presunto)*
Diamantina Blancmange *(Manjar Diamantinense)*

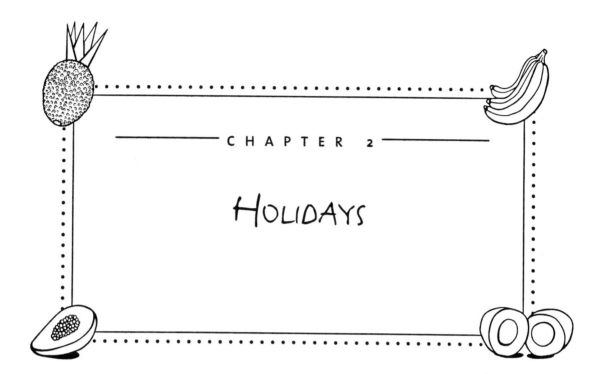

CHAPTER 2

HOLIDAYS

Christmas and St. John's day are commemorated in Brazil with many traditional and folkloric observances along with the custom of serving special foods for these holidays. Other holidays, like Easter and Carnival, which entails a three-day procession of parades, galas and samba schools,[1] are not accompanied by the customary culinary preparations surrounding Christmas and St. John's.

The most important *dia de festa* is Christmas. Replicas of the Holy Child in the Manger are displayed throughout the land and many times these *presépios* or crèches are a fascinating conglomeration of requisites for modern living, in so far as miniature trains, airplanes and factories appear among the pastoral figurines associated with Christ's Bethlehem. The rural Brazilian Christmas is especially interesting and lovely for it embodies so many picturesque manifestations of Brazilian folklore.

The Christmas Cycle in rural areas begins on December 24 and terminates on the Day of the Kings, January 6. During this period, several traditional pageants, tableaux and dances are enacted and there is much singing and music. The folkloric part of the Christmas Cycle is not celebrated in the large cities of Brazil where residents content themselves with a spectacular appearance of Santa Claus *(Papai Noel)* and erect beautifully-decorated Christmas trees in the public squares. There are also programs involving distribution of toys to the underprivileged children and gifts of food to the needy. Presents are exchanged and, in late years, the custom of sending greeting cards has come into prominence.

---

[1] Samba Schools are very colorful organizations whose members make regular contributions used for the sole purpose of participating in the three-day Carnival celebration. The funds received are spent for their costumes and banners, and such other properties as are required for Carnival. Members prepare all year writing music, rehearsing dance steps and designing their costumes, for there is a prize awarded to the best School. Lately, the government has been giving a small subsidy to some of the Schools.

Inhabitants of both rural and urban areas attend Midnight Mass, which in Portuguese is called *Missa do Galo* (Mass of the Rooster). After Mass, each family repairs to its home where a *ceia* or late supper awaits them. Usually, the *ceia* is only for the family, but guests are invited to partake of the Christmas Day lunch or dinner.[1]

MENU FOR A CHRISTMAS SUPPER

Roast Turkey, Brazilian Style with
"Farofa"
French Toast made with Port Wine
Raisins and Dried Fruits
Nuts, both Domestic and Imported
Party Punch
Demitasse

ST. JOHN'S DAY

June 24 is St. John's day in Brazil and also a very special holiday in the northern part of the country. It is also the day of the feast of the maize, hence the reason why so many dishes prepared with corn enter into the festivities surrounding celebrations of St. John's Day. But, first and foremost, St. John is looked to as a marrying saint and maidens seeking a husband appeal to him for a spouse. At parties on this day they sing:

---

[1] For more details concerning Christmas, see *Christmas in Brazil* by Margaret de Andrade, distributed by the Brazilian Government Trade Bureau, 551 Fifth Avenue, New York.

Dai-me noivo, S. João, dai-me noivo,

Dai-me noivo, que me quero casar.

(Give me a bridegroom, St. John, give me a bridegroom,

Give me a bridegroom, I pray, for I fain would wed.)[3]

Preparing the Corn

Usually St. John's Day parties take place at night in the open air. Lanterns are hung from the trees and fireworks enliven the occasion. A traditional part of the celebration are the bonfires, not unwelcome, for June 24 is supposed to be one of the coldest days of the year. Not unwelcome either are the steaming mugs of *quentão* (hot spiced Brazilian rum) passed among the guests. Sweet potatoes and corn are roasted in the fire as guests make merry by singing and dancing. Midnight signals the time for two young people to join hands and jump over the fire. This is to ensure they become lifelong friends or, as is said in Portuguese, *compadres.*

An important part of the St. John's Day activities is fortune telling. This is done in a myriad of ways, but some of the most popular are by "reading" an egg white dropped into a cup of water; by deciphering the spots left on a knife which has been plunged into a banana tree or by tucking an ear of corn under one's pillow to dream of the one who comes to eat it. Pouring hot wax into cold water and interpreting the shapes is another method used to determine the profession of one's future husband. This is also done on St. Anthony's Day, since this saint is also connected with love interests.

St. John's Day parties are distinguished by a special costume. This is called the *caipira,* which is the Brazilian counterpart of what a country peasant would wear. For the girls, this involves a full skirt of flowered material, a blouse and a straw hat. The boys wear old trousers, shirts that have seen better days and kerchiefs tied around their necks. Their costume is also topped by a straw hat.
Foods made with corn, pumpkin and sweet potatoes are typical refreshments for a St. John's Day party.

---

[3] Gilberto Freyre, *The Masters and the Slaves* (New York: Alfred A. Knopf, 1956), p. 255.

St. John's Day Refreshments

Mungunzá[4]
Pamonha
Pumpkin Candy
Baked Sweet Potatoes
Quentão
Demitasse

While Brazil has its own traditional, and exceedingly beautiful way of heralding the birth of Christ, and naively imploring, in a completely Brazilian manner, the good St. John for a satisfactory spouse, many European usages have been imported in commemorating Easter. Those familiar with the American Easter Basket (which the Easter Bunny was said to have left under the children's beds) will find a similarity in the nest containing chocolate eggs that Brazilian parents place under their offsprings' beds. The Easter Rabbit has also made its appearance in Brazil!

However, in Victoria, an island which is the capital of Espírito Santo State, many households observe Easter as in days of old. The famous *Torta da Semana Santa* (Holy Week Pie) is the typical dish prepared for the Easter table of Victoria. Also known as *Torta Capixaba*,[5] this deliciously-seasoned mixture of fish and shell-fish is featured in most homes of Victoria during Holy Week. And should it not be prepared in a given home, rest assured that before the Holy Week is over some neighbor or friend will send one to the household, for it is the custom at this time of the year to present one's friends and neighbors with a *Torta*; a sort of emblem of

---

[4] This is a pudding made of hominy, milk, sugar and cinnamon, which is called *Canjica* in São Paulo and Minas Gerais and *Chá-de-Burro* (Mule's Tea) in some parts of Brazil. Canjica is also made from grated fresh corn. See also footnotes on pages 184/302.

[5] *Capixaba* is the name given to inhabitants of Espírito Santo State. It is interesting to note that the *Torta* has become such an important tradition of this locale that it has even penetrated literary circles of the area. In 1962, Guilherme Santos Neves published a book which he called *Torta Capixaba*, which is actually a collection of poems and literary works of the men of letters of Victoria. He also gives a recipe for the *Torta*.

good fellowship commemorating the sadness and gladness of the Easter Season. And for those away from home at Easter let it be said that many planes leaving Victoria have consignments of *Tortas* destined for *Capixabas* away from home!

But let us see what one *Capixaba* — the journalist, Newton Freitas — wrote about Easter in his homeland and about its principal culinary product. The following is a translation of his article which appeared in the Rio de Janeiro daily newspaper, *Diário de Notícias,* on April 2, 1961.

EASTER TRADITION AND "SAUDADES"[6]

by Newton Freitas

Of all the celebrations I attended during my childhood in Victoria, in spite of the strict routine we were obliged to follow at home, those of Holy Week were the ones I liked best! My Mother forbade us to show any signs of gaiety; to laugh or sing or to shout to anyone; playing cards or whistling were likewise frowned upon. Yet, we waited patiently for the dawn of Easter Saturday when we could club and burn the effigy of Judas, which made its appearance at daybreak, hanging on the abandoned gaslamp in front of the big old house on our street.

During Holy Week, we also looked forward to the arrival of the fishing canoes. We helped to pull my Uncle Beno's trawl net to neighboring islands. We gathered crabs on the banks of the rivers flowing into the bay of Victoria; we dived to pull away the lobsters clinging to marine caves; and at night, with small-meshed nets, we would fill our baskets with shrimp. Our seafaring work would be completed with long trips to adjoining islands, pulling live clams, oysters and crabs from the rocks. It was more sport than work! With what happiness we jumped into the canoes to sail in the moonlight, when there was a moon! Later, came the domestic

---

[6] When a Brazilian says he has *saudades* he means several different sentiments or emotions: a yearning or longing for someone or something or a nostalgia or homesickness for some place.

work — preparing the shellfish for the famous Holy Week Pie — a typical dish of my homeland. It is our invention — unique — and it definitely identifies our island as a maritime civilization. It is eaten once a year, on Good Friday. Here is the recipe — a *saudosa* recipe:

Two strings of crabs,[7] one plate of shucked mussels and oysters, one plate of cleaned shrimp, one plate of lobster meat, one pound of codfish or other dried fish, palm hearts, palm oil (optional), coconut milk (also optional) and seasonings (coriander, powdered cumin, cloves). Cook all these ingredients, then sauté them in a good *Refogado*,[8] pulling the fish apart into strips. Mix well in an earthenware dish. Pour beaten eggs on top, garnish with thinly sliced onions and olives and bake in a medium heated oven until the eggs are set and the top of the dish is browned.

Eat this *Torta*, either hot or cold, distributing it amongst friends and neighbors, in accordance with regional custom, is the great tradition of *Espírito Santo*. It is a form of friendly communion, which brings men of good will together around fish and wine.

---

[7] In Espírito Santo (its capital is the Island of Victoria) the crabs are strung by the fishermen, usually six to a string. And that is the way they are sold at the markets and by the street venders.

[8] See chapter on "Meats," p. 369.

Holy Week Pie

adapted from Newton Freitas' recipe

1 pound salted codfish • 3/4 cup olive oil (or palm oil) • 2 large minced onions 1/2 chopped malagueta pepper • 2 cloves of garlic • 1 teaspoon salt • 4 large tomatoes, peeled and chopped • 1/4 cup chopped parsley • 1 pound cleaned, deveined fresh shrimp 1 pound crabmeat • 1 dozen raw oysters and 1 dozen clams (shucked and separated from their juices) • 1 pound lobster meat • 1/4 cup lemon juice • 1 small can sliced palm hearts • Black pepper • 1 dozen eggs • Thinly-sliced onions and sliced olives for garnish

Remove the salt from the codfish following one of the methods suggested in the chapter on Fish, and set aside. Heat oil in a very large skillet and sauté onions, malagueta pepper, and garlic pounded with the salt, and then add the tomatoes and parsley. Cover and cook all the vegetables for 10 minutes over medium heat, stirring so that they will all blend together. If coriander, cumin or cloves are desired for seasoning, they should be added at this time.

Add codfish, shrimp, crabmeat, oysters, clams and lobster meat to the sautéed vegetables and cook over medium heat until they are done. Sprinkle with lemon juice and let stand 10 minutes.

Add the oyster and clam juices, palm hearts, black pepper and check seasonings. Transfer contents to a large buttered earthenware casserole. Beat eggs with a little salt and pour over the mixture. Garnish with onion slices and olives. Bake in oven preheated at 375° until the *Torta Capixaba* is dry and browned on top. It is necessary that it be dry because the pie is also served cold in wedges.

In days gone, by this traditional *Torta da Semana Santa* was served around 8:00 p.m. on Good Friday. Nowadays, it is served as lunch, dinner or supper on Good Fridays and also Holy Saturday and Easter Sunday.

CHAPTER 3

A WORD ABOUT COCONUT

Coconut is such an important ingredient in Brazilian cookery that it merits a few words apart. You will find coconut or coconut milk used in almost every chapter of this book! The coconut lends itself equally well to the preparation of sweets (cakes, candies, cookies, puddings and desserts) as it does to the delicious dishes made with fish, shellfish and poultry. You will even find coconut milk in soup and made up into a thick mush to accompany the famous Brazilian *Vatapás* and *Moquecas*, not to mention many excellent cocktails.

In large Brazilian cities one can buy coconut milk already prepared, but extracting the milk in your own kitchen is not difficult. This is accomplished by piercing the coconut on the end having the three small dimples, and allowing the water to drain into a vessel. This may be reserved to use in extracting the *thin* milk described below, if desired. Place the whole coconut in a hot oven for 5 or 10 minutes. Take it from the oven, crack the outer shell and remove pieces of coconut. The heavy dark skin has to be peeled with a paring knife.

Grate the coconut very finely and heat gently in a double boiler. When the coconut is hot, add 1/2 cup warm water and press out the *thick* milk through a very fine sieve or a heavy cheese cloth. It may be necessary to squeeze the coconut by hand and then strain. One coconut should average about 3/4 cup thick milk. From the residue, after the *thick* milk has been removed, extract the *thin* milk in accordance with that required by the recipe. Thus, if a recipe calls for 3 cups of *thin* milk, this can be obtained by extracting with a little over 3 cups of warm water.

Large city markets sell freshly grated coconut, usually at the stands that sell fresh horse-radish. The freshly grated coconut may be frozen and used as needed.

Packaged shredded and grated coconut may be used in some of the recipes, but you cannot extract the *thick* milk from these commercialized products. I have had good results in using packaged coconut in some of the candy recipes.

It is also possible to purchase a coconut flavoring extract, which has not been on the market very long. I have used it in some recipes calling for *thin* coconut milk by flavoring cow's milk and proceding with the recipe.

In buying fresh coconut be sure that the shell is not cracked and shake it to see if there is still water inside.

An average coconut yields approximately 1 pound of freshly-grated nut meat, sufficient to prepare about 3/4 cup of *thick* milk and from 2 1/2 to 4 cups of *thin* milk.

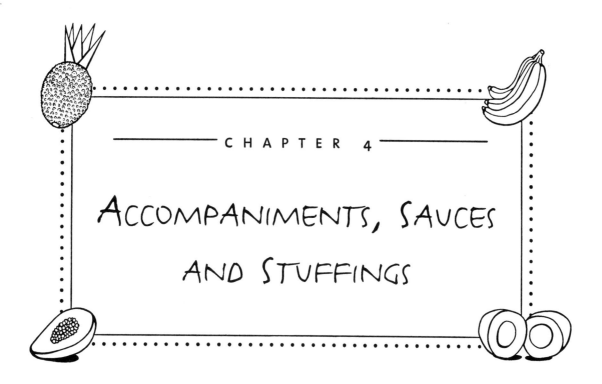

CHAPTER 4

ACCOMPANIMENTS, SAUCES AND STUFFINGS

Socrates said that best sauce in the world
for meats is to be hungry.

ERASMUS, "APOTHEGRAMS 2" (UDALL TRANS. 1542)

N o one can deny that various dishes are improved by serving an auxiliary accompaniment: something which will enhance both the taste and appearance of the dish. Brazilian culinary artists are great exponents of this axiom. Many food courses simply demand a proper accompaniment. Like a beautiful painting without a frame, the dish would be considered incomplete unless its own special accessory food were brought to the table with it.

From a gourmet standpoint, this arrangement is excellent as it presents the dish in its very best light. The sauces served with Afro-Brazilian foods — the *Angus* and *Farofas* — are perfect complements to the foods with which they are associated.

Angu and *Pirão* are types of heavy, salted porridge. They can be made into a mush from corn meal, the same as is so popular in the Southern United States. However *Angu* and *Pirão* — unlike the mush served in Southern United States — are also made from the many meals and flours used so adeptly by the Brazilian housewife (such as manioc meal, tapioca, rice or corn flours). The liquid employed can be plain water, coconut milk or a highly-seasoned broth. These *Angus* and *Pirões* are usually moulded and served either hot or cold as an accompaniment to meat, fish or fowl.

This practice of presenting auxiliary foods as complements to a main dish applies not only to salted dishes, but it also extends from the soup to the dessert course. Guava Paste,[1] for example, is a dessert, but very often cheese or bananas are eaten with it. Many popular Brazilian desserts also call for cheese and, unless you have tasted coconut pudding with a wedge of one of Brazil's popular cheeses, you cannot judge just how delicious such combinations can be. Referring to cheese with sweets, Freyre states: "The tourist tastes our *Goiaba* or *Caju* in compote — here,

---

[1] See chapter on Desserts, p. 285.

as all over Brazil, eaten with cheese. This is the orthodox manner of eating any sweet in Pernambuco."[2]

Cheese happens to be a very important food item in Brazil — just as popular as in this country. Not only does it go to the table with the dessert course or as a course by itself, but it is used extensively in cooking, especially the Brazilian-produced Parmesan, which finds its way into many tasty candies, puddings and cakes as well as soups, entrées and salads. This domestic Parmesan, along with Ricotta, Mozzarella, Gorgonzola and other types of Italian cheese are all now produced in Brazil, but the imported varieties are also available.

Even though Brazil ranks third in cheese production among American nations,[3] it still does not produce enough for its own consumption. In 1962, it was necessary to import 84,000 pounds.[4]

An estimated 35 kinds of cheese are produced in Brazil. These are classified as follows:[5]

SOFT CHEESES: *Gongonzola, Ricotta (fresh), Minas, Roquefort, Requeijão, Strachino, Camembert, Fundido, Itálico.*

SEMI-HARD CHEESES: *Reino, Estepe, Emental, Fontina, Gouda, Gruyere, Mozzarella, Siciliano, Tilsit, Minas, Prato, Minas Pasteurized, Minas (Serro), Port Salut.*

HARD CHEESES: *Caccio Cavalo, Parmesão, Ricotta (smoked), Provolone, Minas (Araxá), Queijo de Coalho, Requeijão do Norte, Pecorina.*

---

[2] Gilberto Freyre, *Guia Prático, Histórico e Sentimental da Cidade de Recife* (Rio de Janeiro: Livraria José Olympio, 1942), p. 149.

[3] According to 1962 figures from "Creamery, Butter and Cheeses Estimates" of the U.S. Department of Agriculture, production was: U.S. 1,571,295,000 pounds; Argentina, 297,621,000 pounds and Brazil 83,775,000 pounds.

[4] 73,000 pounds were imported from Argentina, according to a U.S. "Report from Brazil to the Dairy and Poultry Branch of the Foreign Agricultural Service".

[5] U.S. Foreign Agricultural Service Report No. AGR 71, May 10, 1960.

The most popular types of cheeses are Minas, similar to Muenster; Prato, like a bland American; and Parmesan.

One of the most glamorous accompaniments in Brazilian cookery is called *Fios de Ovos* (egg threads). Actually, this is a sweet. As such it could normally be classified among the Brazilian desserts. However, since the *Fios* are usually served as an accompaniment, the recipe finds an honored place in this chapter. As a general rule, *Fios de Ovos* is more at home with desserts, but lately it has come into use as an accompaniment to roast turkey.

The delicate golden strands of eggs are artistically arranged around the turkey, or they may be wrapped in thin slices of boiled ham to serve as a garnish. Sometimes prunes or dates are stuffed with the glistening yellow threads and the fruit is then used as a means to glorify other dishes. Dramatization of the *Fios* by using them with turkey and other entrées has only taken place within the last few years.

Ingredients for preparing *Fios de Ovos* are simple: egg yolks and a medium sugar syrup — but the cooking process demands a great deal of skill and good judgement. Because of the large number of egg yolks required to make this garnish, *Fios de Ovos* is an expensive dish to prepare. The threads are made by slowly dropping egg yolks through a special funnel having three points into the hot sugar syrup. When the egg threads have solidified, they are removed with a strainer and then plunged into water to which a little syrup or rose water has been added. They are then shaped into mounds or beehives and used to "spectacularize" another dish.

Manioc is listed last among the accompaniments for no special reason. Based upon its importance it should be first, for this versatile tuber, together with the various uses to which it is put, is one of the outstanding food accompaniments used in Brazil. While only a food accessory, it is so adaptable in its use and so extensive in its application, that it has become one of the basic foods of the Brazilian diet, as well as an important part of the Brazilian economy.

Manioc is a tuber, *Manihot Utilissima,* or the bitter cassava. The widely used *farinha de mandioca*[6] is derived from this root and is of great economic importance to Brazil. To prepare *farinha de mandioca* it is first necessary to press and roast the

---

[6] The Brazilian *farinha* is not to be confused with the patented cereal Farina.

tubers in order to expel the deadly poisonous hydrocyanic acid. Plantation owners who do their own processing take great care that farm animals are not exposed to the mash, as even a taste causes death.

Farinha de mandioca — a "must" with black beans and the famous *Feijoada*[7] — also serves as the principal ingredient in many food accessories, such as *Farofas*, *Angus* and *Pirões*.[8] As if this contribution to Brazilian cookery were known as a *farinheira*, from which the *farinha* may be sprinkled over one's food.

Maria Graham, who was married to a British Naval Officer stationed in Brazil, noted the dependence of both rich and poor on this product. In 1821, she wrote in her Journal: "The great article of food here is the mandioc meal, or farinha; it is made into thin bread cakes as a delicacy, but the usual mode of eating it is dry: while at the tables of the rich, it is used with every dish they eat, as we take bread; with the poor, it has every form — porridge, brose, bread; and no meal is complete without it."[9]

The *Manihot Palmata, Variety Aipi,* or sweet cassava, is non-poisonous. Its root is used as a vegetable, principally by peeling and boiling and then frying, with only salt, pepper and butter for seasoning, or simply by boiling. As it is tuberous, it is more satisfying than the smooth potato. Unlike potato, manioc root is firm and requires a long time to cook. Actually, this cassava root is known by different names in Brazil; in Northeastern Brazil it is called *macaxeira*, while in Rio de Janeiro it is called *Aipim*.

Foodstuffs produced from manihot are various, including the tapioca of commerce, alcohol and the *Polvilho* flours, unknown outside Brazil, from which a large variety of baked goods are produced.

Today, well over one hundred years after Maria Graham wrote of the importance of *Farinha de Mandioca* in the Brazilian diet, this versatile foodstuff maintains the same supremacy as it did in that bygone time.

---

[7] The national dish of Brazil, see p. 119.

[8] Recipes on p. 50, 51, 52, 53, 54, 55.

[9] Maria Graham, *Journal of a Voyage to Brazil and Residence There During the Years 1821, 1822 and 1823* (London: Longman, Hurst, Rees, Orme, Brown and Green, 1824), p. 160.

The Brazilian who has to live in North America for any length of time misses this staple upon which he was reared. But he has no need to despair! Excellent substitutes are at hand in the form of the breakfast cereals. "Farina" and "Cream of Wheat." Any use to which the *Farinha de Mandioca* can be put will fare very well with these substitutes.

Many Brazilians prefer to gently toast the *farinha de mandioca* in the oven, stirring often to ensure even toasting. A shallow pan is used for this purpose. When the color just begins to change from white to a pale tan, the *farinha* is removed, stirred well and poured into the *Farinheira*. It can then be used to sprinkle over the foods at the table or to prepare *Farofa* or *Pirão* or any of the other dishes in which the *farinha* is an ingredient.

The American substitutes can also be prepared in this manner, but for those who prefer the genuine *Farinha de Mandioca*, it may be obtained in the United States, usually in stores specializing in Latin American foods.

Egg Threads

Fios de Ovos

Fios de Ovos is not as simple to make as its few ingredients would imply. In fact, many experienced Brazilian cooks would think twice before embarking on such a venture, as the technique involved in preparing these "threads" is very special. But the end justifies the means.

Thirty years ago, it was quite usual to serve *fios* at high teas or special parties. Nowadays, however, because they are costly to prepare and involve much time and patience, *fios* are less frequently seen.

The utensils required are the proverbial wooden spoon (without which it would be impossible for many of Brazil's good cooks to turn out the fine examples of their art), a strainer, a large bowl, a saucepan to boil the sugar syrup and a special utensil to introduce the egg yolks into the hot syrup.

Actually, this utensil consists of three small funnels protruding from a round piece of metal about one inch high and four inches in diameter. The funnels are as far apart as possible and their points are just large enough to allow a fine stream of egg yolk to pass through. The round piece of metal securing the funnels is set in a wire frame with a handle. To make the *Fios* one places the funnel part in the handle and, holding it over the boiling syrup, pours in the egg yolks and gently guides the funnels around the edge of the saucepan, diminishing the heat.

In the absence of this special utensil, one could press the egg yolks through a pastry bag fitted with a nozzle containing one fine hole or, better still, if possible, through a nozzle with three fine well-separated holes. Again, great skill and patience are necessary, for this is a very slow and tedious process, regardless of which type of funnel is used.

36 egg yolks • 3 egg whites (optional) • 4 pounds sugar • 3 cups water
Vanilla or orange flower water

Carefully separate yolks from whites, taking care not to break yolks. Add the 3 whites to yolks and mix very well with a wooden spoon (do not beat). Press through a coarse sieve to remove membrane. Make a syrup with the sugar and water (adding rosewater or vanilla, if desired) and cook until it spins a thread. When it spins a thread, keep it at a rolling boil, and funnel egg yolk mixture into boiling syrup, guiding the funnels around edge of saucepan. This must be done slowly so that the threads come out evenly. Skim off the threads and plunge into cold water to which a little syrup has been added. Remove to a collander to drain. Repeat this process until all the egg liquid has been used.

If syrup becomes too thick, thin it down with hot water.

If the threads stick together, dip two forks into cold water and gently pry the threads apart.

Pile the threads into molds and moisten with a little of the syrup. Unmould next day. Beehive moulds are very effective. The threads may also be used in strands.

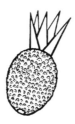

Butter Farofa
Farofa de Manteiga

3 tablespoons butter • 1/2 onion, thinly sliced • 1 egg • manioc meal
1 tablespoon finely-chopped parsley

Melt butter in a skillet and gently sauté onion. (Onion may be omitted, if desired.) Keep heat low, add the egg, scramble, mixing it well with the onion and butter. Gradually add the manioc meal, stirring well. Add enough of the meal to produce a mixture somewhat like the consistency of loose toasted bread crumbs. Mix in parsley and season to taste with salt. This is served as an accompaniment to *Feijoada* or with roast chicken or turkey, either as a stuffing or an accompaniment. It is also excellent with steaks, chops or roasts. In cases when it is used as a stuffing, sometimes olives, raisins or small pieces of cooked ham are added.

[REPRINTED FROM AUTHOR'S ARTICLE IN JULY, 1963 ISSUE OF **GOURMET** MAGAZINE]

Carrot Farofa
Farofa de Cenouras

1 cup grated raw carrots • 4 tablespoons butter • manioc meal
Salt • 1/2 cup raisins

Sauté carrots in half of the butter for about 10 minutes, stirring, constantly over low heat, then add the rest of the butter and cook until tender. Gradually add enough manioc meal, always stirring over low heat, until the mixture is comparable with loose toasted bread crumbs. Remove from heat, salt to taste and add the raisins. Serve with roasts, steaks or poultry.

Cheese Farofa
Farofa de Queijo

3 eggs, separated • 1/2 teaspoon salt • 1/4 cup cheese cubed, quarter-inch
4 tablespoons butter • manioc meal

Beat egg whites until stiff, add yolks, salt and cheese. Melt butter and, when hot, pour in the egg mixture, stirring well with a fork. As soon as the eggs begin to set, pour in the manioc meal in a steady stream, the stirring constantly. Use enough manioc meal to form a mixture comparable with loose toasted bread crumbs. Serve at once with pork or tongue.

Golden Farofa
Farofa de Ouro

6 hard-boiled eggs • manioc mead • 1/2 cup melted butter • salt

Peel eggs, cut in halves and remove yolks. Chop yolks and reserve the white halves. Heat manioc meal (about 2 cups) in oven in a shallow pan until it begins to turn a pale beige, stirring frequently so that it roasts evenly. Melt butter in a skillet, add the manioc meal (enough to form a loose mixture, like toasted bread crumbs) and stir until butter is absorbed. Mix in chopped yolks, and salt to taste. Garnish with hardboiled egg whites into each of which an olive has been placed. Serve with roast meat, poultry or steaks.

Prune Farofa
Farofa de Ameixas

3 tablespoons butter • manioc meal
5 or 6 large prunes, soaked or parboiled, then dried and slivered

Melt butter, slowly pour in the manioc meal (enough to form a loose mixture, like toasted bread crumbs). Remove from heat, add prune slivers and salt to taste. Serve with roast pork.

Ham Cigars
Charutos de Presunto

1 tablespoon butter • 1 tablespoon chopped onion • 1 tablespoon chopped parsley
1 1/2 cups stale cubed bread • 1 cup milk • 1/2 tablespoon all-purpose flour
1/2 teaspoon Worcestershire sauce • salt and black pepper to taste
1/4 pound chopped cooked ham • sifted all-purpose flour
beaten egg • bread crumbs • oil

Melt butter and sauté onion and parsley. Add bread cubes that have been soaked in the milk, then add flour, Worcestershire sauce, and salt and pepper to taste. Cook over medium heat until mixture holds its shape. Allow to cool completely. Mix in the chopped ham. Shape into cigars. Roll in sifted flour, then beaten egg and, lastly, the bread crumbs. Fry in hot oil until delicately brown. Lift onto absorbent paper towel. Use as an accompaniment to chicken.

Cornmeal Mush
Angu de Milho [10]

4 cups water • 1/2 tablespoon salt • 1 cup corn meal
1 tablespoon bacon fat or butter

Heat 2 cups water with the salt and, when it boils, add the other 2 cups of cold water which have been mixed with the corn meal. Add shortening and cook over medium heat, stirring constantly until mixture is thick enough to hold its shape. Turn into a buttered mould. Unmould and serve with *Couve à Mineira* (p. 553), black beans and smoked meats.

---

[10] Brazilians also make a sort of mush with cheese, like polenta, by adding grated cheese to the recipe and about 1/4 teaspoon of nutmeg. The mixture is then turned into a buttered oblong pan to cool, cut into squares, which are dipped into beaten egg yolks and bread crumbs, then fried in hot fat. These squares are served with meats or poultry.

Manioc Mush

Angu de Farinha de Mandioca

6 cups coconut milk (mixture of thick and thin milk from 2 coconuts)
1 teaspoon salt • 1 cup rice flour

Heat 5 cups of the coconut milk with salt. Add the rice flour to the remaining cup of coconut milk and mix until smooth, then gradually stir into the hot mixture. Cook over low heat, stirring constantly, until mixture falls away from sides of pan. It should be of the consistency of a stiff cooked cereal. Turn into individual moulds or one large mould and serve cold with *Bobó* or *Vatapá*.

[LAURITA PIRES, MINAS GERAIS]

Rice Pirão No. 1

Pirão de Arroz Nº 1

1 cup rice • water • salt • thick milk from 1 coconut

Wash rice and soak overnight in enough water to cover. Next day, add salt and cook in same water until rice is pasty. It may be necessary to add more water. When rice is cooked, mash with a wooden spoon and stir in the coconut milk and mix well. Taste to check the salt. Press into a buttered mould and unmould to serve cold with fish or shellfish.

Rice Pirão No. 2
Pirão de Arroz Nº 2

1/2 cup rice flour • 1/2 teaspoon salt • 2 1/2 cups water

Mix flour and salt with cold water in blender, then cook over a low flame, stirring constantly until mixture falls away from sides of pan and holds its shape. Beat well, turn into a well-buttered mould. Unmould and serve cold with *Carne (Picadinho)* (Chopped Beef), p.378.

Corn Pirão
Pirão de Milho

3/4 cup corn flour • 1/2 teaspoon salt • 2 cups cold water • 2 tablespoons butter

Mix flour, salt and cold water in blender. Heat gently, stirring constantly, until mixture falls away from sides of pan. If mixture thickens too rapidly, add small amounts of water. When it is cooked and holds its shape, remove from heat, add butter, beat well and turn into a mould. Unmould and serve cold with meat.

Anchovy Sauce

Molho de Enchovas

1 tablespoon butter • 1 tablespoon olive oil • 1 grated onion • garlic salt
1/4 teaspoon powdered coriander • 1 bayleaf • 1 cup tomato sauce
1/2 cup water • 2 cans drained anchovies • salt and pepper

Heat butter and oil and sauté onion, garlic salt, coriander and bayleaf. Add tomãto sauce and water and bring to a rolling boil. Season with salt and pepper to taste, reduce heat to simmer and cook until mixture thickens. Strain and add mashed anchovies. Yields about 1 1/2 cups sauce. Serve with fish.

[TRANSLATED FROM: **A COZINHA DELICIOSA E MODERNA** BY MARIA THEREZA SENISE]

Carrot Sauce

Molho de Cenouras

2 tablespoons butter • 1 tablespoon all-purpose flour • 1 cup chicken broth
1/2 teaspoon marjoram • 1/2 cup tomato sauce • 1 cup grated raw carrots

Melt butter and blend with flour in a heavy skillet. Gradually add broth and marjoram and cook over low heat until mixture thickens, then bring to a boil, add tomato sauce and carrots. Cook until carrots are done, taste and check seasoning. Serve with meat loaf.

Egg Sauce for Fish
Molho de Ovos Para Peixe

2 tablespoons butter • 1 tablespoon prepared mustard • 1 tablespoon all-purpose flour
1/4 teaspoon salt and black pepper to taste • 2 egg yolks
1/2 cup milk • 1 tablespoon lemon juice

Melt butter, add mustard and flour and stir over low heat until well-blended. Remove from heat. Beat yolks, add milk then combine with first mixture and heat gently over low flame until sauce is smooth. Remove from heat. Add lemon juice a drop at a time. Check seasoning. Add capers, if desired.

Madeira Wine Sauce
Molho de Vinho Madeira

1 tablespoon chopped onion • 1 bay leaf • 1 tablespoon chopped celery
2 tablespoons butter • 2 tablespoons all-purpose flour • 3/4 cup broth
3 ounces Madeira wine • Salt and pepper

Brown onion, bay leaf and celery in butter and add flour, then small amounts of broth. Cook until sauce thickens (about 10 minutes). Strain, add wine and salt and pepper to taste. Serve over veal or fish.

[TRANSLATED FROM: **NOÇÕES DE ARTE CULINÁRIA** BY MARIA THEREZA A. COSTA, SÃO PAULO]

Palm Heart Sauce
Molho de Palmito

1 14-ounce can palm hearts • 1/4 cup milk • 1/2 cup light cream
2 tablespoons all-purpose flour • 2 egg yolks • 2 tablespoons butter
1/4 teaspoon Worcestershire sauce • 4 tablespoons grated Parmesan cheese

Drain the palm hearts and measure 1 cup of the liquid. Slice the palm hearts and reserve. To the liquid, add milk, cream, flour and egg yolks, and mix in electric blender. Pour into a sauce pan, add butter and cook until mixture thickens. When sauce is thick, add Worcestershire sauce and cheese. Cook 2 or 3 minutes, stir in the sliced palm hearts, and season with salt and pepper to taste. Serve over vegetables or fish.

[TRANSLATED FROM: A COZINHA DELICIOSA E MODERNA BY MARIA THEREZA SENISE]

Sardine Sauce No 1
Molho de Sardinha Nº 1

1 can sardines, drained • 1 tablespoon lemon juice • salt and cayenne pepper
3/4 cup mayonnaise • few capers

Mash sardines well, add lemon juice and seasonings. Blend in the mayonnaise and capers. Taste to check seasoning. Serve with cold fish or shellfish.

Sardine Sauce No. 2
Molho de Sardinha N° 2

1 can sardines, drained • 1 tablespoon butter • 1 minced onion • 1 cup stock
2 egg yolks • 2 tablespoons lemon juice • 1/4 cup white wine
salt and pepper • 1 teaspoon capers

Melt butter and sauté sardines with onion. When onion is delicately brown, add the soup stock and cook for 10 minutes or until liquid evaporates to about 3/4 cup. Add the slightly-beaten egg yolks and cook 3 minutes over low heat. Strain, add lemon juice, wine, salt and pepper to taste and capers. Serve hot over fish.

Shrimp and Coconut Sauce
Molho de Camarão e Coco para Peixe

1 grated coconut • 1/2 cup boiling water • 1 tablespoon butter
2 tablespoon all-purpose flour • 3/4 cup cleaned fresh shrimp
1 tablespoon butter • 1 tablespoon chopped onion
1 cup tomato sauce • Seasoning

Add boiling water to the coconut and press out the coconut milk. Make a medium white sauce with butter, flour and the coconut milk and reserve. Sauté shrimp and onion in the other tablespoon of butter, add tomato sauce and seasoning. Combine both mixtures, check seasoning and thicken with more flour, if necessary. Serve over fish.

Shrimp Cream Sauce for Fish
Molho de Camarão para Peixe

2 tablespoons olive oil • 1 thinly-sliced onion • 1 small hot pepper, chopped
1 cup clean, fresh shrimp, chopped • 1/2 teaspoon nutmeg • 2 cups milk
2 tablespoons cornstarch • salt and pepper

Heat oil and sauté onion, pepper, shrimp (and oysters, if desired). When shellfish is cooked, add nutmeg and milk. Thicken with cornstarch and season to taste.

Tomato and Peanut Sauce
Molho de Tomate com Amendoim

1 tablespoon butter • 2 to 4 fresh, sliced tomatoes (or 1 cup tomato sauce)
1/4 cup cream • 3 ounces ground, roasted peanuts • seasoning

Melt butter, add tomatoes, cover saucepan and cook over low heat until tomatoes are done. (If fresh tomatoes are used, press mixture through a coarse sieve.) Add cream, ground peanuts, and salt and pepper to taste (also a pinch of sugar, if desired). Return to stove, bring to a slow boil and serve over vegetables.

Corn Bread Stuffing
Recheio de Pão de Milho

1/2 cup butter • 1 minced onion • 1/4 cup chopped parsley
4 cups crumbs from leftover corn bread (see recipe, p. 173) • 6 stuffed olives, sliced
3 hard-boiled eggs, sliced • salt and pepper

Melt butter in a skillet and sauté onion over medium heat, then add parsley. Gradually add crumbs, olives and hard-boiled eggs. Season to taste with salt and pepper. Use to stuff either poultry or fish.

Fish Stuffing No. 1
Recheio para Peixe Nº 1

1 tablespoon butter • 1 cup manioc meal • 1/4 cup stuffed olives • 3 hard-boiled eggs,
chopped • 1 tablespoon parsley, chopped • salt to taste

Melt butter in a skillet and gradually add manioc meal stirring well until all butter has been absorbed and mixture is smooth. Remove from heat and add rest of ingredients.

61

Fish Stuffing No. 2
Recheio para Peixe N° 2

6 slices firm bread • 1 cup milk • 1/2 tablespoon butter • 1 tablespoon olive oil
1/2 onion, chopped • 2 tablespoons parsley, chopped • 1 tablespoon tomato sauce
1/2 cup drained canned tuna or flaked fish • 2 egg yolks • olives and seasoning

Remove crusts and soak bread in milk. Heat butter and oil, sauté onion with parsley and tomato sauce. Add tuna fish or flaked cooked fish and then the bread and milk mixture. Cook for 5 minutes, remove from heat, stir in egg yolks, check seasoning and cool. When cool, add olives. Stuff fish and bake according to recipe used.

Chestnut and Raisin Stuffing
Recheio de Castanhas e Passas

12 chestnuts • chopped cooked giblets • 1/2 teaspoon salt • prepared butter farofa p. 50
1/2 cup raisins • seasoning

Boil, shell and chop the chestnuts. Add the giblets and salt. Stir in the *farofa* and raisins and correct seasoning. Use to stuff fowl.

Fruit Stuffing for Duck
Recheio de Frutas para Pato

1/3 cup butter • 4 cups bread crumbs • 1 cup chopped pineaple • 1/2 cup chopped prunes
• 1/2 cup slivered tart apple • 1/4 cup chopped Brazil nuts • seasoning

Mix ingredients in the order given. Taste to check seasoning.

Shrimp Stuffing for Fish
Recheio de Camarão para Peixe

1 pound fresh, cleaned shrimp • 2 tablespoons butter • 1 chopped onion
1 chopped tomato • 1/4 cup chopped parsley • 1 cup water • 1 thick slice of bread, cubed
1 raw egg • 3 hard-boiled eggs • seasoning

Sauté shrimp in butter with onion, tomato and parsley. Add water and simmer until shrimp is cooked. Remove shrimp and strain the broth. Add bread and raw egg to broth, and cook until mixture thickens. Chop the shrimp and hard-boiled eggs, and add to cooked mixture. Season.

Stuffing for Goose
Recheio para Ganso

6 medium onions, roasted in skins in moderate oven for 30 minutes
3 tart apples • 2 ounces butter • chopped, cooked goose giblets
4 cups bread crumbs • salt and pepper

Peel and chop onions. Peel and chop apples, and sauté in the butter. Add onions and chopped giblets, and mix with bread crumbs. Season.

Banana Scallops
Croquetes de Banana

Cut bananas into thirds, roll in bread crumbs, then in beaten egg and again in crumbs. Fry in fat heated to about 375°. When golden brown, remove to absorbent paper. Serve with roasts or steaks.

Baked Oranges
Laranjas Assadas

5 thin-skinned oranges • 2 cups sugar • 1/2 teaspoon ground cloves • butter

Cover washed oranges with boiling water and cook in a covered saucepan until tender. When oranges can be pierced with a fork, remove from saucepan and reserve one cup of the water. Cut oranges in halves, arrange in a covered baking dish, and dot generously with butter. To the cup of water in which the oranges were cooked, add sugar and cloves and bring to the boil. Simmer for 5 minutes, then pour over oranges in the casserole. Replace the cover and bake in a 400° oven until oranges are semi-glazed. Serve with fowl or baked ham.

Stuffed Apples
Maçãs Recheadas com Passas

6 apples • butter • raisins

Slice tops from washed apples, then core. Fill cavity with raisins and dot with butter. Place apples in a shallow buttered baking pan and bake in 375° oven until they are fork tender. Serve with poultry or pork.

Cearense Omelet
Mal Assado"

1/2 cup fine olive oil • 6 eggs, separated • 1/2 teaspoon salt • 1/2 cup manioc meal

Divide the oil in 2 skillets of equal size. Heat oil in first skillet while preparing the omelet. Beat egg whites until stiff, add yolks and salt, and continue beating and while gradually introducing the manioc meal. Mix well and pour into the skillet with the hot oil. Cook over medium heat until mixture begins to brown and shrink away from sides of skillet. Meanwhile, heat oil in the second skillet and when omelet is delicately browned at the edge, using a pancake turner, invert it to the second skillet to brown other side. Serve immediately with roasts or chopped beef (p. 378).

[WILSON AGUIAR, CEARÁ]

" Mal assado means "underdone" or "rare" in the large cities of Brazil. The term is applied to beef or steaks.

CHAPTER 5

AFRO-BRAZILIAN COOKERY INCLUDING SAUCES

The palate is more appreciative than the other Senses.
Music may go in one ear and out the other. The vision of
a beautiful picture soon disappears from a short memory.
But the remembrance of a good "vatapá" is eternal.

MANUEL QUERINO, COSTUMES AFRICANOS NO BRASIL, P. 224.

ost Brazilians are of one accord that the strongest element in their national cuisine is African in origin. As stated in the Foreword, the Portuguese colonists and native Indians contributed their share to Brazilian cookery, but it remained for African slaves centered around Bahia to give a truly Brazilian character to many noted dishes that are today famous throughout Brazil.

The Africans not only imported and introduced several of their own spices and herbs into their cooking, but they changed some Portuguese dishes by substituting ingredients which they deemed more palatable. Thus, in the typical Portuguese dish called *Frigideira* (or *Fritada* in Southern Brazil), which consists of codfish, olive oil, eggs, tomatoes and seasoning, the Negroes added coconut milk;[1] they replaced the olive oil with palm oil and substituted cashew nuts for the codfish.[2]

Many native Indian dishes were subjected to the same treatment by being modified in accordance with African taste and customs. As Gilberto Freyre points out, the Indian *Pokeka* was "deliciously Africanized, or, better, Brazilianized, in the form of the *Moqueca* of the Big House kitchens.[3]

In days gone by, this was a ragout of fish or shellfish cooked with oil and pepper and then wrapped in banana leaves, and roasted in coals. That was the real *Moqueca,* but today it has been modernized. Few take the time to wrap the succulent mixture in tender leaves and cook it beneath glowing embers. Nowadays,

---

[1] See "A Word About Coconut," p. 37.

[2] Manuel Querino, *Costumes Africanos no Brasil* (Rio de Janeiro: Civilização Brasileira, S. A., 1938), p. 177.

[3] Gilberto Freyre, *The Masters and the Slaves* (New York: Alfred A. Knopf, Inc.; 1946), p. 131.

Moqueca is made in a saucepan on a stove. This cooking process, however, while it may eliminate a picturesque and unusual way of serving, does not detract from the excellence of the dish when prepared by a *quituteira*[4] of the old school.

Afro-Brazilian cookery is characterized by the lavish use of palm oil, malagueta pepper and other condiments. This excessive use of palm oil and strong condiments has been highly criticized by nutritionists and Brazilian men of letters. Yet others, such as Darwin Brandão, who states that palm oil enters into all Bahian dishes, from *Farofa* to *Feijoada*, have taken up their pens to defend the accused.[5]

This oil, distinctive of Northern Brazilian cookery, is extracted from the palm *elaesis guineensis*, an African palm grown in Brazil that is responsible for the flavor and gusto of such well-known dishes as *Vatapá* and a host of others. Palm oil, called *dendê*, a rich source of vitamin A, is heavy, dense and of a yellowish color. Although it may be purchased in other areas of Brazil, most consumers claim that they would rather obtain it directly from the Bahia State. You will see many a returning visitor from Bahia leaving the airport with a bottle of *dendê* in tow, guarded with as much care as if it were the elixir of the Gods.

I can attest to this desire of the epicure to "go all out" in obtaining ingredients for what are commonly referred to as "gourmet dishes." Not only did I ask a returning traveler to bring me a bottle of *palm* oil to Rio de Janeiro, but I blithely carried the bottle aboard a plane bound for New York. Unfortunately, when the plane landed at Idlewilde, the bottle was leaking and it left a trail from the plane to the Customs counter. Many a good Afro-Brazilian dish was lost underfoot between the ramp of the plane and the Customs, an episode which I have never been able to consider in any other light than lamentable.

Since *palm* oil is not easily come by in the United States, one might reasonably enquire as to the advantage of collecting, translating and testing various recipes for which one of the principal ingredients is so scarce. The reasons are twofold. First, any introduction to Brazilian cookery must, of necessity, include recipes of Afro-Brazilian origin, otherwise the work would be incomplete and, therefore, not

---

[4] See end of chapter.

[5] Darwin Brandão, *A Cozinha Brasileira* (Bahia: Edição da Livraria Universitária, 1948), p. 15.

entirely authentic. Secondly, in this world of shrinking distances, who is to say whether palm oil may be on every gourmet shelf?

An article that appeared in many American newspapers reported that in 1960 Americans spent an estimated $250 million on gourmet foods imported from 30 countries, comprising some 10,000 items.[6] Maybe palm oil will soon be added to this list.

Actually, I know of two sources of palm oil in the United States: La Sevillana, 2469, 18 street, N.W., Washington, D.C. and the firm of Welch, Holme and Clark Company of New York. The latter firm markets a "crude plantation palm oil" which is extracted from the same palm as *dendê*, the *elaesis guineensis*. This is not sold as an edible oil, but I have used it many times and so have several of my friends from Bahia. The only difference from the Brazilian *dendê* cooking oil is one of density, as the crude plantation palm oil solidifies at room temperature, while the Brazilian dendê solidifies at a lower temperature. For this reason, it is recommended that, before measuring, the crude plantation palm oil be slightly warmed to a liquid state.

In connection with the use of *dendê* in cookery, it should be pointed out that it is necessary for the novice gourmet to acquire a taste for it. Once his palate has become used to this exotic flavor, he may be willing to go along with the Brazilian poets and also sing the praises of their *Vatapá, Moqueca* or other famous dishes using *dendê*.

I am convinced that there is no substitute for *dendê*, as no other oil imparts the same "different" flavor to these much heralded Bahian dishes. A Baiana living in Washington told me that when she was out of dendê oil she used paprika with olive oil, and went ahead with the recipe. My own feeling is that when dendê is not available, it is better to forego making the dish. I should point out, however, that most of the recipes in this chapter can be prepared without *dendê* and the results are tasty and palatable, but it is the *dendê* that transforms them into exotic gourmet preparations.

---

[6] Clementine Paddleford's article, "Discover Our Land of 10,000 Delicacies," published January 29, 1961 in the "This Week" section of many American newspapers.

The "maligned malagueta" — another constitutent of Afro-Brazilian cookery, is of the *solanaceae* family. It is a small, hot aromatic pepper, an indispensable item in preparing all Bahian dishes, as well as a culinary ingredient that has made history. Had it not been for the quest for spices and pepper from the Orient, who knows what the ultimate fate of the New World would have been?

Rich in ascorbic acid, this pepper is used indiscriminately by many Brazilians, principally the inhabitants of Bahia. In the olden days, despite the fact that these seasonings were expensive, people of that region were so accustomed to the use of ginger and pepper that they even seasoned wine and beer with these condiments. Pepper was so highly-prized that to say that a man was worth a bag of pepper signified that he was a man of great means.

Thirty-five years ago, when I first went to Brazil, I was invited to play cards in the home of a mineiro[7] friend of my husband's who had married *a lady* from Bahia. When the card game was over, our hostess served some small sandwiches and refreshments together with a dish of malagueta peppers. Although this is an exceedingly strong pepper, the lady from Bahia opened each one of her sandwiches and added a layer of these extraordinarily hot peppers to the filling.

I have never forgotten this incident because it not only shows that many people of Bahia have built up a resistance to the strength of the malagueta, but it proves that they have also adopted it as part of their daily seasoning. In Bahia, the malagueta pepper is placed on the table side by side with salt and black pepper. It not only figures as a prominent ingredient in many Afro-Brazilian dishes, but it is also incorporated into several traditional sauces that accompany the special dishes of the Bahian area.

If you are unable to obtain malagueta, Tabasco peppers may be substituted, keeping in mind that they should be used with a light hand as the taste tolerance of North Americans for pepper does not equal that of the Bahiano. It is therefore recommended that, in preparing the following Afro-Brazilian dishes, the quantity of the malagueta used be governed by your taste.

---

[7] This is the name given to natives of the Minas Gerais State.

The four principal sauces served with Afro-Brazilian dishes are: *molho de acarajé* (bean cake sauce), *molho de pimenta e limão* (pepper and lemon sauce), *molho de azeite de dendê e vinagre* (palm oil and vinegar sauce) and *molho de Nagô* (Nagô sauce) all of which contain malagueta. Usually, the malagueta pepper is used Ginger, okra and cooked *jiló* are also used.[8]

The most popular is the "Pepper and Lemon Sauce" which accompanies roasts, *Moquecas, Feijoadas, Escaldado de Peru* and Shrimp *Frigideira*. Acarajé Sauce is served wich *Acarajé, Haussá* Rice, *Caruru, Efo,* and *Xin-Xin* or *Oxim-Xim*. The Oil and Vinegar Sauce is served with such dishes as Codfish with Coconut Milk, *Escaldado* and fish or crabs. Nagô Sauce is reserved for *Cozidos* or stews.

While Africans introduced pepper and *dendê* to Brazilian food habits, one must not discount the influence of the native Indian. The Indians were familiar with coconut and the many uses of the palm tree, although they did not exploit this knowledge to any extent. They were content to lackadaisically follow the habits and customs of their ancestors without improving them. It remained for the Africans to appropriate what the Indians already knew and to prepare tastier dishes through their improvisation of new culinary methods and ingredients.

The African slaves made great use of the banana and okra. They introduced coconut milk and dried shrimp into many recipes. They seasoned with ginger, many species of pepper, and leaves from exotic plants, as well as pounded melon and pumpkin seeds. They were very fond of wrapping foodstuffs in leaves and roasting them in embers, such as the original *Moqueca*.

At the same time, the slaves created their own traditions and a folklore that applied especially to the art of cookery, for the cooking of many Afro-Brazilian dishes hinges on special utensils, methods and superstitions.

For instance, the true Afro-Brazilian cook would disdain the use of modern cooking utensils that were used in colonial times. Earthenware cookery utensils are always used in a Bahian kitchen and the wooden spoon[9] is proverbial. Gourds are commonly fashioned into bowls, meaures and other cooking utensils. Fibers

---

[8] See "Vegetables," p. 537. For recipes see chapter on "Accompaniments," p. 41.

[9] Besides the superstition and the pleasant feel of a wooden spoon, it is ideal for long stirring, as it is not a heat conductor.

are woven into sieves and baskets to store or carry foodstuffs. Grating stones form a part of the African technique for pulverizing corn, beans or rice. The Bahian cook always has a mortar and pestle for pounding garlic, dry peppers, seeds and condiments which are made into a paste and mixed with salt before they are introduced into a recipe.

Caruru,[10] *Vatapá* and *Feijoada* were by far the best-liked Afro-Brazilian dishes set on colonial tables. These dishes have retained their popularity and are regarded as synonymous with the best of Bahia. *Caruru* and *Vatapá* are still considered regional, but *Feijoada* has attained the place of Brazil's national dish.[11]

Caruru is also the traditional dish served in Bahia in honor of the twin saints, Cosme and Damion.[12] This very interesting custom, called "*caruru* of the two-two," is celebrated in households where there are twins. Whether rich or poor, the head of the household having twins invites friends and neighbors to partake of a *caruru* in honor of his twins and Saints Cosme and Damion. The festival takes place during the month of September and often the host is aided in preparing the party by his relatives and friends.

Children also have their part in the celebration as a special invitation is sent to them. A large platter of the *Caruru* is set before them from which they all eat together, while the adults keep order clapping and singing:

"Come here, come here Two-Two
Come here, como here Two-Two"

When the children are through eating, the grownups take over.

---

[10] The dish called *Caruru* is prepared with okra, taioba (a leafy green vegetable), onions, shrimp, malagueta peppers, palm oil and fish. Sometimes, the leaves of the capeba (of the *peperacea* family) enter into its preparation. This is also the name of a herb of the amaranth family, which was probably brought to Brazil by the Africans.

[11] Recipes for *Feijoada* are given in the chapter on "Beans and Rice," p. 124.

[12] The policemen of Rio de Janeiro, because they patrol in two's, are known as Cosme and Damion.

In preparing the dish for this celebrations, it is customary for the hostess to see that seven okra pods remain whole. Each person served one of these whole okra pods is required to duplicate the party the following year. Thus, it is possible to preserve these traditional customs of years gone by.

Brazilian literary men who have written about Bahia sing high praise to those skilled cooks noted for their preparation of these special dishes of Bahia. They have given them the name *quituteira*, which means an expert in preparing tidbits, since the word *quitute* in Portuguese means tidbit.

The *quituteira* guarded their secrets well. They gave their recipes only to their children or to those very much in their confidence. Even to the literary men who sang their praises, like Manoel Bandeira, Darwin Brandão, Sodré Vianna, Manoel Querino, Gilberto Freyre, Nina Rodrigues and others who wrote music and dedicated poetry to their talents, they imparted very little information. Quantities and proportions were very often not given, and, in the instances when measurements were indicated, they could not be relied upon because they were too indefinite. The *cuia*[13] that one cook used as a measure may not have been the same size as that of her neighbor; just as a "handful of this" or a "pinch of that" varies from person to person.

But this uncertainty is a distinguishing factor in preparing all old recipes, or, for that matter dishes made by some cooks of today who are guided by instinct in selecting exact proportions of each ingredient and who, seemingly, never measure their ingredients.

Alas and alack! We do not all have this aptitude in judgment. Although the great men, who set the talents of the *quituteira* to music and prose, have faithfully transcribed the ingredients and methods in preparing their favorite dishes, most have failed to mention the all important factor of accurate quantities. Only the *quituteiras* can tell us, and many of their secrets passed away with them.

Fortunately, some astute housewives and some of the Brazilian men of letters did take time to record these dishes in terms of modern weights, measures and methods. To these unsung heroes and heroines the present-day cuisine of Brazil is indebted for the preservation of many colonial dishes, which otherwise would have perished and been lost to the modern world.

---

[13] A gourd fashioned into a small bowl.

AFRO-BRAZILIAN SPECIALTIES

Abará

Once the recipe for Acarajé *(below)* • *2 tablespoons palm oil* • *Malagueta pepper to taste* *banana leaves* • *1 whole dried shrimp for each Abará*

PREPARING ABARÁ

After the acarajé batter is smooth, add the palm oil and pounded malagueta, and mix very well. Drop by spoonfuls on pieces of banana fronds and insert 1 whole dried shrimp in each frond. Corn husks or foil paper may be substituted for the fronds. Roll up and secure well. Abará should be steamed, and the best way I have found for obtaining the desired results is to follow the procedure for cooking cuscuz (see p. 277). If you cover the colander with banana fronds, the abará is cooked when the covering fronds are tender. If the abará is in foil paper, allow about 1 hour. Serve cold in the wrapping in which it was cooked.

Acarajé

No Bahia *festa* is complete without acarajé, a famous Brazilian *quitute* made from a batter of dried shrimp and skinless dried beans. Spoonfuls of the mixture are dropped into hot palm oil and deep fat fried until they puff up like elongated dumplings. Removed from the oil, they are drained on absorbent paper and served cold, split down the center, with acarajé sauce spread inside the wedge.

The bean used is called *fradinho* and the nearest to it would be dried black-eyed peas, cow peas (which are actually of the bean family) or navy beans. After removing impurities, they can be soaked to remove all outer skins. This can be accomplished by rubbing with the palms of the hands to loosen skins and then pulling them off, or by placing beans in a folded napkin and lightly pressing with a rolling pin. The skins are then discarded. No matter what process one uses, each bean going into acarajé should have its outer skin removed.[14] The beans are mashed or put through the meat grinder with the onion and the ground dried shrimp and seasonings are added. The batter is dropped by spoonfuls into hot palm oil and deep-fat fried.

2 cups dried black-eyed peas or navy beans • 1 onion
1/2 cup ground dried shrimp (use only 1/4 cup in recipe and reserve the other
1/4 cup for the acarajé sauce, page 89) • salt and pepper • palm oil

Prepare beans as directed above and discard the outer skins. Grind in a food chopper with the onion. Add ground shrimp and season well with salt and pepper. The mixture should then be very well beaten. Place enough dendê oil in

GRINDING BEANS FOR ACARAJÉ

a saucepan to deep-fat fry. When the oil is very hot, drop spoonfuls of the batter into it. Each spoonful will puff up and take the shape of an elongated dumpling. Drain on absorbent paper and serve cold with acarajé sauce.

---

[14] In Bahia a grinding stone is used for this purpose. It is a flat rectangular stone with a rough surface. The beans are placed on the stone and rolled back and forth with a stone rolling pin until the outer skins are broken. They are then removed and discarded, and the beans mashed.

Haussá Rice (also Aussá)
Arroz de Haussá [15]

Prepare the recipe for Brazilian Rice (p. 131) omitting all seasoning except salt. Scald 1 pound jerked beef cut into small pieces and let stand overnight in cold water. Next day, fry the meat in a small amount of butter with a thinly-sliced onion until jerked beef is well browned. Spoon rice into center of a large serving plate and surround with the jerked beef. Serve with Acarajé Sauce (p. 89).

Bobó [16]

1/2 cup Portuguese olive oil • 2 chopped onions • 6 peeled tomatoes, chopped
2 green peppers, chopped • 4 tablespoons parsley, chopped • 2 pounds manioc (cassava)
3 freshly-grated coconuts (save 1 for the Pirão de Arroz, p. 54)
2 pounds fresh shrimp, peeled, deveined and cleaned • palm oil

Place half the olive oil in a skillet and sauté half the onions, tomatoes, peppers and parsley. Add the manioc root, which has been peeled, washed and cut into small pieces. Simmer, covered, for 30 minutes with the vegetables, stirring frequently to prevent burning.

Squeeze out thick milk from 2 coconuts, saving the third coconut for the accompaniment, *Pirão de Arroz*. To the remainder, add 3 cups boiling water and remove

---

[15] The name applies to a tribe of African Negroes of mixed blood.
[16] In Bahia this is also the name given to a dish made of mashed beans and bananas mixed with *dendê* palm oil and manioc meal.

the thin milk. Add this thin milk to the manioc and vegetable mixture and cook slowly, mashing once in a while. This may take 2 or 3 hours. If the mixture becomes too thick, add a small quantity of water. When the root is cooked, mash thoroughly. The mixture should then have the consistency of a heavy lumpy batter.

Meanwhile, sauté the other half of the vegetables with the remaining 1/4 cup of oil. Add the raw shrimp and cook over low heat for 5 minutes. Add the thick coconut milk from the 2 coconuts and cook until the shrimp is done. Combine the two mixtures (shrimp and manioc) and season to taste. If desired, add enough palm oil to make the mixture yellow.

Because of its consistency, which is like a batter, *Bobó* is served in a soup dish with the *Pirão de Arroz* in the center. It is eaten with a soup spoon.

[LAURITA PIRES, MINAS GERAIS]

Shrimp Caruru
Caruru de Camarão

1 pound fresh shrimp • 1 tablespoon butter • 1 tablespoon chopped onion
1 tablespoon chopped parsley • 1 tablespoon chopped green pepper • 1 peeled and
chopped fresh tomato • 1 1/2 cups sliced okra • 1/4 pound dried shrimp
1 1/2 tablespoons manioc meal • 1 grated coconut • 1/2 cup dendê oil

Sauté cleaned, raw shrimp in butter with onion, parsley, green pepper and tomato. Add sliced okra. Grind dried shrimp and mix with manioc meal. Grate coconut and remove thick milk. To remainder add 1 cup boiling water and remove thin milk. Into this, mix the dried shrimp and manioc mixture. Add shrimp okra mixture and cook over low heat until okra is done. Just before serving, add the thick coconut milk and palm oil. Note: Sometimes ground peanuts are added.

[TRANSLATED FROM AS RECEITAS PARA VOCÊ DA TIA EVELINA, 4TH ED.]

Chicken Marajoara[17]

Galinha Marajoara

1 cut-up stewing chicken • 1/2 recipe for Vinha d'Alho (see Brazilian Turkey, p. 470) 1/2 cup olive oil • 2 sliced onions • 4 tablespoons chopped parsley • 1/2 cup tomato sauce or 2 chopped tomatoes • 2 ounces dried shrimp • 1/4 cup palm oil • thick milk of 1 coconut

Marinate chicken overnight in *Vinha d'Alho*. Next morning remove and sauté in a large skillet in the oil, with half the onions, parsley and tomato sauce or tomatoes. Cover and cook until the chicken is tender, adding some of the marinade if necessary (about 1 hour). When chicken is cooked, remove to another pan to keep warm and make a sauce with the drippings by gently sautéing remaining half of onion, parsley and tomatoes. Add 1 cup of water and cook the vegetables down. Strain the liquid and add the dried shrimp that were pulverized in the blender. Add palm oil and the thick milk of 1 coconut. Heat gently. Taste to check seasoning. Arrange warm chicken on a bed of plain boiled rice and pour sauce over the chicken.

[TRANSLATED FROM **AS RECEITAS PARA VOCÊ DA TIA EVELINA**, 4TH ED.]

---

[17] Pertaining to the Island of Marajó.

E f ó

1 pound dried, shelled shrimp or 1 pound fresh shrimp • 1 small dried hot pepper
1/2 garlic clove • 1 onion • 1/8 teaspoon coriander seed • 1 package frozen spinach [18]
1 pound grouper fish or haddock fillet • 1 tablespoon oil • 1/2 cup palm oil (optional)

Pound the dried shrimp with the next four ingredients or put in the blender. (If fresh shrimp is used, shell, devein, clean and sauté in the tablespoon of oil with next four ingredients, then put in blender.) Cook spinach in its own juice in a covered saucepan. When cooked, drain off all the liquid and add to the shrimp mixture. Season to taste and set aside. In another skillet, fry the fish in a small amount of oil. When done, remove skin and bones, and cut into small portions. Add to spinach mixture with the palm oil. Heat and keep warm. Serve with Rice *Pirão* No. 1.

---

[18] Other greens used are mustard leaves and the native *taioba* or *língua de vaca*.

Turkey Stew
Escaldado[19] de Peru

1/2 cup chopped bacon • 1/2 cup chopped onions • 1 mashed garlic clove
1 chopped malagueta pepper • 2 tablespoons chopped parsley
1 chopped green pepper • 3 peeled chopped tomatoes • 1 pound lean veal, cubed
1 pound cooked, smoked tongue, cubed • 2 teaspoons salt • black pepper • ham bone
(optional) • 3 quarts water • 1 bunch kale or collards, broken into pieces • 2 cups cut-up
raw pumpkin • 3 chayotes, peeled and quartered • 4 potatoes, peeled and quartered
1/2 recipe for Ragout of Jerked Beef (p. 392) • 2 pounds cut-up left-over turkey

Render the bacon and sauté the onions, garlic, malagueta pepper, parsley, green
pepper and tomatoes. Gently fry the veal and tongue with the sautéed vegetables.
Add salt and black pepper, the ham bone and water. Bring to a boil. Add kale,
pumpkin, chayotes and potatoes and reduce heat. Cover and cook for 2 hours over
medium heat. Add Ragout of Jerked Beef and the turkey and simmer until half the
liquid has evaporated. Check seasoning. Make a *Pirão* (p. 54) from some of the pot
liquor. Arrange the meats in the center of a large platter and surround with the
vegetables. Serve the *Pirão* on a separate plate. The *Escaldado* should be accompanied
by Pepper and Lemon Sauce (p. 91) or Nagô Sauce (p. 90). Serves 8.

---

[19] *Escaldado* means "scalded."

Shrimp Frigideira
Frigideira de Camarão

1/2 pound dried shrimp • 3/4 cup oil • 2 1/2 pounds fresh shrimp, cleaned, deveined and seasoned with lemon juice and salt • 3 large onions • 6 tomatoes • 1 garlic clove 3/4 cup chopped parsley • 1 teaspoon coriander powder • 1 fresh grated coconut 1 malagueta or Tabasco pepper • 5 eggs

Soak dried shrimp. Heat oil in a skillet and sauté fresh shrimp for 5 minutes. Grind 3/4 of the fresh shrimp in meat grinder with onions, tomatoes, garlic, parsley, coriander and dried shrimp. Add the 1/4 fresh shrimp which were reserved and 1 cup of the grated coconut. Extract the thick milk from the rest of the coconut and add it to the mixture. Check seasoning. Heat, stirring well until most of the liquid has evaporated. Beat eggs and reserve a small amount for the topping. Add the rest to the shrimp mixture, little by little, stirring vigorously. Pour into a baking dish, cover with reserved beaten eggs and brown in a 375° oven. Serve garnished with slices of raw onions and *farofa* (page 50).

[TRANSLATED FROM: **AS RECEITAS PARA VOCÊ DE TIA EVELINA**, 4TH EDITION]

Shrimp Moqueca
Moqueca de Camarão

*1/2 garlic clove • 1/2 teaspoon salt • 1 pound fresh shrimp, deveined and cleaned
1 thinly-sliced onion • juice of 1 lemon • 2 tablespoons vinegar • 1 tablespoon
finely-chopped parsley • 2 tablespoons tomato paste • black pepper • 2 tablespoons tomato
paste • black pepper • 2 tablespoons dendê oil • 1 large grated coconut*

Crush garlic with salt and add to shrimp. Let stand 15 minutes. Make a marinade from onion, lemon juice, vinegar, parsley tomato paste and pepper. Mix in the palm oil and the raw shrimp. Grate the coconut and extract thick milk. Add 1 cup hot water to the residue and extract thin milk. Add thin milk to the shrimp mixture and cook over a low flame. When the shrimp is cooked, add thick milk and continue to cook slowly for a few minutes. Serve with rice that has been cooked in coconut milk.

VARIATON : Substitute cooked fish or chicken for the shrimp.

[JANDARC SILVA SANCHEZ, BAHIA]

Fish Moqueca

2 1/2 pounds fish fillet (small fish are best) • 5 or 6 coriander seeds • 1 onion
1 small hot pepper • 2 tomatoes • 1/4 teaspoon salt • juice of 1 lemon
1 cup water • 1/2 cup palm oil

Grind coriander seeds, onion, hot pepper and tomatoes or pound with a mallet to reduce to a paste. Add salt and lemon juice. Marinate fish in this mixture for at least one hour. Place fish and marinade in a covered skillet, add water and oil and cook over medium heat until fish is done. Serve with Brazilian Rice.

Quiabada

1 tablespoon oil • 1 pound cut-up stewing veal • 1 veal bone • 1 onion, chopped
1 garlic clove • 1/4 cup parsley, chopped • 1/2 teaspoon salt • 1/4 teaspoon pepper
1 pound okra • 1 ounce bacon rind • 1/4 cup dried ground shrimp

Pound onion, garlic, parsley and mix with salt and pepper. Heat oil in skillet, add veal and bone and pounded seasonings. Gently sauté, but do not brown. Slice okra in 1/2 inch slices. Add to veal with bacon rind and ground shrimp. Cover skillet, cook over medium heat until done, adding small amounts of water when necessary. Check seasoning. Serve with Manioc Mush (page 54).

Quibebe

1 pound very lean jerked beef, cut in cubes • 1 tablespoon oil
1 onion, chopped • 1 tomato, chopped • 1/4 cup parsley, chopped
2 pounds raw, yellow pumpkin, cubed • seasoning

Soak jerked beef overnight. Next day, change water and scald to remove salt, drain, then sauté in oil with the onion, tomato and parsley. When meat is brown, add enough water to cover and cook in covered saucepan until meat is tender. Add pumpkin, mix well and cook until it is done and the mixture has thickened.

Vatapá Naná Sá

1 pound clean fresh shrimp • 2 pounds grouper or sea bass (cut into strips)
1/4 cup olive oil • 1 fresh tomato, chopped • 1 onion, minced • 1 malagueta pepper, chopped 1
grated coconut • 1/2 cup ground roasted peanuts • 1/4 pound dried ground shrimp
rice flour • 3 or 4 tablespoons palm oil • salt and pepper

Sauté fish and shrimp in oil and then add the tomato, onion and malagueta pepper. Do this in a large saucepan equipped with a tight-fitting cover. When delicately brown, cover, but do not add water. Cook gently until done, then remove most of the fish and shrimp and set aside. Also reserve the fish liquor and any pieces of shrimp or fish left inside it. Extract the thick milk from the coconut and reserve. To the grated residue, add 2 1/2 cups water, peanuts and dried ground shrimp. Bring to boil and simmer 15 minutes. Then add the fish liquor and press through a sieve. Season. Return to stove and thicken with rice flour. This should be done by mixing some of the flour with a small amount of the liquid and gradually adding the boiling sauce. (You may also add the flour to cold water and then add to the hot mixture.) Cook slowly until the mixture has the consistency of a heavy white sauce. Remove from heat, add fish and shrimp that were reserved and the palm oil and thick coconut milk. Check seasoning. Serve in a soup plate accompanied by *Pirão* of Rice with Coconut Milk (p. 54).

[NANÁ SÁ, MINAS GERAIS]

Vatapá Renata Aragão Silveira

2 grated coconuts • 1/2 loaf French bread • 2 1/2 pounds dried, peeled shrimp
5 pounds fish steaks which have been fried with 2 tablespoons oil, 2 grated onions and
2 chopped tomatoes • 2 green peppers • 2 onions • 1 pound fresh tomatoes • 3 coriander seeds
2 cups palm oil • 2 1/2 pounds cleaned fresh shrimp

Remove the thick milk from coconuts and set aside. Add 4 quarts water to residue and squeeze out thin milk. Remove crusts from bread and soak in thin coconut milk. Grind up dried shrimp or put in the blender. Cut the cooked fish into strips, add the ground shrimp and the bread and coconut milk in which it has been soaking. Grind, or put in blender, green peppers, onions, tomatoes and coriander and add to fish mixture. Season with salt, pepper and garlic (optional), add the palm oil and the raw shrimp and cook over low heat until shrimp is cooked and some of the liquid has evaporated. When cooked, remove from heat and add thick coconut milk. Serve with *Pirão* of Rice with Coconut Milk, p. 54.

[RENATA ARAGÃO SILVEIRA, SÃO PAULO]

Chicken Vatapá
Vatapá de Galinha

1 onion, sliced • 1/4 cup parsley, chopped • malagueta peppers (optional)
2 or 3 chopped peeled tomatoes • 2 tablespoons olive oil • 1 chicken, cleaned and cut at joints
2 grated coconuts • 1/2 pound ground dried shrimp • 1/2 pound ground roasted peanuts
2 tablespoons palm oil • salt and black pepper

Sauté onion, parsley and tomatoes in oil. If desired, add one or two chopped malagueta peppers. Cook the chicken in this *refogado*, adding water as necessary until chicken is cooked and falls away from bones. Remove chicken and separate it from bones. Extract thick milk from the coconuts and set aside. Add 5 cups water to the residue and simmer gently until coconut is soft. Add shrimp and peanuts and cook again, then add the chicken gravy. Season with salt and pepper and strain. Thicken with rice flour which has been mixed with a little cold water. Add the chicken and thick coconut milk and heat slowly. Mixture should be of the consistency of a heavy white sauce. Remove from heat, add the palm oil. Serve in a large deep platter surrounded by individual moulds of Corn *Pirão* (p. 55), which is a heavy, salted cornstarch pudding.

Acarajé Sauce
Molho de Acarajé

4 dry malagueta peppers • 1/4 cup dried ground shrimp • 1 small chopped onion
1/2 teaspoon salt • 1/2 teaspoon ginger (optional) • 2 tablespoons palm oil

Pound first 5 ingredients together and mix thoroughly or put through a blender. Heat in the palm oil for about 10 minutes. Serve on *Acarajé*.

Xinxim[20]

1 cut-up stewing chicken • 1 teaspoon salt • 2 cups water • 1 cup dried ground shrimp
1 cup palm oil • 1/4 cup chopped parsley • 1 teaspoon ground coriander seed
1 chopped onion • 1 chopped Tabasco pepper

Stew chicken in covered saucepan with salt, water, shrimp, 1/2 cup palm oil, parsley, coriander, onion and pepper, replacing water as it evaporates. When chicken is cooked, reduce heat, remove cover and allow most of the liquid to evaporate. Then, add the other half cup of palm oil, raise the heat and fry the chicken. Serve with Haussá Rice (p. 78).

[DAURA ALVES DA COSTA, RIO DE JANEIRO]

---

[20] Brazilian authorities on Afro-Brazilianism also refer to this dish as *Chim-Chim* and *Ochim-Chim*. Some of the recipes call for pounded pumpkin seeds.

Palm Oil and Vinegar Sauce
Molho de Azeite de Dendê e Vinagre

1/2 teaspoon salt • 3 or 4 malagueta peppers • 1 thinly sliced onion
green coriander or 1 teaspoon coriander seed • 1/4 cup palm oil • 1/2 cup vinegar

Pound first 4 ingredients with wooden mallet or put through blender, then add oil and vinegar.

Nagô Sauce
Molho de Nagô [21]

3 or 4 malagueta peppers • 1/2 teaspoon salt • 1/4 cup dry ground shrimp
1/4 cup lemon juice • 1/2 cup sliced okra, cooked

Pound first 3 ingredients with a wooden mallet or put through blender, then add lemon juice and okra. This sauce is usually served with Brazilian stew, and it should be diluted with some of the broth from the stew. Sometimes a small amount of *jiló*, a vegetable, is also used in this recipe.

---

[21] Nagô was a tribe of Negroes brought to Brazil from the Yoruba region of the African slave coast.

Pepper and Lemon Sauce
Molho de Pimenta e Limão

3 or 4 malagueta peppers • 1/2 teaspoon salt • 1 sliced onion
1 garlic clove, optional • 1/2 cup lemon juice

Pound first 4 ingredients to make a paste or put through the blender. Add lemon juice and let stand 1 hour before using. This sauce cannot be kept because it ferments.

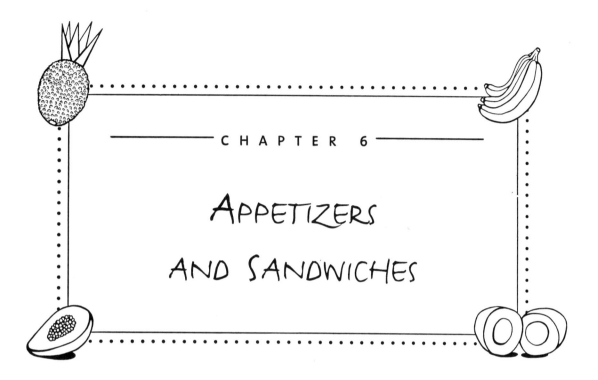

CHAPTER 6

APPETIZERS AND SANDWICHES

*The Creator, though condemning man to eat
to live, invites him to do so by appetite, and rewards
him by enjoyment.*

BRILLAT-SAVARIN

*I*n a general sense, appetizers have a twofold usage. They may be exciting and tempting tidbits served before a meal or they may be accompaniments to a cocktail. In any event, whether they are the prelude to a formal dinner or a snack served with plebian beer, aristocratic champagne or even the popular martini, their function is the same: to induce one to eat.

Physiologically, the appetizer alerts the alimentary tract to the good things to come and prepares the contented diner for a savory repast with, one hopes, pleasant company.

It is therefore the goal of the conscientious host or hostess to fulfill this expectation by planning an attractively served, tasty meal and by taking care that the guests are congenial.

Classification of appetizers in Brazil is the same as in North America. There are finger foods, such as highly decorated small open-faced sandwiches (canapés) or piquant morsels of food, which may be eaten with the fingers or from tooth picks (hors d'oeuvres). The appetizer may also include such things as cocktails consisting of fruits, vegetables, fish or sea food, which are served at the table, or fruit juices.

Recipes for these can be found in any complete cookbook and are not repeated here, even though they are frequently served in Brazil. A Brazilian fruit salad, which may also be served as a cocktail, is included among the dessert recipes, p. 285.

The Brazilian hors d'oeuvres are brought to the guests both hot and cold. For the most part, canapés are served cold, but sometimes they are slightly broiled. Several Brazilian recipes for sandwich fillings and spreads are included in this chapter because, with a little imagination, they can be employed admirably in the preparation of canapés, or worked up as fillings for the — Oh! so versatile, *Empadinhas* and *Pasteizinhos*.[1]

---

[1] See special chapter, p. 421.

One should never underestimate the many uses to which these tasty little foodstuffs can be adapted. It is suggested that you take advantage of these valuable adjuncts to typical Brazilian appetizers at the very first opportunity if you want to serve something different from what the Joneses serve.

The Hot Rolled Sandwich recipe is given in this chapter because it may be served in small finger-sized portions. This does not apply to the Around-the-Clock Sandwich, which must be served on plates.

Incidentally, the sandwich, as we know it in this country, does not enjoy the same popularity in Brazil. I believe this is true all over the world, as in no other place does one find the sandwich playing such an important role in a nation's food habits as in the United States, where it frequently is used as a meal. The sandwich forms a lunch for scores of school children, office workers, business men and laborers. Perhaps most of the United States lunches on a sandwich. This does not hold true in Brazil where lunch is a hot meal.

However, in Brazil, you may order a ham or cheese sandwich or a combination of both, luncheon size, at some restaurants or bars. Other fillings are reserved for tea sandwiches.

Such American standbys as bacon, lettuce and tomato, sardine and egg, chicken or tuna fish salad and many others are not listed on Brazilian menus, although one undoubtedly could obtain them if explicit directions were given for their preparation. Hot Dogs were introduced into large Brazilian cities in the late twenties, followed by Hamburgers and Cheeseburgers. The latter two retain their English names but the Hot Dog was translated into its Portuguese equivalent, *Cachorro-quente*. The latest snack to make its way to Brazil are the small wedges of pizza pies sold throughout the big cities.

However, the number of Brazilians who would regard any of this fare as a lunch is very small, indeed.

Codfish and shrimp are popular ingredients of Brazilan appetizers, but so are bananas and cheese. As a matter of fact, the Brazilian poet's delight, *Vatapá*, has also been called upon to render service in this connection. Since *Vatapá* is neither a liquid nor a solid, you may wonder how this could be served as an appetizer. The innovation was accomplished by an enterprising Brazilian hostess who presented this agreeable surprise to her guests in small paper cups accompanied by a demitasse spoon!

SALGADINHOS FRIOS

American Cheese

Queijadinhas

Insert toothpicks in one-inch cubes of American cheese and arrange in serving dish. Sprinkle a few drops of Worcestershire sauce on top of each cube.

Anchovy and Nuts

Anchovas e Nozes

Mix equal amounts of ground nuts and butter. Spread on crackers and place an achovy on top of each.

Shrimp Moulds
Forminhas de Camarão

1 pound fresh shrimp, shelled, deveined and cleaned • 2 tablespoons olive oil
1/4 cup minced onion • 1 tablespoon chopped parsley • few grains garlic salt
salt and black pepper • 1/4 cup tomato sauce • 1 cup milk • 3 tablespoons cornstarch

Sauté shrimp in oil with onion, parsley, garlic salt and salt and pepper. When shrimp is cooked, add tomato sauce, cover skilled and simmer 3 or 4 minutes longer. Remove shrimp from gravy. Mix milk and cornstarch, add to gravy and cook over medium heat, stirring constantly until mixture has a creamy consistency. Butter small individual moulds or *empadinha* tins. Place a whole shrimp in the bottom of each tin. Chop the rest of the shrimp, add to the gravy and pour some of it into each mould. Smooth tops with a fork and refrigerate until firm. Turn each mould out on a lettuce leaf on a toasted round of bread which is a little larger than the mould. Yields 12.

Stuffed Olives
Azeitonas Recheadas

Remove stones from large olives and fill cavity with sardines that have been mashed with a few drops of lemon juice and ketchup.

Stuffed Prunes
Ameixas Recheadas

Remove stones from large tenderized prunes and stuff cavities with *pâté de foie gras*. Sprinkle chopped peanuts on top.

Cariocas [2]

Spread a sharp cheese on rounds. Place a slice of banana on top of each and bake in 400° oven until cheese melts.

Cheese Balls No. 1
Bolinhas de Queijo Nº 1

2 eggs whites • 1/4 pound grated American cheese • 1/4 pound grated Parmesan cheese
1/2 teaspoon Worcestershire sauce

Beat egg whites until stiff, add cheeses and Worcestershire sauce. Shape into balls, fry in deep fat and drain on absorbent paper. Yields approximately 16.

---

[2] Name applied to a native of Rio de Janeiro City.

Cheese Balls No. 2
Bolinhas de Queijo Nº 2

*2 ounces butter • 1 cup sifted all-purpose flour • 2 ounces grated American cheese
2 ounces grated Gruyère cheese • 1 egg*

Cut butter into flour and mixed cheeses. Blend with finger tips and add salt, if needed. Shape into small balls, dip in beaten egg and bake in 400° oven.

[JEANETTE VIANNA, RIO DE JANEIRO]

Cheese Balls No. 3
Bolinhas de Queijo Nº 3

*2 eggs whites • 4 ounces grated Parmesan cheese • 1 teaspoon baking powder
• 1 teaspoon all-purpose flour*

Beat egg whites until very stiff and gradually fold in the rest of the ingredients. Shape into small balls and fry in deep fat. Drain on absorbent paper and serve in small paper cups.

Cheese Tasties
Mineiros[3]

1/2 cup cold mashed potatoes • 1/2 cup sifted all-purpose flour • 1/2 cup butter
1/2 teaspoon salt • grated cheese

Make a dough of potatoes, flour and butter and salt. Knead, let stand, then roll out to 1/4 inch and cut into shapes. Place on buttered cookie sheet, sprinkle cheese on top and bake in 400° oven until delicately brown.

Codfish Appetizers
Salgadinhos de Bacalhau

1/2 pound codfish • 1 tablespoon butter • 1 tablespoon parsley, chopped
1 tablespoon ketchup • 1/2 cup all-purpose flour • 1/2 cup milk • 2 eggs, separated
1 teaspoon baking powder • seasoning

Prepare codfish according to directions given in chapter on "Fish and Shellfish," p. 313. Sauté in butter with parsley, ketchup and seasoning. Shred the codfish and return to skillet. Dissolve flour in milk and stir until smooth, then add to the shredded codfish and cook over a low flame, stirring constantly. Remove from heat, add egg yolks. Mix and check seasoning. Let cool to room temperature then refrigerate for 30 minutes. Fold in the stiffly beaten egg whites and baking powder. Drop by small spoonfuls into hot oil and drain on absorbent paper.

---

[3] Name applied to a native of Minas Gerais State.

Golden Shrimp
Camarões Doré

2 pounds fresh jumbo shrimp • 1 cup olive oil • 8 or 10 garlic cloves • 1 tablespoon salt

Wash shrimp very well and do not remove shells. Devein by inserting a toothpick under the shell or with a proper shrimp deveiner and wash and dry. Heat oil, garlic cloves and salt in a heavy skillet. When garlic cloves are brown, remove and discard. Fry shrimp in the oil until golden brown and serve as an appetizer or part of a meal.

[MARÍLIA PEIXOTO AQUINO, RIO DE JANEIRO]

Prune and Ham Appetizers
Ameixas Pretas com Presunto

Remove stones from large, tenderized prunes and fill with stuffed olives. Wrap in small oblongs of boiled ham and secure with a toothpick. Bake 5 minutes in 375° oven.

VARIATION: Use bacon in place of ham.

[REPRINTED FROM AUTHOR'S ARTICLE IN JULY, 1963 ISSUE OF **GOURMET MAGAZINE**]

Rice and Sardine Balls

Bolinhos de Arroz com sardinha

1 cup Brazilian rice, cold (p. 131) • 1/4 cup Parmesan cheese, grated
1 can sardines, drained and mashed • 1 egg • 1 beaten egg • bread crumbs • oil

Reheat rice with cheese, sardines and egg, cooking over medium heat until mixture holds its shape. Stir constantly. Check seasoning and cool. Shape into small balls, dip in beaten egg and roll in crumbs. Fry in hot oil until delicately brown. Drain on absorbent paper.

Sardine Rounds

Rodelas de sardinha

1 can sardines, drained and mashed • 1 tablespoon butter
3/4 cup bread, cubed, without crusts • 3/4 cup cream • 2 hard-boiled eggs, chopped
salt and pepper

Mix sardines with butter and add the bread that has been mashed with the cream. Heat gently. When mixture is thick enough to hold its shape, remove from heat, add the chopped eggs and seasoning. Cool. Spread on rounds of bread and broil. Serve hot.

Shrimp Appetizers
Bolinhos de Camarão

*1/2 pound bread • milk, enough to reduce bread to a mush • 1/2 pound fresh shrimp,
cleaned and deveined • 2 tablespoons butter • 2 tablespoons onion, minced
1/8 teaspoon coriander powder • salt and pepper • 1 tablespoon chopped parsley
3 eggs • bread crumbs • oil for frying*

Remove crusts from bread and soak the remainder with just enough milk to make a mush. Sauté shrimp in butter with onion, coriander, salt and pepper. When shrimp is cooked, cool and pass mixture through a blender. Mix the ground shrimp with the mush and finely-chopped parsley and 2 of the eggs that have been lightly beaten. Cook over medium heat until mixture is thick enough to hold its shape. Adjust seasoning and allow to cool completely. Shape into bite-size balls, roll in bread crumbs, then in the other slightly beaten egg and once again in the crumbs. Let stand 1 hour. Fry in hot oil until golden brown, drain on absorbent paper and serve hot.

Carrot Filling
Cenoura

Mix 1 cup grated raw carrots with 1/2 cup chopped ham and enough highly-seasoned mayonnaise to hold.

Chicken, Ham and Cabbage
Galinha, Presunto e Repolho

1/2 cup chopped cooked chicken • 1/2 cup chopped boiled ham
1/2 cup shredded raw cabbage • 1/4 cup chopped celery • 1 tablespoon lemon juice
1/2 tablespoon chopped green olives • 1 tablespoon capers • mayonnaise • salt and pepper

Mix all ingredients with sufficient mayonnaise to hold. Add salt and pepper to taste.

VARIATION: Substitute grated raw carrot for cabbage.

Egg and Spinach Filling
Ovo com Espinafre

1/2 package chopped frozen spinach • few drops lemon juice • 2 hard-boiled eggs, chopped
4 tablespoons chopped celery • 1 grated raw carrot • salt and pepper • mayonnaise

Cook spinach as directed and drain out all the liquid. Cool thoroughly and then sprinkle with lemon juice. Let stand 5 or 10 minutes. Add eggs, celery, carrot, salt and pepper to taste (also dry mustard, if desired) and enough mayonnaise to hold.

Egg White and Pickle Filling
Claras de Ovos com Picles

8 hard-boiled egg whites • 1/4 cup chopped pickles • 1 teaspoon prepared mustard
1 tablespoon minced onion • 1 tablespoon grated raw carrot • 1 teaspoon capers
seasoning • mayonnaise to hold

Chop egg whites and mix with pickles, mustard, onion, carrot and capers. Season to taste. Add mayonnaise to hold.

Eggplant Filling
Berinjela

1 cup cooked eggplant • 3 seedless green olives • 1/4 clove garlic • 1/2 teaspoon vinegar
salt and pepper • mayonnaise to hold

Blend eggplant with olives and garlic in electric blender or chop very fine. Add vinegar and season to taste. Mix well with enough mayonnaise to hold. May also be used as a hot canapé.

Ham and Bacon Filling
Presunto com Bacon

2 ounces bacon • 4 ounces cooked ham • 1 tablespoon prepared mustard
1 teaspoon Worcestershire sauce • 2 tablespoons chopped peanuts
salt and pepper • mayonnaise to hold

Fry or broil bacon and drain off all the grease. Grind with ham, or chop very fine. Add mustard, Worcestershire sauce, peanuts and mayonnaise to hold. Season to taste. May also be used as a hot canapé.

Nut Filling
Nozes

Mix equal quantities of chopped nuts, chopped olives and chopped pickles with half the amount of chopped seedless raisins. Moisten with a highly seasoned mayonnaise — enough to hold.

Palm Heart Filling
Palmito

1 10-ounce can palm hearts • few drops lemon juice • 1 tablespoon butter
2 beaten eggs • salt and pepper • 2 tablespoons ketchup

Drain the palm hearts, pull apart and mash with a fork. Sprinkle lemon juice on top and let stand 15 minutes. Melt butter in a skillet and scramble the eggs. Sprinkle with enough salt and pepper to taste. Remove from fire and when slightly warm add the ketchup. When the mixture is cold, add the mashed palm hearts.

Pineapple and Chicken Filling
Abacaxi e Galinha

1/3 cup butter • 1 tablespoon prepared mustard • 1 tablespoon chopped parsley
1 cup cooked, chopped chicken • 1/2 cup chopped pineapple, drained
seasoning • mayonnaise to hold

Cream butter with mustard, parsley, chicken and pineapple. Season to taste. Add mayonnaise to hold.

Sardine Filling
Recheio de Sardinha

1 can sardines, drained • 1 tablespoon lemon juice • 1/4 cup cold mashed potatoes
1 tablespoon chopped shallots • 1/4 cup chopped black olives
1 tablespoon mayonnaise • salt and pepper

Drain all the oil from the sardines and mash with the lemon juice. Add cold mashed potatoes and rest of ingredients. Check seasoning. Serve on bread rounds grilled under the broiler.

Spinach Filling
Recheio de Espinafre

1/2 package chopped frozen spinach • 1 tablespoon butter • 1 teaspoon prepared mustard
1 tablespoon grated cheese • salt and pepper

Cook spinach as directed on package. Press out all the liquid. Return to saucepan with butter, mustard and cheese and heat until mixture is thoroughly blended. Cool and correct seasoning.

Shrimp Couples No. 1
Casadinhos de Camarão Nº 1

36 small, cleaned, fresh shrimp marinated in 1 tablespoon lemon juice with salt and pepper
1/2 cup rice flour • 1/4 teaspoon salt • 1 egg, separated • 1/2 cup beer
1 tablespoon melted butter • oil for deep frying

Sift flour with salt and add beaten egg yolk that has been mixed with the beer. Beat until smooth, add butter and let stand 1 hour. Fold in beaten egg white. Coat 2 shrimp with the batter, pierce with a toothpick, and brown in deep fat at 370°, until all shrimp are used. Drain on absorbent paper and serve with the toothpicks still in the shrimp.

VARIATIONS: This batter may be used for many kinds of fritters. Add 1 1/2 cups highly seasoned chopped fish, shrimp, ham, chicken or meat and drop by spoonfuls in hot fat or oil.

Shrimp Couples No. 2
Casadinhos de Camarão Nº 2

Marinate shrimp as in No. 1 and let stand 1 hour. Arrange in pairs on a toothpick, roll in bread crumbs, beaten egg and in crumbs again. Fry as in No. 1.

[TRANSLATED FROM: **NOÇÕES DE ARTE CULINÁRIA** BY MARIA THEREZA A. COSTA]

Around-the-Clock Sandwich
Sanduíche para Todas as Horas

8 slices buttered toast with crusts removed • sliced Swiss cheese • sliced boiled ham
2 cups milk • 1 tablespoon butter • 3 tablespoons grated Swiss cheese
3 beaten eggs • seasoning

Arrange toast, Swiss cheese and sliced ham in layers in a baking dish until ingredients are all used. Add milk, butter and grated cheese to beaten eggs and seasoning. Pour mixture over toast. Bake in a 400° oven 10-15 minutes. Serve for breakfast, for lunch, as a first dinner coarse or for a midnight snack.

Hot Rolled Sandwich
Sanduíche Enrolado

DOUGH (MASSA)

2 envelopes granulated yeast • 1 cup warm milk • 1 tablespoon butter • 2 tablespoons salt
1 tablespoon sugar • 4 eggs • 4 boiled potatoes, riced • 8 1/2 cups sifted all-purpose flour

Dissolve yeast in warm milk, add butter, salt, sugar, eggs and boiled potatoes and mix well. Sift in 4 1/2 cups of the flour and knead until bubbles form. Let stand 20 minutes, cut down, add the rest of the flour and knead. Let stand another 20 minutes.

FILLING (RECHEIO)

1/2 pound butter • 1/2 pound thinly-sliced boiled ham • 1/2 cup seedless raisins
6 ounces grated mozzarella cheese

Roll out the dough as thinly as possible and spread the butter evenly on top. Fold dough over into 3 parts and roll out a second time. Divide dough into 3 parts and roll each out to the same size, either square, round or oblong. Place one portion on a large buttered baking sheet and spread with the thinly sliced ham and raisins. Cover with a second portion of the dough, rolled out to fit the first. Sprinkle evenly with the mozzarella cheese. Place the third portion on top, rolled out to the same size. Cover with a towel and let stand until double in bulk.

TOPPING

Egg yolk • Butter • Grated Parmesan cheese

Brush top with egg yolk and dot with butter. Sprinkle with Parmesan cheese and bake in a 400° oven for 25 minutes.

N O T E : This recipe is sufficient to cover a 15" by 20" baking sheet. If a smaller one is used, make half the recipe.

[MARIA AMALIA AZEVEDO LEITE, MINAS GERAIS]

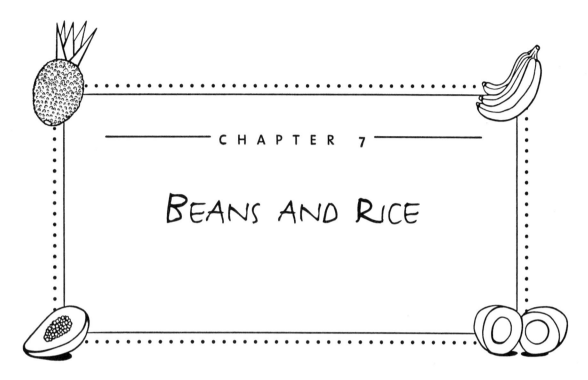

CHAPTER 7

BEANS AND RICE

To say of a man that "He knows how many beans make five," is to speak highly of his shrewdness.

G. F. NORTHALL, FOLK-PHRASES, P. 16

It is better not to stir the rice, although it sticks.

CERVANTES, DON QUIXOTE, PT. II, CH. 37

B eans, rice and manioc meal are without doubt the most important staples in the Brazilian's diet. They are served throughout Brazil at least once a day and, many times, twice daily. In fact, their use, to the exclusion of other foodstuffs, like salads and vegetables has been highly criticized, not only by Brazilian nutritionists, but by many visitors to Brazil during the last hundred years. Nearly all foreigners residing in Brazil know that unless beans and rice are at hand, servants will not remain on the premises. And in all industry, whether in factories, mines or in construction fields, when lunch time approaches, the worker wants his rice and beans. The sandwich that satisfies the American laborer does not appease the appetite of his Brazilian counterpart.

Generally, it is the laboring class that makes beans and rice the mainstay of its diet, but many intellectuals also do not consider that they have properly eaten unless these foodstuffs have been available during the course of the day, usually at lunch. This predilection is easily comprehended in drought areas, where it is difficult to come by fresh vegetables. However, a great many inhabitants of populated areas, where such is not the case, still subsist on rice, beans and manioc meal.

Although Brazil produces more beans than any other country in the world, double the amount produced in the United States,[1] consumption sometimes exceeds production, and it is necessary to important more. Per capita annual consumption of beans in Brazil amounts to 54 pounds ,[2] while that of rice amounts to 59.5 pounds.[3]

---

[1] U.S. Department of Agriculture, Foreign Agriculture Circular F.D.P. 8-59 of October 20, 1959. In 1960-1961 dry bean production in Brazil reached 1,822,000 metric tons. *Production Year Book* of FAO, 1961, p. 85.

[2] *Ibid.*

[3] Unpublished report of the U.S. Department of Agriculture.

There are many types of beans grown in Brazil, ranging in color from black to white with various shades of brown, but the black bean constitutes about 80 percent of the beans consumed. Bread may be the staff of life in many countries, but in Brazil rice and beans assume this position. Brazil depends so much on these staples that any act of man or nature cutting off their supply plays havoc with the nation's sustenance.

During World War II, when it was necessary to ration cooking fuel, the Brazilian housewife was faced with a serious dilemma. Cooking beans and rice without a pressure cooker and lacking the necessary fuel posed a difficult challenge. Resourcefulness was put to the test and the Brazilian housewife emerged triumphant. Those who had a backyard, set up a brazier and cooked their black beans outside. But they cooked more than beans! A washed, unlabeled can of condensed milk went into the bean pot and *Doce de Leite*[*] was made at the same time the beans were cooking.

Apartment dwellers did not have this advantage of saving fuel. But when they cooked their beans, they too made their *Doce de Leite* in the same pot, which also served to economize fuel for the war effort.

Napoleon once told Gaspard Gourgaud that rice is the best food for the soldier. Brazilians have extended this view, as they consider rice an indispensable item in their daily fare, both civilian and military. Like beans, cooking rice during the war was fraught with difficulties. But the Brazilian housewife surmounted these just as she did in preparing the beans. She would prepare the rice in a heavy earthenware vessel (or lacking this, she used heavy aluminum) up to the step where boiling water was added. Then, the saucepan was removed from the heat and the fuel was extinguished. The saucepan or earthenware pot was enveloped in old newspapers, placed in a closed, unlit oven where the cooking process was completed by means of the stored heat in the vessel.

Cooking rice in this manner proved so satisfactory that many cooks still employ this method. As a matter of fact, there is a young Brazilian housewife in Washington who continues to prepare her rice in this fashion, claiming that the taste is far superior than when the cooking process is completed with direct heat.

---

[*] This is a very popular Brazilian sweet made by simmering milk and sugar together until it thickens. It is now available in cans.

Actually, beans and rice properly prepared in the Brazilian style are excellent dishes even though they fall short of being complete foods in themselves. They are tasty adjuncts to a meal, combining well with other foods, and they are satisfying.

Rice should be flaky and tasty; when served, each grain should fall separately from the spoon. Although the grains are loose, they are well-seasoned. This is accomplished by frying the raw, washed rice with the seasoning so that each grain is coated with it. The water added is only sufficient to steam the rice. Once cooked, the rice may be removed to a mould, pressed down firmly, unmoulded, and served attractively-garnished with meat, fish or fowl.

Black beans, which seem to be the most popular kind consumed in Brazil, are an indispensable ingredient in the national dish *Feijoada*. There is no record of this dish prior to the nineteenth century, but its popularity has grown steadily.

Preparing and serving a *Feijoada Completa* is almost ritualistic in character. It is served all over Brazil, with slight variations.

The *Dicionário do Folclore Brasileiro*[5] states that "it would be impossible to list all the ingredients that go into a *Feijoada*, but the standard items are beans, sausages of different varieties, jerked beef, pork, cured meats, bacon, tongue, and the ear, foot and tail of a pig." In Bahia and the Northern Regions, vegetables such as pumpkin and kale are included in the recipe, and also orange juice. The beans used in the Northern *feijoada* are the type known as *mulatinho*, while in Southern Brazil black beans are used.

Most families have their own ideas and recipes as to what constitutes a good *Feijoada*. However, while recipes and ingredients vary slightly, one style of serving the *Feijoada* is observed throughout the country.

The cooked meats are separated from the beans, then sliced and arranged attractively on a platter. Traditionally, the tongue goes in the center of the platter, and some of the bean liquor is ladled over the meats. The beans are served from a tureen. Sliced oranges are served with the beans and also a sauce, *Molho de Pimenta e Limão*[6]

---

[5] Luís da Câmara Cascudo, *Dicionário do Folclore Brasileiro* (Rio de Janeiro: Ministério da Educação e Cultura, Instituto Nacional do Livro, 1954), p. 262.

[6] See recipe, p. 91.

to which a small amount of the bean liquor has been added, together with thin rounds of sliced onions. A dram or two of *cachaça*[7] is placed before each guest to aid digestion. It goes without saying that rice and the popular manioc meal are always at hand.

Preparing a *Feijoada* takes anywhere from 5 to 24 hours. As it is a heavy dish, it is usually served at luncheons. While Brazilian cuisine has one or two other ceremonial dishes, *Feijoada* is *the* ceremonial dish.

Bean Croquettes
Croquetes de Feijão

2 cups cooked white dried beans • 1 cup tomato sauce • 2 tablespoons butter
1 tablespoon minced onion • 2 tablespoons all-purpose flour • 2 eggs yolks
salt and pepper • 1 beaten egg • bread crumbs • oil for frying

Liquify beans with tomato sauce (or grind to a purée and then add tomato sauce). Melt butter in a saucepan and gently sauté onion. Stir in the flour. Pour in the bean purée, add egg yolk and season with salt and pepper. Cook over medium heat, stirring constantly until mixture is thick enough to hold its shape. This takes from 20 to 30 minutes. Cool thoroughly. Shape into croquettes, roll in bread crumbs, then beaten egg and again in bread crumbs. Fry in hot oil.

---

[7] See chapter on "Beverages," p. 149.

Black Bean Cake
Bolo de Feijão Preto

2 cups cooked plain black beans (page 129) • 1 1/4 cups bread crumbs
1/2 cup tomato sauce • Crisp slices of bacon and hard-boiled eggs for garnish
1/4 cup chopped onion • 1 slightly beaten egg • Seasoning

Beans should be of the consistency of a medium cream sauce. Add bread crumbs, tomato sauce, onion and egg. Season to taste. Turn into a well-buttered 1 1/2-quart pudding mould and bake in a 375° oven for approximately 45 minutes. Unmould and garnish with wedges of hard-boiled egg and crisp slices of bacon. Cover with tomato sauce, if desired.

[DAURA ALVES DA COSTA, RIO DE JANEIRO]

Black Bean Tutu No. 1
Tutu de Feijão Nº 1

2 cups cooked plain black beans (page 129) • 2 ounces of bacon, cut up and delicately
fried with grease removed • 1/2 bay leaf • manioc meal

Heat beans with bacon and bay leaf for 10 to 15 minutes until the flavor of the bacon and bay leaf permeates the beans. Add salt and pepper, if necessary. As the beans are cooking, gradually add enough manioc meal for the mixture to thicken to the consistency of mush. Stir carefully when adding the meal so as to prevent lumps.

N O T E : *Tutu* is served with *Roupa-velha* (p. 420) that has been made from jerked beef taken from the *Feijoada* and also with *Couve à Mineira* (p. 553).

[OLGA DE SÁ PIRES, MINAS GERAIS]

Black Bean Tutu No. 2
Tutu de Feijão N° 2

3 cups cooked plain black beans (page 129 • manioc meal • 2 tablespoons vinegar
1/4 cup chopped bacon • 1/2 pound smoked sausage, finely sliced • 1 onion, finely sliced

Beans should be of the consistency of a medium cream sauce. Heat, add enough manioc meal, stirring constantly, until mixture thickens to the consistency of a mush. Stir well, remove from heat and add vinegar. Fry bacon and sausage together and drain on absorbent paper. Place on top of the *Tutu* which has been spooned into a serving dish. Fry onion in some of the bacon fat and pour over the *Tutu*. Serve surrounded by *Couve à Mineira* (p. 553) and hard-boiled eggs.

[FLORINDA K. MACHADO, RIO GRANDE DO SUL]

Brazilian Baked Beans
Feijão Branco Assado

1 pound dry white beans • 1 pound breast of lamb, cubed with as much fat cut away as possible
1 pound smoked ham or tongue, cubed • 1 bayleaf • 1/2 pound bacon, cubed
1/2 cup chopped onions • 1 cup peeled, chopped fresh tomatoes (or 1 cup tomato sauce)
1 crushed garlic clove • salt and black pepper • bread crumbs • butter

Pick over beans and soak until the next day. Add water to cover and cook with lamb and ham (or tongue) and bayleaf. Simmer until meats are tender and beans are cooked. Fry bacon in a skillet, drain off most of the grease and sauté the onions. Add the tomatoes (or sauce), garlic, salt and pepper. Simmer for 10 minutes, then add to the beans. Continue to simmer beans for another 40 or 50 minutes, taste and check seasoning. Pour 1/3 of the beans into a buttered casserole and place the pieces of meat on top, then add the rest of the beans. Sprinkle bread crumbs on top, dot with butter and bake in a preheated 375° oven for 30 minutes.

[TRANSLATED FROM: **AS RECEITAS PARA VOCÊ DA TIA EVELINA, 4TH ED.**]

Feijoada No. 1[8]

(SUFFICIENT TO SERVE 12 TO 15 HUNGRY PEOPLE)

5 cups black beans • 1 pound jerked beef • 1 small smoked tongue
1/2 pound Canadian bacon • 1 pound fresh pork sausages • 1 pound corned spareribs
1 pound smoked sausages or Portuguese sausages • 2 pig's feet
1 pound lean beef, cut in half • 1/4 pound lean bacon • 1 tablespoon shortening
2 large chopped onions • 3 crushed garlic cloves • 1 chopped tomato (optional)
1 tablespoon chopped parsley (optional) • 1 crushed hot pepper (optional)

1. Remove any impurities from beans, wash and soak overnight in cold water.

2. Soak jerked beef, tongue, Canadian bacon overnight in separate pans of cold water.

3. Next morning, drain the beans (if any liquid remains), cover with fresh cold water and cook for about 2 1/2 hours in covered saucepan, adding, as needed, sufficient water to keep the beans covered. When beans are cooked and tender, remove about 1/4 cup of the bean liquor and set aside to cool and be used in preparing the special hot sauce served with *Feijoada*.

4. Meanwhile, as the beans are cooking, prepare the meats, as follows, always removing them from the liquid in which they were cooked:

    a) Drain the jerked beef, cover with cold water, bring to boil and simmer for 1 hour, or until fork tender. Remove, cut into 1-inch strips and set aside.

    b) Parboil tongue long enough to be able to remove skin, and set aside.

    c) Prick fresh sausages, parboil and set aside.

    d) Parboil Canadian bacon, spareribs, smoked sausages, and pig's feet, and set aside.

---

[8] Reprinted from an article on *Feijoada* by the author that appeared in the *Washington Post*, February 7, 1963.

5. Place all the meats, except the fresh pork sausages, but including the beef and bacon, in a very large saucepan, cover with tepid water, slowly bring to boil and simmer until meats are tender (about 1 1/2 hours).

6. Drain all the meats and add to the beans with the pork sausages. Simmer until meats are very tender and beans are soft enough to mash easily. Season with salt.

7. About 1/2 an hour before serving, melt the shortening in a large skillet and gently sauté the onions and garlic. If the optional ingredients are desired, they also should be sautéed at this time.

8. Add about 2 cups or ladles of the beans and mash with a wooden spoon or mallet.

9. Pour about 2 cups of the bean liquor over the mixture, simmer until mixture thickens, then return to the pot containing beans and meats.

10. Simmer until thoroughly blended, about 1/2 an hour.

11. Taste to check seasoning.

TO SERVE : Remove the meats from the beans and slice so that each person may have a small portion of the various kinds of meat. According to long established custom, the tongue is placed in the center of the platter and the smoked meats at one end while the fresh meats are arranged attractively at the other end of the platter. Moisten the meats with a small laddle of the bean liquor.

The beans are served in a soup tureen or deep serving dish. The guest helps himself to an assortment of meats and places a serving of Brazilian Rice (p. 131) to one side of the plate. The beans with their rich sauce are ladled over the rice while manioc meal or Butter Farofa (p. 50) is sprinkled over the beans or meats.

Sliced oranges and *Couve à Mineira* (p. 553) accompany the *Feijoada* as well as a special hot sauce, *Molho de Pimenta e Limão* to which some of the bean liquor is added.[9] Brazilian rum *(cachaça)* is also served with this meal or else a *Batida* (p. 150).

---

[9] See chapter on "Afro-Brazilian Specialties," p.67.

Feijoada No. 2[10]

The creation of music in honor of food and drink is nothing new. Bach wrote a cantata in praise of coffee and Schubert a quintet about trout. One of the most recent and spontaneous compositions of this sort was a musical essay written by one of South America's most illustrious composers, the late Heitor Villa-Lobos.

When Maestro Villa-Lobos was a guest in the home of the Brazilian Consul General in New York, Dona Dora Vasconcellos, a special *feijoada*, Brazil's national dish, was prepared for him. On that occasion, the kitchen staff was, as it is now, headed by Noemia Faria, a shy good-humored woman.

The meal was an outstanding success and the composer was inspired to pen a brief composition in Miss Faria's autograph book titled "A Fugue Without End." The composer wrote beneath the piece that it is a "feijoada set to music for Noemia to remember Villa-Lobos." The composition was in four parts called "Farina," "Meat," "Rice" and "Black Beans," four of the essential components of the meal.

Although there are many parts of a feijoada, it is easy to prepare and an excellent idea for autumn and winter entertaining.

Noemia Faria's feijoada consists of black beans, several cooked meats including sun-dried beef, sausage and salt pork; fluffy rice; golden sweet orange slices, chopped collards and onions marinated in a powerfully hot French dressing.

Each of the foods is served from separate dishes to dinner plates and all is sprinkled liberally with an uncooked meal the Brazilians call "farinha de mandioca."

---

[10] Craig Caliborne, *New York Times Cook Book* (New York: Harper & Brothers, 1961). Reprinted with permission of the author.

3 cups black beans • 1 pound carne seca (sun-cured salted beef) that has been soaked overnight in water • 2 pounds raw smoked tongue • 1/2 pound lingüiça defumada (Portuguese sausage) • 1/2 pound chuck beef • 1/2 pound salt pork • Salt and pepper 2 large cloves garlic, chopped • 2 teaspoons shortening

1. Wash beans well and soak overnight water to cover. Drain, add six cups water and cook, covered, adding water as needed till beans are tender, about two and a half hours. As soon as beans are cooked, begin adding other ingredients.

2. Cut carne seca (dried beef) into inch and a half squares and add to beans.

3. Peel tongue and cut it into large cubes. Cover with water and bring to a boil. Simmer ten minutes, drain and add to beans.

4. Prick sausages with a fork, cover with water, boil a few minutes, drain and add to beans.

5. Cut chuck in half and add to beans.

6. Cut salt pork into half-inch slices and add to beans. Season stew with salt and pepper.

7. When beans are tender, brown garlic lightly in shortening. Add about a cup of the beans, mash and return mixture to large pot of beans. Adjust seasonings.

8. Remove pieces of meat to a large platter and turn beans into a chafing dish or bowl. Serve with rice, onions in sauce, sweetened orange slices, collards and braised pork loin.

Feijoada No. 3

3/4 pound jerked beef • 3 cups black beans • 1 pound smoked sausage • 1 pound smoked pork
1 pound smoked tongue • 1/4 pound bacon • 1 pig's foot

Soak jerked beef overnight in plenty of cold water. Soak beans overnight. Drain beef, cover with cold water, bring to a boil and boil 15 minutes. Drain again and cool. Add all the meats, cover with tepid water, bring slowly to a boil and simmer until meats are almost tender. Meanwhile, in another pot, place the drained beans, cover with cold water and no seasoning and cook until almost tender.

Combine contents of the 2 pots and cook beans and meats together, simmering until meats are very tender and beans are soft enough to mash. While the meats and beans are cooking, prepare the following:

1 shallot, chopped • 1 onion, chopped • 1 piece fresh sausage, cut up
1 garlic clove, minced • dash of cayenne pepper

Fry shallots and onions with sausage until lightly browned, then add garlic and pepper. Stir, frying until lightly browned. Add 1 cup of cooked beans, mix well and mash all together, then stir in some of the bean liquor and simmer 5 or 10 minutes, until the seasonings are blended. Return this sauce to the beans and meats and simmer until well-blended. Adjust seasoning.

Separate the meats from the beans and slice in uniform pieces and arrange on a platter. According to a long established custom, the tongue is placed in the center and the other meats surrounding it. Moisten the meats with some of the liquor from the beans. Serve the beans in a hot tureen, with flaky boiled rice, sliced oranges, pepper and lemon sauce, and *cachaça* as accompaniments.

Plain Black Beans
Feijão Preto Simples

1 pound black beans • 1 tablespoon bacon fat • 1 grated onion • 1 crushed garlic clove
1 teaspoon salt • black pepper

Pick over beans the night before. Wash and soak in clear, cold water. In the morning, drain and cover with cold water and simmer until beans are tender. This may take from 1 to 3 hours, depending upon the quality of the bean used. A pressure cooker may also be used. When the beans are tender, remove from heat.

Melt bacon fat in a skillet, add onion and garlic, and sauté. With a large ladle, take some of the cooked beans and bean liquor, and mix in skillet with onion and garlic. Mash the beans with a potato masher or the bottom of the ladle. Add some of the liquid from the beans and bring to boil. Season with salt and pepper.

Pour contents of the skillet into the rest of the beans and simmer for at least 30 minutes. Correct seasoning and cook until mixture thickens to the consistency of a medium white sauce. Serve with manioc meal or a *Farofa* made from the meal (p. 50).

[OLGA DE SÁ PIRES, MINAS GERAIS]

Baked Rice No. 1
Arroz de Forno Nº 1

5 cups cooked Brazilian Rice (p. 131) • sliced boiled ham • 4 hard-boiled eggs
sliced olives • grated cheese • salt and pepper

Fill a buttered baking dish with layers of cooked rice, ham, sliced eggs, olives and seasoning. Sprinkle grated cheese over top and bake 20 minutes in a preheated 375° oven.

VARIATION: This may also be prepared with shrimp or chicken, cooked in a sauce, in which case the baking will take longer.

[MARIA BARBOZA NUNES, RIO DE JANEIRO]

Baked Rice No. 2
Arroz de Forno Nº 2

4 cups cooked Brazilian Rice (p. 131) • 1/2 cup tomato sauce • 1/2 cup grated cheese
• salt and pepper • bread crumbs

Place Brazilian Rice in a buttered baking dish and cover with a paste made of the tomato sauce, cheese and seasonings. Lightly sprinkle with bread crumbs and bake in a 375° preheated oven until brown.

Baked Rice — Country Style
Arroz de Forno da Roça

1 chicken bouillon cube dissolved in 3/4 cup hot water • 2 egg yolks
5 cups cooked Brazilian Rice (p. 131) • seasoning • 1 beaten egg • bread crumbs

Dissolve bouillon cube in hot water and cool. Add egg yolks to dissolved bouillon cube and mix with rice. Taste and correct seasoning. Remove to a buttered baking dish and pour beaten egg on top. Sprinkle with bread crumbs and bake in a preheated 400° oven to brown.

Brazilian Rice
Arroz Brasileiro

2 cups uncooked rice • 3 tablespoons shortening • 1 onion, thinly sliced
1 peeled, chopped tomato or 2 tablespoons tomato sauce
2 — 2 1/4 cups boiling water • 1 teaspoon salt

Wash and pick rice very well (preferably using long-grain rice). Melt shortening in a medium-size skillet. Use oil, lard, margarine, or bacon fat, but *not* butter. Fry the rice with onion, gently stirring with a wooden spoon until the mixture has a swishing sound. This takes about 10 minutes over a low flame and is a very important factor in producing the dry final product, which is one of the prime requisites of Brazilian Rice.

Add tomato, stir once or twice, remove from heat and pour 2 cups of boiling water which have been mixed with the salt over the fried rice. Care must be taken at this point because the mixture will spatter. Stir once or twice (no more), return to heat and bring to boil. Then cover and reduce heat to very low. Cook 20 or 25 minutes, until all the water has evaporated. Taste 1 or 2 grains of the rice to see if they are cooked. If not, add the other 1/4 cup boiling water. Do not stir. When rice is done, remove from heat, uncover and allow some of the steam to evaporate. Place in a serving dish or press into a warm mould and unmould on a platter. When the rice is properly made, each grain falls separately from the spoon. Makes approximately 6 cups.

[REPRIMED FROM AUTHOR'S ARTICLE IN JULY, 1963 ISSUE OF GOURMET MAGAZINE]

Rice Cakes
Bolinhos de Arroz

2 cups cooked Brazilian Rice (p. 131) • 2 eggs, separated • 2 tablespoons butter
1/2 cup milk • seasonings • corn oil

Firmly pack rice in a measuring cup to measure. Put rice in blender, add egg yolks, butter and milk. Remove and fold in stiffly-beaten egg whites. Check seasoning. Fry by spoonfuls in corn oil at 375°. Drain on absorbent paper. Yields 12.

Casserole of Rice
Caçarola de Arroz

1 pound veal • 1 pound lean pork • 1/4 cup oil • 1/2 cup chopped onion

2 tablespoons chopped parsley • 2 chopped tomatoes or 1 cup tomato sauce

1 16-oz. can peas (drain and reserve the liquid) • 1 teaspoon salt

4 cups cooked Brazilian Rice firmly packed (p. 131) • 1 tablespoon butter

1/2 cup grated Parmesan cheese • 1 tablespoon bread crumbs • Salt and pepper to taste

Cut meat into small pieces and sauté in the oil with onion, parsley and tomatoes. If tomato sauce is used, do not add until meats are browned. When meats are browned, add the liquid from the canned peas and salt. Cover and simmer until meats are tender, then add rice, butter, cheese, crumbs and peas. Check seasonings. Butter a mould and sprinkle lightly with bread crumbs, which are in addition to the crumbs used in the recipe. Firmly press the rice and meat mixture into the mould and bake in a 375° preheated oven for 20 minutes. Unmould and serve with a piquant tomato sauce.

Drayman's Rice
Arroz de Carreteiro"

Prepare jerked beef as for Ragout of Jerked Beef (p. 392) by boiling beef with garlic clove and omitting bayleaf, parsley, spring onions and butter. Next, fry the beef in 3 tablespoons of bacon fat with 1 chopped onion, 1 chopped, peeled tomato, and 3 tablespoons chopped green pepper. Cover skillet and cook until tender, then add 1 cup of uncooked rice, which has been washed. Mix and cook 5 minutes. Season to taste with salt and pepper (cayenne or malagueta). Add enough boiling water or beef stock to cover. Boil 2 minutes. Replace cover and cook slowly until rice is done.

Palm Hearts with Rice & Shrimp
Palmito com Arroz e Camarão

1 pound fresh shrimp • 2 tablespoons olive oil • 1/2 crushed garlic clove
1 tablespoon minced green pepper • 1 tablespoon minced onion • 1 tablespoon minced parsley
2 tablespoons tomato sauce • 2 cups cooked rice • 1 small can palm hearts

Shell, devein and clean raw shrimp. Heat oil and sauté next four ingredients, then add raw shrimp. Add tomato sauce and cook until shrimp is tender. Season, add cooked rice, cook over low flame until mixture is thoroughly blended and heated and grains of rice are separate. Taste to check seasoning. Add the palm hearts that have been drained. Stir and mix gently, so as not to break the palm sections. Pile onto a platter and garnish with sliced green pepper, *pimiento* and a mixture of chopped black and green olives.

" This dish is very popular in Rio Grande do Sul State.

Florida Rice
Arroz Flórida

6 medium-sized tomatoes • 2 tablespoons butter • 1 12 cup grated onion • 2 eggs
1 tablespoon cornstarch dissolved in 1 cup milk • 1 cup cooked shrimp, chopped and seasoned
2 tablespoons grated cheese • 1 cup cooked peas • 2 egg yolks
6 cups cooked Brazilian Rice (p. 131) • bread crumbs

Slice tops off tomatoes and scoop out the centers. Melt 1 tablespoon of the butter and sauté onion with the chopped tomato pulp until tender. Add eggs, milk-cornstarch mixture and stir over a slow flame to thicken. When sauce is of the consistency of a thick white sauce, remove from heat, strain through a coarse strainer, add shrimp and check seasoning. Fill the tomatoes with the shrimp mixture. Mix cheese, peas, the other tablespoon of butter and the 2 egg yolks with the rice. Taste to check seasoning. Turn into a buttered Pyrex baking dish and make 6 indentations with the bottom of a glass. Place one stuffed tomato in each cavity. Sprinkle bread crumbs on top and bake in a preheated 375° oven for about 50 minutes.

[TRANSLATED FROM: **NOÇÕES DE ARTE CULINÁRIA** BY MARIA THEREZA A. COSTA, SÃO PAULO]

Rice Croquettes
Croquetes de Arroz

2 cups cooked rice • 1/4 cup meat gravy, stock or tomato sauce • 3 eggs, separated
3 tablespoons Parmesan cheese • 1 tablespoon grated onion • 1 tablespoon butter
1 tablespoon chopped parsley • seasoning • corn oil

Mix rice, gravy, egg yolks, cheese, onion, butter and parsley. Taste and correct seasoning. Cook over low heat until you have a thick mixture, then cool, thoroughly. Shape into croquettes, roll in the beaten egg whites and fry at 375° in hot cornoil. Drain on absorbent paper and serve plain or with a sauce. Yields 6.

VARIATION: Use leftover chicken, fish or meat with same mixture.

Rice — Minas Style
Arroz à Moda de Minas

Proceed as for Rice and Pork (p. 137) substituting 1 pound smoked sausages cut into 1-inch slices. Do not marinate the sausages. Proceed up to the point where the pork has been fried with the onions and parsley and then add 2 cups of raw shredded cabbage, which has been thoroughly washed and scalded. Cook 5 minutes to blend sausages with the vegetables. Omit cheese, peppers and ham. Add uncooked rice and cook for 10 minutes, stirring constantly to prevent sticking. Season well with salt and pepper. Add boiling water, cover and cook as for Rice and Pork.

Rice and Clams
Arroz com Mariscos

2 dozen raw, shucked clams with their juice • 1 tablespoon lemon juice • salt and black pepper
2 tablespoons olive oil • 1/4 cup chopped onion • 2 tablespoons chopped parsley
1/8 teaspoon tomato paste • prepared Brazilian Rice (p. 131)

Drain clams and reserve liquid. Marinate whole clams in lemon juice, salt and pepper for 30 minutes. Heat oil, and gently sauté clams with onion, parsley, garlic salt and tomato paste. Add 1/2 cup of the cold clam juice, stir, check seasoning and remove from heat. Prepare the recipe for Brazilian Rice using any leftover clam juice for part of the 2 – 2 1/4 cups of boiling water that recipe calls for. Proceed as in recipe for Brazilian Rice and when rice is almost cooked, stir in clam mixture. Cover, and return to complete cooking over a low flame.

Rice and Pork
Arroz com Porco

3 pounds fresh, lean pork, cut into small strips • marinate, same as for Stewed Guinea
Fowl, p. 476 • 1/4 cup oil or fat • 2 minced onions • 1 tablespoon chopped parsley
3 tablespoons grated Parmesan cheese • 2 chopped green peppers • 1/4 pound diced boiled ham
2 cups uncooked rice • 3 – 4 cups boiling water • 1 teaspoon salt

Marinate pork overnight. Next morning cut into smaller pieces and sauté in oil with onions and parsley until meat is cooked. Add cheese, peppers, ham and washed rice. Cook for 10 minutes to blend, then add water and salt. Bring to boil, reduce heat to low, cover and cook until done, adding small amounts of hot water as necessary. When cooked, turn into a slightly oiled mould, press firmly and invert on a serving plate. Serve with your favorite sauce.

Rice Soufflé
soufflée de Arroz

1 cup uncooked rice • salted water • 1 cup tomato sauce • 1 peeled and chopped tomato
3 eggs, separated • 1 cup canned peas, drained • salt and pepper

Boil rice in slightly salted water. When done, strain and hold under cold tap water to wash off starch. Drain thoroughly. Add chopped tomato to the tomato sauce and mix with rice. Season to taste. Add beaten egg yolks and peas and fold in the stiffly-beaten egg whites. Turn into a buttered 2-quart soufflé dish and bake in a preheated 375° oven for 30 minutes, then serve immediately.

[TRANSLATED FROM: **AS RECEITAS PARA VOCÊ DA TIA EVELINA, 4TH ED.**]

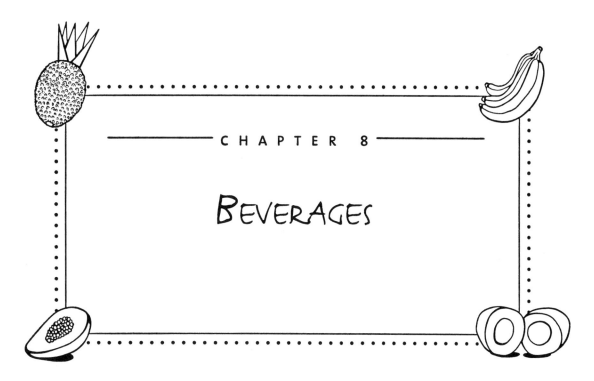

CHAPTER 8

BEVERAGES

The government of a nation is often decided over a cup of coffee, or the fate of empires changed by an extra bottle of Johannesberg.

G.P.R. JAMES, RICHELIEU, CHAP. 16

Coffee is an accepted and highly appreciated beverage in most parts of the world, especially in the United States where the annual per capita consumption is about 16 pounds.[1] However, there is no other country where coffee is such an important adjunct to everyday living as in Brazil. The "drink called coffa" — as Bacon called the beverage — is served in demitasse cups at frequent intervals throughout the day, when all Brazil takes time off to sip this, the Brazilian "pause that refreshes." It is not unusual for a Brazilian to consume anywhere from 12 to 24 of these little demitasses per day.

Many Brazilian businessmen conduct their business over a *cafezinho*, while the ladies of the family always welcome visitors with a cup of the delicious brew, for, in Brazil, coffee is a symbol of hospitality. All government agencies and private companies serve coffee at least twice a day. Even the beauty shops in Rio have one of their employees passing among the patrons offering coffee. Coffee in Brazil is the delight of both rich and poor, and one ventures to predict serious trouble if coffee were removed from their daily life.

It is small wonder, then, that the art of brewing coffee has developed to a very fine degree in Brazil. This has been aided by scientific research, as it has been proven conclusively that if you want to make uniformly good coffee, in any manner, you must start with thoroughly clean utensils, freshly drawn cold water, correct measurements and never, never let the water boil or serve coffee that has been reheated or boiled. If you *must* reheat coffee, do so in a double boiler, or set the coffee pot in another pan of boiling water.

To prepare the Brazilian demitasse, in addition to observing these principles, you must also select the blend and have it ground properly. I have found it most

---

[1] *Statistical Abstract of the United States for 1962*, p. 90.

satisfactory to order two parts French roast and one part American roast. When it is not possible to obtain the coffee bean, there is a vacuum packed Italian coffee on the market that will serve. The coffee should be pulverized, preferably as used. Grandmother had the right idea when she ground her coffee to order, although modern packaging makes this unnecessary. However, if you brew coffee only occasionally, it is wise to grind it as you use it because the volatile oils evaporate once it is exposed.

The next step is to have the proper utensils. In spite of the fact that there are numerous complicated coffee makers available, the Brazilian's requirements to make a good *cafezinho* are quite simple — a saucepan to heat the water, a flannel strainer and a plain coffee pot to serve the coffee. The flannel strainer, called *coador*, can be purchased in any Latin American market or can be made by sewing a V-shaped bag onto a strainer frame. When not in use, the *coador* is kept soaking in clear, cold water, and when it is newly acquired, it should be boiled in a coffee bath to absorb the flavor. The strainer has to be replaced from time to time as it becomes "stale."

Demitasse Coffee

Now you are ready to brew the genuine Brazilian coffee. The proportions are 2 level tablespoons of pulverized coffee for 3/4 cup of fresh-drawn cold water. Heat the water just below boiling, about 203° (boiling is 212°), because boiling would vaporize the essential oils. When the water has reached the proper temperature, stir in the measured coffee and remove from heat. Let stand 1 minute and stir again, then pour into the flannel strainer and strain directly into the coffee server. The latter should be thoroughly scoured and scaulded first. The demitasses should be served immediately, very hot, with plenty of sugar.

Brazilian Breakfast Coffee
Café com Leite

The demitasse coffee is served diluted with hot milk.

Iced Coffee
Café Gelado

It comes somewhat as a surprise to find that the largest coffee producing country in the world has not learned to like iced coffee, but due to its popularity in the United States, a favorite recipe is included here. To make good iced coffee, it is necessary to brew fresh coffee. If you are using the regular American roast, the proportions are 4 tablespoons for each cup, but if a darker roast is used, the quantity of coffee can be diminished by half. If you use instant coffee, the proportions are usually indicated on the jar. Fill tall glasses with ice cubes and pour freshly made coffee on top. Serve with cream and sugar.

Coffee Egg Nog
Gemada de Café

1 egg yolk • 1 teaspoon sugar • 1 cup hot coffee • 1 cup hot milk

Beat egg yolk with sugar and gradually add hot coffee and milk. Heat.

Mocha
Chocá

3 squares semi-sweetened chocolate • 2 1/2 cups scalding milk
3/4 cup strong coffee • sugar

Melt chocolate in half the scalding milk, stirring constantly. Add rest of milk, coffee, sugar to taste and scald. Serve hot with a teaspoonful of whipped cream in each cup.

Hot Chocolate with Egg Yolks
Chocolate com Gemas

2 squares unsweetened chocolate • 1 quart milk • 2 egg yolks • sugar

Melt chocolate, gradually add milk, but do not boil. When chocolate is thoroughly dissolved, remove from stove. Beat egg yolks with 2 tablespoons sugar and add milk and chocolate mixture. Return to heat, scald. Taste and add more sugar if desired. Serve hot, with or without whipped cream.

Caramel Milk
Leite Queimado

Heat 1 tablespoon sugar in a saucepan, stirring constantly until it is caramelized. Add 1 cup of milk, heat to dissolve the caramel and strain.

Mate

The beneficial qualities of *mate*, a kind of tea, have been acclaimed by many scientists and by both Presidents Theodore Roosevelt and Franklin Delano Roosevelt. It is a tonic for brain and nerves, reduces the feeling of hunger and fatigue, and is the principal beverage consumed by the Brazilian Gaucho or cowboy, who brews and drinks it from an elongated gourd called *Chimarrão*. All health food stores and fancy grocery stores sell *mate* which is prepared and served like tea, hot or cold.

HOT MATE *(Mate Quente):* Preheat the teapot by filling with boiling water. Use proportions of two tablespoons of *Mate* to three cups of boiling water or follow directions on the package. Let the *mate* steep at least five minutes. Flavor with sugar or honey and lemon or cream, or drink it plain.

ICED MATE *(Mate Gelado):* Brew hot *Mate* double strength and steep until it is cool. Pour over cracked ice and serve with sugar and lemon.

FOAMY MATE *(Mate Espumoso):* Beat iced *Mate* in liquifier.

MATE PUNCH *(Ponche de Mate):* Mix iced *Mate* in equal parts with either ginger ale or cider.

Guaraná

Even though it is not obtainable in this country, one cannot omit a brief word or two about *Guaraná*. This is a Brazilian shrub from which a dried paste for medicinal use is prepared and also a base for a very refreshing and stimulating soft drink. Brazilian American importers have long speculated on the idea of introducing the *Guaraná* beverage to thirsty Americans, but because of its tendency to ferment, importation of ready-prepared *Guaraná* has not been successful. I believe this could be overcome if it were imported in the form of a syrup or paste.

When one considers that not only is the beverage refreshing and pleasing to the taste, but also that it is a nerve stimulant and restorative, its potential value as a good seller cannot be overemphasized. The fact that it contains 5% caffeine lends this drink properties similar to those of coffee, that is, its slight acceleration of the brain and muscular control.

The *Guaraná* beverage is very popular in Brazil. Like Coca-Cola, it can be served plain with ice, or, far more important, it can be incorporated into several very good cocktails and punches.

In the hope that this useful refreshment may some day be imported from Brazil, I am printing the following recipe for a Guaraná Cup. Perhaps, in the not too distant future, some enterprising importer will realize the vast potentialities he is passing up and create a market for this delicious Brazilian soft drink.

Guaraná Cup

Make an infusion of 1 tablespoon black tea and 2 cups of boiling water. Let steep until cool, then strain and add the following:

2 bottles guaraná • 1 bottle sparkling mineral water • 2 cups orange juice
2 cups peach juice, drained from a large can of peaches
4 canned peaches, cut into slivers • 1 apple, cut into slivers

Let stand in the refrigerator from 4 to 6 hours and then pour in the punch bowl over a piece of ice.

ALCOHOLIC BEVERAGES
Bebidas Alcoólicas

There's naught, no doubt, so much the spirit calms
As rum and true religion.

BYRON, DON JUAN, CANTO II, STANZA 34

The Brazilian host is familiar with nearly all cocktails and other alcoholic beverages that are served in this country and on the Continent. But he has also concocted one of his own called a *batida*. The translation of *batida* is "beaten" or "whipped." However, as Ambassador Maurício Nabuco[2] says: "*Batida* in Brazil, already has a special significance. It is not, as one might suppose, any kind of an apéritif prepared with a beater or in a shaker. Also known as *batida Paulista*, the *batida* is becoming known beyond our frontiers as *batida brasileira*! It is a 'sour' always made with *cachaça* — a rum made from sugar cane." This is the drink that is served with the famous *Feijoada* although, again quoting Ambassador Nabuco: "In Brazil, we old timers like, with a *Feijoada,* simply a dram of good *cachaça* — also called *aguardente* — which is nothing but rum made from sugar cane molasses, like any other rum."

---

[2] Maurício Nabuco was Brazilian Ambassador to Washington, 1948-1951.

149

Batida Paulista

1 jigger rum • 1 teaspoon fine egg white, to bind the mixture • Sugar
1/4 jigger lemon juice • Ice

Shake well in a cocktail shaker. Generally, the rim of the glass is moistened with a damp cloth and then dipped into the sugar bowl, before pouring in the *batida*. Many are of the opinion that the sugar which adheres to the glass gives an inviting aspect to the *batida*. The above recipe, without the egg white, but with the addition of club soda, becomes a Pinga Fiz.

[AMBASSADOR MAURICIO NABUCO]

Coconut Batida
Batida de Coco

1 tablespoon grated coconut • 1 teaspoon sugar • 2 jiggers rum • 2 tablespoons shaved ice

Mix all ingredients in the liquifier.

Coconut Milk Batida
Batida de Leite de Coco

1 cup thick coconut milk • 1 cup cow's milk • sugar to taste • 1/2 cup gin
1/2 cup rum (cachaça)

Shake well with small amount of ice and refrigerate before serving.

[OLIVIA LODER, MINAS GERAIS]

Coffee Batida
Batida de Café

1 jigger rum • 1 teaspoon sugar • cracked ice • 1/4 cup very strong cold coffee • 1 egg white

Mix all ingredients in a cocktail shaker with the cracked ice.

Pineapple Batida
Batida de Abacaxi

1 jigger pineapple juice • 1 teaspoon sugar • cracked ice • Juice of 1/2 lemon • 2 jiggers rum

Shake well in a cocktail shaker.

The Dulce

1 cup tomato juice • 1/4 teaspoon salt • few grains black pepper
1 teaspoon Worcestershire sauce

For each jigger of the above, add the following and beat in a blender.

2 jiggers rum • 1 jigger lemon juice • 1/2 jigger sugar • crushed ice

[AMBASSADOR MAURICIO NABUCO]

Champagne Cocktail
Coquetel de Champanha

Place an ice cube in a large-size wine glass. Add 2 tablespoons orange juice, 1 teaspoon Grande Marnier and fill glass with champagne. Stir with a swizzle stick.

Homestead
Coquetel do Lar

Shake well in a cocktail shaker with cracked ice, 1/2 jigger crème de menthe, 1/2 jigger peach brandy, 1/2 jigger fresh cream and serve with a few grains nutmeg sprinkled on top.

Negroni

Pour into a cocktail shaker containing ice cubes, 1 jigger of Campari bitters, 1 jigger of dry vermouth and 1 jigger of gin. Stir with a swizzle stick; do not shake. Pour into a chilled glass.

[SIZÍNIO PONTES NOGUEIRA, MINAS GERAIS]

Brazilian Grog

Grogue Brasileiro

Into a measuring cup, put 3 teaspoons sugar, 2 jiggers of orange curaçao, small piece of cinnamon stick and a small piece of lemon rind. Stir and fill with boiling water.

Quentão

(SERVED ON ST. JOHN'S DAY, JUNE 24)

1 cup of rum • 1 lemon, sliced in thin rounds • 3 ounces of water • 1 clove
small piece of ginger, size of a lima bean • 1 cinnamon stick • sugar to taste

Mix all the ingredients in a saucepan and bring to boil. Strain. Serve hot in china or porcelain mugs.

Wine Quentão

Quentão de Vinho

1 bottle of wine, any kind • 1 1/2 quarts mineral water • 12 cloves • 6 cinnamon sticks
2 lemons, sliced in thin rounds • 1/2 cup sugar

Boil water, cloves, cinnamon sticks, lemon and sugar for 1/2 hour. Cover and let brew about 1 hour. Strains. Add the wine and serve hot in china or porcelain mugs.

Punch

Ponche

It seems too bad to see the beautiful old cutglass or silver punch bowl relegated to the attic or to the realm of collector's items. But that is what is happening, both in Brazil and in this country. Thirty years ago you could not have a party without the traditional punch bowl duly filled with some mild alcoholic refreshment and the ladies, bless their dear hearts, could drink four or five glasses and still be ladies. I think some clever hostesses should revive the use of the punch bowl! Not only does it lend a dramatic effect as a lovely table ornament, but the old time punches, with their soft blending of non-alcoholic and alcoholic beverages, added a delicate touch of taste and color to the most prosaic of gatherings. There is something nostalgic about the punch bowl, suggestive of happy family gatherings and good times.

While the punch bowl is still used at wedding receptions and christenings, it could also be a valuable asset at other functions.

So, if you own a punch bowl, do not underestimate its manifold uses. If it is glass, rinse it in ammonia water until it sparkles, and polish the silver ladle until it shines. If you are fortunate enough to possess a silver one, don't wait for a wedding or a christening to use it. Give it the place of honor at your next buffet supper and glamorize your party by filling it with one of the following mixtures taken from old Brazilian recipes.

Party Punch
Ponche para Festas

1 lemon, sliced thin • 1 orange, sliced thin • 3 tablespoons sugar
thin pieces of fresh fruit (pineapple, peaches, peeled grapes, pears, etc.)
1/2 bottle sparkling water • 1 jigger maraschino • 1 jigger curaçao • 1 bottle claret tinto

Place sugar and sliced fruits into the punch bowl and let stand until sugar is dissolved. Add the maraschino, curaçao, claret, and sparkling water and set in refrigerator for two hours to ripen. Remove punch bowl to table and place a large piece of ice in center of bowl.

[ZEUMAR WAXLER, MINAS GERAIS]

Coffee Cocktail
Coquetel de Café

Shake well in a cocktail shaker with cracked ice, 1 jigger strong, cold coffee, 1 jigger cointreau, 1/2 jigger crème de cacao, and 1 jigger cognac.

High Life

Arrange in a liquor glass without mixing, in the following order: one part crème de cacao, one drop of angostura bitters, one part fresh cream and one part peach liqueur.

Wine Punch
Ponche de Vinho

2 cups pineapple juice • 1 1/2 apples, finely-sliced and then cut into slivers
1/4 bottle port wine • 2 cups orange juice • 1 bottle fine white wine
1/2 cup red wine • 1 jigger créme de cacao

Mix all ingredients and, when ready to serve, add one bottle sparkling water and 1/4 bottle sparkling wine or champagne. Serve over ice.

Champagne Punch No. 1
Ponche de Champanha Nº 1

1 bottle champagne • 1 jigger curaçao • 2 jiggers dry sherry • 2 jiggers cognac
1 thinly-sliced orange • 1 thinly-sliced lemon

Mix all ingredients and chill. Pour into punch bowl over a large piece of ice.

[MARIA BARBOZA NUNES, RIO DE JANEIRO]

Champagne Punch No. 2
Ponche de Champanha Nº 2

1 tablespoon sugar • juice of 1 lemon • 2 thin slices of pineapple
1 tablespoon grenadine syrup • 2 thin slices of orange

Mix the above ingredients in the punch bowl and let stand in refrigerator for a few hours. Before serving, add a piece of ice and a bottle of champagne.

[MARIA BARBOZA NUNES, RIO DE JANEIRO]

Rhine Wine Punch
Ponche de Vinho do Reno

1 bottle champagne • 1 bottle Burgundy • 2 bottles Rhine wine • 4 chopped apples
2 cups pineapple juice • 1 cup orange juice • 2 jiggers curaçao • sugar to taste

Mix all ingredients and pour into punch bowl over a large piece of ice.

[MARIA BARBOZA NUNES, RIO DE JANEIRO]

CHAPTER 9

Breads, Rolls, and Muffins

Man does not live by bread alone, but by faith,
by admiration, by sympathy.

EMERSON, "THE SOVEREIGNITY OF ETHICS."

*I*n the early days of Brazil's colonization, the Fathers of the Society of Jesus tried to grow wheat to prepare the Sacred Host, but the climatic and soil conditions were not conducive to reaping a good harvest. However, they persisted in their efforts to at least produce the small measure of wheat required to attend their specific needs.

In the absence of wheat, the Portuguese colonizer had to change his food habits — a change that was to endure for well over 200 years. Lacking bread, which was not introduced into Brazil until the nineteenth century, the early settlers adopted the use of manioc[1] and corn from the Indians. The results of this choice are still evident in present-day Brazilian food habits, as there are many regions in Brazil where corn and manioc are preferred to wheat.

Wheat was never cultivated to the same extent as corn. Brazil today ranks third in world production of corn[2] and is the largest importer of wheat in Latin America.[3]

The uses of manioc were highly developed by the Indian woman who was already preparing a cake for children *(Carimã)* and a paste or porridge *(Mingau)* when the first colonists arrived.[4] The *Carimã* cake was soaked in water and given to children who had worms.

The Indians were also skilled in the use of corn from which they prepared many dishes that are still served. It was the *cunhã* or Indian Tupi woman who brought to modern Brazilian culture not only the use of corn, which is tremendously popular in Brazil, but also the personal neatness and cleanliness upon which modern Brazilians pride themselves.

---

[1] For more information on manioc, see chapter on "Accompaniments," p. 41.
[2] *FAO Production Yearbook for 1961*, p. 44-46.
[3] *FAO Trade Year Book for 1961*, p. 82.
[4] Gilberto Freyre, *The Masters and the Slaves* (New York: Alfred A. Knopf, 1946), p. 127.

A lack of wheat, however, did not deter the colonizers from preparing good substitutes for wheat bread and biscuits. Following the lead of the Indian, they used crushed corn and manioc extensively and later, when the process of making flour was better developed, they extended the use of these products. As a result, Brazil today is producing and using many flours which are unknown in other countries. *Polvilho* flours, for example, are of one such type. A host of excellent baked goods is prepared from these *Polvilho* flours.

Northern and Western Brazil still prefer corn and manioc to wheat. Southern Brazil, on the other hand, has long enjoyed the use of wheat and so have the large Brazilian cities, even though it has to be imported. Despite the fact that Brazil has made a great advance in wheat production, it is still far from growing enough for its own consumption.

"In the four wheat-producing states of Southern Brazil, which contain 33 per cent of the country's population, wheat products have long been a staple item in the diet of both urban and rural population. Thanks to improvements in distribution facilities and income levels, they have also become important in the diet of many people living in other states of the country, which produce little or no wheat at all." [5]

The most common type of bread used in Brazil resembles French bread and is aptly named *Pão Francês*. This is baked in different lengths. The slang word *bisnaga* or "tube," designates the smallest size. Often this kind of bread is sliced and either dried in the oven or toasted. It is then stored in a special tin box and served at the table like Melba toast.

As in the United States, it is possible to buy sandwich bread at the *padaria* or baker's, and have it sliced lengthwise for rolled sandwiches, canapés, etc., or crosswise for toast or regular sandwiches. This bread corresponds to the firm sandwich loaf which can be ordered specially from caterers. The soft, packaged loaf of bread is unknown in Brazil, although one can purchase packaged bread.

The twist, which is disappearing from American bakery shelves, since many of the supermarkets have replaced the old-fashioned bakeries, is still available in large Brazilian cities. It is called *trança* or braid.

---

[5] U.S. Department of Agriculture Bulletin, No. FAZ M60, *Brazil's Future as a Wheat Producer*, p. 8.

Rolls, whether their leaving agent is yeast or baking powder, are called *pãezinhos* or "little breads." These may also be sweet, like buns.

Cornbread or *broa de milho* is highly appreciated in Brazil, just as in the Southern United States.

There does not seem to be any translation for muffins. I have seen them served in Brazil, made of flours other than corn, but they were not called *broas*. It appears that this name only applies to the muffins made of corn meal or containing corn meal as one of the flours. The recipe from Mrs. Aersylia Pereira Pinto exemplifies this fact. Actually, it is a muffin in accordance with standards set by the American housewife, and it has been translated as "Cornstarch Muffins." But, in Portuguese, the recipe was called *Pãezinhos de Maizena* or Cornstarch Rolls.

A slang expression that was very much used during the depression of the early thirties was "Coffee and…." The Brazilian counterpart is *média com canoa*, which, finally translated, means "coffee and milk with bread and butter." *Média* means a cup of coffee with milk and the *canoa* is the small French bread cut in half lengthwise with the insides scooped out and the crusts buttered.

Algerian Cookies
Biscoitos Algerianos

1 small cooked potato • 2 tablespoons butter • 1 cup grated Swiss cheese
1 cup sifted all-purpose flour • 1/2 teaspoon salt • 1/2 teaspoon baking powder

Mash potato and cool. Add butter and cheese. Sift flour, salt and baking powder and add to the potato mixture. Knead. Pat or roll out to 1/3 inch thickness and cut with a biscuit cutter. Place on ungreased cookie sheet, brush with milk or egg yolk, if desired. Bake in preheated 375° oven until done.

[LAURITA PIRES, MINAS GERAIS]

Beer Rolls
Pãezinhos de Cerveja

1 package dry granular yeast or 1 cake compressed yeast • 1/2 cup warm milk
1 tablespoon sugar • 1 cup light beer • 2 cups sifted all-purpose flour • 1 tablespoon salt

Dissolve yeast in warm milk. Add sugar, flour, salt and beer. Mix, cover and let stand in a warm place overnight.

Approximately 6 cups sifted all-purpose flour • 4 eggs, separated
1 tablespoon sugar • 1/2 cup butter

Next morning add 2 cups of the sifted flour and the beaten egg yolks, sugar and butter. Beat well, then knead in 2 more cups of the sifted flour and the stiffly-beaten egg whites. Knead in sufficient sifted flour (about the remaining 2 cups) to produce an elastic dough. Let stand in a warm place until double in bulk. Shape into rolls. Place on greased baking tins. Cover and let stand another 15 or 20 minutes. Brush with melted butter and bake in a preheated 375° oven for about 20 minutes. Yields 40 rolls.

Beer Twists or Rusks
Rosquinhas de Cerveja

2 cups all-purpose flour • 1/4 pound margarine • 1/4 pound butter
1 tablespoon sugar • 1/2 cup beer • powdered sugar

Blend flour with shortening and sugar, and add the beer. Knead well and refrigerate overnight. The next morning, cut off chunks the size of a walnut or smaller, if desired. Place each piece on breadboard, and roll with the palm of the hand into about 2-inches lengths. Twist and lay on ungreased cookie sheet in the form of crescents. Bake in preheated 400° oven around 30 minutes. Roll in powdered sugar while warm.

VARIATION: This dough may also be shaped into one large twist. Roll out with hands to a cylindrical shape, twist a few times and place in a buttered tubular baking tin. Let rise 30 minutes, then bake in a preheated 375° oven about 1 hour.

[OLGA DE SÁ PIRES, MINAS GERAIS]

Bread Twist or Rusk
Pão Rosca

1 package dry granular yeast or 1 cake compressed yeast • 2 cups warm milk
1/2 cup butter • 1 tablespoon sugar • 2 teaspoons salt • 3 cups sifted all-purpose flour

Dissolve yeast in milk, add butter, sugar, salt and sifted flour. Mix well, cover and let stand in a warm place for 2 hours. After 2 hours begin Step 2.

2 beaten eggs • 1 cup sugar • 4 1/2 – 5 1/2 cups sifted all-purpose flour

Add to the dough, the beaten eggs, sugar and 3 cups of flour. Knead well. If the dough is not stiff enough, add more flour until you are able to roll it out. This may be anywhere from 1 1/2 cups to 2 1/2 cups. Divide dough into 2 or 3 equal parts. Shape into cylindrical lengths by rolling on a floured board, and, holding both ends, twist and lay on a buttered baking sheet in the form of crescents. Cover, set in a warm place until double in bulk. Brush with egg yolk and bake in a preheated 375° oven for 30 to 40 minutes.

[YVONNE AMARANTE, MINAS GERAIS]

Cassava Bread
Pão de Aipim

2 packages dry, granular yeast or 2 cakes compressed yeast • 3 tablespoons sugar
1 cup cold milk • 7 cups sifted all-purpose flour • 2 1/2 pounds cassava root
2 tablespoons salt • 2 tablespoons butter • 2 tablespoons lard • 3 eggs

Mash yeast with sugar and milk. Add 1 cup sifted flour and mix well. Cover and let set for 1 hour. Peel cassava root, cut into slices and boil in water with 1 tablespoon salt until it is fork tender. Drain and while still warm put through the meat grinder or purée in liquifier. Add butter, lard and beaten eggs to the yeast mixture, then add the warm cassava and mix well. Mix in the other tablespoon of salt and enough flour (about 6 cups) to make dough the same consistency as bread dough. Knead until it does not stick to the hands. Divide into 2 or 3 parts and shape into loaves. Place each loaf in a bread pan which has been buttered and lightly sprinkled with flour. Cover and let rise until double in bulk. Brush with melted butter and bake, like bread, in a preheated 400° oven for about 15 minutes, then reduce heat to 375° and bake about 40 more minutes, until crust is golden brown and crisp and the loaves sound hollow when tapped on the bottom. Turn loaves out and cool thoroughly on cooling racks for at least 3 or 4 hours before slicing.

[TRANSLATED FROM: **A COZINHA DELICIOSA E MODERNA** BY MARIA THEREZA SENISE]

Cornstarch Muffins
Pãezinhos de Maizena

*1 tablespoon butter • 1 egg • 1/2 cup sifted all-purpose flour • 1/2 cup cornstarch
1 cup milk • 2 teaspoons baking powder*

Cream butter, add egg and flour which has been sifted with cornstarch. Mix well, gradually add milk in which baking powder has been dissolved. Beat well. Pour into well-buttered small cupcake tins and fill 3/4 full. Bake in a preheated 400° oven for 25-30 minutes. Yields approximately 24 muffins.

[AERSYLIA PEREIRA PINTO, PERNAMBUCO]

Cornstarch Rusks
Roscas de Maizena

*1 1/2 cups cornstarch • 3 tablespoons sugar • 1 tablespoon butter
1 egg yolk • 1/2 cup cream*

Mix cornstarch and sugar, blend in butter and egg yolk. Add cream and mix with finger tips. Shape into small balls the size of a walnut. Place on a buttered cookie sheet and with prongs of a fork, press down edges. Bake in a preheated 350° oven for 25 minutes. Yelds approximately 2 dozen.

[MARIA BARBOZA NUNES, RIO DE JANEIRO]

Corn Cake
Bolo de Fubá

4 tablespoons butter • 6 tablespoons sugar • 3 eggs, separated
2 tablespoons all-purpose flour • 6 tablespoons fine cornmeal
1/2 tablespoons baking powder • 1/2 teaspoon salt • thick milk of 1/2 coconut

Cream butter and sugar, add beaten egg yolks. Sift flour, cornmeal, baking powder and salt together and add to the creamed mixture. Stir in the coconut milk and fold in stiffly-beaten egg whites. Turn into buttered cake tin and bake in a preheated 375° oven until done.

[ALDA FONTENELLI, RIO DE JANEIRO]

Cheese Rolls
Pão de Queijo

1 package dry, granular yeast or 1 cake compressed yeast • 1 cup warm milk
2 tablespoons sugar • 2 teaspoons salt • 1/4 pound butter • 3 slightly-beaten eggs
7 – 8 1/4 cups all-purpose flour • 3/4 cup light beer
2 cups grated Muenster or Swiss cheese

Dissolve yeast in warm milk. Add sugar, salt, butter and slightly-beaten eggs. Let stand 10 minutes, then add beer and 3 cups of sifted flour. Stir with a wooden spoon until bubbles appear. Add the cheese. Cover and set in a warm place to rise. When batter has doubled in bulk, cut it down with a knife and knead in another 3 cups sifted flour. Knead well and then add the extra sifted flour (from 1 to 2 1/4 cups) until you have a smooth, elastic dough that does not stick to the hands. Cover and let rise again. Shape into butterhorn rolls by dividing into portions that will roll out into rounds about 10 inches in diameter and 3/8 inch thick. Brush with melted butter and cut into 12 pie-shaped wedges. Roll up each piece beginning with the wide end, stretching dough slightly as you roll. Lay straight or in a crescent shape on a greased cookie sheet with tip underneath to keep from unrolling. Cover, set in a warm place again to rise. Brush with melted butter or an egg yolk slightly diluted with milk. Bake about 20 minutes in a preheated 375° oven. Yields approximately 48 rolls.

[GRADYS MARIE SILVA, MATO GROSSO]

Corn Bread
Pão de Milho

1 tablespoon butter • 1 tablespoon lard • 1 cup hot milk • 1/2 cup cold water
1 tablespoon sugar • 1 1/4 teaspoons salt • 1 package dry, granular yeast or
1 cake compressed yeast • 2 eggs • 3 cups all-purpose flour sifted with 2 cups very fine
cornmeal • 1/4 to 3/4 cup extra all-purpose flour

Add butter and lard to hot milk, then add cold water, sugar and salt. When the mixture is tepid, dissolve the yeast in the liquid. Add eggs, mix well, then add the flour and cornmeal that have been sifted together. Beat well. Sift in more all-purpose flour (about 1/2 cup), enough to make a spongy dough. Beat again, cover bowl and let stand 2 hours in a warm place. Add more all-purpose flour (about 1/4 cup), sufficient to knead, and knead very well. Divide the dough into 2 parts. Butter 2 loaf pans, shape each part of dough to fit into the pan, cover and let stand 30 minutes. Brush with egg yolk, cream or milk and bake in a preheated 375° oven for about 45 minutes.

[FABIANA PIMENTA, MINAS GERAIS]

Cuca

1 compressed yeast cake or 1 package dry, granular yeast • 1/2 cup warm milk
9 cups all-purpose flour • 3 teaspoons salt • 5 tablespoons sugar • 1 tablespoon butter
1 tablespoon lard • 5 eggs • 1 1/2 cups warm milk • melted butter • cinnamon sugar

Dissolve yeast in the 1/2 cup warm milk and reserve. Sift 8 cups of the flour, salt and sugar into a bowl and blend in the butter and lard. Add the eggs, slightly beaten and the 1 1/2 cups milk and knead, then add the other 1/2 cup of milk in which yeast was dissolved. Knead until the dough falls away from the sides of the bowl. Cover and let stand in a warm place for 4 hours. Punch down and knead in the other cup of flour. Divide dough into 3 portions and fit into buttered bread pans. Let rise another 2 hours. Brush each loaf well with melted butter and pile on a very heavy coat of cinnamon sugar. Bake in a preheated 375° oven for around 40 minutes.

VARIATION: Many times the cuca is baked with bananas on top. After brushing tops of loaves with melted butter, bananas, cut in half lengthwise, are placed across the top. The cinnamon sugar is them piled generously over the bananas and the loaf baked according to the above directions.

[ALDA FONTENELLI, RIO DE JANEIRO]

Queen's Twist No. 1
Rosca da Rainha N° 1

2 packages dry granular yeast or 2 cakes compressed yeast
1 1/2 cups warm water • About 17 1/2 cups sifted all-purpose flour • 9 eggs • 2 cups sugar
1 1/2 tablesopoons salt • 1 cup milk • 1 teaspoon grated nutmeg • 1/3 cup anisette
1 cup butter • 1 cup hydrogenated shortening

Dissolve yeast in warm water and gradually add 3 1/2 cups of the sifted flour to make a dough. Knead very well, cover, and let stand 3 hours. Beat eggs in electric mixer, gradually adding the sugar and beating until the mixture is lemon colored. This mixture should be very well beaten. Add it to the raised yeast dough. Dissolve salt in warm milk, add nutmeg, anisette and butter that has been melted with the shortening. Mix very well. Begin adding the second quantity of flour (about 14 cups depending upon the absorbency of the flour used). Knead until dough is smooth and elastic and forms air bubbles. As last additions of flour are made, it will be necessary to turn dough out onto a flat surface for kneading. Divide dough into 8 parts. Roll each part into a cylinder and twist 2 cylinders together then lay out on a buttered cookie sheet, joining the ends.

N O T E : As this is a recipe for making 4 large twists, it is recommended that you start with extra large mixing bowls. Cover and let rise until double in bulk. Bake in a preheated 400° oven for 15 minutes. Reduce temperature to 350° and bake another 25-35 minutes. Remove to cake racks to dry out. Top while still warm with a plain sugar icing or an orange icing.

V A R I A T I O N S : Before baking, brush with an egg yolk that has been mixed with a little milk and decorate with crystalized fruits. These twists are served at Easter time with a whole egg in the shell placed in the center and baked. Sometimes, smaller twists are attached to the center one, scollop-wise. For New Year's parties, chopped filberts or hazelnuts are sprinkled over the icing.

[TRANSLATED FROM: **A COZINHA DELICIOSA E MODERNA** BY MARIA THEREZA SENISE]

Queen's Twist No. 2
Rosca da Rainha N° 2

Approximately 8 1/2 cups sifted all-purpose flour
1 package dry, granular yeast or 1 cake compressed yeast • 1/2 cup warm water
1/4 cup strong cinnamon infusion • 1/2 cup milk • 3/4 cup sugar • 6 eggs
1 tablespoons salt • 1/4 pound butter • 2 ounces lard

Sift and measure flour. Dissolve yeast in warm water and cinnamon infusion, then add warm milk, 1/8 cup sugar and 1 cup sifted flour. Beat very well, cover and let stand in a warm place for about 2 hours. Beat eggs, gradually adding the rest of the sugar. This mixture should be very well beaten. Add the salt and then combine with the yeast batter. Beat very well, then add the butter and lard that have been melted together. Knead in the rest of the flour, kneading until dough is smooth and elastic and forms air bubbles. Divide dough into 3 parts and shape each into a twist, bringing both ends together and placing on a buttered cookie sheet. Brush with a mixture made of melted butter and egg yolk. Cover and let rise until double in bulk. Bake in a preheated 400° oven for 15 minutes, then reduce heat to 350° until done. Top while warm with a plain sugar icing.

[IZAURA PINTO, MINAS GERAIS]

Minute Cookies
Pão de Minuto

2 cups all-purpose flour • 4 teaspoons baking powder • 4 tablespoons butter • 2 eggs
1/2 cup milk • 1 teaspoon salt • 1 tablespoon sugar (optional)

Sift flour and baking powder together and cut in the butter. Slightly beat eggs with milk and salt (also sugar, if used) and add to flour mixture. Knead lightly with finger tips. Let stand 5 minutes. Pat out 3/4 inch thick and cut with a 2-inch cookie cutter. Place on buttered cookie sheet and bake in a preheated 400° oven approximately 20 minutes. Yields 18-20 biscuits. Serve immediately.

[YVONNE MUNIZ, PARIS]

Sweet Potato Rolls
Pãezinhos de Batata-Doce

6 cups all-purpose flour • 1 cup fine corn meal
2 packages dry, granular yeast or 2 cakes compressed yeast • 1 cup warm milk
1 tablespoon sugar • 4 slightly-beaten eggs • 1 1/2 pounds warm puréed sweet potato
1/4 pound butter or margarine • 2 teaspoons salt • 1 teaspoon aniseed

Sift flour and corn meal together. Dissolve yeast in warm milk, add sugar, slightly beaten eggs and aniseed. Mix well. Add about 2 cups of the flourcorn meal mixture to make a spongy batter. Stir well. Cover and set in a warm place to rise. Cook the peeled sweet potatoes in salted water, and, when tender, drain and mash to a purée with the butter and salt. While still warm, but not hot, combine with the first mixture. Stir and begin adding the rest of the flourcornmeal mixture. When dough gets heavy, start kneading. Knead until you have a dough which does not stick to your hands. It will be necessary to add more sifted flour, possibly up to 2 or 3 cups. Cover the dough and let rise until doubled in bulk. Shape into cloverleaf rolls by breaking off pieces of dough and rolling into balls the size of a small walnut (the size should be determined by size of muffin tins.) Place 3 balls in each greased muffin tin. Cover and let rise until doubled in bulk. Brush with melted butter and bake in preheated 375° oven approximately 20 minutes. Yields 4 dozen rolls. Serve immediately, as these rolls dry out within 5 or 6 hours.

[GLADYS MARIE SILVA, MATO GROSSO]

Peanut Corn Muffins
Broa de Amendoim

1 cup roasted peanuts • 1 cup fine corn meal • 1 cup sugar • 3/4 cup water • 4 eggs
1/2 teaspoon ground cloves

Grind peanuts and corn meal in food chopper as finely as possible or pass through the electric blender. Make a syrup of the sugar and water by boiling until it spins a thread and then add to the first mixture. Let stand a few hours to cool and set. Add the beaten eggs and cloves and mix well. Spoon into buttered muffin tins and bake in a preheated 400° oven for about 15 minutes.

Three-Flour Biscuits
Biscoitos de Três Farinhas

2/3 cup arrowroot flour • 1/4 cup fine cornmeal • 1/2 cup all-purpose flour
1/2 teaspoon salt • 1/2 cup butter • 1 tablespoon sugar • 2 eggs yolks

Sift together arrowroot flour, cornmeal, all-purpose flour and salt. Cream butter with sugar, add egg yolks and mix. Stir and then knead in the sifted dry ingredients. Pat out on a floured board to 1/2 inch thickness and cut with a biscuit cutter 2 inches in diameter. Place on a buttered cookie sheet. Bake in a preheated 375° oven for 15 to 18 minutes and then lightly brown tops under the broiler. Serve hot. Yields approximately 1 1/2 dozen.

[GLADYS MARIE SILVA, MATO GROSSO]

CHAPTER 10

CAKES, CUPCAKES AND TARTS

Oh, cakes and friends we should choose with care,
Not always the fanciest cake that's there
Is the best to eat! And the plainest friend
Is sometimes the finest one in the end.

MARGARET E. SANGSTER, "FRENCH PASTRY", ST. 3

The variety of cakes made in Brazil is simply tremendous, but remembering Margaret Sangster's poem, in editing and selecting these recipes I have tried to adhere to simple, palatable ones that have proven their merit. This has not been an easy task. The number of cake recipes from which I had to choose exceeds those produced in American kitchens. And this, without the aid of commercial food manufacturers who maintain experimental kitchens for developing recipes and promote contests designed to step up consumption of their products.

There are two prime factors responsible for the great variety of Brazilian cakes. The first can be attributed to the vast number of flours available, and the second to custom or tradition.

Generally, the American housewife confines herself to wheat flour, but the Brazilian housewife is adept in the use of several different flours and meals, some of which are unknown in the Northern Hemisphere. She makes frequent use of flours or meals derived from potatoes, corn, rice, arrowroot, manioc and some *polvilhos*. Her pantry boasts of all these flours in addition to wheat flour. They are used singly in the preparation of breads, biscuits, cakes and cookies, and sometimes they are mixed. Some recipes may call for a mixture of even three kinds of flour!

When the Brazilian *dona-de-casa*[1] gets bored using the varied flours and meals available to her, she reverts to other basic materials. She grinds nuts or stale cake, sponge cake or cookies, sifts the result through a fine sieve and uses the crumbs as flour. At least 4 years before the American housewife was using packaged pudding mixes as an ingredient in cakes and cookies, her Brazilian counterpart had already made this "discovery" (see Joaquim's Torte, p. 204). Likewise, packaged gelatin dessert mixes find their way as ingredients into candy making (see p. 234).

---

[1] Housewife.

Often you will find that coconut milk is substituted for cow's milk, like the African slaves used to do, and sometimes the sugar content of a recipe is introduced as a syrup.

Custom is the other factor producing the large number of Brazilian cake recipes. An afternoon snack, called *lanche* (not to be confused with "lunch," which in Portuguese is *almoço*) is very popular in Brazil. Usually, a *lanche* consists of a beverage and some cookies or a piece of cake. To meet this exigency, the housekeeper in Brazil has concluded that a "cake in the larder is worth two in the oven." Usually, therefore, most middle class homes have a plain cake in the pantry for the *lanche* or snack.

Cocktail parties are popular, but teas play an important role in the social life of the Brazilian middle and upper class ladies. The cake is practically an indispensable item at these functions, and often more than one is served.

Many of the traditional cakes of today, such as Louis Felipe, Cavalcanti, Souza Leão, etc. were developed in the kitchens of the well-known sugar plantations in the North.[2] While the African slaves who presided over the kitchens in the large plantations introduced some of their native cakes, such as *Cuscuz*[3] and improved on Portuguese recipes through the addition of coconut milk and sugar, to the Indian goes the credit for *Canjica* or *Mungunzá*[4] and *Pamonha*.

It was the Indian Tupi Guarani woman who prepared a paste of corn called *acanijic* which is today *canjica* or *mungunzá* — depending upon which part of Brazil one comes from. The Indian woman was also responsible for the *pamonha*, which

---

[2] Gilberto Freyre's book, *Assucar*, goes into this in detail and gives the traditional recipes he obtained from direct descendents of the plantation owners in the sugar producing areas.

[3] A popular special Brazilian dish made of steamed rice, manioc, corn meal or tapioca. See special chapter for "Cuscuz," p. 277.

[4] A dish of hominy, milk, sugar and cinnamon, and sometimes, peanuts. *Mungunzá* is the name used in Northern Brazil, but in São Paulo and Minas Gerais this dish is known as *Canjica*. *Canjica* has a special significance for me! It was, I think, one of the last requests my husband made during his fatal illness. Fortunately, although it was many years ago, New York markets stocked everything required to prepare this dish, and I shall always be grateful for the benign providence that made it possible to prepare this native Brazilian dish in New York City! See recipe in chapter on Desserts.

was called *pamuna*. This is made of fresh corn, sugar, coconut milk, cinnamon and aniseed, and is cooked in corn husks.[5]

These sweets, one of which is actually a pudding-like dessert resembling a glorified hominy *Canjica*, while the other, *Pamonha,* resembling small cakes, are known throughout Brazil and are traditionally served on St. John's Day along with confections made of pumpkin.

At the time Europeans regarded sugar as a luxury, available only in apothecary shops, the Negro slaves of the Big Houses were mixing it into their cakes with a lavish abandon. Foreigners claim that Brazilians lean towards excessively sweet foods, but it can readily be seen that this is a natural legacy from their forebears. On the other hand, inasmuch as Brazil ranks third in world production of sugar, there is little need to stint in the use of this product.

Recipes from the Big Houses were faithfully recorded by the owners of the plantations and handed down to their heirs as part of the inheritance. Many times a veil of secrecy surrounded the ingredients and the quantities called for, and sometimes, in order to preserve complete secrecy, one item, known only to the master, would be purposely omitted from the written recipe.

Some recipes took the surname of the owner of the Big House, like Bolo (cake) Cavalcanti, Souza Leão and Fonseca Ramos — names which are still prominent in the Brazil of today. Other cakes were named after historical events of that era. There was *Bolo Cabano,*[6] *Bolo 13 de Maio,*[7] *Bolo Legalista,*[8] *Bolo Dom Pedro,*[9] *Bolo Republicano,*[10] and *Bolo Santos Dumond*[11] these being but a few of the cake names with historical connotations.

---

[5] The recipe appears later in this chapter, p. 218.

[6] The Cabano was a political social movement that agitated Northeastern Brazil. It began in Pernambuco in 1832 and spread to surrounding regions, until it was quelled in 1835.

[7] Princess Isabel liberated the slaves on May 13, 1888.

[8] A *legalista* is one who fights to uphold the law.

[9] Dom Pedro II was Emperor of Brazil from 1841 to 1889.

[10] Brazil was declared a Republic on November 15, 1889.

[11] Brazilian aeronaut, constructor of dirigible airships who won two prizes for the first flight in a given time from St. Cloud to the Eiffel Tower, October 19, 1901.

I Want More, Sneezer, Fatten Your Husband, Hurry Hurry, Shaggy Towel, and Hunger Killer are typical of the suggestive names given to cakes developed in the Big Houses.

Cakes in Brazil represent a culinary heritage. I know of no other course of the Brazilian menu that has adhered so steadfastly to tradition, other than some of the Afro-Brazilian dishes.

Arrowroot Sponge Cake
Pão-de-Ló de Araruta

6 eggs, separated • 6 tablespoons sugar • 6 tablespoons arrowroot flour
1/2 teaspoon baking powder

Beat egg yolks and gradually add sugar. Sift flour with baking powder and slowly add to egg yolks. When combining mixtures, use a folding motion. Do not beat. Fold in the stiffly-beaten egg whites. Pour into a buttered baking dish and bake in preheated 375° oven for 20 minutes. Reduce heat to 350° and bake another 20 minutes.

VARIATION: This recipe may also be made substituting rice flour for arrowroot flour.

[LAURITA PIRES, MINAS GERAIS]

Beer Cake
Bolo de Cerveja

1 1/2 cups all-purpose flour • 1/2 tablespoon baking powder • 1/4 teaspoon salt
1/2 cup butter • 1/2 cup sugar • 2 eggs, separated • 1/2 cup beer

Sift flour, baking powder and salt together. Cream butter, add sugar and beaten egg yolks. Add flour mixture alternately with the beer to the creamed mixture. Fold in the stiffly-beaten egg whites. Pour into a well-buttered 1 1/2-quart cake tin and bake in a preheated 350° oven for 35 minutes, then reduce heat to 275° and bake another 30 minutes until done.

[OTTILIA JANSEN DE MELLO, MINAS GERAIS]

Cake of the Saints
Bolo dos Santos

4 tablespoons butter • 1 3/4 cups sugar • 4 eggs, separated • 1 teaspoon salt
3/4 cup all-purpose flour • 3/4 cup cornstarch • 3/4 cup tapioca flour
1 cup coconut milk • 3 tablespoons baking powder • 1/2 cup milk
1/4 cup chopped dates

Cream butter with sugar, egg yolks and salt. Sift together the flour, cornstarch and tapioca flour and add to creamed mixture alternately with the coconut milk. Dissolve baking powder in the 1/2 cup milk and add to the mixture. Fold in the stiffly-beaten egg white and the chopped dates. Pour into a well-buttered 2-quart cake tin which has been lightly sprinkled with flour. Bake for approximately 1 hour in a 350° preheated oven.

[GLADYS MARIE SILVA, MATO GROSSO]

188

Cake to Please Mothers-in-Law
Bolo para Agradar as Sogras

1 cup chopped, seedless raisins dredged in 1/2 cup sifted all-purpose flour • 1 cup butter

2 1/2 cups sugar • 1/2 teaspoon salt • 1 teaspoon grated orange rind

1 teaspoon grated lemon rind • 5 eggs, separated • 1 cup orange juice

2 1/2 cups all-purpose flour • 1 cup cornstarch • 3 teaspoons baking powder

Reserve raisins. Cream butter with sugar, salt and grated orange and lemon rinds. Add egg yolks, one at a time and beat mixture well. Continue beating and add orange juice alternately with the flour, cornstarch and baking powder that have been sifted together. Fold in the stiffly-beaten egg whites and the raisins. Bake in a well-buttered angel food tin in a preheated 350° oven for approximately 1 hour. Cool and serve plain or spread jam on top and sift with powdered sugar.

VARIATION: Prepare *Strawberry Frosting* by mixing:

1/2 cup strawberry preserves • 1 egg white • 3/4 cup sugar

a few grains salt • 1 tablespoon water

Cook all ingredients in a double boiler, beating constantly with an egg beater until frosting stands in stiff peaks. Spread on cake while frosting is hot and allow to stand about 2 hours before slicing.

[TRANSLATED FROM: **A COZINHA DELICIOSA E MODERNA** BY MARIA THEREZA SENISE]

Carioca Lemon Spice Cake
Bolo de Carioca

1/2 cup butter • 1/2 cup brown sugar • 4 eggs, separated • 1/2 teaspoon ground ginger
1 teaspoon ground cinnamon • 1 teaspoon mace • 1 tablespoon grated lemon rind
2 1/4 cups sifted all-purpose flour • 1/2 teaspoon salt • 1 tablespoon baking powder
1 cup heated stout beer • 3/4 cup molasses • 1 teaspoon baking soda

Cream butter with sugar and add egg yolks that have been beaten with ginger, cinnamon, mace and lemon rind. Resift the flour with salt and baking powder. Heat the beer to lukewarm and mix in the molasses and soda. Gradually combine the flour mixture with the creamed butter, alternating with the beer. Fold in stiffly-beaten egg whites and turn into 2 well-buttered 9-inch layer cake tins. Bake 35 minutes in a preheated 350° oven or until a steel knife inserted in center comes out clean. Remove from oven, loosen edges and turn out onto wire rack to cool. Put layers together with your favorite Lemon Frosting and cover top layer with the frosting. Garnish with paper-thin slices of lemon.

VARIATION: Join layers together with apple sauce and flavored whipped cream. Top cake with a layer of apple sauce and garnish with the whipped cream.

[GLADYS MARIE SILVA, MATO GROSSO]

Cassava Cake
Bolo de Mandioca [13]

2 pounds grated cassava root (this yields about 3 cups) • 2 ounces butter • 3 beaten eggs
1 cup thick coconut milk • 1 teaspoon salt • sugar to taste • cinnamon sugar

Peel the raw cassava root and cut into small pieces. Put in the blender and purée. This should yield about 3 cups. Add 1/2 cup boiling water and press through a coarse sieve to remove some of the starch. To the puréed cassava, add butter, beaten eggs, coconut milk, salt and sugar to taste. Grease a cake tin and line with wax paper. Butter the wax paper. Spoon the batter into the form and sprinkle lightly with cinnamon sugar. Bake in a preheated 400° oven 60 to 70 minutes. Cool slightly and remove from tin. Peel off the paper and invert on serving plate.

[LIA MAGRO, PERNAMBUCO]

---

[13] Actually, the sweet cassava root has three different names in Brazil, depending upon the region. In Northeastern Brazil it is called *macaxeira*, while in Rio de Janeiro State it is known as *aipim*. In São Paulo and Minas Gerais, the same root is called *mandioca* — not to be confused with the *mandioca utilissima*, which is poisonous. (See page 45.)

Chocolate Cake
Bolo de Chocolate

2 1/2 cups sugar • 2 cups butter (1 pound) • 5 eggs, separated
3 3/4 cups all-purpose flour, sifted • 1 cup milk • 1/2 teaspoon salt
5 ounces melted chocolate • 1 tablespoon baking powder • 1/4 cup milk • 3 ounces rum

Cream sugar with butter, add beaten egg yolks and sifted flour alternately with the milk and salt. Fold in the stiffly-beaten egg whites and melted chocolate. Finally, dissolve the baking powder in the 1/4 cup milk and stir into the mixture. Butter and dust with flour a 4-quart cake tin and turn the mixture into the tin. Bake in a preheated 350° oven 60 to 70 minutes. *Note:* if other-sized cake pans are used, regulate the oven temperature and the baking time in accordance with the pans. After the cake has been removed from oven allow to partially cool in the pan and then make several incisions and pour the rum into them. Turn the cake onto serving dish and, while still warm, top with the following icing:

2 ounces chocolate • 2 ounces butter • 1 can condensed milk

Melt butter and chocolate and add the condensed milk. Cook over low heat until mixture is thick enough to hold its shape.

[LAURA LOPES DA SILVA, SÃO PAULO]

Chocolate Layer Cake
Bolo de Chocolate

3 ounces unsweetened chocolate • 1/2 cup hot water • 2/3 cup butter • 1 1/2 cups sugar
3 eggs • 1 cup sour milk or buttermilk • 2 cups sifted all-purpose flour
2 teaspoons baking powder • 1/2 teaspoon baking soda • 1/2 teaspoon salt

Dissolve chocolate in hot water. Cream butter, add sugar, slightly-beaten eggs and sour milk. Add cooled chocolate mixture. Sift flour with baking powder, salt and soda, then combine flour and liquid mixtures. Beat thoroughly. The batter will be thin. Turn into 2 eight-inch layer cake tins, which have been very well-buttered, and bake in 350° preheated oven about 25 minutes or until cake springs back when lightly pressed with finger tips. Allow to stand in pans for 5 minutes, then turn out on cake racks to cool. Fill and frost with the following:

1 cup sugar • 4 ounces unsweetened chocolate • 1 2/3 cups milk • 1/4 teaspoon salt
1/4 cup crème de cacao

Boil all ingredients (except the crème de cacao) together until mixture falls away from sides of pan, stirring with a wooden spoon. This takes about 1 hour. Cool and beat in the crème de cacao.
Variation: Chopped cashew nuts may be sprinkled on top of cake.

[CECILIA FERREIRA LOPES, SÃO PAULO]

Corn-Meal Cake
Bolo de Fubá

1/2 cup butter • 1/2 cup other shortening • 5 tablespoons sugar • 1 egg
1 cup all-purpose flour • 1 cup fine yellow cornmeal • 1 teaspoon salt
4 teaspoons baking powder • 1/2 teaspoon aniseed • 1 1/2 cups milk • cinnamon

Cream shortenings, add sugar and egg. Sift flour, cornmeal, salt, baking powder and aniseed. Add alternately with the milk to the sugar-and-egg mixture. Pour into a well-buttered baking dish and sprinkle cinnamon on top. Bake in a preheated 400° oven 35 to 45 minutes.

VARIATION: Prepare same recipe omiting aniseed and cinnamon and adding 1/2 cup cubed American cheese (1/2 inch size) to batter.

[OLGA DE SÁ PIRES, MINAS GERAIS]

Diamantina Cake
Bolo de Diamantina [14]

1 yeast cake • 1/4 cup warm water • 1 tablespoon sugar • 1 cup all-purpose flour
1/2 cup cooked potato • 1/2 cup cooked pumpkin • 1 cup thick molasses
1 pound rice flour • 3 eggs • 1 cup melted shortening • 1/2 teaspoon aniseed
2 tablespoons sugar • 1 teaspoon salt

Dissolve yeast in warm water and add the sugar and flour, then the potato and pumpkin. Beat very well, cover and set aside in a warm place to rise until double in bulk. Boil molasses and add the rice flour, mixing throughly with a wooden spoon. When yeast mixture is double in bulk, add the molasses mixture. Add eggs, melted shortening, aniseed, sugar and salt and mix well with the wooden spoon. The batter should have the consistency of a thick porridge. It does not matter if small pieces of the potato or pumpkin are visible in the batter. Butter 2 baking tins and line with banana leaves or wax paper. Pour in the batter and let rise until double in bulk. If you make this at night to bake in the morning, do it as late as possible because the batter rises rapidly. Baking time varies considerably. The cakes should be baked in a preheated 375° oven and should be removed to dry on a cake rack when the cake tester comes out clean.

[LAURITA PIRES,[15] MINAS GERAIS]

---

[14] Diamantina is a small mining town in Minas Gerais State. The publication of Helena Morley's book, *Minha Vida de Menina* — a diary kept by the author from 1893 to 1895, when she was 12 to 15 years of age, focused great attention on this provincial diamond-mining town. The book has been translated into several languages, including English. Elizabeth Bishop did the English translation, calling it *The Diary of Helena Morley* and it was very well received by the English-reading public. Helena Morley is the pseudonym used by Senhora Augusto Mario Caldeira Brant. Former President Juscelino Kubitschek de Oliveira was born in Diamantina.

[15] Mrs. Gudesteu Pires (Laurinda Rabello Pires) brought this recipe with her from Diamantina. It was one of the recipes taken from her old recipe book that her daughter, Mrs. Paulo Cirne, made available to me. The recipe probably is a very old one.

Delicious Papaya Cake
Bolo de Mamão Delicioso

1 1-pound can papaya packed in heavy syrup • 1/4 pound butter • 1 cup sugar
4 eggs, beaten • 1 teaspoon vanilla • 3 cups sifted all-purpose flour
3 teaspoons baking powder • 1/2 teaspoon salt • 1/2 cup milk

Drain papaya. Measure 1 cup of the fruit and reserve 3/4 cup of the syrup. Mash the fruit with a fork. Cream butter, add sugar and eggs slightly beaten with vanilla. Stir in the mashed papaya. Sift flour, baking powder and salt together and add alternately with the milk to the creamed mixture. Pour into a well-buttered 13 x 9 x 2 inch tin and bake in a preheated 350° oven for about 40 minutes. When cake is done turn out on cake rack to dry while you prepare the icing.

I C I N G : Heat the 3/4 cup of syrup with 1 cup brown sugar and boil until it spins a thread. If any pieces of the papaya are left, add 3 or 4 and mash in the syrup while it is cooking. When the syrup spins a thread, remove from heat, add 1 tablespoon butter, a few grains of salt and 3 or 4 drops lemon juice. Make several incisions in the top of the cake and cover with icing.

[GLADYS MARIE SILVA, MATO GROSSO]

Fruit Cake
Bolo de Frutas

1/2 cup seedless raisins • 1 cup chopped crystalized fruits • 3/4 cup port wine

2 tablespoons butter • 1 cup bread crumbs • 1 cup sugar • 5 eggs, separated

1/2 ounce unsweetened grated chocolate • 1/2 teaspoon ground cloves

1 tablespoon lemon juice • 1 teaspoon baking powder • guava jelly • powdered sugar

Soak raisins and fruits in 1/4 cup of the wine. Cream butter and bread crumbs, add sugar, beaten egg yolks, chocolate, cloves, lemon juice and baking powder. Mix in the fruits add the remaining 1/2 cup of wine. Fold in stiffly-beaten egg whites. Pour into 2 buttered 9-inch layer cake tins and bake in a preheated 350° oven 30 to 35 minutes. Remove, loosen edges and let cool in pans for 10 minutes, then turn onto cake racks. When cool, put layers together with the guava jelly and sprinkle powdered sugar on top layer.

[REPRINTED FROM AUTHOR'S ARTICLE IN JULY, 1963 ISSUE OF **GOURMET** MAGAZINE]

Gladys Marie's Cake
Bolo Gladys Marie

3/4 cup dates • 3/4 cup raisins • 1/2 cup rum • 1/4 pound butter • 1 cup sugar
4 eggs, separated • 1/2 teaspoon cinnamon • 1/2 teaspoon nutmeg • 1/2 teaspoon allspice
1 teaspoon either grated orange or lemon peel • 2 1/2 cups sifted all-purpose flour
1/2 teaspoon salt • 4 teaspoons baking powder • 1 cup yoghurt

Soak dates and raisins in the rum for 3 or 4 hours. Cream butter, add sugar and the egg yolks, one by one, beating well after each yolk is added. Stir in the cinnamon, nutmeg, allspice and orange or lemon peel. Add the soaked fruit and rum. Resift the flour with the salt and baking powder and add to creamed mixture alternately with the yoghurt. Beat until smooth. Fold in the stiffly-beaten egg whites. Turn into an angel-food tin that has been well-buttered and slightly dredged with flour. Bake in a preheated 350° oven for 60 to 70 minutes. Serve plain or ice lightly with an orange or lemon icing.

[GLADYS MARIE SILVA, MATO GROSSO]

Green Corn Cake
Bolo de Milho Verde

1 cup raw corn kernels, fresh of frozen • 1 cup fresh coconut • 3/4 cup milk
1 cup butter • 1 cup sugar • 4 eggs, separated • 2 cups all-purpose flour
2 teaspoons baking powder • 1/2 teaspoon salt

Put first 3 ingredients in blender and then strain. This should equal 1 cup of liquid. If you do not have this amount, add enough milk to fill the cup. Cream butter, add sugar and beaten egg yolks. Sift dry ingredients and add to creamed butter alternately with the liquid obtained from the corn and coconut. Fold in the stiffly-beaten egg whites. Turn into buttered 1 1/2-quart cake pan and bake in a preheated 350° oven about one hour. Cool slightly before removing from pan

[OTTILIA JANSEN DE MELLO, MINAS GERAIS]

Hoping-for-a-Husband Cake
Bolo Espera Marido [16]

1 freshly-grated coconut • 1 cup warm milk • 2 cups all-purpose flour
3 tablespoons cornstarch • 3 teaspoons baking powder • 1 teaspoon salt • 1 cup butter
2 cups sugar • 4 eggs, separated

Divide the coconut in half and reserve one part for the frosting. To the other half add the warm milk and press out as much of the coconut milk as possible. Sift flour, cornstarch, baking powder and salt. Cream the butter with sugar and add egg yolks, beating until mixture is smooth. Beat the egg whites until they are stiff. Add whites to the creamed mixture alternately with the sifted dry ingredients. Add the coconut milk last. Divide batter into 2 layer cake tins and bake in a preheated 350° oven 30 to 35 minutes. Remove to a cake rack to cool and when layers are cold put together and top with the following frosting:

1 cup cream • 1 cup sugar • 3 egg yolks • 1/2 cup butter or margarine
1 teaspoon vanilla • remaining half of grated coconut

Cook milk, sugar, egg yolks and butter over medium heat for 20 minutes, until mixture thickens. Remove from heat, cool, add vanilla and coconut and beat until mixture is thick enough to spread.

[TRANSLATED FROM: **A COZINHA DELICIOSA E MODERNA** BY MARIA THEREZA SENISE]

---

[16] The cake, from Mrs. Senise's book, *A Cozinha Deliciosa e Moderna*, does not have the frosting, which I adapted to be used for a layer cake.

Orange and Cashew Nut Cake
Bolo de Castanha de Caju

1/4 pound butter • 4 eggs, separated • 2 cups sugar • 3/4 teaspoon salt
1 cup ground cashew nuts • 1 teaspoon grated orange rind • 2 1/2 cups all-purpose flour
3/4 cup bread crumbs • 3 teaspoons baking powder • 1 1/2 cups orange juice
1/2 teaspoon cinnamon mixed with 1/3 cup bread crumbs

Cream butter with egg yolks and 1 cup of sugar. Add salt, nuts and orange rind. Sift together flour, crumbs and baking powder, and add to creamed mixture alternately with one cup orange juice. Fold in the stiffly-beaten egg whites and beat until bubbles appear in the batter. Turn into a very well-buttered 3 quart cake tin that has been sprinkled with the cinnamon crumb mixture, and bake in a preheated 350° oven for about 1 hour and 15 minutes. While still warm, make incisions with a sharp knife and pour over the remaining 1/2 cup of orange juice. Sprinkle with the remaining cup of sugar and remove to serving plate.

[TRANSLATED FROM: A COZINHA DELICIOSA E MODERNA BY MARIA THEREZA SENISE]

I-Want-More Cake
Bolo Quero Mais

4 tablespoons butter • 1 tablespoon margarine • 2 cups sugar • 4 eggs, separated
1/4 cup Parmesan cheese • 1/2 teaspoon salt • 1/4 teaspoon each, ground cinnamon, cloves
and nutmeg • 1 cup plain yoghurt • 1 cup cornstarch • 3 teaspoons baking powder
1/2 cup milk • 2 cups sifted all-purpose flour • 1 cup dried or crystalized fruits, chopped
fine or 1 cup goiabada cascão cut into pieces

Cream butter and margarine with sugar and beaten egg yolks. Continue beating while you add cheese, salt, spices and yoghurt. Stir in cornstarch. Dissolve baking powder in milk and add alternately with sifted flour. Fold in stiffly-beaten egg whites and fruits. Pour into a buttered shallow (15 1/2 x 10 1/2 x 1 inch) baking tin that has been lightly sprinkled with flour and a little cinnamon. Bake in a 350° preheated oven 40 to 45 minutes. Remove to cake rack to dry. Cut into small squares and serve plain or with a fruit icing.

[TRANSLATED FROM: **A COZINHA DELICIOSA E MODERNA** BY MARIA THEREZA SENISE]

My Friend's Cake
Bolo do Meu Amigo [17]

1 cup butter • 2 cups sugar • Grated rind of 1 lemon • 2 cups all-purpose flour
1 cup cornstarch • 1 teaspoon salt • 1/2 teaspoon grated nutmeg
2 teaspoons bicarbonate of soda • 1 cup milk • 1/2 cup port wine
7 egg whites • 1 cup guava jelly • powdered or confectioner's sugar

Cream butter with sugar and add lemon rind. Sift flour, cornstarch, salt and nutmeg then add to creamed mixture alternately with the bicarbonate of soda dissolved in the milk. Add port wine, mix well and fold in the stiffy-beaten egg whites. Turn into a well-buttered 2 1/2 quart ring mold and bake in preheated 375° oven 45 to 50 minutes. When partly cooled, spread on the guava jelly (or strawberry or current jam) and sprinkle lightly with the sugar. This is also very good with a mixture of sugar and cinnamon sprinkled on top, and omitting jelly or jam.

N O T E : The recipe for "Maiden's Delight," p. 301, calls for 7 egg yolks, so if you plan to make these two recipes at the same time, all the eggs will be used.

---

[17] This is one of those recipes I mentioned in the Acknowledgement as becoming separated from the name of the donor. It has been in my possession since 1927 and it probably came from some member of the Accioly, Rabello, Sá, Lessa, de Mello, Brant, Prates, Muniz or Brandão families. At any rate, since I am unable to credit the exact donor, I have renamed the recipe "My Friend's Cake" in honor of the families mentioned.

Joaquim's Torte
Torta Joaquim

4 tablespoons butter • 1 cup sugar • 2 cups all-purpose flour • 1 tablespoon baking powder
1 4 1/2-ounce package butterscotch pudding mix • 3 eggs, separated • 1 cup milk
1/2 cup pineapple syrup or any cordial • whipped cream • pineapple

Cream the butter and sugar, add flour sifted with baking powder and the package of pudding mix. Add egg yolks that have been beaten with the milk, a little at a time. When batter is thoroughly mixed, fold in the beaten egg whites. Pour into a buttered cake tin and bake in preheated 375° oven about 50 minutes. When cool, turn onto a baking rack and let stand until the cake is completely cooled. Make incisions with a sharp knife and pour pineapple syrup or cordial over the cake. Refrigerate. Garnish with sweetened whipped cream and slices of pineapple. Serve very cold.

[IRACEMA DIAS LEITE, MINAS GERAIS]

Peanut Cake
Bolo de Amendoim

2 tablespoons butter • 2 tablespoons peanut butter • 1 cup light brown sugar
1 cup granulated sugar • 3 eggs, separated • 3 cups all-purpose flour
3 tablespoons baking powder • 1/2 teaspoon salt • 1/2 teaspoon ground cloves
1/2 teaspoon cinnamon • 1 cup milk

Cream butter and peanut butter with the sugars and add beaten egg yolks. Sift flour, baking powder, salt and spices and add alternately with milk to the first mixture, then fold in stiffly-beaten egg whites. Pour into buttered 2-quart cake tin and bake in preheated 350° oven for approximately 1 hour.

[FABIANA PIMENTA, MINAS GERAIS]

Picnic Cake
Bolo Piquenique

1 cup butter • 2 cups sugar • 3 eggs, separated • 1/2 cup cornstarch
2 cups all-purpose flour • 1 teaspoon baking powder • 1/2 teaspoon salt • 1 cup milk

Cream butter and sugar and add beaten egg yolks. Sift together cornstarch, flour, baking powder and salt. Add to yolk mixture alternately with the milk. Fold in stiffly-beaten egg whites. Pour into well-buttered 1 1/2 quart cake pan and bake in preheated 375° oven for approximately 1 hour.

VARIATION: 1 teaspoon grated lemon rind may be added to batter.

[HILDA LEITE QUEIROGA, MINAS GERAIS]

205

Nut Cake
Bolo de Nozes

2 cups walnuts, ground to a powder • 8 eggs, separated • 1 cup sugar
1 tablespoon all-purpose flour • 1 tablespoon bread crumbs

Grind nuts in blender or meat grinder. Beat egg yolks, add sugar and powdered nuts, flour and bread crumbs. Fold in the stiffly-beaten egg whites. Pour into two 9-inch layer cake tins that have been buttered and lightly floured and bake in a preheated 350° oven from 35 to 40 minutes. Turn on to cake racks to cool. When cool, spread the following filling between layers and top with a meringue made from leftover egg whites.

1 cup water • 1 cup sugar • 1 tablespoon butter • 4 egg yolks • Vanilla

Boil water and sugar until it spins a thread when dropped from the prongs of a fork. Let cool. Add butter and strained egg yolks, stirring constantly and beating until thick. Flavor with vanilla.

FROSTING : Make a meringue with the 4 egg whites left over from the filling, using 4 tablespoons sugar. Cover top and sides of cake.

[ELZA MORAES, RIO DE JANEIRO]

Prune Cake
Bolo de Ameixas

20 prunes • 1/2 cup water • 1 cup butter • 2 cups sugar • 5 eggs, separated
2 cups all-purpose flour • 2 teaspoons baking powder • 1/2 teaspoon salt
1/2 cup milk • 3 ounces Cointreau

Steam prunes with water for about 20 minutes. Remove the stones and reserve the liquid. Cream butter with sugar until mixture is light. Add egg yolks, beat well and fold in the mixture alternately with the milk. Do not beat. Stir prunes into the batter. Pour into a well-buttered 2 1/2 quart cake tin. Bake in a preheated 375° oven 60 to 70 minutes. Remove from tin and dry out on a cake rack. Perforate the top of the cake with a knife. Mix Cointreau with the prune liquid and sprinkle over the cake.

[TRANSLATED FROM: **RECEITAS CULINÁRIAS** BY MYRTHES PARANHOS]

Raisin Cake
Bolo de Passas

1 cup sugar • 1 cup melted butter • 1/4 teaspoon salt • 1 egg
2 cups all-purpose flour • 1 teaspoon cinnamon • 2 teaspoons baking powder
1 cup milk • 1/2 cup raisins

Cream sugar with melted butter, salt and egg. Sift flour, cinnamon and baking powder together and add to sugar mixture alternately with the milk. Stir in raisins. Pour into a well-buttered aluminiun loaf tin and bake in a preheated 375° oven for approximately 1 hour.

Ribbon Cake
Bolo de Fita

cups sugar • 12 eggs, separated • 2 cups butter • 2 3/4 cups all-purpose flou
2 ounces melted unsweetened chocolate

Beat one half sugar with beaten egg yolks and cream the other half with the butter. After these have been well beaten, combine the mixtures. Add sifted flour, beating well, and then the stiffly-beaten egg whites. Divide batter into 2 equal portions and add the melted chocolate to 1 portion. Pour the white batter into two 9-inch buttered layer cake tins and repeat the same process with the chocolate batter. Bake in a preheated 375° oven about 14 minutes. Cool on cake raks and put layers together, alternating the white and chocolate, with a vanilla syrup, made as follows:

3/4 cup water • 1 1/2 cups sugar • vanilla

Bring water and sugar to boil, then reduce to a medium heat and cook until it spins a thread. Add vanilla to suit taste. The syrup should be *brushed* on each of the 4 layers with a small brush, so that when it dries, its taste mingles with that of the cake. This cake does not have an icing as such, but when the layers are in place a mixture of powdered sugar and cinnamon is sprinkled on top and sides.

N O T E : This is a typical recipe from old notebooks of the North in the sugar-producing area, and from a time when the use of baking powder was unknown. It is a rich cake and should be served in small wedges, preferably the day it is made.

[IGNEZ CORREIA D'ARAUJO, PERNAMBUCO]

Sand Cake
Bolo de Areia

1 cup butter • 1 cup sugar • 5 eggs, separated • 1 3/4 cups arrowroot flour
1/4 teaspoon salt • 1 tablespoon baking powder • 1 tablespoon lemon juice • 1/4 cup cognac

Cream butter and sugar. Beat egg whites until stiff and then add the beaten yolks. Sift flour, salt and baking powder together. Add egg mixture and sifted dry ingredients alternately to the butter. Beat very well. Stir in lemon juice and cognac. Pour into a well-buttered 2-quart aluminium or tin ring mould and bake in a preheated 375° oven for approximately 45 minutes.

[LAURITA PIRES, MINAS GERAIS]

White Short Cake
Bolo de Claras com Morangos

7 egg whites • 1/2 cup sugar • 1/2 cup rice flour • 1/2 teaspoon salt
2 tablespoons soft butter • sliced sweetened strawberries • sweetened, flavored whipped cream

Beat whites until stiff. Add sugar gradually, then rice flour and salt, beating constantly. Beat in the butter. Spoon batter into two 9-inch layer cake tins that have been well-buttered. Bake in a preheated 400° oven around 17 minutes. Remove. Cool in pans for 10 minutes. Loosen edges with a sharp knife and invert to cool on a cake rack. Divide berries and cream into halves. Put layers together with half the berries and cream, and top with the remainning half.

VARIATION: Mix 2 tablespoons of a fruit liquour with the berries.

Wafer Cake
Torta em Camadas

4 eggs, separated • 1/2 cup sugar • 1 cup all-purpose flour, sifted • 1/4 teaspoon salt
flavoring, if desired, or chopped orange or lemon peel.

Beat egg whites in electric mixer until stiff and add a little at a time, 1/4 cup of sugar, until meringue stands in stiff peaks. Beat yolks and add other 1/4 cup of sugar and combine mixtures. Fold in flour (which has been mixed with salt) with a spatula until dry flour has been absorbed.

Invert two 9-inch cake tins and butter bottoms, then sprinkle lightly with flour. Pour about 1 cupful of batter on each and spread with spatula to 1/2 inch of edge. Bake in a preheated 350° oven for 10 or 15 minutes until golden brown and center springs back when lightly touched. Cool on cake racks and also cool cake tins before buttering and flouring for second batch. This makes four layers. Cut each in half and put together with the following filling. To make a whole round cake, double the recipe for both batter and filling. Cover the top wafer with a syrup made by caramelizing 1 cup of sugar with water.

CHOCOLATE CREAM FILLING

1 cup butter • 1 cup sugar • 3 ounces melted chocolate • 1 egg
1/4 cup crème de cacao or peach liqueur

Cream butter and sugar. Add melted chocolate, egg and crème de cacao. Beat well.

[REGINA SANTOS, BAHIA]

Bom-Bocados [18]

2 cups sugar • 6 ounces water • 3 ounces butter • 3 ounces grated Swiss cheese
3 egg whites • 5 egg yolks • 3/4 cup sifted all-purpose flour

Heat sugar and water until it spins a thread. Cool until tepid, then add butter and cheese, and mix well. Set aside to cool completely. Beat egg whites, add yolks, then the cold syrup. Fold in the flour. Pour into small buttered individual muffin tins that have been lightly sprinkled with flour (or use *Empadinha* tins). Bake in a 350° preheated oven for 25 to 30 minutes, depending upon the size of the tins used. Remove from tins and set in small paper cups to serve. Yields approximately 36.

[HILDA MADASI, BAHIA]

Coconut Bom-Bocados
Bom-bocados de Coco

2 cups sugar • 1 cup water • 4 tablespoons butter • 3/4 cup all-purpose flour
3 cups freshly-grated coconut • 6 eggs, slightly beaten • 4 tablespoons grated Parmesan cheese

Heat sugar and water until it spins a thread. Add butter and cool completely. Mix sifted flour with the coconut and cheese, and stir in the slightly-beaten eggs. Combine the 2 mixtures. Pour into well-buttered *empadinha* tins or small individual muffin tins and bake in a preheated 375° oven for approximately 25 minutes. Yields approximately 30 small *Bom Bocados*.

---

[18] The translation is "a good bite or mouthful."

Pernambuco Bom-Bocados
Bom-bocados Pernambucanos

1 cup sugar • 3 ounces water • 2 tablespoons butter
1/2 cup Swiss or Muenster cheese, grated • 2 tablespoons all-purpose flour
1/2 cup thick coconut milk • 4 eggs yolks

Cook sugar and water until it spins a thread (230°-238°). Remove from heat and allow to cool, beating occasionally with a wooden spoon. While still warm, add butter and cheese. Mix well. Add flour to coconut milk and stir so as to prevent lumps from forming. Beat egg yolks and add gradually to coconut milk and flour mixture, then add to syrup mixture. Fill buttered individual cup cake or *empadinha* tins with batter and set the tins in a shallow pan of warm water. Bake in a preheated 350° oven, like custard until done (45 to 50 minutes). Yields approximately 12.

N O T E :   Allow to cool partially before loosening edges from sides of tins with a sharp knife. If recipe is doubled, use 1 of the egg whites together with yolks.

[IGNEZ CORREIA D'ARAUJO, PERNAMBUCO]

Orange Bom-Bocados
Bom-bocados de Laranja

2 cups sugar • 6 ounces water • 6 eggs • 1/2 cup sifted all-purpose flour
1/2 cup orange juice • 1/2 teaspoon orange flower water • 1/4 cup grated Muenster cheese

Cook sugar and water until it spins a thread. Let stand until cold. Add whole eggs, sifted flour, orange, juice, orange flower water and strain. Add grated cheese. Pour into buttered *empadinha* tins or individual muffin tins. Bake in a preheated 350° oven 25 to 35 minutes, according to the size of pans. When cold, loosen from sides of tins, and turn into small paper cups to serve.

Papaya Bom-Bocados
Bom-bocados de Mamão

1 1-pound can papaya melon[19] • 1 cup sugar • 3 tablespoons butter
3 tablespoons sifted all-purpose flour • 4 whole eggs • 2 eggs yolks

Drain papaya and reserve liquid, which should be equal to 3/4 cup. If liquid does not measure this amount, add enough water to make 3/4 cup. Add sugar to the liquid and boil until it spins a thread. Add the butter and cool thoroughly. Mash the papaya and blend in the sifted flour. Mix well, then add the cooled syrup. Add the eggs, one at a time, beating well as each egg is added. Butter *empadinha* tins and fill with the batter. Bake in 375° oven for about 35 minutes. As this is a very delicate confection, allow to cool several minutes before removing to the little paper cups in which they are served. Yields approximately 28.

[IGNEZ MORRIS, RIO DE JANEIRO]

---

[19] If fresh papaya is used, measure 2 cups, add 2 cups of sugar, cover and cook until melon is done. Remove the melon, boil down the syrup until it spins a thread, and proceed as above.

Cassava and Rice Flour Cupcakes
Bolinhos de Mandioca e Arroz

1/2 cup cooked, mashed manioc root (cassava root) • 1/2 cup shortening • 1/2 cup sugar
1/2 package dry, granular yeast or 1/2 cake compressed yeast • 1/2 cup warm milk
1 teaspoon salt • 1/4 teaspoon aniseed • 1/4 cup grated Muenster cheese
1 1/2 cups rice flour • 5 eggs

Boil and mash manioc root and while still warm add shortening and sugar. Dissolve yeast in warm milk and add to manioc. Stir in salt, aniseed, cheese and rice flour. Beat eggs, add to manioc and beat until air bubbles form. The mixture should have the consistency of a batter. Cover, let stand in a warm place until double in bulk. Spoon into buttered cup cake tins and bake in a preheated 400° oven for about 25 minutes. Yields 12 cupcakes.

[TRANSLATED FROM: **AS RECEITAS PARA VOCÊ DA TIA EVELINA, 4TH ED.**]

Coconut Cupcakes
Bolinhos de Coco para Chá

2 ounces butter • 1 cup sugar • 2 eggs, separated • 1 cup freshly grated coconut
1/2 cup milk • 1 cup all-purpose flour • 1 1/2 teaspoon baking powder
1/4 teaspoon salt • 1 teaspoon vanilla

Cream butter and sugar and add beaten egg yolks. Add coconut and milk. Sift flour, baking powder and salt, and add to the creamed mixture. Fold in stiffly-beaten egg whites. Pour into bite-size buttered muffin tins and bake in a preheated 425° oven 15 to 20 minutes. Yields 3 dozen bite-size cupcakes.

[LIA MAGRO, PERNAMBUCO]

Heaven's Bacon
Toucinho de Céu

1 1/2 cups sugar • 1/2 cup water • 3/4 cup butter • 3/4 cup ground almonds
3 egg whites • 6 eggs yolks • 3/4 cup all-purpose flour

Boil sugar and water until it spins a thread, and while still warm add butter and almond meal. Let cool. Beat egg whites until stiff and beat in yolks, and then add to cooled syrup mixture. Sift flour into mixture and beat until flour has all been absorbed. Pour into a shallow buttered (square or oblong) baking tin and bake in a preheated 375° oven for approximately 20-25 minutes. Remove from oven, sprinkle top with powdered sugar, cool and cut into squares.

[HILDA MADASAI, BAHIA]

Pamonha

12 ears of fresh corn • 1/2 cup coconut milk, or cow's milk • 1 tablespoon butter
1/2 teaspoon salt • 1/4 teaspoon aniseed • 3/4 cup sugar • grated cheese (optional)

Shuck the corn and save the husks. Scrape off the kernels and grind in the electric blender, or grate directly from the corn cob. Strain through a coarse sieve. Add coconut milk, butter, salt, aniseed and the sugar and mix. The mixture should be of the consistency of a very thick sauce. Select whole pieces of the husks and make little sacks by sewing three sides together. Fill with the mixture and tie open end with strips of corn husk or thread. Plunge into boiling salted water and cook until corn husk turns yellow. Cool and serve in the small sack in which it was cooked. When opened, the pamonha should be like a thick paste. This is one of the specialities served on St. John's Day.

VARIATION: Many people believe that cheese imparts a better flavor and they advocate adding as much as one cupful with the above recipe. The cheese used should be a hard cheese of the Holland variety.

[BERNADETE LOUREIRO, PERNAMBUCO]

Mother Benta
Mãe Benta [20]

1 1/4 cups butter • 3 eggs • 1 1/4 cups sugar • 2 3/4 cups rice flour
1 grated coconut, divided into 3 parts • 3 egg yolks

Cream butter and add the whole eggs. Beat well and add sugar and rice flour. Mix thoroughly. Using 2 parts of the grated coconut, extract the pure coconut milk and add to the mixture. Lastly, stir in the beaten yolks and the third part of the grated coconut. Spoon into small-size paper baking cups 3/4 full and bake in a preheated 350° oven 30 minutes or until golden brown. Yields approximately 40 small cupcakes.

[IGNEZ CORREIA D'ARAUJO, PERNAMBUCO]

---

[20] The name of this cupcake could be translated as "Holy Mother" and the recipe itself could have been brought to Brazil by the Portuguese nuns and the coconut introduced by the Negro slaves. On the other hand, because the recipe calls for coconut, so closely associated with African cookery, the name could be that of Mother Benta — one of those famous Negro cooks of the Big Houses. Mrs. Myrthes Paranhos, in her book, *Receitas Culinárias*, p. 241) says that during the time of the Regency in Brazil there lived in Rio de Janeiro a Mrs. Benta Maria da Conceição Torre, whose son, Geraldo Leite Bastos, was a high church dignitary of that time. Mrs. Benta was noted for her pastries and confections, and it is said that Regent Feijó used to frequent her house on the Rua das Violas (today called Rua Teófilo Otôni) to partake of her delicious cakes, one of which took the name Mother Benta. So there are many ways in which the name could have originated and the reader is free to take his choice or the historian to research the matter.

Quindins de Yáyá

"Yáyá" or *"Iaia"* was the slaves' way of addressing the young girls of the Big House, just as *"Sinhá"* — a contraction of *"Senhora"* — was used to address the mistress. The slaves also called the young girls *"Sinhá Moça"* which corresponds to "Missy." Likewise, the Masters were called *"Sinhô"* and their sons *"Ioiô."*

The *Quindim* is a very sweet cupcake that was popular in the Big House of the sugar plantations in the North of Brazil. They were always available for either intimate meals or elaborate parties. Baked in small individual cupcake tins, such as are used for the *empadinha* in *bain marie*, they are then inverted and served in the little paper cups frequently used in Brazil for serving many kinds of candies and cakes.

The *Quindim* (the singular is spelled with an "m" while the plural changes the "m" to an "n" and an "s" is added) is golden brown on top while the bottom is congeled, like gelatin.

The following recipe is from Gilberto Freyre's book. *Assucar.*

1 pound sugar • 1/4 pound butter • 16 egg yolks • 3 egg whites • 1 grated coconut cloves • cinnamon • orange flower water • 1/2 pound sifted all-purpose flour

Mix first eight ingredients very well and beat. Add flour and continue to beat thoroughly. Turn into buttered cupcake tins and bake in *bain marie* in 350° preheated oven. Yields 60.

N O T E : Modern Quindins omit the flour.

Rice Flour Cup Cakes
Bolinhos de Fubá de Arroz

2 eggs, separated • 1/3 cup sugar • 1/4 cup butter • 1/2 cup coconut milk or cow's milk
1/2 cup rice flour • 1/2 cup all-purpose flour • 1/4 teaspoon salt

Beat egg whites, add beaten egg yolks and the sugar that has been creamed with the butter. Then add the coconut milk and the rice flour sifted with all-purpose flour and salt. Mix well. Pour into well-buttered small-size cupcake tins and bake in a 375° oven for 20 to 30 minutes. Yields 1 dozen.

Tarts
Tortas

PASTRY *(Massa)*

2 tablespoons butter • 2 tablespoons lard • 1 tablespoon sugar • 1 egg
1 cup all-purpose flour • 1/8 cup milk

Blend butter with lard and sugar and add lightly-beaten egg. Add sifted flour alternately with the milk. Mix and press dough together. Roll out to fit small cupcake tins. Press into shape in buttered cupcake tins and sprinkle tarts lightly with cinnamon. Bake 15 minutes in preheated 375° oven. Yields approximately 18 tarts.

LEMON FILLING *(Recheio de Limão)*

1 can condensed milk • 2 eggs • juice of 2 lemons • grated rind of 1 lemon

Heat all ingredients over medium heat and cook, stirring constantly for 5 minutes. Pour into baked tarts and return to 350° oven for 10 minutes. Yields approximately sufficient filling for 12 small tarts.

PRUNE FILLING *(Recheio de Ameixas)*

48 prunes • 1/2 cup port wine • 1/2 cup water • 3/4 cup sugar
1/2 cup seedless raisins, soaked in rum or brandy • 1 teaspoon grated orange rind
1 tablespoon butter

Cover prunes with cold water and soak for a few hours. Drain off all the water, remove the stones and add wine, water and sugar and cook until thick. Remove from heat, add grated orange rind, butter and the raisins and cool. Fill tarts. Yields approximately enough filling for 36 tarts.

VARIATION: Dot each filled shell with sweetened whipped cream and garnish with chopped crystalized fruit or maraschino cherries.

[LIA MAGRO, PERNAMBUCO]

Cybele Magro's Butterfly Cake [21]

The making of confections has developed into a fine art in Brazil. From the Colonial days, when the nuns maintained their convents, sometimes exclusively, by preparing and selling their delicate sweets and tidbits, until the present day when many Brazilian ladies of both middle and upper classes have attained great skill in creating and decorating cakes as a hobby, this art has progressed. By incorporating well-proven and traditional ingredients and methods with the newer materials now available, the Brazilian amateur confectioner has produced results that, in the United States, could only be compared with the work of a professional.

Cake decorating in Brazil has become an important hobby and is one expression of the creative ability of a people devoted to art in all its ramifications — both primitive and trained. Whenever there is a wedding, a christening or some extra-special event, you will often find that the stellar attraction — the cake — has originated from and been executed by a female member or friend of the family. You will see beautiful examples of their handicraft. It may be in the form of a box of bonbons; an ornately decorated open box and lid of a cake containing real bonbons, or a child's spinning top, striped and resting at an angle, a rabbit jumping over a small fence or a dog on a sandy beach, a castle, a canoe gliding on a placid river, a Cinderella complete with pumpkin, or, you name it — and I am sure these wonderful Brazilian amateurs can design and execute your wish.

Miss Cybele Magro's Butterfly Cake is a fine example of this delicate art. A veritable Rembrandt of a cake, if you follow directions, the only things required besides the ingredients are the pan, a greal deal of time and patience and an appreciative audience to sample and enjoy the resulting masterprice!

If you profess to patience and time and can assemble a sufficient number of people who enjoy beauty and have a sweet tooth, please call upon me to lend you the special baking pan in which it is made in Brazil. Naturally, this is contingent upon the prompt return of the pan, because I am sure there will be many applicants from those wanting to duplicate Miss Magro's lovely cake.

---

[21] This recipe was featured in *The Washington Post* of May 7, 1964.

223

In case you do not wish to assume the responsability for the butterfly pan, cut a paper butterfly pattern to fit over a rectangular tin 17 1/2 x 12 x 3 inches, bake the cake in the tin, and then cut to the size of the pattern. Use the cake trimmings for puddings or in recipes calling for cake crumbs. Bake the cake in two layers, each one separately. The following ingredients are for one layer only.

BATTER

3 cups butter • 6 cups granulated sugar • 10 eggs, separated • 8 cups sifted all-purpose flour
2 tablespoons baking powder • 2 teaspoons salt • 2 cups cornstarch • 2 cups milk
2 tablespoons grated lemon peel

Cream butter and sugar well and add egg yolks, one at a time, beating after each addition. Sift flour again with baking powder, salt and cornstarch. Add these dry ingredients to the creamed mixture alternately with the milk. Fold in stiffly beaten egg whites and the lemon peel. Turn into the well-buttered butterfly cake tin or a rectangular pan and bake in a 375° oven for 30 minutes, then reduce the heat to 350° and bake 30 minutes more. Before removing cake from oven, insert cake tester in the center. If it comes out clean, the cake is done. Repeat same process and bake the second layer. The layers should be baked so that the top surface is flat. Cool layers on cake racks while you prepare the icing.

I C I N G : This recipe is for one-third the total amount needed. Make in three batches because it hardens rapidly.

2 pounds of powdered sugar • 3 eggs whites • juice of 1 lemon

Sift sugar through a very fine sieve. Note that the sugar should be *powdered* rather than confectioner's. Mix egg whites, 1/2 cup of the sugar and the lemon juice in the mixer at high speed. Gradually add the rest of the sugar, a little at a time, continuing to beat until icing is of the proper consistency to spread. You can test this by lifting out a spoonful and pointing the spoon downwards. If the icing does not drop from the spoon it is of the proper consistency. If it is necessary to store the icing, cover with a clean, damp cloth and refrigerate.

ARRANGEMENT AND DECORATION

Filling (cream, jelly or any smooth filling) • pastry bag with nos. 3 and 16 tubes
colored sugar crystals • vegetable coloring (Miss Magro used green)
silver shot, 2 sizes if possible • cut-out cardboard pattern to represent body of the butterfly

1. Spread the filling between the two layers evenly so that the top of the cake will be flat and smooth. Cover entire cake with a thin layer of the icing (white) and smooth out with a spatula. Let dry overnight. **2.** Decide on the color scheme to be used. Miss Magro made her cake a delicate green, as the photograph shows. Then proceeded as follows: **3.** Color enough icing in a *light* green and spread thicky on sides of cake. Smooth out and let dry. **4.** Place the cardboard representing the body in position. Ice it heavily so that it will stand out in relief. Allow to dry completely. **5.** With a pencil, lightly mark the wing veins and ornamental designs on the butterfly. **6.** Using tube no. 3, outline the veins in icing and sprinkle colored sugars on top, removing all excess sugars. **7.** Follow same process for other designs, using different shades of sugars. **8.** Dye some of the icing in a darker shade of green, but still in a pastel hue. **9.** Using the flowered tube, no. 16, press out flowers on entire surface of cake not yet decorated. **10.** Shape the antennae with wire and cover with successive layers of the same colored icing, using a no. 3 tube. Place one small silver shot at the end of each antenna and use the larger silver shot to represent the eyes. **11.** Complete the decoration by outlining the side edging using the same tubes, as follows: with the no. 3 tube, outline the borders of the design; use no. 16 tube to fill in any vacant spaces with small buds.

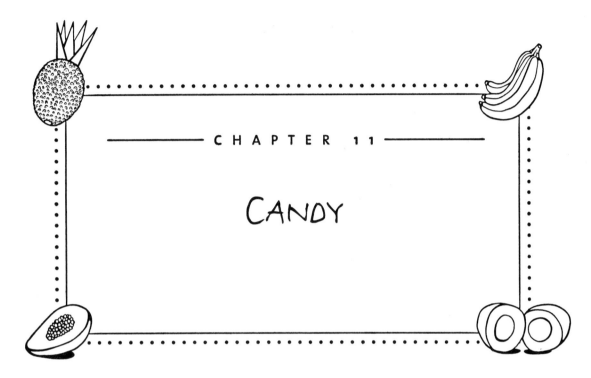

CHAPTER 11

CANDY

Ah, that such sweet things should be fleet,
Such fleet things sweet!

SWINBURNE, FÉLISE, ST. 22

One cannot disassociate the preparation of candies and cakes in Brazil from their early association with the Big House[1] and the convents built in Northeastern Brazil. It was to these establishments that the Portuguese nuns brought their recipes for candies, cakes and cookies when they left their homeland to settle in the new country. Later, the African slaves added their own touch and also incorporated some aboriginal ingredients.

Of native Indian cookery, Freyre says: "The national cuisine — let it be said in passing — would have remained impoverished and its individuality would have been profoundly affected if these delicacies of native origin had not survived, for they give a flavor to the Brazilian diet that neither Lusitanian dishes nor African cookery could supply. But it should be noted that it was in the kitchens of the Big Houses that many confections lost their regional and exclusively Indian character to become truly Brazilian."[2]

Later, Freyre goes on to say: "Portugal's cuisine, as well as its hagiology, in the old names that are given to certain confections, in the semi-phallic forms and trimmings of certain sweetmeats, and in the piquant, not to say aphrodisiac seasoning of garnishings, dressings, and gravies, has preserved for us the erotic vibrancy, the procreative tension, which the country of necessity sought to maintain in the fervent era of Imperial colonization. The same is true for the Brazilian colonial kitchen, where we find similar stimuli to love and fecundity. Even in the names of convent sweets and cakes, made by the seraphic hands of the nuns, there is to be perceived at times an aphrodisiac intention, an obscene touch, confounded with the mystic — such names as Nun's Sighs, Heavenly Salt Pork, Heavenly Manna, Angel's Tidbits.

---

[1] See Foreword, p. 11.
[2] Gilberto Freyre, *The Masters and the Slaves* (New York: Alfred A. Knopf, Inc., 1946), p. 128.

These were the cakes and sweets for which the sisters' male friends sighed at the convent doors. Not being able to give themselves in the flesh to their admirers, the nuns made use of the cakes and caramels as a substitute, and these came to take on a sort of sexual symbolism. Speaking of the patriarchal desserts, Afrânio Peixoto, in one of his Brazilian *romans de moeurs*, observes that 'it was not we who enjoy them who gave them such names, but their feminine creators, the respective abbesses and nuns of Portuguese convents, who were more occupied with the making of such dishes than they were with divine service.'"[3]

Many of the convents sold their sweets, and sometimes ladies from the Big Houses ordered them to be made and then sent a slave girl to the market place to sell them. It is said that the nuns even received orders from abroad for special dried sweets, which is easy to understand, since sugar was very scarce in Europe and yet so plentiful in Brazil.

Sugar was the principal product of the area. Therefore, it was only to be expected that Pernambuco would be the center for cooking and baking foodstuffs of sugar. As it was! Traditional cakes and sweets were developed in the kitchens of the Big Houses, some of which we have already mentioned in the chapter on Cakes and Cup Cakes. These recipes, handed down from one generation to another, are still in use today, and many are still to be found on the *tabuleiro*[4] of the Bahian sweet vender.

The Negro slave women of Pernambuco not only learned to make the confections as they worked in the kitchens of their masters or in the convents, but they also acquired the picturesque and interesting art of cutting out paper lace doilies to decorate their trays. This fascinating custom was brought from Portugal. Although it is disappearing both in Portugal and Brazil, just as the sweet vender is herself disappearing, one still encounters original examples of this folkloric art.

---

[3] Freyre, *op. cit.*, p. 259.

[4] This is the tray used for displaying sweets, which may be balanced on the vender's head when she is walking, or resting on a folded stand when she is seated.

Emanuel Ribeiro, the Portuguese folklorist, has declared that the cutting out of lace paper doilies and small figures like birds, hearts, fruits, flowers, etc. is "one of the most beautiful manifestations of popular art" in Portugal.[5]

My first experience with these paper lace cutouts was in 1926 when I was living in Rio de Janeiro. We had a maid from Bahia whom I had asked to clean the kitchen shelves and the pantry. I was completely amazed when I found she had produced a most attractive lacy shelf covering from old newspapers. The symmetrical design of cutouts and the effect of black and white paper was striking. Even the insides of the cupboards were adorned with this exciting form of primitive art.

Probably the *Baiana* and her *tabuleiro* originated in Recife, but it was in Bahia that she received fame and took her place as one of the most colorful figures in all Brazil. The *Baiana* is known not only throughout Brazil, but she has been projected to other shores by means of the posters and advertising material distributed by travel agencies. Dressed in her voluminous petticoats and skirt, just as in colonial times, the *Baiana* lends grace and interest to the modern street scene. Although many have come to believe that her costume is the Brazilian national costume, this is not true. The costume is regional in character, like that of the Gaucho or Brazilian cowboy who rides the range in Rio Grande do Sul State.

Carnival times in Brazil produces many authentic *Baiana* costumes appearing at masquerades, but as the Brazilian ladies have taken some flamboyant liberties in adapting the style and enriching the materials for carnival use, there are also several versions which are not genuine. The authentic *Baiana* dress today remains basically the same as when it was first worn by African slaves. It consists of either a plain or gaily-colored very full skirt worn over several petticoats and topped by a white short-sleeved blouse of eyelet embroidery or trimmed with Brazilian handmade lace. The genuine *Baiana* costume boasts a plain turban worn tightly draped around the head.

The *pano da costa* (cloth from the coast) is a long piece of material (like a stole) worn slung over the shoulder and pinned under the opposite arm. It also may be wrapped once or twice in a wide fold about the waist and tied rather tightly.

---

[5] Gilberto Freyre, *Assucar* (Rio de Janeiro: Livraria José Olympio, 1939), p. 62.

Without the abundant strings of glass beads, gold chains, bracelets, amulets and earrings that accompany the costume, and the open sandals on her feet, the *Baiana* is not complete. Originally, many of these ornaments were worn as charms and were supposed to ward off the evil eye and protect the wearer against harm. One of the better known of these figures is the *figa* which is also styled into expensive jewelry worn by fashionable Brazilian ladies.

The *figa* represents the figure of an outstretched left arm and clenched fist with the thumb thrust between the first and second fingers. It is a charm used as a protection against bad spirits. There is some possibility that it was introduced into Brazil by the Bantu Negroes imported as slaves, however there is a wide divergence of opinion on this subject.

Luís da Câmara Cascudo's book on Brazilian folklore traces the wearing of the *figa* back to the Roman Empire and cites references from Dante's *Divine Comedy* and from Shakespeare's *Othello*. Cascudo goes on to state that Freudian implications were associated with its use and origin.[6]

Alexandre Dumas, who was just as good a gourmet as he was as a novelist, gives us still another version of the *figa*. In his *Dictionary of Cuisine* under the heading "figs" he relates the following story, attributed to Rabelais: "When the Milanese revolted against Frederick, his wife, the Empress, was driven from the city on an old mule, facing the tail. When Frederick reconquered the city, he captured all the rebels and ordered his executioner to insert a fig under the tail of the same mule. The rebels were required to remove the fig, offer it to the executioner, saying 'Ecco il fico!' and then replace it. Many were hung rather than submit to such humiliation, but until today the Milanese are infuriated when anyone 'figs' them."

However, as Dumas took some liberties in compiling his Dictionary — liberties which are pardonable in a novelist of his stature — one does not have to accept this theory, although it could be true.

The *figa* travelled from Europe to Africa to Brazil, losing its humiliating connotation on the way and acquiring its reputation as a charm agains evil. Today, the *Baiana* in full regalia must display a *figa* on her person, else she is not entirely authentic.

---

[6] Luís da Câmara Cascudo, *Dicionário do Folclore Brasileiro* (Rio de Janeiro: Ministério da Educação e Cultura, Instituto Nacional do Livro, 1954), p. 262.

The classic and colorful figure of the *Baiana* is found in all large cities of Brazil. She is more evident, though, in Salvador da Bahia, the city where she forms part of a tradition and culture. There you will see her, elegantly poised, as she balances the tray on her head. Sometimes, she is sitting on the small stool she carries with her — the *tamborete* — as she leisurely tends the tapioca sticks toasting on a brazier.

The *tabuleiro* is usually lined with the traditional cutout paper, but I have seen many with a clean piece of fringed linen instead of the paper. The sweets arranged on the tray are: *Cocadas*,[7] *Acaça*,[8] *Mães-Bentas*,[9] *Quindins*,[10] *Pé-de-Moleque*,[11] *Broa*,[12] *Grude*,[13] *Manué*,[14] *Pamonha*,[15] and *Cuscuz*.[16]

---

[7] Coconut Kisses, see recipe, p. 244.

[8] A confection of rice flour and cornmeal wrapped in banana leaves.

[9] See recipe and explanation in chapter on "Cakes and Cupcakes," p. 219.

[10] *Ibid.*, p. 220.

[11] Pé-de-moleque (Pé means foot; moleque in the days of slavery meant a pickaninny or small Negro boy). Today, its meaning has been expanded to signify a ragamuffin, urchin or rascal. In Brazilian cookery there are two recipes known as "Pé de Moleque." In this instance the "Pé de Moleque" on the Baiana's tabuleiro was probably a sort of cake described by Gilberto Freyre as being served in Pernambuco and prepared from eggs, brown sugar, cashew nuts, butter, aniseed, salt, cloves and flour made from sun-dried manioc root, and *baked as cake*. This flour from the manioc or cassava root is called "massa de mandioca" and is not to be confused with the "farinha de mandioca."

[12] A corn bread made with rice or tapioca and beaten eggs.

[13] A baked cake made of dried tapioca and grated coconut, wrapped in banana leaves.

[14] A cake prepared from corn flour and honey.

[15] A cake made from grated corn, coconut milk, and sugar, wrapped in corn husks and boiled. Served especially on St. John's Day. See recipe in chapter on "Cakes and Cupcakes, p. 218.

[16] See chapter on Cuscuz, p. 277. The one sold by the Baiana is probably the sweet variety used as a dessert and made of tapioca.

Although the *Baiana* sells mostly sweets, she also has a few salty specialities which inspired poems by several important Brazilian men of letters.

Among the salty foodstuffs on the *tabuleiro* one could find fried fish or fish cakes, *Acarajé*,[17] *Mocotó*,[18] *Vatapá*,[19] *Abará*,[20] and *Feijão de Coco*.[21]

Many of these foods that the poets raved about are disappearing from her *tabuleiro*. If someone interested in preserving Brazilian folkloric cookery does not record these recipes soon, not just listing ingredients — as most of the literary people have done — but giving detailed information as to quantity, as well as exact procedure, these valuable epicurean delights of the Brazilian table will be lost forever to the gourmets of the world.

A WORD ABOUT CANDYMAKING: If you do not have a candy thermometer, there are certain physical changes in the mixture that serve as a guide. All experienced confectioners know about "spinning a thread," "soft-or hard-ball stage," etc. But to take the guesswork out of candymaking, there is no substitute for the inexperienced like a good candy thermometer graded up to 400°. Check the thermometer in boiling water for accuracy. It should register 212°. When using the thermometer, first place it in water and bring to the boiling point, shake it and then transfer to hot syrup to avoid too sudden heating. Recipes in this chapter are geared to meet the needs of those who work with and without the thermometer.

---

[17] A patty made of beans, highly seasoned, and served with a special hot sauce. See chapter on "Afro-Brazilian Foods," p. 76.

[18] Ordinarily, this would be a kind of calf's-hoof jelly, but the Mocotó of the *Baiana's tabuleiro* was a heavy meat dish, made from calves' hooves, tripe, and lungs and highly seasoned. It requires many hours to prepare.

[19] A creamy dish made of fish, shrimp, peanuts, coconuts and palm oil. See recipes in chapter on "Afro-Brazilian Foods," p. 86.

[20] Acarajé batter steamed in banana fronds.

[21] A creamy dish made of beans and coconut, and served in soup plates. See recipe in chapter on "Soups," p. 519.

COOKING TEMPERATURES FOR CANDY

Thread stage ....230°-234°F
Soft-ball stage ....234°-238°F
Medium-ball stage...238°-245°F
Firm-ball stage ....245°-250°F
Hard-ball stage..250°-265°F
Soft-crack stage ....265°-272°F
Medium-crack stage..272°-290°F
Hard-crack stage..290°-310°F
Caramel stage ....320°-345°F

TESTING CANDIES:[22] The cold-water test is a valuable aid in determining when the candy is done, whether or not a thermometer is used.

Into a cup of cold water (not iced) let fall several drops of boiling-hot candy. Form a ball with the fingers. At the *soft-ball stage*, the drops will form a ball that can just be picked up, but which will fall apart when removed from the water. At the *medium-ball stage*, the ball, in water, will be firm but will lose its shape when removed from the water. At the *firm-ball stage*, the ball, in water, feels like putty and will hold its shape out of water. At the *hard-ball stage*, the ball when removed from water will be hard enough to make a sound when tapped against a plate.

At the *soft-crack stage*, the candy will be too hard to shape into a ball in water, but the firm ribbon it forms will bend when lifted out. At the *medium-crack stage*, it will hold its shape out of water without being brittle. At the *hard crack stage*, it will remain brittle when removed from the water. The *caramel stage* begins at the point where the color becomes a light amber, and continues through a dark amber color; if allowed to progress too far, the caramel will develop a disagreeably burned flavor.

CAUTION: The pan of candy should always be removed from the heat while the cold water test is being made; otherwise there is danger of overcooking while testing is done.

---

[22] Meta Given, *Modern Encyclopedia of Cooking* (Chicago: J. G. Ferguson and Associates, 1949), v. 1, p. 623.

A WORD ABOUT THESE CANDY RECIPES: It will be found that many of the candy mixtures that are cooked *up to the medium-ball stage* (238°-245°F) improve if left standing overnight before shaping into small balls. In fact, this is highly recommended, especially for Brigadiers, Little Apples, Kisses, Date Plums, Fruit Candy, Peanut Creams and most of the recipes calling for sweet potato or pumpkin purée.

It will also be noted that several recipes call for condensed milk. Before this short-cut product appeared on the market, the recipes started with *doce de leite* (see recipe for Milk Sweet in chapter on Desserts, p. 285), and to prepare it was a time-consuming process.

Sometimes, if the candy mixture has passed the desired stage, or has been removed from the heat before it reaches the proper stage, the addition of a raw egg white to each 2 cups of the candy mixture will give sufficient body to work the candy into balls. When this correction is applied, it is necessary to allow the mixture to "set" several hours or even overnight.

Several universal favorites are also made in Brazil, but for obvious reasons recipes for fudge, penuche, fondant, caramels, etc. are not included in this chapter.

Usually, candies and other confections are shaped into small bite-size balls by rolling in the palms of slightly buttered hands. They are then placed in small paper cups before arranging in the serving dish. The little bonbon cups are available in pastel colors and silver and gold, as well as in various sizes. Small tissue paper wrappers with fringed edges are used to wrap hard candies.

Almond Balls
Bolinhas de Amêndoa

*3 cups sugar • 1 cup water • 1/4 teaspoon cream of tartar • 1/4 teaspoon salt
3 egg yolks, slightly beaten • 1 cup finely-chopped almonds • 1/2 teaspoon vanilla
2 egg whites • 2 tablespoons dark cocoa powder*

Cook sugar, water and cream of tartar over medium heat, stirring constantly with a wooden spoon until it spins a thread (230°-234°F). Remove from heat and add salt and egg yolks, and beat well. Return to medium heat and cook until mixture begins to pull away from sides of saucepan (238°-245°F). Remove from heat, beat well, add 3/4 cup of the almond and cool. Beat in vanilla and when cool enough knead in the 2 egg whites. Let stand overnight or until you are able to work candy into small balls. Roll the balls in the cocoa that has been mixed with the other 1/4 cup of nuts, and place in small paper cups. Yields 50-60 small balls.

Apricot Delight
Delícias de Damasco

*1/2 pound dried apricots • 1 cup water • 2 cups sugar • 5 egg yolks
1 tablespoon butter • sprinkles or grated coconut*

Steam dried apricots in water, add sugar and lightly-beaten egg yolks. Cook over low heat, stirring constantly with a wooden spoon until the mixture falls away from sides os saucepan (234°-238°F). Remove from heat, beat in the butter and allow to dry out overnight. Next day, shape into small balls and roll them in sprinkles or coconut. Yields 50.

Brazil Nut Balls
Docinhos de Castanha do Pará

1 can condensed milk • 1 cup Brazil nuts, chopped or ground • 1 tablespoon butter
flavoring (vanilla or almond)

Heat condensed milk over low flame, stirring constantly. When mixture is thick enough to hold its shape away from sides of pan (238°-245°F), add butter and nuts. Beat well, remove from heat and cool. Add flavoring, shape into small balls and allow to dry. Place in small bonbon cups. Yields 25.

[JEANETTE VIANNA, RIO DE JANEIRO]

Brigadiers No. 1
Brigadeiros Nº 1

2 cans condensed milk • 4 tablespoons grated unsweetened chocolate • 2 tablespoons butter
1/2 cup milk • 1/4 teaspoon vanilla • chocolate sprinkles or cocoa

Heat condensed milk, chocolate, butter and milk and cook over low heat until mixture falls away from sides of pan (238°-245°F), stirring constantly with a wooden spoon. Remove from heat, beat in the vanilla and turn onto a buttered platter to cool. Shape into smal balls, roll in or top with chocolate sprinkles or cocoa and place in paper bonbon cups. Yields about 40.

Brigadiers No. 2
Brigadeiro Nº 2

1 can condensed milk • 1/4 cup milk • 2 tablespoons grated bitter chocolate
1 tablespoon butter • 1 egg yolk • 1 tablespoon honey • 4 ounces stale plain cake or
cookies, vanilla or social tea biscuits, or champagne biscuits mixed with enough crème de
cocoa, rum or whiskey to make a mush (about 1/3 cup) • chopped nuts

Cook first 6 ingredients as in Brigadiers No. 1 to 238°-245°F. Remove from heat, beat in the mush and let stand overnight. Shape into small balls and roll in or top with chopped nuts. Place in paper bonbon cups. Yields 50.

[TRANSLATED FROM: **A COZINHA DELICIOSA E MODERNA** BY MARIA THEREZA SENISE]

Brigadiers No. 3
Brigadeiros Nº 3

2 cans condensed milk • 1/2 cup fresh milk • 4 tablespoons grated unsweetened chocolate
1/4 cup sugar, mixed with 1 tablespoon cornstarch • 1 tablespoon butter
1/2 cup grated Parmesan cheese • 2 cups grated coconut • 4 egg yolks

Heat condensed milk, milk and chocolate over low heat and when mixture is evenly blended, stir in sugar-cornstarch mixture. Add butter, cheese, coconut and egg yolks and cook over low heat, stirring constantly with a wooden spoon until mixture falls away from sides of pan (238°-245°F). Cool and follow procedure for Brigadiers No. 1. Yields about 60.

[TRANSLATED FROM: **A COZINHA DELICIOSA E MODERNA** BY MARIA THEREZA SENISE]

Cherries
CEREJAS

1 1/2 cups mashed ripe bananas • 1/2 of a 3-ounce package cherry gelatin dessert mix
1 1/4 cups sugar • 1/4 cup honey • 1 tablespoon butter

Mash bananas thoroughly, measure, and cook over medium heat with dessert mix, sugar and honey, stirring with a wooden spoon until mixture falls away from sides of saucepan (238°-245°F). Add butter, cool, shape into small balls and roll in or top with crystalized sugar. Place into small paper bonbon cups and garnish with a small piece of maraschino cherry. Yields about 40.

Chocolate Balls
Bolinhas de Chocolate

1 ounce unsweetened bitter chocolate • 1/6 cup sugar • 1 1/2 tablespoons milk
2 ounces ground almonds • 2 ounces lady fingers or sponge cake crumbs
2 ounces crème de cacao • 1 ounce melted sweet butter • 1 egg white

Melt chocolate with sugar and milk. Cool. Add rest of ingredients in order given. Let stand until mixture is thick enough to hold its shape (overnight, if possible). Roll into small balls and coat with powdered sugar and chocolate sprinkles. Place in small paper bonbon cups. Yields 28.

Coconut "Alfenins"

Alfenins de Coco

3 cups water • 2 pounds sugar • thick and thin milk from 1 coconut
1/2 tablespoon white vinegar • 1/4 teaspoon salt

Heat water, sugar, coconut milk, vinegar and salt to boil, then reduce heat to low and *cook without stirring* until it reaches the medium crack stage (272°-290°F). Once in a while scrape down sides of the saucepan with a knife. It may take around 3 hours for the syrup to reach the proper stage. Once the syrup responds to the medium crack test, pour it onto a buttered platter to cool sufficiently to handle. Butter hands and pull the mixture until light. This works better when two people do the pulling. With the final pulls, draw out into a cord about 1/2 inch in diameter and twist the cord several times. While still pliable, cut into half inch lengths or tie into knots. Wrap each piece in a fringed colored tissue paper. Yields about 2 pounds.

N O T E : At first hand it may appear that this recipe would produce a hard candy, like toffee. Actually, the final result, although brittle, like a meringue, literaly melts away at the first crunch. It is one of the most delicate and delicious of Brazilian confections and a favorite of the Big Houses.

[MARIA LUIZA NARDON, SÃO PAULO]

241

Coffee Drops
Balas de Café

3 cups sugar • 1 cup strong instant coffee • 1 cup milk • 2 egg yolks • 3 tablespoons honey
1 tablespoon butter • 1 tablespoon all-purpose flour • pinch of baking soda

Mix all ingredients in blender and then cook over low heat, stirring with a wooden spoon until mixture forms a hard ball when dropped into cold water (250°-265°F). Remove from heat and cool in saucepan by beating so that mixture does not become grainy. Shape into small balls or twists and wrap each piece in a small strip of wax paper and twist ends. Add nutmeats to the mixture, if desired.

[MARIA LUIZA NARDON, SÃO PAULO]

Fruit Candy
Docinhos de Frutas

1 cup tenderized figs, uncooked • 1 cup tenderized prunes, uncooked
1 cup tenderized apricots, uncooked • 6 ounces freshly-grated coconut
3 cups granulated sugar • 5 eggs, unbeaten • 2 tablespoons butter

Grind all the fruits in a food chopper or blender. Combine all the ingredients in a saucepan, *without adding any water* and cook over high heat, stirring constantly with a wooden spoon until mixture thickens enough for you to "see the bottom of the pan" (238°-245°F). This takes about 1/2 hour. Transfer mixture to a bowl and allow to cool, preferably overnight.

When ready to shape, have ready small paper cups about 1 1/2 inches in diameter. These can be made from aluminium foil cut into 2-inch squares and shaped over a bottle cap about 1 1/2 inches in diameter. Trim off excess foil with scissors leaving even with rim of the cap, and then slip off the finished cup. Grease palms of hands with a small amount of butter and shape the mixture into little balls about 1 inch in diameter. Roll in crystalized sugar before placing in the cups. Yields 50 to 60.

High-Society Candy
Docinho Grã-fino [23]

1 can condensed milk • 2 egg yolks • 1 tablespoon butter • 1 cup grated coconut
3 ounces chopped prunes • 3 ounces chopped dates • 1/4 cup chopped nuts • 1 jigger rum

Cook condensed milk, egg yolks, butter, coconut, prunes and dates over medium heat, stirring constantly until mixture thickens and falls away from sides of pan (238°-245°F). Add nuts, beat well and cool. Add rum. Work into small balls, roll in crystalized sugar and place in small paper cups. Yields 38.

---

[23] Suggested by *"Docinho de Festa"* from Maria Thereza Senise's book, *A Cozinha Deliciosa e Moderna*

Kisses
Beijos

3/4 cup sugar • 1/4 cup cold water • 1/2 cup ground almonds • 3 egg yolks
1 teaspoon all-purpose flour • flavoring, as desired

Make a syrup by boiling sugar and water, and when it boils, add the ground nuts. Cook until mixture is just beginning to hold its shape when stirred from sides of the pan, then add the egg yolks, one by one and the flour. Stir very well and cool for a few hours. Shape into small balls, roll in crystalized sugar and place in bonbon cups. Yields approximately 24 small balls.

VARIATION: Use as a filling for tenderized prunes, dates or dried figs.

[HILDA MADASI, BAHIA]

Coconut Kisses
Beijos De Coco — Cocadas

1 1/2 cups milk • 3 cups sugar • 1 tablespoon butter • 6 egg yolks (optional)
5 cups freshly-grated coconut • vanilla

Heat milk, sugar and butter over low heat, stirring constantly until mixture spins a thread (230°-234°F). Remove from heat and cool. Add beaten egg yolks and coconut and return to low heat, stirring constantly and scraping down sides of pan to prevent the mixture from becoming grainy. Cook until it is thick enough to hold its shape. Allow to cool completely, add vanilla, then grease palms of the hands with a small amount of butter and shape into small balls. When hands become too sticky, wash them and apply more butter so as to make bonbons smooth. Let stand an hour or so, roll in granulated sugar or coconut and place in small paper cups. Approximate yield: 80 kisses.

VARIATION: Use as a filling for tenderized prunes, figs or dates or roll into kisses and top with a clove or small piece of cherry and arrange in the paper cups.

Papaya Kisses
Beijos de Mamão

2 1-pound cans of papaya packed in heavy syrup. If fresh papaya used, measure 2 cups,
add 2 cups of sugar, cover with water and cook until melon is tender.
1 cup chopped pineaple, or 1 8-ounce can crushed pineapple • 4 cups sugar
3 thin slices of orange, including the rind but with seeds removed • 4 whole cloves
1/2 cub freshly-grated coconut (optional)

Mix above ingredients and bring to boil. Reduce heat to low and cook for about 2 hours or until mixture holds its shape when scraped away from sides of the pan. Cool overnight. Remove cloves. Lightly butter palms of the hands and shape into small balls. Top with small pieces of candied fruit and place in paper bonbon cups. Yields approximately 70 kisses.

Orange Coconut Kisses
Beijos de Laranja e Coco

2 cups sugar • 1 cup milk • 1 tablespoon butter • 2 cups freshly-grated coconut
1 tablespoon grated orange rind • 1/4 cup orange juice • 2 egg yolks
2 tablespoons orange flower water

Heat first three ingredients until mixture spins a thread when dropped from the prongs of a fork (230°-245°F) which takes about 25 minutes. Add coconut, orange rind and juice, and cook, stirring constantly until mixture falls away from sides of pan or holds its shape (about 30 minutes). Remove from heat, add egg yolks and mix well. Cool, add orange flower water. Let stand a few hours to dry out or even overnight. Shape into small balls, roll in grated coconut and place in small bonbon cups. Yields approximately 40 kisses.

VARIATION: Add vegetable dyes to the grated coconut before rolling the kisses.

Little "Apples" No. 1
Maçãzinhas Nº 1

1 1/4 cups sugar • 1/2 cup water • 1 1/2 cups grated coconut
3 egg yolks, slightly beaten • Red vegetable coloring

Boil sugar and water until it spins a thread (230°-234°F). Add coconut and egg yolks, and return to heat. Cook over medium heat, stirring constantly until mixture falls away from sides of pan (238°-245°F) or holds its shape. Add a few drops of red coloring, remove from heat and cool thoroughly. Work into small balls. Insert a clove in the center of each "apple" to represent the stem, top with crystalized sugar and place in bonbon cups. Yields 34.

[OTTILIA JANSEN DE MELLO, MINAS GERAIS]

Little "Apples" No. 2
Maçãzinhas Nº 2

*1 1-pound, 4-ounce can sliced apples for pie or 2 1/4 cups sliced raw apples with
1/4 cup water • 1 cup granulated sugar • 1 cup brown sugar • 1/4 teaspoon ground cloves
1/4 teaspoon grated lemon rind • 1 egg yolk • 2 tablespoons butter*

Cook apples with sugars and mash as they are cooking. When apples are thoroughly
cooked, add cloves and lemon rind and continue cooking and stirring until mixture
holds its shape or falls away from sides of the pan (238°-245°F). Add egg yolk and
cook for 4 or 5 minutes more, then add butter and beat well. Remove from heat
and beat again. Let stand overnight to dry out. The next morning, shape into small
balls (about 40), roll in the egg white that was left over and then in a coating made
as follows:

1/2 cup grated coconut • 1/2 teaspoon cinnamon • few drops green coloring

Little "Apples" No. 3
Maçãzinhas Nº 3

1 1/2 cups thick applesauce • 1 cup cooked pumpkin purée • 3 cups sugar
1 cup crushed pineapple with most of the juice removed
1/2 of a 3-ounce package lime gelatin dessert mix • 6 or 7 whole cloves

Mix ingredients in order given and cook over low heat, stirring constantly with a wooden spoon until mixture is thick enough to hold its shape (238°-245°F). This takes about 2 hours. Remove cloves and discard. Cool mixture overnight. Shape into small balls and roll in red or green sprinkles. Insert a clove to represent the apple stem and place in small bonbon cups. Yields 50-60.

Little Hams
Presuntinhos

LIGHT MIXTURE

2 cups sugar • 1 cup water • 1 cup ground blanched almonds • 3 egg yolks

Boil sugar and water over medium heat until it spins a thread (230°-234°F), then add the almonds. Continue cooking over low heat, about 5 minutes, stirring constantly with a wooden spoon until mixture thickens. Remove from heat and, with a rapid motion, stir in the egg yolks. Cook until mixture falls away from sides of pan. Total cooking time is about 1 hour.

DARK MIXTURE[24]

2 ounces unsweetened chocolate • 1/2 cup sugar • 1 cup milk • 1 cup ground almonds
2 eggs yolks • 1 tablespoon butter

Melt chocolate, add sugar and milk, and simmer until mixture is creamy, taking care to stir constantly. This takes from 30 to 40 minutes. Add nuts, egg yolks and butter and cook until mixture holds its shape.

To shape the "hams," take a heaping 1/4 teaspoonful of the Light Mixture (use a measuring spoon) and shape into a ball (The Light Mixture yields about 3 dozen). Elongate the ball by pinching between the thumb and forefinger. Cover the elongated end of the "ham" or hock, with the Dark Mixture to represent the skin. Press joining edges together so as to form a smooth surface. Dip top end of "ham" or butt in crystalized sugar. Insert a toothpick in the elongated or hock end of "ham" and cover the toothpick with narrow strips of fringed paper secured by lightly moistening ends with egg white.

[OTTILIA JANSEN DE MELLO, MINAS GERAIS]

---

[24] The Dark Mixture is more than enough to simulate the "hocks." Left over mixture can be worked into balls, rolled in ground nuts and served in little paper cups. If time is of the essence, omit Dark Mixture and dip hock ends of "hams" in chocolate sprinkles.

Mother-in-Law's Eyes
Olhos-de-Sogra[25]

1 pound extra large tenderized prunes (about 42)

Wash prunes, remove stones and, if they have not been tenderized, steam with a few drops of water in a covered saucepan (not to cook, but just enough to tenderize them). Cool and fill with the following:

1 1/2 cups sugar • 1/2 cup water • 5 egg yolks, slightly beaten and strained

Boil sugar and water until it spins a thread (230°-234°F). Cool, add egg yolks and return to stove. Cook, stirring constantly until mixture pulls away from sides of pan (238°-245°F). When mixture stirs free, it is done. Allow to cool, fill cavities of prunes and roll in crystalized sugar.

[MARIA BARBOZA NUNES, RIO DE JANEIRO]

[25] These are traditional Brazilian confections served at parties or special afternoon teas or even among desserts at important buffets. Other fillings used are: Kisses (double the recipe); Coconut Kisses (one-half the recipe) or Almonds Balls (the full recipe). Figs and dates are also made up into confections with these fillings and sometimes they are coated with a caramel icing.

Mulatta's Eyes
Olhos de Mulata

1 tablespoon butter • 1/4 cup rich cocoa powder • 2 egg whites • 1 cup superfine sugar
1/4 teaspoon vanilla • 1/8 teaspoon salt • 1 cup finely-chopped peanuts • whole peanuts

Mix ingredients in the order given (omitting the peanuts). Beat out all the lumps and let stand 1 hour. Beat in the chopped peanuts. Let stand until the mixture can be shaped into small balls. Insert 1 whole peanut in center of each ball and place in small paper cups. Yields about 28.

[TRANSLATED FROM: **A COZINHA DELICIOSA E MODERNA** BY MARIA THEREZA SENISE]

Nut Croquettes No. 1
Croquetes de Nozes Nº 1

1/2 pound shelled walnuts • 1 cup sugar • 1/2 cup milk • 2 egg yolks

Grind nuts in blender. Mix with other ingredients and cook over low heat, stirring constantly until mixture holds its shape (238°-245°F) and falls away from sides of the saucepan. Cool, shape into miniature croquettes and roll in crystalized sugar or a rich cocoa powder. Yields 20.

[HILDA LEITE QUEIROGA, MINAS GERAIS]

Nut Croquettes No. 2
Croquetes de Nozes Nº 2

1 pound ground nuts (Brazils, almonds or walnuts) • 2 tablespoons lemon juice
3 egg whites • 1/8 cup milk • 1 teaspoon vanilla • 1/8 cup rum or crème de cacao
2 cups confectioner's sugar

Mix ingredients in the order given, beat well and let stand overnight. Next morning, shape into small croquettes, dip end in crystalized sugar and arrange for serving. Yields 50.

Peanut Brittle with Egg Threads
Pé-de-moleque com Fios de Ovos

1 cup white Karo • 3 cups sugar • 1 1/2 cups water • 3 egg yolks
2 cups roasted peanuts, coarsely chopped

Heat Karo, sugar and water until it reaches the hard ball stage (250°-265°F) and mix in the lightly-beaten egg yolks, twirling them around with a fork to form the "threads." Add the peanuts, turn into a buttered shallow pan and mark off squares (or allow to cool and break into pieces). Yields about 2 pounds.

Peanut Candies
Balas de Amendoim

2 cups scalded milk • 2 whole eggs • 4 egg yolks • 4 cups sugar • 2 cups grated coconut
1/4 cup grated Parmesan cheese • 2 cups ground peanuts

Beat eggs and yolks lightly and mix with sugar. Add coconut, cheese, peanuts, and milk. Cook over low heat, stirring constantly with a wooden spoon until mixture holds its shape away from sides of saucepan (238°-245°F). This takes about 2 hours. Turn onto a buttered platter to cool. When cold, shape into small balls, roll or dip one side in crystalized sugar and place in small paper bonbon cups. Yields 80.

Peanut Creams
Docinhos de Amendoim

1 cup white Karo • 3 cups sugar • 1 1/2 cups water • 3 egg whites, stiffly beaten
1 cup roasted peanuts, finely chopped

Heat Karo, sugar and water until it reaches the medium-ball stage (238°-245°F). Pour over stiffly beaten egg whites, beat well and add peanuts. Let stand overnight. Next day, shape into balls, coat with chocolate sprinkles and set into small paper bonbon cups. Yields 60.

Brazilian Peanut Brittle
Pé-de-moleque Brasileiro[26]

2 1/2 cups brown sugar, tightly packed • 3/4 cup water • 2 tablespoons butter
1/2 cup roasted peanuts, coarsely chopped, with a few left whole
1/2 cup sifted manioc meal • 1/2 teaspoon powdered ginger • 1/2 teaspoon salt (optional)

Cook sugar and water until it reaches the hard ball stage (250°-265°F). Add butter, peanuts, salt (providing the peanuts are unsalted), manioc meal and ginger, and mix lightly. Turn onto a buttered marble slab or into a buttered shallow pan. Cut into squares while warm or allow to cool thoroughly and break into pieces. Yields about 2 pounds.

[TRANSLATED FROM: **A BOA COZINHEIRA Nº 2009 — 150 RECEITAS DE DOCINHOS** BY LÍGIA JUNQUEIRA]

Peppermint Roses
Rosas de Hortelã

1 unbeaten egg white • 1 tablespoon cream or evaporated milk • 2 cups confectioner's sugar
a few drops oil of peppermint • 1/2 teaspoon vanilla • green vegetable food coloring

Mix egg white and milk. Add sugar gradually. When a thick paste is formed, beat in oil of peppermint and vanilla. Add green food coloring and beat thoroughly. Force through a pastry tube, using the attachment to shape roses. Let dry. When roses are completely dried out, fit into the small paper cups and arrange on serving dish.

---

[26] This is the other Pé-de-moleque referred to in note 11 on page 233. It is like Peanut Brittle and is sometimes sold on the streets, warm, cooked on the spot over kerosene stoves or hot embers.

Prune Candies No 1
Bolinhas de Ameixa Nº 1

1 cup prunes • 1 cup sugar • 2 tablespoons orange juice
1 cup grated coconut • 1 tablespoon butter

Remove pits from prunes, wash and grind in meat grinder, or blender. Add sugar and orange juice, and cook over low heat, stirring constantly until mixture falls away from sides of pan (238°-245°F). Add grated coconut, remove from heat, mix well and beat in the butter. Pour into a buttered bowl to cool. When mixture is cool, shape into small balls, roll in crystalized sugar and place each ball in paper bonbon cup. Yields 30.

Prune Candies No. 2
Bolinhas de Ameixa Nº 2

1/3 pound prunes • 2 1/2 ounces ground Brazil nuts • 1 can condensed milk
1/4 cup milk • 1 ounce whiskey

Slightly steam the prunes and remove pits. Add nuts, both kinds of milk, and cook over low heat, stirring until mixture is thick enough to hold its shape, about 15 or 20 minutes (238°-245°F). Cool, add whiskey or other flavoring, if desired. Roll into small balls, dip one end into crystalized sugar and place in small paper bonbon cups. Yields between 24 and 28.

[JEANETTE VIANNA, RIO DE JANEIRO]

Pumpkin Candy No. 1
Docinhos de Abóbora Nº 1

2 cups sugar • 1 cup water • 2 cups boiled, strained pumpkin or canned puréed pumpkin
6 cups grated coconut

Make a syrup of the sugar and water, cooking over medium heat, stirring constantly for about 20 minutes. Add pumpkin and coconut and continue cooking until candy reaches the soft-ball stage (234°-238°F). Remove from heat and let stand until next day. Drop by demitasse spoons into a shallow pan lined with wax paper and set to dry in the sun for about 2 days. Serve in paper bonbon cups. Yields 60-70. *Note:* This is a favorite for St. John's Day.

[FLORINDA K. MACHADO, RIO GRANDE DO SUL]

Pumpkin Candy No. 2
Docinhos de Abóbora Nº 2

1 cup puréed pumpkin • 1 cup sugar • 2 cups grated coconut
1/4 teaspoon cinnamon • 1/4 teaspoon ground cloves

Cook all ingredients together, stirring constantly until the mixture is thick and stands up, or until it reaches the medium-ball stage (238°-245°F). Turn onto a buttered platter to cool. Shape into small balls or mounds and sprinkle with powdered sugar. Set in paper bonbon cups. Yields 50.

Sweet Potato Candy No. 1
Docinhos de Batata-doce Nº 1

1 cup mashed sweet potatoes • 1 1/2 cups sugar • 1 tablespoon Swiss cheese, grated
1/2 cup thick coconut milk, or cow's milk flavored with coconut extract
2 tablespoons butter • 1/4 cup chopped nuts

Add sugar to sweet potatoes and cook over low heat for 5 minutes. Add coconut milk and continue to cook, stirring with a wooden spoon until mixture holds its shape (238°-245°F). Remove from heat, add cheese, nuts and butter, beat and cool. Shape into small balls, roll in grated coconut or crystalized sugar, garnish with a clove or small piece of nut meat, and place in small paper bonbon cups. Yields 40.

Sweet Potato Candy No. 2
Docinhos de Batata-doce Nº 2

1 cup purée of sweet potato • 1 1/2 cups sugar
1 cup crushed canned pineaple, with juice removed • crystallized sugar

Mix sweet potato, sugar and pineapple and cook over low heat, stirring constantly with a wooden spoon until mixture holds its shape away from sides of saucepan (238°-245°F). Cool thoroughly, or let stand until next day and then shape into small balls, and roll in the crystallized sugar. Yields about 35.

[TRANSLATED FROM: **A COZINHA DELICIOSA E MODERNA** BY MARIA THEREZA SENISE]

Stuffed Figs
Figos Recheados

1 pound tender dried figs • full recipe for Maiden's Delight, p. 301 • 1 cup chopped nuts

Steam figs if necessary and make an opening in each. Prepare the full recipe for Maiden's Delight and allow to cool thoroughly, then add the nuts. Stuff the figs with the Delight and press edges together. Roll in crystallized sugar and place in small individual paper cups.

[TRANSLATED FROM: A COZINHA DELICIOSA E MODERNA BY MARIA THEREZA SENISE]

Sweethearts
Amorzinhos

1 can condensed milk • 1 cup grated Muenster cheese • 1 tablespoon butter
1/8 teaspoon salt • 1/4 teaspoon vanilla
chocolate sprinkles or crystallized sugar or cinnamon sugar

Heat condensed milk, cheese, butter, and salt, stirring constantly with a wooden spoon until mixture falls away from sides of saucepan (234°-238°F). Cool, beat in vanilla, shape into small balls and roll in either sprinkles, crystallized sugar or cinnamon sugar. Place in small bonbon cups. Yields about 35.

CHAPTER 12

COOKIES

Instead of by battles and Ecumenical Councils, the rival portions of humanity will one day dispute each other's excellence in the manufacture of little cakes.

FOURIER

Philosophically speaking, this would not be a bad idea. To begin with, it is based on a common ground: namely, that both contestants in the battle are fond of cookies. This, in itself, has a great advantage, because if two warring factions can agree on one point, the chances are that they may discover other points upon which they are in accord. Such contemplations, facetious though they may be, lead one into great realms of thought. And, could this possibility be extended to nations, there is no end to what could be accomplished! Universal peace could be assured through the simple expedient of settling differences through cookie contests!

By definition, this hypothetical instrument of peace is a small, flat, sweet cake. But this does not apply to many Brazilian cookies. Although they are sweet, several are as round as a ball. Like Brazilian cakes, they are known by very suggestive names: *Não Me Toque* (Don't Touch Me), *Sonhos* (Dreams), *Suspiros* (Sighs),[1] *Língua de Gato* (Cat's Tongue) and several taking the names of girls. Many of these cookies are traditional legacies from the Big Houses[2] that figured so prominently in Brazil's colonial history, and are served today with a certain reverence for the past.

As indicated in the chapter on Cakes and Cupcakes, the custom of serving afternoon tea still prevails in Brazilian homes. This is the time when cookies and cakes come into their own. The cookie also plays an important part at receptions, birthday parties and christenings.

---

[1] The Suspiro in Portuguese is actually a meringue. It is included in this Brazilian cookbook because of the great versality with which Brazilian cooks employ it. Not only do they add small amounts of different flours to the egg whites, but they have perfected many fillings which are inserted into the meringues as one does in filling cream puffs.

[2] See Foreword, p. 11.

There seems to be a misconception that cookies are more appealing to children, but adults and the elderly are also very fond of cookies. The fact is that cookies are universal favorites without heed to geographical boundaries. Everybody enjoys a cookie! This applies not only to the female sex, but to downright vigorous and good examples of the "stronger sex." At a poker table in Rio, where all the players were men, I once saw a plate of Brazilian cookies disappear as fast as the locusts devastated "The Good Earth." I wanted one of those cookies myself, but during the time that I stopped to say "Hello" to a guest and the couple of minutes it took me to reach the cookies, they had all been devoured! So, who says cookies are "kid's stuff?" They are for all ages, both sexes, any occasion and any place.

To our regret, many delicious Brazilian cookies are made with ingredients not available abroad and for which there are no satisfactory substitutes. This was mentioned in the chapter on "Breads and Biscuits." Most of these cookies are made with the *polvilho* flours, *doce* and *azedo* (sweet and sour), which lend themselves so well to the preparation of baked goods.

There is no proverbial cookie *jar* in Brazil to which the small fry betake themselves for renewed energy. Instead, there usually is a tin box in which cookies are stored and to which the small fry beat a hasty path when they come home from school or need a *biscoitinho* to tide them over between meals. The tin box makes its appearance at tea time, too. In addition, it is subject to periodic "snack raids" by all members of the household and at any hour. The good Brazilian housewife, who keeps the tin box amply stocker is never at a loss in filling it for she has a large stock of recipes from which to select.

Arrowroot Cookies
Biscoitos de Araruta

3/4 cup arrowroot flour • 1/2 cup all-purpose flour • 1/4 teaspoon salt
1/4 cup butter • 1/4 teaspoon aniseed • 1 egg • 1/4 cup sugar • 1/4 cup milk

Sift flours and salt and cut in the butter and aniseed. Beat egg and add sugar and milk, then add to first mixture. Drop by small teaspoonfuls on a buttered cookies sheet and bake in 375° oven for 15 to 20 minutes. Yields about 20.

Arrowroot & Rice Flour Cookies
Biscoitos de Araruta e Arroz

1 cup arrowroot flour • 1 cup rice flour • 1/2 teaspoon salt • 2 ounces butter • 3 or 4 eggs
1/2 cup sugar • 3/4 cup all-purpose flour • 1/2 teaspoon aniseed
grated lemon rind • Cinnamon sugar

Sift arrowroot, rice flour and salt into butter and 3 lightly beaten eggs. Add sugar and all-purpose flour, and aniseed. Knead with hands. (At this point the dough should be similar to pie crust dough, but not as elastic. If the dough is too dry, add the fourth egg, lightly beaten.) Knead, roll or pat out on a floured board to 1/3 inch thickness. Cut with a cookie cutter, dust with the lemon rind and sprinkle lightly with cinnamon sugar. Place on a buttered cookie sheet and bake in 375° oven 18 to 20 minutes. Yields 4 dozen.

Beer Cookies
Sequilhos de Cerveja

1 1/2 cups all-purpose flour • 3/4 teaspoon baking powder • 3 ounces salt butter
beer to hold • Cinnamon sugar

Sift flour and baking powder and cut in butter. Add enough beer to make a dough, the consistency of pie crust. Let stand 10 minutes. Break off walnut size pieces and shape in the palm of the hand into small balls. Roll in cinnamon sugar. Place on a buttered cookie sheet which has been lightly dredged with flour and bake in a preheated 350° oven for 25 or 30 minutes.

[HILDA MADASI, BAHIA]

Belgiums
Belgas ou Sequilhos Baianos

1 cup all-purpose flour • 1 teaspoon baking powder
1/2 cup butter at room temperature • 2 egg whites • 1/2 cup sugar

Blend sifted flour and baking powder into butter with a pastry blender or finger tips. Beat egg whites until stiff and gradually add sugar. Fold egg white mixture into flour and butter mixture and, after combining the two mixtures, put into a pastry tube with a ribbon nozzle (about 1/2 inch wide). Press onto buttered cookie sheet in 3-inch lengths. Bake in a preheated 350° oven for 10 or 15 minutes. Yields 2 dozen.

[HILDA MADASI, BAHIA]

Brevities
Brevidades

3 eggs, separated • 1 cup sugar • 2 cups arrowroot flour

Beat egg whites until stiff and add yolks, continuing to beat well. Gradually mix in the sugar and beat until mixture is light. Add arrowroot, a little at a time and beat until mixture is spongy. The important element in making this cookie is that the batter must be well beaten. Spoon into small buttered muffin or *empadinha* tins, 1/2 full and bake in a preheated 350° oven for about 25 minutes. Yields about 30.

VARIATION: 1/2 teaspoon grated lemon rind may be added to batter.

[OLIVIA LODER, MINAS GERAIS]

Brazil Nut Cookies
Biscoitos de Castanhas do Pará

3/4 cup butter • 1/2 cup sugar • 1 cup all-purpose flour • 3/4 cup cornstarch
3/4 cup chopped Brazil nuts • 1 egg white

Cream butter and sugar and add flour and cornstarch which have been sifted together. Chop nuts finely or put in the liquifier and mix in the dough. Add egg white. Knead slightly with hands and shape into small balls. Place on slightly-buttered cookie sheet and bake in 400° preheated oven for 15 to 20 minutes. Yields approximately 2 dozen.

[LAURITA PIRES, MINAS GERAIS]

Brazilian Mocha Cookies
Biscoitos de Moca

3 cups all-purpose flour • 1/4 cup cornstarch • 3/4 tablespoon salt
2 1/2 teaspoons baking powder • 1 tablespoon instant powdered coffee
1/2 teaspoon baking soda • 3/4 cup chocolate syrup • 1/4 cup cachaça[3]
3/4 cup stout beer • 1 cup margarine or butter • 1 cup brown sugar
2 eggs, slightly beaten • 3 tablespoons ground Brazil nuts • Powdered sugar

Sift first 6 ingredients. Combine syrup, cachaça and stout beer. Cream butter with the sugar and add the eggs. Alternately add sifted dry ingredients to the creamed mixture with the combined liquids. Mix in the nuts. Beat well, cover and let stand overnight. Drop by demitasse spoons on a lightly-buttered cookie sheet, leaving about 2 inches all around for the cookies to spread. Bake in a preheated 350° oven for 12 minutes. Remove to wire rack to cool and sprinkle with powdered sugar. Yields about 90 cookies.

[GLADYS MARIE SILVA, MATO GROSSO]

---

[3] See Ambassador Nabuco's description, p. 149.

Brazilians
Brasileiras

1 cup sugar • 1/2 cup water • 2 cups freshly-grated coconut • 2 tablespoons butter
4 eggs yolks • 4 tablespoons all-purpose flour • 1/2 teaspoon vanilla

Cook sugar and water until it spins a thread. Add all the other ingredients, except vanilla and cook over low heat, stirring constantly with a wooden spoon until mixture is thick enough to hold its shape away from sides of pan. Cool, add vanilla. Shape into small balls, arrange on a buttered and floured cookie sheet and bake in a preheated 375° oven until brown (about 10 minutes). Serve fresh. Yields approximately 40 cookies.

[TRANSLATED FROM: **NOÇÕES DE ARTE CULINÁRIA** WRITTEN BY MARIA THEREZA A. COSTA, SÃO PAULO]

Cat's Tongue Cookies
Biscoitos Língua de Gato

5 ounces butter • 3/4 cup sugar • 2 cups all-purpose flour • 4 egg whites

Cream butter and sugar, and add sifted flour, beating well. Add stiffly beaten egg whites. Place in a pastry bag with ribbon nozzle and squeeze on buttered cookie sheet in strips 3 to 4 inches long. Bake in a preheated 375° oven for 10 to 15 minutes. Yields approximately 32 cookies.

[OLIVIA LODER, MINAS GERAIS]

Coconut Cookies No. 1
Biscoitos de Coco N° 1

3 tablespoons butter • 1/2 cup sugar • 2 eggs, separated • 2 tablespoons milk
1 cup all-purpose flour • 1/2 teaspoon salt • 1 teaspoon baking powder
1/3 cup grated coconut

Cream butter with sugar and egg yolks. Add milk and stiffly-beaten egg whites. When well mixed, add the sifted flour, salt and baking powder, then the coconut. After stirring well, drop by small teaspoonfuls on a buttered cookie sheet. Sprinkle lightly with cinnamon sugar and bake in a preheated 350° oven 16 to 20 minutes. Yields approximately 30 cookies.

Coconut Cookies No. 2
Biscoitos de Coco N° 2

1/2 cup condensed milk • 2 cups grated coconut • 1 teaspoon almond or vanilla extract

Mix all ingredients together and roll teaspoonfuls into balls in the palm of the hand. Place on a buttered cookie sheet and bake in a preheated 350° oven until they start to brown on top. Reduce heat to 325° and remove from oven when they are golden brown (about 15 minutes). Allow to cool partially on cookie sheet and then transfer to a cake rack using a spatula. Allow to dry out. Yields approximately 2 dozen cookies.

Cornstarch Cookies No. 1
Biscoitos de Maizena N° 1

1/2 cup butter • 1/2 cup sugar • 2 eggs, separated • 1/2 cup all-purpose flour
1 cup cornstarch • 1/4 teaspoon salt • 1/4 cup raisins

Cream butter, add sugar and egg yolks. Sift flour with cornstarch and salt, and knead into first mixture. Add raisins. Stir in the unbeaten egg whites, beat 4 or 5 times, then drop by demitasse spoonfuls onto a buttered cookie sheet. Brush with melted butter. Bake in a preheated 375° oven 11 to 13 minutes. Yields 32 cookies.

Cornstarch Cookies No. 2
Biscoitos de Maizena N° 2

2 cups cornstarch • 1 cup sugar • 1/2 teaspoon salt • 1 egg
3/4 cup butter • few drops vanilla

Mix cornstarch, sugar, salt and egg, and blend in the butter. Add a few drops vanilla and knead well. Let stand 10 or 15 minutes. Shape into balls in the palm of the hand and place on a buttered cookie sheet. Bake in a preheated 375° oven 5 to 7 minutes. Yields approximately 3 dozen cookies.

[ESTHER HILL GARCIA LEÃO, NEBRASKA⁴]

---

⁴ It may seem strange to see Nebraska mentioned in a Brazilian cookbook. However, the recipe is Brazilian. Esther Garcia Leão, although born in Nebraska, has spent over 40 years in Brazil.

S i g h s

Suspiros

6 egg whites at room temperature • 3/4 teaspoon salt • 3/4 teaspoon cream of tartar
1 1/2 cups sugar • Flavoring

Beat whites with salt and cream of tartar until mixture forms peaks. Start adding sugar, a tablespoon at a time, and continue beating until all sugar has been used and mixture forms glossy, soft peaks. Add flavoring (vanilla, almond, maple, etc.) and coloring, if desired. Squeeze through a pastry bag on unglazed paper that has been placed on cookie sheet. In the absence of a pastry bag, the Sighs may be dropped by small spoonfuls. Bake very slowly in a very slow 250° oven from 30 minutes to 1 hour depending on the size. When thoroughly dry, turn off heat and open oven door, allowing the Sighs to cool in the oven.

VARIATIONS: Add 1 tablespoon arrowroot flour to batter and when baked, make a small opening in top of each and fill with the mixture used for Coconut Kisses, p. 244, or add 1/4 cup ground peanuts to batter and fill with the following Date Filling.

1/2 pound pitted dates • 2 cups water • 2 cups sugar

Soak dates in the water for 1 hour, then cook over slow heat for 1 hour. Add the sugar, mix and continue to cook down until mixture holds its shape. Stir constantly.

270

Peanut wafers
Tarecos de Amendoim

2 egg whites • 3/4 cup sugar • 1 cup ground roasted peanuts

Beat whites until they form stiff peaks, add sugar a tablespoon at a time and continue to beat until all sugar has been used. Gradually stir in the ground peanuts. Drop by small teaspoonfuls on buttered cookie sheet and bake in a preheated 300° oven for 15 minutes. Yields 45-50 wafers.

[GLADYS MARIE SILVA, MATO GROSSO]

Don't-Touch-Me
Não me Toques

2 tablespoons butter • 1/2 cup sugar • 2 egg yolks • 1/4 teaspoon salt
thick milk of one coconut (1/3 to 1/2 cup) • arrowroot flour to hold (about 1 3/4 cups)

Cream butter and sugar, add egg yolks, salt and coconut milk. Mix in arrowroot, stirring and kneading until you have a stiff dough. Shape into small balls, size of a walnut, place on buttered cookie sheet and bake in a preheated 375° oven approximately 15 minutes. Yields about 40 cookies.

Dreams

Sonhos

1 cup all-purpose flour, sifted • 2 teaspoons baking powder • 1/4 teaspoon salt
1 can condensed milk • 2 tablespoons butter • 2 eggs, separated
1/4 cup chopped Brazil nuts • 1/4 cup milk

Mix flour, baking powder and salt. Heat condensed milk with butter. When mixture is hot, add dry ingredients all at once, stirring rapidly. Return to low heat, stir constantly and cook for 5 minutes. Cool 5 minutes. Beat in egg yolks, then fold in stiffly-beaten whites. Add the nuts and milk. Spoon into buttered small-size muffin tins, filling 3/4 full. Bake in preheated 400° oven for 8 minutes. Reduce heat to 300° and bake another 8 minutes. Yields approximately 30 small-size Dreams.

Fine Cornmeal Cookies

Biscoitos Finos

1/2 cup very fine cornmeal • 1 cup arrowroot flour • 1/2 cup all-purpose flour
1/2 cup sugar • 1/4 teaspoon salt • 1/4 cup butter • 2 egg yolks
1/4 cup milk • Cinnamon sugar

Sift dry ingredients, cut in the butter. Add egg yolks and milk. Mix and let stand 15 minutes. Roll teaspoonfuls into balls in the palm of the hand, and then flatten and place on a buttered cookie sheet. Sprinkle with cinnamon sugar and bake in a 400° oven 20-25 minutes. Yields approximately 24 cookies.

Brazilian Sablés
Sablés Brasileiros

3/4 cup butter • 1/2 cup sugar • 1 3/4 cups all-purpose flour, sifted
1/4 cup milk • 1/4 cup chopped peanuts • 1/4 teaspoon cinnamon

Cream butter and sugar, and add sifted flour and milk to make a dough. Knead and let stand 10 minutes. Break off walnut size pieces of dough and roll in palm of hand to make small balls. Mix peanuts and cinnamon, and roll the balls in this mixture, then place on a buttered cookie sheet and bake 15 minutes in preheated 400° oven. Yields approximately 3 dozen cookies.

Milk Sweet Cookies
Biscoitos de Doce de Leite

1 can condensed milk • 2 tablespoons butter • 3 egg yolks • 1 3/4 cups all-purpose flour
1 tablespoon cinnamon • 2 egg whites • chopped almonds

Heat condensed milk in a saucepan and add 1 tablespoon of butter. Cool and pour into a bowl. Add the other tablespoon of butter and egg yolks. Sift flour and cinnamon and add to the mixture. Shape into small balls and dip them or drop by teaspoonfuls into the raw egg white. Roll in chopped almonds. Place on buttered cookie sheet and bake in 375° oven for 20-25 minutes. Yields approximately 3 dozen.

Marvellous Cookies
Biscoitos Maravilhosos

*1/2 cup butter • 1/2 cup sugar • 1 cup cold mashed potatoes • 1 teaspoon salt
grated rind of 1 lemon • 1 1/4 cups sifted all-purpose flour • cinnamon sugar*

Cream butter and sugar, and add mashed potatoes. Blend thoroughly, add salt and lemon rind. Sift in the flour, a little at a time, stirring and kneading as last of the flour is added. Knead until dough is pliable. Let stand 1/2 hour, then turn onto a slightly-floured board and press or roll out 1/4 inch thick. Cut with a cookie cutter, place on ungreased cookie sheet and bake in a preheated 375° oven for about 20 minutes. Sprinkle with cinnamon sugar. Yields about 40 cookies.

[TRANSLATED FROM: **A ARTE DE FAZER DOCES**, BY I. LUND]

Nut Cookies
Biscoitos de Nozes

*1 cup sugar • 1/2 cup water • 1 cup finely-ground nuts • 6 egg yolks, slightly beaten
3 unbeaten egg whites • 3 beaten egg whites*

Heat sugar and water in a 2-quart saucepan until it spins a thread. Add nuts, yolks, and unbeaten whites and then fold in the stiffly-beaten whites. Cook over very low heat, stirring constantly with a wooden spoon until mixture holds its shape away from sides of pan. Cool thoroughly. Drop small spoonfuls on unbuttered cookie sheet, or shape in small balls and bake in a preheated 375° oven for 15 minutes. Yield is approximately 35 cookies. Serve fresh.

Missy Cookies
Biscoitinhos de Sinhá⁵ Moça

2 cups arrowroot flour • 3/4 cup sugar • 1/4 teaspoon salt • 1/2 cup butter
2 egg yolks • 1/2 cup thick coconut milk

Blend first 3 ingredients with butter and then add egg yolks. Add the coconut milk to make a soft dough. Shape into small balls in palm of the hand and place on a buttered cookie sheet. Bake in preheated 375° oven for 15-17 minutes. Yields approximately 30 cookies.

Wafers
Tarecos

4 eggs, separated • 1 cup sugar • 1 cup all-purpose flour
1/4 cup either cornstarch or arrowroot flour • 1/4 teaspoon salt

Separate eggs, beat whites until stiff, add yolks and continue beating. Add sugar. Sift flour with the cornstarch or arrowroot flour and salt, and then add to the first mixture. Drop by demitasse spoonfuls on a buttered cookie sheet leaving plenty of space for them to spread. Bake in preheated 400° oven 8 to 10 minutes. Yields approximately 50 cookies.

---

⁵ Negro slave corruption of *Senhora* or Mistress. *Moça* is a young girl.

W e d d i n g   C o o k i e s
Bem-casados [6]

3 eggs, separated • 1/2 cup sugar • 1/2 cup potato starch • 1/2 cup all-purpose flour

Beat egg whites until stiff, add sugar and continue beating. Add beaten yolks and continue beating. (The secret of this recipe lies in the beating.) When mixture is thick, add the potato starch and flour which have been sifted together. The flour mixture should be added all at once and folded in with a spatula. Drop by demitasse spoonfuls on a buttered, lightly-floured cookie sheet and bake in 375° oven from 8 to 10 minutes. Cool on cake rack and join two together with Maiden's Delight, p. 301, or any other filling. Yields approximately 50 single cookies or 25 doubles. Sprinkle with powdered sugar. *Note:* These are served at weddings. They are wrapped in white crepe paper with fringed edges and tied together with white satin bows from which orange blossoms protrude.

[OLIVIA LODER, MINAS GERAIS]

---

[6] A free translation would be "Happily-Married."

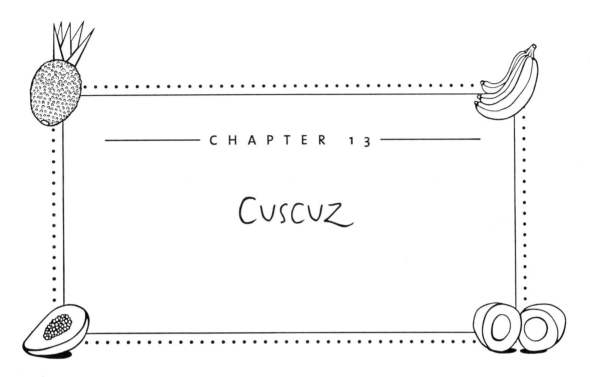

CHAPTER 13

Cuscuz

Always something new out of Africa.

PLINY THE ELDER

Cuscuz, thought of today as so very Brazilian, traveled far before it arrived in Brazil. Originating in Arabia, it was brought to Africa and Portugal by Arabians and, later, introduced into Brazil by Africans. Nearly all modern Brazilians use the newer spelling, but one still encounters the African spelling of *Couscous.*

The *Cuscuz* of the North is a dessert made from tapioca, rice, corn or manioc flours or meals, coconut milk, sugar and grated coconut. It is steamed and served like a cake. There is a tapioca cuscuz recipe which does not require steaming, however, and this is the one included as *Tapioca Cuscuz.*

My introduction to this well-known dish of Northern Brazil was way back in 1927 at the home of the late Professor Antonio Austragesilo in Rio de Janeiro. The Professor took great pains to explain that there were two different dishes in Brazil known by this name, one sweet and the other salty. It developed that sweet cuscuz was very popular in the Professor's home state of Pernambuco and so he went to great lengths to make sure I understood which of the *Cuscuz* dishes I was eating.

It was years later that I came to know and appreciate the salty *Cuscuz.* This is popularly known as *Cuscuz Paulista.* It can be made from chicken, animal meat, fish or shrimp. The African version uses lamb or mutton and differs from the Brazilian recipe in that the meal is not mixed with the meat or seafood.[1]

The principal farinaceous ingredient is cornmeal, noistened with salted water and shortening to which highly-seasoned fish, meat or poultry is added with palm hearts, sliced tomatoes and hard-boiled eggs, olives, etc. Some recipes add manioc meal to the cornmeal and, at times, this type of *Cuscuz* is also prepared from rice flour.

---

[1] I have also seen recipes for the African *Couscous* using Cream of Wheat.

Cuscuz is cooked by steaming in a proper vessel manufactured for this purpose and called a *cuscuzeiro*. This is a sort of large double boiler arrangement with the exception that the bottom of the upper part is perforated·so that the steam comes into direct contact with the mixture. It is not necessary to have a *cuscuzeiro* to make this especially delicious Brazilian dish, so Brazilianized that today it actually is Brazilian. A *cuscuzeiro* can be improvised by placing a colander in a large covered saucepan resting on an inverted cake tin. A better improvisiation is to use a covered roasting pan with a trivet. When steaming, it is necessary to take great care that the water level does not reach the bottom of the collander, and to maintain sufficient water to produce the steam.

In preparing *Cuscuz Paulista*, many people place fresh kale or collards over the top of the mixture before covering with the napkin. When the greens are cooked, the *Cuscuz* is done. It is necessary to allow the *Cuscuz* to stand a while before unmoulding. Then it should look like a cake with the hardboiled eggs and tomatoes garnishing the sides.

In an age when everything is done according to the time element, preparing *Cuscuz* may seem to consume a great deal of this valuable commodity. But to gourmet cooks, time and ingredients are not "of the essence." The finished product is what counts. If you have the patience to prepare this dish with calm and perseverance, you will be rewarded with a gastronomic delight.

C h i c k e n   C u s c u z
Cuscuz de Galinha

PRELIMINARY PREPARATION

Prepare the full recipe for Stewed Chicken, p. 468, making sure you have 1 1/2 cups of gravy. Remove skin and bones from chicken and let meat stand in the gravy. Prepare the cornmeal mixture, as follows:[2] Take 4 cups white cornmeal and heat in a shallow baking dish in a preheated 350° oven for 5 minutes, stirring 3 or 4 times with a long-handled spoon, so that the meal bakes evenly. As soon as the meal begins to turn to a light beige, remove from oven, sprinkle 1 cup of boiling salted water over it, stir well with a fork and return to oven for 2 minutes. The meal should then have irregular flakes. Add 1/4 pound butter and mix well.

CUSCUZ MIXTURE

1 stewed chicken with about 1 1/2 cups gravy • 2 or 3 malagueta peppers, pounded (optional)
1/2 cup melted butter or olive oil • 1/4 cup parsley, chopped • cornmeal mixture
1/2 pound smoked pork sausages, fried, or leftover meal • 1 16-ounce can of peas, drained
1 10-ounce can palm hearts • 3 sliced hard-boiled eggs • 3 sliced tomatoes • olives

Heat boned chicken with gravy, add peppers, butter or olive oil, parsley, and check the seasoning. Remove from heat, add cornmeal mixture, knead, then add sausages or leftover meat. If you can form a small ball with the mixture that will retain its shape, it is of the proper consistency. If it is too dry, moisten with some of the liquid from the can of peas used in the next step. Slice the palm hearts and have ready sliced hard-boiled eggs, tomatoes and olives.

---

[2] In Brazil, because of the way the meal is prepared, it is not necessary to heat and steam in the oven. But to obtain the best results from North American cornmeal, experiments have shown that heating in the oven improves the *cuscuz.*

ARRANGEMENT OF INGREDIENTS in the *cuscuzeiro* or collander
— First Layer: In the bottom and on sides place sliced tomatoes, eggs and olives in a symmetrical design, along with a little of the meal mixture.
— Second Layer: Add more meal mixture, press against the sides and bottom, then cover with peas, palm hearts, tomatoes, eggs and olives, and alternate with the meal mixture until all ingredients are used.

Cover with a napkin and steam in the *cuscuzeiro* or the improvised double boiler arrangement, taking care that the water does not reach the level of the collander or *cuscuzeiro*. The cuscuz is done when the napkin is very wet. Remove napkin, let cuscuz stand a few minutes and unmould on a serving platter. Garnish with slices of sour oranges.

N O T E : The secret of making the *Cuscuz* lies in the use of shortening, or butter, which holds the mixture together.

In some regions, instead of placing the napkin on top, collard greens are used. When the greens are steamed, the *Cuscuz* is done.

[RENATA SILVEIRA DE ARAGÃO, SÃO PAULO]

Shrimp Cuscuz
Cuscuz de Camarão

First prepare the cornmeal mixture as for Chicken Cuscuz, and then prepare the shrimp mixture as follows:

SHRIMP STEW

1/2 pound fresh jumbo shrimp • 1 pound medium-size raw shrimp
2 tablespoons lemon juice • black pepper • salt • 1/2 cup butter or oil
1/2 cup onion, minced • 1/4 cup parsley, chopped • garlic salt
1 cup tomato sauce • hot pepper

Shell, devein and wash shrimp. Dry, cover with lemon juice, black pepper and salt, and let stand 1 hour. Melt butter in a skillet, add onion, parsley and garlic salt; sauté 2 or 3 minutes, then add the shrimp and continue cooking until shrimp is hot. Add the tomato sauce and hot pepper, cover and simmer until shrimp is tender. Pick out jumbo shrimp for garnish. Add rest of shrimp mixture to the corn meal, after having checked seasoning.

ARRANGEMENT IN THE CUSCUZEIRO

2 canned sardines in tomato sauce • 3 hard-boiled eggs • 3 sliced tomatoes
olives • jumbo shrimp for garnish

On the bottom and sides of the cuscuzeiro, place tomatoes, eggs and olives in symmetrical design and add a little of the cornmeal mixture to hold garnishes in place. Press some of the jumbo shrimp on bottom and sides, also pieces of the sardines in tomato sauce. Proceed as for Chicken Cuscuz.

283

Tapioca Cuscuz — A Dessert
Cuscuz de Tapioca

1 large freshly-grated coconut • 3 cups boiling water • 1/2 teaspoon salt
2/3 cup sugar • 1 8-ounce package minute tapioca

Remove thick milk from the coconut and reserve. Add boiling water to residue and press through a coarse sieve to extract thin milk. Add salt and sugar to thin milk, bring to boil and remove from heat. Add tapioca, stir well and cool. Moisten a mould with some of the thick coconut milk and pour in the tapioca mixture. Cover and refrigerate overnight. Next day, turn onto a serving plate, pour rest of thick coconut milk over it and garnish with freshly-grated coconut. Serve in wedges, like a cake.

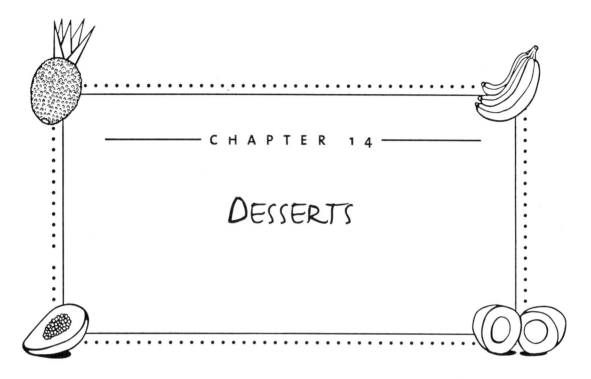

CHAPTER 14

DESSERTS

At the end of the dinner dessert is sweet,
though it follows the fullest feast.

PINDAR, **DIRGES**, FRAG. 124, SANDYS

essert is defined as a food course taken at the close of a meal. It would, therefore, include fruits, pies, puddings, cakes, gelatins, ices, moulds, whips and even cookies. However, inasmuch as there are so many cakes, puddings and cookies representative of Brazilian cookery, separate chapters have been prepared on these subjects while all other recipes for fruits, ices, gelatins, etc. have been included here in this chapter.

Most of the recipes in this chapter have fruits or nuts as a base. Also included are other desserts that can not be classified as puddings, cakes or cookies. *Baba-de-Moça* and *Papo-de-Anjo* are two very well-known Brazilian desserts falling into this latter category. Actually, they are confections, but they are always served as a dessert, hence their inclusion in this chapter.

As a general rule, Brazilian desserts are very sweet, just like the cakes and puddings appearing on Brazilian tables. There is a type of dessert called *doce* (sweet) which is followed by the preposition *de* and the name of the fruit. Although it is usually made of fruits, sometimes vegetables like pumpkin and sweet potato are used. This *doce* corresponds to a thick compote of fruits in a very heavy syrup. There is also a solid fruit sweet, or paste that can be cut with a knife and that takes the name of the fruit, followed by a suffix consisting of the letters *ada*. Thus, we have fruit pastes called *Goiabada* (guava), *Bananada* (banana), *Marmelada* (quince), *Pessegada* (peach), *Mangada* (mango) and *Cocada* (coconut).

Both the compote and the paste types of sweets are exceedingly popular all over Brazil and are available in every home and restaurant. They are packed commercially in cans and prepared as preserves in Brazilian homes.[1] One of my Brazilian friends has a summer home in Teresópolis surrounded by guava trees. She had an

---

[1] Many of the recipes in the chapter on "Candies," p. 227, can serve as compotes by following the recipe and removing from the heat before the mixture is thick enough to shape into balls.

outdoor grill constructed so she could boil the guava fruit to make *goiabada*. When the fruit is ripe, she places it in a huge kettle and boils it down with sugar in much the same manner as early settlers in this country prepared their apple butter.

Many Brazilian desserts are served with a wedge of cheese, principally those desserts which I call the *adas*. Sometimes a banana accompanies this dessert.

In colonial times, desserts consisted mainly of the fruits grown in Brazil and the puddings and cakes made from milk, honey, coconut and sugar as well as the staple, corn, which was prepared by the African women who ran the kitchens. But when ice was introduced into Brazil a new class of desserts came into being. The first ice arrived in 1834 in the American ship "Madagascar." Then the Brazilians made use of their many native fruits! They extracted the juices and made them into delicious, cooling refreshments. They also learned to freeze these exotic tropical juices into the mouth-watering sherberts and ices that one finds in the Brazil of today.

Considering the vast number of fruits indigenous to Brazil, it is easy to see that this innovation would produce a great many new recipes, which it did, *in Brazil*. Unfortunately, although the introduction of ice in Brazil was of great importance insofar as the Brazilian menu was concerned, especially the dessert course, to the North American it brought nothing new from Brazil. Even today, despite modern methods of transportation and preservation, many of the common fruits of Brazil remain unknown to us in the United States.

Two of the most delicious fruits I have ever encountered are the *jaboticaba* and *fruta-do-conde*, which in English are called jabuticaba and the sweetsop or sugar apple. They are pleasing to every taste — delicate — and never to be forgotten. The jabuticaba is very perishable and is seldom found far from its habitat. Actually, it is practically a parasite, since it grows directly on the tree trunk, rather than on branches. It has the appearance and color of a dark purple plum.

FRUTA-DO-CONDE

The sweetsop or sugar apple, known in Brazil as *fruta-do-conde*, is truly a conversation piece. This fruit of the tropical sweetsop tree is shaped like an artichoke, and is also green in color, with small scales covering its surface. Inside, the fruit is pulpy and tastes somewhat like a pear. If the adjective "distinguished" could be applied to a fruit, truly the *fruta-do-conde* would be the most distinguished of them all!

Brazil produces apples, apricots, avocados, bananas, berries, breadfruit, cherries, figs, grapefruit, grapes, lemons, limes, mangos, melons, oranges, peaches, pears, pineapples, persimmons (introduced recently by the Japanese — now rapidly-growing in popularity), plums, pomegranates, quinces, watermelons and at least 26 fruits unknown to North American markets.

This tremendous number of unknowns would certainly render our daily diet much more varied and interesting if some of them could be exported.

On the other hand, the only fruit grown in North America and not found in Brazil that comes to mind is cranberries. Rhubarb, also, is not grown there.

Bananas and oranges are the Brazilians' favorite fruits and are produced in great abundance. Brazil ranks second to the United States in production of oranges, producing enough for her own consumption, which is great, and also for export to Europe. Brazil is the world's largest producer of bananas,[2] but her exports are comparatively small due to the large domestic consumption.

---

[2] *Statesman's Year Book, 1960-1961.*

Angel's Double Chin
Papos-de-anjo

9 egg yolks • 1 egg white • 2 cups sugar • 1 cup water • 1 teaspoon vanilla

Beat egg yolks until light and frothy, then add the beaten white. Continue beating and when mixture is spongy in texture, pour into individual-size muffin or *empadinha* tins that have been buttered. Set tins in a shalllow pan of hot water and bake in 350° oven until an inserted knife comes out clean (about 17 minutes). Meanwhile, boil sugar and water until it spins a thread Flavor with vanilla Remove "chins" carefully from their tins, make 3 or 4 perforations with a toothpick and drop into the boiling syrup. Remove from heat and let cool until following day. Serve as a compote with the syrup or remove from syrup to small paper cups. In the latter case, the "chins" should be dusted with powdered sugar. Yields 16 *empadinha*-sized "chins."

[THEREZA NOVAES, SÃO PAULO]

Ambrosia

1 cup sugar • 1/2 cup water • 3 egg yolks • 1 cup milk

Make a syrup of the sugar and water, cooking until it is just ready to spin a thread. Cool. Beat egg yolks a little and add the milk. Add this to the syrup and reheat, boiling until it forms into large lumps. Reduce heat to a simmer and allow to thicken or even brown a little. Serve cold with an American-type cheese.

[FLORINDA K. MACHADO, RIO GRANDE DO SUL]

Avocado Cream
Creme de Abacate

3 ripe avocados • 1 tablespoon lemon juice • 3/4 cup sugar • 1/4 teaspoon salt
1 1/2 cups milk • 2 ounces port wine

Peel avocados, remove stones and cover with lemon juice and sugar. Let stand 5 or 10 minutes. Add salt and put in blender with milk, or mash with milk and press through a coarse sieve. Beat in the wine and chill. Yields about 1 quart.

AVOCADO ICE CREAM: Follow above procedure and use same ingredients, but substitute 1 cup of whipped cream for the wine. Add whipped cream to the mixture, folding it in gently. Turn into a 1 1/2 quart Pyrex dish and partly freeze in the refrigerator. When mixture is beginning to freeze around edges, remove and beat with egg beater. Return to freezer compartment of refrigerator.

VARIATION: Beat in 1/2 pint of vanilla ice cream instead of the whipping cream and freeze as above.

Baked Bananas and Cheese
Banana Assada com Queyo

4 bananas • butter for frying • sliced Muenster cheese • cinnamon sugar

Cut bananas in halves, then split. Fry in butter until delicately brown. Place in baking dish and cover with sliced cheese. Sprinkle with cinnamon sugar and bake in a preheated 375° oven until cheese is melted.

Baked Papaya
Mamão Assado

5 cups ripe, mashed papaya • 1 1/2 cups freshly-grated coconut • 4 cups milk
4 eggs, slightly beaten • 1 cup sugar • grated rind and juice of 1 orange

Place papaya pulp in a baking dish and cover with the coconut. Make a boiled custard with the milk, sugar, eggs and orange juice and stir in the rind. Pour over the papaya and bake in a preheated 375° oven until the custard is well set. Serve chilled.

Baked Pears
Peras Assadas

8 peeled pears • condensed milk • raisins • 1/2 cup sweet wine • powdered sugar • butter

Remove cores from pears and fill with condensed milk and raisins. Arrange in a buttered baking dish, pour wine on top and sprinkle with sugar. Dot with butter and bake in a preheated 375° oven until done. Cool and chill. Serve with sweetened whipped cream.

VARIATION: Peaches may also be prepared using this same recipe.

[CONCEY BITTENCOURT, SÃO PAULO]

Bananas with Brazil Nuts
Bananas com Castanhas-do-pará

6 bananas • 2 tablespoons lemon juice • 1/4 cup peach liqueur
1 cup ground Brazil nuts • 1 egg white • 1/2 cup heavy cream
3 tablespoons powdered sugar • berries coated with sugar

Slice bananas, add lemon juice, liqueur and the ground nuts, which have been slightly browned in the oven before grinding. Beat egg white and cream separately, then combine and add powdered sugar. Place the bananas in a pudding dish, cover with the cream mixture and garnish with raspberries or strawberries rolled in powdered sugar. Chill.

[TRANSLATED FROM: **A ARTE DE COMER BEM** BY ROSA MARIA (MME H. LEONARDOS)]

Banana Torte
Torta de Banana

6 bananas • butter • 1 cup water • 1 cup sugar, plus 6 tablespoons
10 eggs, separated • grated rind of 1 lemon

Slice the bananas and gently fry in butter until they are golden brown. Reserve. Boil water and the cup of sugar until it spins a thread. Cool to room temperature. Slightly beat egg yolks and add to the cooled syrup. Beat egg whites until stiff, adding the 6 tablespoons of sugar in small quantities and beating after each addition. Mix in the lemon rind. Butter a 3-quart ovenware dish that can be taken to the table. Pour in the egg yolk syrup and then the fried bananas and mix. Top with the meringue. Bake in a preheated 350° oven for 12 to 15 minutes.

[TRANSLATED FROM: **RECEITAS CULINÁRIAS** BY MYRTHES PARANHOS]

Brazil Nut Torte
Torta de Castanha-do-pará

6 eggs, separated • 1 cup sugar • 1/2 pound ground Brazil nuts • 1 teaspoon baking powder
1/4 teaspoon salt • 1/2 pint heavy cream, whipped and sweetened
1 can peaches, drained • Maraschino cherries

Beat egg yolks and add sugar, beating well. Add nuts, baking powder, salt and then fold in stiffly-beaten egg whites. Turn into an oblong buttered baking tin 13 x 9 x 2 inches or 2 buttered 9-inch layer cake tins. Bake in preheated 350° oven for 45 to 60 minutes or until knife blade inserted in center can be removed clean. When baked, remove from tin and allow to cool. If baked in an oblong tin, cut in half, fill and cover with the whipped cream and, on top, arrange the peaches garnished with cherries. If layer cake tins are used, join layers with some of the whipped cream mixture, spread the rest on top and garnish with the cherries.

[IGNEZ CORREIA D'ARAUJO, PERNAMBUCO]

Burned Eggs
Ovos Queimados[3]

2 cups sugar • a few whole cloves • 1/2 cup water • 7 egg yolks • cinnamon
2 egg whites • 2 tablespoons butter

Heat sugar in a skillet until it is melted and beginning to brown. Add the cloves and water, and cook until mixture spins a thread. Add beaten egg yolks and whites, and cook in the syrup, stirring only when the syrup starts to thicken. Cook, or even brown a little, remove from fire, beat in the butter and turn into a compote dish. Sprinkle powdered cinnamon on top and serve cold, plain or with cheese.

[REPRINTED FORM AUTHOR'S ARTICLE IN JULY 1963 ISSUE OF **GOURMET MAGAZINE**]

---

[3] This dessert is said to have been a favorite of Dom Pedro II, Emperor of Brazil.

Chocolate Pavé
Pavê de Chocolate

6 ounces sweet chocolate • 1/4 pound sweet butter • 3 egg yolks • 16 lady fingers, split
1 cup milk • 4 ounces Cinzano or crème de cacao

Melt chocolate over hot water. Remove from heat and cream with the butter, beating well with a wooden spoon. Add egg yolks and continue to beat. Butter a 1 1/2 quart Pyrex dish. Line bottom and sides with the split lady fingers, dipped first in the liquor and then in the milk. Spread first layer with the chocolate mixture and top it with another layer of dipped lady fingers. Continue until chocolate and lady fingers are all used. The last layer should be chocolate. Refrigerate before serving.

[TRANSLATED FROM: RECEITAS CULINÁRIAS BY MYRTHES PARANHOS]

Coconut Floating Island
Espuma Baiana

2 cups milk • 1 cup freshly-grated coconut • 1/4 teaspoon salt • 1/3 cup sugar
4 eggs, separated • 1/2 teaspoon vanilla

Scald milk and pour over coconut. Press through a sieve to extract coconut milk. Scald the liquid obtained in top of a double boiler with salt and 3 tablespoons of sugar. Beat egg yolks well and slowly stir in the hot milk mixture. Strain, if necessary, and return to double boiler. Cook over 1 inch of boiling water until mixture coats a metal spoon. Remove from heat, stir in vanilla and pour into a baking dish. Beat egg whites until fluffy, add rest of sugar and spoon meringue on top of custard. Bake in preheated 375° oven to brown meringue. Chill and serve. Yields from 1 to 1 1/2 quarts.

Coconut Gelatin

Gelatina de Coco

1 15-ounce can condensed milk (1 1/2 cups) • 1 1/2 cups thin coconut milk[4]
1 1/2 cups hot milk • 3 envelopes unflavored gelatin • 1/2 cup cold water

Empty the condensed milk into a bowl and use the can to measure the coconut milk and the hot milk. Soften gelatin in cold water, add the hot milk and stir. Mix in electric blender at medium speed, adding condensed milk and coconut milk. Pour into a 1 quart ring mould. Refrigerate and unmould.

V A R I A T I O N : For a spectacular dessert, after unmolding, fill the center of the ring with halved preserved apricots and place a red maraschino cherry in each apricot. Tint fresh coconut pale pink or green. Use to outline the mold or to garnish the top. Pour 1 cup of chilled custard sauce on apricots, using 1/4 recipe of the sauce for Snow Pudding, page 492.

---

[4] As a substitute, measure 1 can of sweet milk and simmer 10 minutes with 1/2 cup grated coconut. Cool, strain and proceed with recipe.

Coconut Ice Cream
Sorvete de Coco

2 cups milk • 6 tablespoons sugar • 1 freshly-grated coconut
2 egg whites • 1/4 teaspoon salt

Heat milk with half the amount of sugar and, when it boils, pour over the coconut. Press through cheese cloth, and allow to cool completely. Beat egg whites until stiff, add salt and the rest of the sugar. Slowly add the coconut milk mixture. Freeze in refrigerator trays. When almost frozen, remove and stir well to prevent ice from forming. Return to freezer compartment.

NOTE: If an ice cream freezer is used, this last step is unnecessary.

[LAURITA PIRES, MINAS GERAIS]

Compote of Mangos
Doce de Manga

4 eggs, separated • 1/2 cup sugar • 1 package orange-flavored gelatin dessert mix
1 cup water • 1 cup orange juice • whipped cream

Beat egg yolks with sugar, add gelatin dessert mix dissolved in water. Add the orange juice and cook in top of a double boiler until mixture coats a metal spoon. Cool thoroughly, then chill until it begins to set. Fold in the stiffly-beaten egg whites, spoon into a lightly-buttered 2-quart mould and refrigerate. Unmould and serve with whipped cream.

[MARIA BARBOSA NUNES, RIO DE JANEIRO]

French Toast
Rabanadas[5]

1 tablespoon sugar • 3/4 cup milk • 8 slices French bread • 2 eggs • butter
cinnamon and powdered sugar

Mix sugar and milk, and pour over sliced bread. Dip each piece of bread in beaten eggs, handling carefully so that bread retains its shape. Gently melt butter in a skillet and fry bread on both sides until golden brown. Remove to serving dish and sprinkle with cinnamon and powdered sugar. Serve hot.

VARIATIONS: **1)** For a holiday recipe, use port wine instead of milk; **2)** substitute coconut milk for regular milk; **3)** omit the sugar and cinnamon, add salt, and serve sandwich-fashion with a·shrimp cream filling or a savory beef or cheese filling.

[ALBINA MARTINS, PORTUGAL]

---

[5] This is a traditional dessert served during the Christmas and Easter holidays.

299

Fruit Salad
Salada de Frutas

1 fresh pineapple • 3 bananas • 1 avocado • 2 oranges • 1/2 small papaya melon
• 1/2 honeydew melon • 1/4 cup lime juice • 1 cup sugar • 1 jigger port wine

Remove skins from fruits and cut into cubes. Sprinkle with lime juice and sugar. Refrigerate for 30 minutes, then add wine. Serve in small fruit cups surrounded by crushed ice to which a few drops of green or red coloring has been added. Garnish with fresh mint or cherries.

Cream Leticia
Creme Leticia

1 1/4 cups sugar • 2 teaspoons cornstarch • 2 egg yolks • 2 cups milk • vanilla
1 cup butter • 1/2 pound ground peanuts • lady fingers • wine or cordial
flavored whipped cream • fresh fruit or berries

Take 1/4 cup of the sugar and mix half with the cornstarch and the other half with the egg yolks. Reserve the remaining cup. Make a sauce by scalding milk and adding cornstarch-sugar mixture. Cook over low heat for 10 minutes, stirring constantly, then add egg yolk-sugar mixture and cook until mixture coats a metal spoon. Remove from heat, cool thoroughly and flavor with vanilla. Set aside. Cream the butter with the reserved sugar and add ground peanuts, then combine with the sauce. Line a buttered mould on sides and bottom with split lady fingers that have been slightly sprinkled with wine or cordial. Pour some of the sauce, terminating with a layer of lady fingers. Place a heavy weight on top, refrigerate overnight and the next day unmould and garnish with flavored whipped cream and fresh fruit or berries.

[MARIA DE LOURDES MURGEL FURTADO, MINAS GERAIS]

Heavenly Cream
Creme do Céu

1/2 cup orange juice • 6 eggs • 1/2 cup sugar • 1 cup milk • 1/8 teaspoon salt

Mix orange juice with lightly-beaten eggs and strain. Add sugar, milk, and salt. Pour into a caramelized 1-quart mould (see chapter on Puddings, p. 479). Set mould in a pan of hot water and bake like custard in a 325° oven for about 1 hour or until a knife inserted in the center comes out clean. Unmould to serving dish, and garnish with peeled sliced oranges.

[TRANSLATED FROM: **NOÇÕES DE ARTE CULINÁRIA** BY MARIA THEREZA A COSTA]

Maiden's Delight
Baba de Moça

2 cups sugar • 1 1/4 cups water • 7 egg yolks[6] • Thick milk from 1 coconut

Mix sugar and water and heat until it spins a thread (230°-234°F). Remove from heat and cool thoroughly. Beat egg yolks very well, add the coconut milk and then add mixture to the cold syrup. Stir well and return to medium heat, stirring constantly until mixture thickens. Serve cold, as a compote, in small glasses or dessert dishes with powdered cinnamon sprinkled on top or use as a cake filling or topping.

---

[6] The egg whites left over may be used to prepare My Friend's Cake, p. 203.

Hominy

Mungunzá[7]

2 cups cooked hominy, drained • 4 cups milk and 1 cup thick coconut milk
3 whole cloves • 1 cinnamon stick • 1 teaspoon salt • 1 cup sugar, or less
1 tablespoon butter • 1/2 cup crushed roasted peanuts
1 teaspoon rose flower water (optional) • rice flour to thicken

Add hominy to scalded milk together with cloves, cinnamon, salt and sugar, and simmer for 45 minutes. Add butter, peanuts and rose flower water and simmer another 45 minutes. Next add coconut milk. Thicken with enough rice flour to impart a creamy consistency to the mixture. Serve cold with cinnamon sprinkled on top.

---

[7] In some areas of Brazil this is called *Chá-de-Burro* or Burro's Tea. In Bahia, although one eats it with a spoon, it is called *Mungunzá para Beber*, or Hominy to Drink. A thicker, more solid type is prepared with the same ingredients and called *Mungunzá para Cortar*, or Hominy to Cut. This is spooned into a plate lined with banana fronds and allowed to cool. It is cut into squares and served cold. Sometimes the banana fronds are slightly scorched over a flame. A plain Pyrex dish is used when banana fronds are unavailable. See also pages 32 and 184.

Luscious Torte
Torta Saborosa

6 eggs, separated • 1/2 pound powdered sugar, sifted • 1/2 pound ground nuts
4 tablespoons butter • 2 tablespoons ground cinnamon
1 tablespoon grated unsweetened chocolate • 2 ounces curaçao

Beat yolks with sugar until mixture is lemon colored. Add ground nuts, then the stiffly-beaten egg whites. Pour into 2 buttered 8-inch layer cake tins and bake in preheated 350° oven until done. Cool on a cake rack. Make a filling by creaming the butter with cinnamon and grated chocolate. Use the remaining 1/4 to spread on the top layer. Refrigerate. Before serving powder with confectioner's sugar.

[TRANSLATED FROM: **RECEITAS CULINÁRIAS** BY MYRTHES PARANHOS]

Mango Sherbert
Sorvete de Manga

Peel mangos and cut into small pieces. Squeeze as much juice as possible from the seed and add to cut-up pieces. Liquify in the electric blender. Sweeten to taste, taking into account that, when freezing, the mixture loses some of its sweetness. Press mixture through a sieve and put it in freezer trays of a refrigerator. When mixture begins to freeze, spoon into the blender and beat, or use egg beater. Return to refrigerator trays and complete freezing.

N O T E : A good Mango Sherbert depends greatly on the quality of the fruit.

[HILDA MADASI, BAHIA]

Milk Sweet

Doce de Leite

Cook 2 cups of sugar with 1 quart of milk until some of the liquid evaporates and the residue is thick and creamy. This is a long process and will take anywhere from 60 to 90 minutes. In the final stages, it is necessary to stir constantly with a wooden spoon. The sweet is ready when it spins a thread when dropped from the tines of a fork or when it is thick enough to fall away from the sides of the saucepan. This is served as a dessert, accompanied by cheese or as an ingredient in other desserts, such as *Queijão*.

VARIATION: A simpler way is to simmer an unopened can of condensed milk for 2 hours. This may be done while cooking beans or making soup stock. Wash the can first and remove the label, then place with the beans or stock which will be cooking for 2 hours or more.

Mrs. Muniz's Dessert
A sobremesa da senhora Muniz[8]

6 eggs, separated • 1/2 cup sugar • 1 1/2 cups milk • 2 3-ounce packages strawberry
gelatin dessert mix (original recipe called for red gelatin which is sold in sheets)
1 cup boiling water • 1 teaspoon vanilla • 8 lady fingers, split
1/2 cup strawberry jam • sherry, rum or cognac • 1 cup heavy cream

Beat yolks, then beat in the sugar until light. Add to the milk and heat gently (do not boil) until mixture coats a metal spoon. Dissolve gelatin mix in boiling water, add to custard mixture and cool. Stir in the vanilla and refrigerate until mixture begins to set. Meanwhile, line sides of a 2 1/2 quart ring mould with the lady fingers that have been well moistened with the liquor. Dot with small spoonfuls of the strawberry jam. Beat egg whites until stiff, then whip the cream. Remove the congealed gelatin mixture from refrigerator and beat in the electric mixer. Fold in beaten egg whites and whipped cream and turn into the lined mould and refrigerate until firm.

[ANA VIRGINIA COSTA MARQUES MUNIZ, MATO GROSSO]

---

[8] This was the first dessert I tasted in Brazil. It was in 1927. Mrs. Muniz, the mother of my good friend, the late João Carlos Muniz, invited me to dinner in the lovely ancestral home she occupied at 140 Rua Paissandu. In 1927, there were many such homes in Rio, but this type of home has all but disappeared from the apartment-lined streets of Rio. The Rocha Miranda family (Mrs. Rocha Miranda is a granddaughter of Mrs. Muniz) lived in the house for some years and then the house was demolished to make room for an apartment dwelling.

Papaya Cream
Creme de Mamão

2 pounds ripe papaya • Sugar to taste • 1/4 cup peach liqueur or muscatel wine

Peel papaya, remove seeds and cut into small pieces. Mash with the sugar or place in blender with sugar. Add liqueur or wine and pile into serving glasses. Serve well chilled.

VARIATION: Avocado is also prepared this way. Both of these creams make an excellent dessert served with vanilla ice cream.

Peaches Supreme
Pêssegos Supremos

2 cups canned, puréed peaches (1 1-pound, 13-ounce can)
3 tablespoons powdered sugar • 3 ounces peach brandy • 1 cup heavy cream
1 cup sliced bananas, strawberries or mixed fruits

Drain canned peaches. Save the juice for future use in preparing gelatin desserts. Purée peaches in a blender and measure 2 cups. Add sugar and brandy and chill for 2 or 3 hours, then whip the cream and combine with puréed peaches. Mix in sliced fruit and chill. Yields 1 quart.

Peanut Chocolate Mousse
Mousse de Amendoim e Chocolate

6 eggs, separated • 1/2 cup sugar • 2 cups milk • 2 ounces unsweetened chocolate
1 tablespoon cornstarch • 1/4 teaspoon salt • vanilla • 1 cup ground roasted peanuts
1 envelope unflavored gelatin dissolved in 1/2 cup milk

Beat egg yolks, add sugar, milk, grated chocolate, cornstarch and salt, and cook over medium heat about 20 minutes, stirring until mixture thickens. Strain and cool slightly. Add vanilla and peanuts. Dissolve the gelatin in 1/2 cup of milk and stir into the mixture, then cool completely. When thoroughly cool add the stiffly-beaten egg whites. Turn into a serving dish and chill. Serve with sweetened whipped cream.

Pear Dessert
Sobremesa de Peras

8 canned pear halves, drained • 1/2 cup whipped cream
1/2 cup guava shells, drained from syrup and chopped
cashew nuts, chopped and slightly toasted

Drain pears and guava on absorbent paper to remove syrup. Arrange pears in a serving dish and fill cavities with whipped cream mixed with guava. Garnish with nuts.

[IRACEMA DE CARVALHO, RIO GRANDE DO SUL]

Pumpkin Delight
Delícia de Abóbora

2 cups canned or cooked, puréed pumpkin • 4 1/4 cups sugar • 1 cup coconut milk (see p. 39)

Cook pumpkin and 4 cups of the sugar, stirring constantly until mixture is thick enough to fall away from sides of saucepan, then add the coconut milk and the other 1/4 cup sugar. Cook until mixture reaches the soft-ball stage. Remove from heat and beat very well. Serve cold with cream cheese.

[HILDA LEITE QUEIROGA, MINAS GERAIS]

Prune Foam
Espuma de Ameixas

2 tablespoons cornstarch • 1 cup sugar • 1/8 teaspoon salt • 2 cups milk • 2 eggs, separated
6 lady fingers or strips of sponge cake, sprinkled with crème de cacao, muscatel wine or rum
5 extra-large prunes steamed in 1/2 cup water with 2 tablespoons sugar

Mix cornstarch, sugar and salt with a little cold milk. Scald rest of milk and add cornstarch mixture and egg yolks. Cook, stirring constantly until mixture thickens. Set aside to cool. Line individual sherbert glasses or a 1 1/2-quart pudding dish with the lady fingers. Pour cornstarch mixture over the moistened lady fingers. Meanwhile, cut up the cooked prunes, which should be very cold, and fold into the stiffly-beaten egg whites. Pile into partially-filled sherbert glasses or on top of the pudding dish and refrigerate.

[HILDA LEITE QUEIROGA, MINAS GERAIS]

Prune Soufflé
Soufflé de Ameixas

1 cup dried prunes (about 20) • 1/4 cup water • thin slice lemon • 1/4 cup port wine
3 cups sliced bananas • 3 egg whites • 3 tablespoons sugar

Wash prunes and steam until tender in water with the slice of lemon. Add port wine and cook slowly until all liquid has evaporated. Cool, remove pits from prunes and add the well-mashed bananas. Beat egg whites until stiff, add the sugar, then fold in the prune-and-banana mixture. Pour into a buttered 1 1/2-quart mould and bake in bain marie in 350° oven for about 35 minutes. Remove when it responds to custard test for "doneness." Serve with the following sauce:

3 egg yolks • 1 tablespoon cornstarch • sugar to taste • 1 cup milk

Beat yolks, add cornstarch mixed with 1 tablespoon sugar, then heat with scalded milk until sauce thickens. Taste and add more sugar, as needed.

[OTTILIA JANSEN DE MELLO, MINAS GERAIS]

Queijão

3 eggs, separated • 1 15-ounce can condensed milk or • 1 1/3 cup Milk Sweet (p. 304)

Beat egg whites until stiff and add to the condensed milk. Stir in beaten egg yolks. Line a 1-quart mould with caramelized sugar (see p. 481), pour in the mixture and bake in bain marie in 350° oven about 30 or 35 minutes or until it responds to the custard test for "doneness."

[ALICE BRANT,⁹ MINAS GERAIS]

Siracaia No. 1

2 cups milk • 4 egg yolks • 1 tablespoon melted butter • 4 tablespoons sugar
Few grains powdered cloves • few grains powdered cinnamon

Mix all ingredients and pour into a baking dish that can be brought to the table. Bake in a 400° oven until custard becomes firm. Serve chilled with cheese.

[OLGA DE SÁ PIRES, MINAS GERAIS]

---

⁹ When Mrs. Alice Brant gave me this recipe 35 years ago, Milk Sweet (p. 304) was used, the versatility of condensed milk in cookery not yet having been discovered.

Siracaia No. 2

6 egg yolks • 6 tablespoon sugar • 1/2 teaspoon salt
milk from 1 coconut, extracted by using 2 cups cow's milk

Beat yolks with sugar and salt. Add the coconut milk. Turn into a buttered 1-quart pudding dish and bake in bain marie in a 350° preheated oven 35-40 minutes or until it responds to the custard test. Cool and chill. Serve with powdered cinnamon sprinkled on top or plain with sweetened berries.

------ C H A P T E R 1 5 ------

FISH AND SHELLFISH

Fish should swim thrice. First, it should swim in the sea,
then it should swim in butter; and at last, sirrah, it
should swim in good claret.

SWIFT, POLITE CONVERSATION, DIAL. II

F   ish and shellfish, especially shrimp, are looked upon with great favor in Brazil. In fact, this Brazilian fondness comes naturally, for the Portuguese predilection for fish is well-known, while "meat of the water" was one of the principal foods of the Indian who occupied the Amazon region long before the advent of the white man.

Several processes of preserving and preparing fish and shellfish were devised by the natives and incorporated into Afro-Brazilian cookery by the slaves. *Moqueca*, which was developed in the kitchens of the Big Houses by the Africans, was adapted from the Indian's *Pokeka*. Made by wrapping fish in banana leaves and roasting it over hot embers, the *Pokeka* soon gave way to the African version, which is actually a ragout or stew prepared from fish or shellfish, oil, coconut milk and hot pepper.[1] This is one of the famous Northern Brazilian fish dishes, along with *Caruru, Efó, Vatapá* and *Bobó de Inhame,* all of which are well-known Afro-Brazilian dishes.

The Indians were also adept in salting and drying fish, but preserving fish by salting was a process known to the Portuguese, as well. It is little wonder, then, that modern Brazilian fish cookery includes numerous hereditary dishes made with salted fish, especially the cod, which has to be imported.

As in meat and poultry cookery, many recipes for preparing fish and shellfish call for the cook to *refogar* or marinate the fish in *vinha d'alho* and then carry out the cooking process through other methods, by creaming, grinding to make soufflés or croquettes, baking in the oven with a dressing or *farofa* (p. 50), or steaming and then making a *pirão* (p. 54) from the fish liquor. Even the salted cod, after the salt has been removed by soaking and parboiling, is treated in this manner. Fish is also served broiled, with a slice of lemon or lime, or breaded and accompanied by a sauce.

---

[1] Gilberto Freyre, *The Masters and the Slaves* (New York: Alfred A. Knopf, Inc., 1946), p. 131.

The versatility of Brazilian fish cookery is enhanced, too, by the many kinds of seasonings, herbs and flavorings used. Coconut milk and wine are favorites, although the wine used is not always the "good claret" advocated by Swift. Usually, just a red or white wine is indicated. Spices and herbs like bayleaf, ginger, coriander and sesame seeds, peppercorns, cloves and thyme are frequently introduced into a recipe. Salt pork is also used, not to mention the onions, garlic, tomatoes and parsley which are the component parts of the Brazilian *tempero* (seasoning). In addition, various fish dishes are served with their own special sauces or accompaniments, while the Afro-Brazilian dishes call for palm oil and hot pepper and special accompaniments like *Angu, Pirão* and *Farofa*, which can be made from any of the many meals and flours that Brazil produces.

A dish very much in style now is *Bobó*, not so highly seasoned as some of the other Afro-Brazilian dishes, but very delicious, and appealing to all palates because it is blander in taste than other Northern Brazilian dishes.

It is claimed that the Amazon River complex contains 800 species of fish. However only a few varieties are used commercially, such as the *pirarucu*, the *bicuda* and the *voador*. These are dried and sold in the interior of the country.[2] The *pirarucu* is a very important food element among the rural population of the far North, substituting, not only for salted codfish, but for the jerked beef's longer preservation. It is salted and then dried in the sun. The Indians also prepared a flour from this dried fish which they called *areia do peixe* or fish gravel.

The species of fish encountered in Brazilian waters differ from those found in the northern waters of the United States, yet we do have several varieties in common, as may be seen from the following chart:

---

[2] Wythe, Wigh and Midkiff, Brazil: *An Expanding Economy* (New York: The Twentieth Century Fund, 1949), p. 167.

SALT - WATER FISH									
ENGLISH	PORTUGUESE	WEIGHT (LBS.)	METHODS OF COOKING (✻ - PREFERRED)						
			BROIL	BAKE	BOIL	STEAM	DEEP FAT	PAN FRY	CHOWDER
Catfish	Bagre	1 - 5				*			
Cod	Bacalhau	2 1/2 - 10	See special explanation and recipes						
Seabass	Badejo	1 1/2 - 4	✻	*			*	*	
Croaker	Corvina	1 - 1 1/2	*	*	*	*	*	✻	*
Flounder	Linguado	3/4 - 2	*	*	*	*	*	✻	*
Grouper, Red	Garoupa	5 - 15	*	✻	*	*			*
Hake; Coddling	Abrotea	1/2 - 1 1/2	*	*			*	✻	
Mackerel	Cavala	2 - 20	✻	*	✻	✻			
Small	Cavaquinha	1/2 - 2 1/2	✻	*	*	*			
Spanish	Sororoca	1 - 4	✻	*			*	*	
Mullet	Tainha	1/2 - 5	✻	*	*	*			*
Snapper, Red	Vermelho	2 - 15	*	✻	*	*			
Snook; Robalo	Robalo	4 - 50		✻	*	*			*
Swordfish	Peixe espada	60 - 600	✻	*			*	*	
Tuna	Atum	10 - 700	*	✻	*	*			
Weakfish	Pescada	1 - 10	*	*	*	*	*	✻	*
FRESH - WATER FISH									
Carp	Carpa	2 - 8	*	✻			*	*	
Catfish	Bagre (Mandi)		*				*	✻	
Minnow	Lambari	2 - 8	*	✻			*	*	
Trout	Truta	1 1/2 - 10	*	✻			*	*	
	Pirarucu³					*			

GENERAL RULES FOR BAKING FISH

In a 400° oven, bake fillets 20 minutes and steaks 30 minutes. For whole fish without dressing, allow 10 minutes per pound which should be increased to approximately 12 minutes per pound when fish is stuffed.

    In addition to those on the chart, there are many other kinds of fish in Brazil not indicated because they are not available in North America.

---

³ This is the largest fresh-water fish in South America, attaining a length of 8 feet and a weight of 300 pounds. It is marketed in Northern Brazil as a dried fish, which must be soaked overnight before cooking.

Shellfish, notably shrimp and lobster are very popular in Brazil and very abundant. Shrimp is available in all sizes and can be purchased either fresh or dried, the latter forming part of the ingredients of *Vatapá, Efó, Muqueca, Caruru* and other well-known dishes.

In 1956, the Fish and Wildlife Service of the United States Department of the Interior made a survey of shrimp fishing in Brazil. They found that between 20 and 25 million pounds of shrimp were caught yearly, and that the resources would allow an annual catch of from 60 to 100 million pounds. Nearly the entire catch is consumed in Brazil, about half being partially dried and salted.[4]

Turtle meat is highly appreciated in the North and the Brazilians in that region prepare several turtle dishes that have won great acclaim from gourmets, reminding one of the refrain from Thomas Hood's "The Turtles":

"Of all the things I ever swallow —
Good well-dressed turtle beats them hollow —
It almost makes me wish, I vow,
To have to two stomachs, like a cow!"

They make *Arabu* out of the flour prepared from turtle eggs or from the eggs of the *tracajá*.[5] Better yet is *Abunã* — turtle or *tracajá* eggs that have been smoked before gestation has been completed. There is also a dish called *Munjangué*, which is a porridge made from manioc and the egg yolks of the turtle or *tracajá*. From turtle livers, these indigenous gourmets prepare a dish called *Paxicá*,[6] a sort of ragout seasoned with lemon and pepper. This is one of the most prized dishes of Amazonia and the surrounding area.

Lobsters are now being exported to the United States, and Brazil is trying to build up a sizeable export trade in this commodity![7] Until recently, very little attention was paid to the necessity of expanding fish production. Between the years 1955 to 1959, fish production rose from 11 to 40 million tons, practically quadrupling the

---

[4] *Special Scientific Report — Fisheries*, no. 235, p. 11.

[5] A fresh water tortoise whose flesh and eggs are considered delicacies. See *Glossary of Brazilian Amazonian Terms, Strategic Index of the Americas*, p. 21.

[6] *Glossary of Brazilian Amazonian Terms, Strategic Index of the Americas*, p. 16.

[7] *Estatístico do Comércio Exterior do Brasil*, p. 236, reports that the 1961 export of freshly killed or frozen lobster was 1,741 metric tons valued at US$ 2,863,414.

1955 catch![8] Enjoying a seacoast of approximately 4,600 miles, with modern equipment and techniques, great strides could be taken in this direction, just as are being accomplished in Japan and Peru, now tops in world fishing.

In 1957, it was estimated that there were 223,000 fishermen in Brazil, concentrated mainly in the Northeastern part of the country. Here, in the very precarious (but picturesque) sailing boat called the *jangada*, they set out to sea in groups, sometimes remaining on the open sea for days at a time. Considering that the *jangada* is merely an open raft of bound logs with a single mast, the two or three men who sail them must not only be skillful, but hardy and brave, as well.

D R E S S I N G   A   T U R T L E : If you want to make *Sarapatel*, remove the head and drain the blood into a large bowl containing lemon juice or vinegar. The U.S. Fish and Wildlife Service recommends that: "After the head and feet have been removed, if the turtle is large, nail it to a post or other object, belly out. Cut along the shell around each of the four limbs and pull the skin over each leg. The belly shell of snapping and soft-shelled turtles may be separated from the back shell by cutting through the suture between the two with a knife. If the incision is made in the right place, the two shells are easily separated. After the bridges are cut, the belly-plate may be removed by carefully cutting it away from the meat underneath. A hatchet or meat saw may be used to part the upper and lower shells of other turtles. The entrails are removed, and the quarters may be easily obtained by cutting to disjoint them from the shell. The tail and neck should also be skinned out. If the turtle is large, the ribs may be cut with a hatchet and the tenderloin removed from the 'ceiling' of the upper shell. One turtle thus provides eight fine sections of meat: the four quarters (dark), and neck, tail and the two tenderloins (light).

"As the fat is very gamey in flavor, this should be removed at once from all portions of meat. The meat may then be cooked directly or be soaked overnight in salt solution concentrated enough to float an egg. Some cooks like to add a tablespoonful of vinegar per quart of salt solution. If it is soaked in salt water, the meat must be washed before being cooked. In either case, no parboiling is necessary."[9]

---

[8] *Correio da Manhã*, October 30, 1960.
[9] U.S. Department of the Interior, Bureau of Sport Fisheries and Wildlife, *Leaflet No. FL-190*, Revised April, 1962, p. 4.

Baked Fish No. 1
Peixe Assado Nº 1

1 large fish suitable for baking (see chart, p. 317) • salt and lemon juice
1/4 cup white wine • 3 sliced onions • 1/4 cup chopped parsley
1/4 teaspoon coriander powder • 1/4 cup olive oil • 1 cup tomato sauce
1 tablespoon butter • 1 teaspoon vinegar

Clean fish, rub with salt and lemon juice. Cover with wine, 2 of the onions, parsley and coriander powder. Let marinate at least 1 hour, turning fish so that both sides can absorb the marinade. Place on foil paper in a baking dish, cover with oil, tomato sauce and the other sliced onion. Pour the marinate over the fish and bake in a preheated 400° oven (see p. 317). Baste frequently with drippings. When the fish is baked, remove to serving platter and serve with parsley potatoes. Strain the drippings, add butter and vinegar, bring to a boil and pour over the fish.

[TRANSLATED FROM: **AS RECEITAS PARA VOCÊ DA TIA EVELINA**, 4TH ED.]

Bake Fish No. 2
Peixe Assado Nº 2

1 large fish, suitable for baking (see chart, p. 317) • 1 large sliced onion
1/2 cup chopped scallions • 1/2 cup chopped parsley • 5 tablespoons butter
1 cup Madeira wine • 1/4 cup quartered cooked mushrooms • 2 egg yolks

Wash and clean fish, sprinkle with salt and place in buttered roasting pan. Surround with onions, scallions and parsley, dot with 4 tablespoons of the butter, and cover with 1/4 cup of the wine. Let stand 1 hour and turn fish once. Bake in oven according to the instructions on p. 317, basting with another 1/4 cup of the wine. When fish is baked, remove to serving platter, keep warm and make a sauce from the drippings, as follows: if roasting pan is too dry, add a little water, heat and scrape to remove all drippings. Strain into another pan, heat gently, add rest of the wine, butter and mushrooms and egg yolks. Check seasonings. Pour hot over fish, but do not boil after adding egg yolks.

[TRANSLATED FROM: **A ARTE DE COMER BEM** BY ROSA MARIA (MME. H. LEONARDOS)]

Baked Fish with Beer
Peixe Assado com Cerveja

1 dressed fish, 2 to 4 pounds, suitable for baking • 2 grated onions
1/2 cup chopped parsley • 1 teaspoon pounded coriander seed
2 pounded garlic cloves • 2 small hot peppers • juice of 2 lemons
1/4 teaspoon salt • 1/2 cup olive oil or butter • 1/2 cup beer

Make a marinade with the onions, parsley, pounded coriander seed, garlic and hot peppers by mixing with lemon juice, salt and olive oil. Marinate fish in this for a few hours, turning occasionally. Remove and wipe dry. If stuffing is to be used, fill with Fish Stuffing No. 1 or 2 (p. 61). Rub with butter, place in a baking dish lined with foil, papel, (or banana leaves) and brush with the rest of the marinade that has been mixed with beer. Bake in 400° oven according to instructions on p. 188. Baste frequently with marinade mixture. Serve with one of the Fish Sauces included in the chapter on "Accompaniments," p. 41. Or serve plain on a bed of shredded lettuce, garnished with olives, hard boiled eggs and tomatoes.

F i s h   P u d d i n g
Pudim de Peixe

1 pound fish fillets • 1/2 cup chopped onions • 1/4 cup chopped parsley
salt, pepper, Tabasco sauce • 1 dinner roll, broken up and soaked in milk
4 eggs, separated • 4 tablespoons butter • 1 teaspoon all-purpose flour
1/4 to 1/3 cup milk • 3 tablespoons grated cheese

Poach the fish in a skillet with a small amount of water to which the onions and parsley have been added. Season with salt, pepper and Tabasco sauce. When poached, remove the fish from the liquid and strain and reserve this broth. Grind the fish and add the milk-softened dinner roll. To stiffly-beaten egg whites, add the beaten yolks and the butter and flour creamed together with the grated cheese. Mix with fish. Pour into buttered baking dish and bake in bain-marie at 375° for 50-60 minutes. Serve with the following sauce:

2 tablespoons minced onions • 1 tablespoon chopped parsley • 1 tablespoon fine olive oil
1 tablespoon flour • 1 egg yolk • a few drops lemon juice
1/2 cup fish broth reserved from poaching • olives or cut-up shrimp (optional)

Sauté onions and parsley in olive oil. Mix flour with egg yolk, add lemon juice and combine with the sautéed onions and parsley. Mix well and gradually add the fish broth, cooking over a low flame and stirring constantly until the sauce thickens. If desired, add olives or cut-up shrimp.

N O T E : This sauce should be made just before serving.

[IZAURA PINTO, MINAS GERAIS]

Fish with "Pirão"

Peixe com Pirão

1 pound firm fish fillets • 1/4 pound butter • 1 medium-sized minced onion
1/4 cup chopped parsley • 1/4 cup chopped green pepper
2 peeled, chopped tomatoes or 1/2 cup stewed tomatoes with 3/4 cup of their juice
2 or 3 drops Tabasco sauce • salt and black pepper • 3 cups hot water • 1 cup manioc meal

Fry fish on both sides in butter with onions, parsley and green pepper. Add the tomatoes, Tabasco sauce, salt and black pepper to taste, plus garlic salt, if desired. When fish is cooked, remove to a covered pan to keep warm. Add the water to the drippings and vegetables in the pan and bring to boil. Gradually stir in the manioc meal, stirring constantly and vigorously to prevent lumps. When mixture has the consistency of corn meal mush, remove and press into a moistened 1 quart mould. Unmould, place the cooked fish around the mould and garnish with olives and hard-boiled eggs.

Fish with Cabbage or Cauliflower
Peixe com Repolho ou Couve-Flor

1 small cabbage, shredded • 2 pounds fish fillets, cut in 2-inch strips
2 bouillon cubes, dissolved in 2 cups hot water • 2 tablespoons butter • 1 chopped tomato
1 tablespoon potato starch • 1 cup fish broth, drained from fish and cabbage
1 cup milk • grated cheese • 1 hard-boiled egg • salt and pepper

Mix cabbage and fish in a large covered skillet and add bouillon cubes dissolved in water. Steam until cabbage is tender, but not over-cooked. Drain off all liquid and reserve 1 cup. Melt butter and sauté tomato for 2 or 3 minutes. Dissolve potato starch in the fish broth and add to the tomato. Stir and cook 10 minutes. Add milk and season. Butter a shallow baking dish and line with cheese. Arrange layers of the fish and cabbage mixture alternately with the sauce. Sprinkle grated cheese over top and bake until brown in a 375° oven 25 to 30 minutes. Garnish with a chopped hard-boiled egg.

VARIATION: This may be made with cauliflower, in which case the fish should be poached separately in the broth and the cauliflower boiled and then mixed with the fish.

Fish Senise

Peixe Senise

8 fillets of fish in serving-size pieces (haddock, flounder or sole), marinated for 3 hours in
1/2 cup lemon juice • 1 teaspoon salt and black pepper • 1/4 teaspoon coriander powder
all-purpose flour • 2 or 3 eggs • frying oil • full recipe for Palm Heart Sauce, p. 58
full recipe for Anchovy Sauce, p. 56 • grated Parmesan cheese

After fish has marinated, wipe dry, cover with sifter flour, dip in lightly-beaten eggs and again in the flour. Deep fat fry in oil until a golden brown, remove and drain on absorbent paper. Pour Palm Heart Sauce into a large Pyrex baking dish and arrange the fish on top. Cover with Anchovy Sauce, sprinkle Parmesan cheese on top and bake in a hot oven. Serve immediately in the Pyrex dish.

[TRANSLATED FROM: **A COZINHA DELICIOSA E MODERNA** BY MARIA THEREZA SENISE]

Fish with Coconut Milk Sauce
Peixe com Molho de Coco

2 tablespoons butter • 4 fish steaks or fillets • 1/2 cup chopped onion • 1 bayleaf
salt and pepper • 1 cup white wine • 1 lemon

Melt butter in a skillet and sauté fish on both sides with onion, bayleaf, salt and pepper. Add wine and poach gently until fish is done. Squeeze 1/2 the lemon over the fish, turn fish and squeeze other half, allowing fish to stand about 5 minutes each time lemon juice is sprinkled. Lift pieces of fish out onto serving platter and strain the broth over top. Serve with the following sauce:

2 tablespoons butter • 2 tablespoons cornstarch • 1 cup coconut milk
1 egg yolk • seasoning • capers

Melt and brown butter in a skillet. Add cornstarch and stir well. Gradually add the coconut milk. Cook 4 or 5 minutes, stirring constantly to prevent lumps. When ready to serve, add egg yolk and cook 2 or 3 minutes. Pour over fish and sprinkle a few capers on top.

[LAURITA PIRES, MINAS GERAIS]

Fish Fillets

Filé de Peixe

8 fillets of fish, cut in strips about 2 inches wide and 7 inches long • lemon juice and salt
8 small apples dotted with butter • full recipe for Shrimp Patty Filling (p. 443)
1/2 cup olive oil • juice of 1/2 lemon • 1 chopped onion • 1/2 cup port wine
salt and pepper • 1 cup tomato sauce

Sprinkle lemon juice and salt over the fish and let stand 20 minutes. Cut tops off apples, core and remove most of the center, saving this for apple sauce. Rub with butter and bake in a buttered baking dish until fork tender. Remove fish from the lemon juice and spread each fillet with the Shrimp Patty Filling. Roll up, fasten with toothpicks and place in a baking dish. Cover with the olive oil, lemon juice, onion and port wine. Bake in a preheated 400° oven about 20 minutes, or until fish is cooked, and baste with the drippings. When fish is done, remove and add any leftover Shrimp Patty Filling to drippings in baking dish together with the tomato sauce. Heat to make a medium thick sauce. Arrange the fillets on a serving dish and remove toothpicks. Fill the cavities of the baked apples with the sauce and use as an accompaniment to the fish. Pour any remaining sauce over the fish and garnish with capers.

[TRANSLATED FROM: **AS RECEITAS PARA VOCÊ DA TIA EVELINA, 4TH ED.**]

Fried Fish
Peixe Frito

2 pounds fillet of haddock or flounder • 2 tablespoons lemon juice • 1/2 teaspoon salt
1/4 teaspoon black pepper • 1/4 teaspoon ground coriander
sifted all-purpose flour • corn oil

Cut fillets in serving-size pieces, wash and wipe dry with absorbent paper. Place in a large shallow bowl and marinate in a mixture made of the lemon juice, salt, pepper and coriander. Let stand at least 1 hour and turn frequently so that both sides are equally impregnated with the marinade. Dredge fillets in flour and fry in deep hot corn oil at 375° until golden brown.

Pickled Fish
Escabeche de Peixe [10]

Full recipe for Fried Fish, p. 329 • 1 cup olive oil • 2 sliced onions
3 chopped, peeled tomatoes (optional) • 1 bayleaf • 1/2 teaspoon powdered ginger
1 teaspoon salt • 5 peppercorns • juice of 1 lime • juice of 1 lemon • 1/2 cup vinegar

Heat oil, sauté onions, tomatoes, bayleaf, ginger, salt and peppercorns. When vegetables are delicately browned, add juice of the lime and lemon, vinegar, and bring to boil. Pour over Fried Fish. Cool uncovered, then cover and store in the refrigerator. Serve cold.

[10] Mrs. Esther Garcia Leão (see footnote page 269) gave me this recipe which she obtained from Mrs. Flora de Oliveira Lima. Dr. Oliveira Lima served as Secretary at the Brazilian Legation in Washington in 1895 and later as Minister to Japan. By his will, his library and many personal objects were given to the Catholic University where the Oliveira Lima Library is now housed. More than 43,000 volumes have been catalogued, in addition to various memorabilia left by Dr. Oliveira Lima.

Stuffed Baked Fish
Peixe Recheado

1 whole fish, 3 to 4 pounds • 1/4 cup lemon juice • 1 teaspoon salt • butter or olive oil
1/2 cup white wine • shrimp or corn bread stuffing

Clean fish and wipe dry. Marinate in lemon juice and salt for 1 hour, turning fish over once. Stuff with Shrimp or Corn Bread Stuffing (p. 61) and place in a buttered baking dish. Dot generously with butter or brush with olive oil. Cover with wine and bake in a preheated 400° oven, according to directions on p. 317. Serve surrounded with watercress, hardboiled eggs and sliced tomatoes.

[TRANSLATED FROM: **A ARTE DE COMER BEM** BY ROSA MARIA (MME. H. LEONARDOS)]

Salmon Pudding
Pudim de Salmão

1/4 pound stale bread • 2 cups milk • 1 1-pound can salmon • 1 minced onion
1 tablespoon chopped parsley • 6 eggs, separated • salt and pepper
bread crumbs • grated cheese

Cook bread and milk, then add the salmon from which skin and bones have been removed. Stir in onion, parsley and the beaten egg yolks. Season to taste. Fold in the beaten egg whites. Turn into a buttered baking dish which has been sprinkled with bread crumbs. Top with grated cheese. Bake in bain-marie preheated at 350° 60 to 70 minutes. Serve with Anchovy Sauce, p. 56.

Salmon with Palm Hearts
Salmão com Palmito

1 1-pound can choice salmon • 4 tablespoon butter • 1 tablespoon minced onion
1 tablespoon minced parsley • 1 tablespoon capers • salt and cayenne pepper
1 tablespoon lemon juice • 1 10-ounce can palm hearts • 1 cup yoghurt
1/4 cup bread crumbs

Drain salmon, discard skin and bones, then shred. Melt half the butter in a skillet, add onion, parsley and capers. Sauté and add the salmon. Gently heat for 3 or 4 minutes. Season to taste with salt and cayenne, then sprinkle with the lemon juice and remove from heat to cool. Drain the palm hearts and reserve the liquid for soup stock or sauces. Slice palm hearts and place in a well-buttered shallow casserole dish. Cover with the salmon mixture. Mix in the yoghurt and cover with the bread crumbs. Dot with the other half of the butter. Bake in 375° oven about 30 minutes. Serves approximately 4.

VARIATION: Cauliflower buds or asparagus tips are excellent substitutes for the palm hearts.

Fish and Shrimp Stew
Moqueca de Peixe com Camarão[11]

3 pounds fish fillets • 2 pounds shelled, deveined shrimp • 1/4 cup lemon juice
1 teaspoon crushed coriander seed • 1 tablespoon salt • 1/2 teaspoon garlic salt
black pepper • 1/2 cup olive oil • 6 peeled and chopped tomatoes
2 minced onions • 2 tablespoons parsley • 1 grated coconut • 1 tablespoon palm oil
4 cups milk • 1 cup rice flour

Mix lemon juice, coriander, salt, garlic salt and black pepper, and spread half over the fish and other half over the shrimp. Blend evenly and let both mixtures stand for 2 or 3 hours, stirring once or twice. Mix olive oil, tomatoes, onions and parsley; divide into 2 parts in 2 skillets and separately sauté fish and shrimp. Extract thick milk from the coconut and cook in with the fish, then stir in cooked shrimp. Blend in palm oil over a low heat and cook for about 10 minutes, or until most of the liquid has evaporated and the mixture has the consistency of a thick stew. Taste, and correct seasonings. Scald milk with the residue of the coconut, force through a coarse sieve and prepare a *Pirão* by cooking the rice flour with this liquid (see p. 54). Mould the *Pirão* if desired or turn onto the center of a large platter and cover with the *Moqueca*. Serve with Pepper and Lemon Sauce (p. 91).

---

[11] This recipe was given to me by Mrs. Flávia Chermont Ararigboia, who in turn received it from Mrs. Marina Hartz of Rio de Janeiro.

Stewed Fish
Peixe Cozido

*1 pound fish fillets or steaks, cut in serving-size pieces • 2 tablespoons lemon juice
salt • 1 tablespoon oil • 1/4 cup minced onion • 2 tablespoons chopped parsley
1 chopped tomato • 1 cup water • 1/4 cup white wine • 1 tablespoon all-purpose flour
3 egg yolks • few drops lemon juice*

Clean fish and wipe dry. Cover with most of the lemon juice, reserving a few drops for the sauce. Add salt and let stand 1 hour, turning fish over once. Heat oil in a skillet and sauté fish with vegetables for 10 minutes. Remove fish and pour water and wine into the skillet. Add the flour and cook until the sauce thickens. Check seasoning and strain. Return fish to the sauce and cook over low heat for about 5 minutes. When ready to serve, add the egg yolks and the few drops of lemon juice saved from the 2 tablespoons. Arrange fish on a serving plate, pour sauce over fish, garnish with capers, hard-boiled eggs and watercress.

D R I E D   C O D F I S H

BACALHAU

M E T H O D S   O F   F R E S H E N I N G   C O D F I S H

1. Soak in cold water for 3 or 4 hours and change water every hour.

2. Let cold tap water run over codfish for 15 minutes, then run warm water over it for 5 minutes. Drain, cover with cold water and let stand overnight.

3. Let cold water run over fish for 15 minutes. Place in saucepan, cover with cold water and gradually heat to boiling. Repeat until fish tastes fresh.

In each of the above methods, the codfish should be left in large pieces. Before starting the recipe, be sure skin and bones have been removed. Also taste to see if most of the salt has been removed. If not, gently parboil.

Codfish Balls
Bolinhos de Bacalhau

1 pound dried codfish • 2 tablespoons butter • 1/2 cup chopped onions
1/4 cup chopped parsley • salt and black pepper • 1 cup milk • 2 cups mashed potatoes
1/4 cup all-purpose flour • 3 eggs

Freshen fish according to directions (p. 335) and sauté in butter with onion, parsley, salt (if necessary) and pepper, flaking with a fork as it sautées. Add milk, potatoes, flour and the eggs, lightly beaten. Mix well, check seasoning and let stand 10 minutes. Shape into balls or cakes and drop into hot oil. Serve hot, plain or with a sauce.

[LYDIA SOARES, ESPÍRITO SANTO]

Codfish with Chick Peas
Bacalhau com Grão-de-bico

1 pound dried codfish • 2 tablespoons olive oil • 1 pounded garlic clove
3/4 cup chopped onions • 1/2 cup chopped parsley • 1 cup tomato sauce
seasoning • 2 1/2 cups cooked chick peas[12] • 7 or 8 stuffed olives

Freshen fish according to directions (p. 335). Sauté in half the olive oil with half the garlic, onions, parsley and tomato sauce. Season to taste and set aside, keeping warm. Sauté chick peas in the other tablespoon of oil with the remaining half of the garlic, onions, parsley and tomato sauce. Season. Place codfish in the center of serving dish surrounded by chick peas and garnished with the olives.

---

[12] If dried chick peas are used, they may be soaked overnight with the codfish, but next morning they should be boiled separately.

Codfish Pudding
Pudim de Bacalhau

3/4 pound dried codfish • 1 bayleaf • 3 1/2 cups milk
2 slices cubed bread, moistened in some of the milk • 1/2 cup butter
1/2 cup all-purpose flour • 4 or 5 very thin slices of onion • 5 eggs, separated
1/4 cup seedless raisins (optional)

Freshen fish according to directions in methods for freshening, then boil with a bayleaf until tender. Drain. Melt the butter and stir in the flour and the rest of the milk gradually, stirring constantly to prevent the formation of lumps. Cook until you have a medium white sauce. Strain through a coarse sieve, if necessary, to remove any lumps, then add the onion and set aside. Put cooked codfish in blender with bread milk mixture and beat with the egg yolks. If you do not have a blender, grind the codfish in a meat grinder, then add the bread and milk mixture and the beaten egg yolks. Fold in the stiffly-beaten whites. Taste and season with salt, freshly ground black pepper, and a few grains of cayenne pepper. Pour into a generously-buttered 2 1/2 quart aluminium ring mould and, if raisins are to be used, sprinkle them on top. Bake in bain-marie preheated at 375° from 1 1/4 to 1 1/2 hours or until a bladed knife comes out clean when inserted in center. Loosen edges and remove from mould to serving plate. Serve immediately with melted butter.

Codfish with Coconut Milk
Bacalhau com Leite de Coco

1 pound dried codfish • 1 freshly-grated coconut • 4 tablespoons butter or oil
2 chopped onions • 2 chopped tomatoes • 2 or 3 drops Tabasco
1 tablespoon palm oil (optional)

Freshen fish according to directions (p. 335). Remove thick milk from coconut and reserve. To the residue add 2 cups hot water and remove thin milk by pressing through a coarse sieve. Fry codfish in butter or oil with the onions and tomatoes and wet with the thin milk of the coconut. Cook over a low flame (do not boil) stirring once in a while. When ready to serve, shake the Tabasco over the fish, add the palm oil and the thick milk of the coconut. Serve on a platter surrounding a mould of *Angu* of rice flour with coconut milk (p. 54).

[TRANSLATED FROM: **A ARTE DE COMER BEM** BY ROSA MARIA (MME. H. LEONARDOS)]

Codfish — Minas Style
Bacalhau à Mineira

1 pound dried codfish • 2 tablespoons fine olive oil or butter • 1 minced onion
1/4 cup chopped parsley • 1 fresh, peeled tomato, cut up
black pepper, salt, garlic salt • 2 cups finely-shredded cabbage

Freshen fish according to directions (p. 335). Heat oil in a skillet and sauté fish with onion, parsley and tomato. Season. Add shredded cabbage, cover the skillet and steam until cabbage is done. Prepare half the recipe for Brazilian Rice, p. 131. Combine the codfish and rice mixtures and serve piled high on serving platter.

[TRANSLATED FROM: **AS RECEITAS PARA VOCÊ DA TIA EVELINA. 4**TH EDITION]

Codfish Pie
Torta de Bacalhau

1 pound dried codfish • 2 tablespoons butter or oil • 1 minced onion
2 tablespoons chopped parsley • juice of 1 lemon • 1 chopped tomato • black pepper
1/4 teaspoon mashed coriander seed • 2 or 3 drops Tabasco sauce • 1 cup mashed potatoes
1 tablespoon grated cheese • 4 eggs • 1 cup milk

Freshen fish according directions (p. 335). Heat butter or oil and sauté onion, parsley and tomato. Add fish when vegetables are beginning to brown. Cook and stir with a fork to break fish into small pieces. Cool. Add lemon juice, black pepper, coriander and Tabasco sauce. Mix. Add the potatoes and cheese and check seasoning. Beat eggs, add the milk and combine with the fish. Turn into a well-buttered baking dish and bake in a preheated 375° oven for 30 minutes or until a knife comes out clean when inserted.

Mother's Codfish Pudding
Pudim de Bacalhau da Mamãe[13]

1/4 pound codfish • 1 tablespoon parsley • 1 small onion • 1/4 clove garlic (optional)
1/2 small Tabasco pepper • 1/2 cup tomato sauce • 1 teaspoon Worcestershire sauce
1 tablespoon chopped pickles or Indian relish • 2 tablespoons butter
3 tablespoons all-purpose flour • 1 cup milk • 7 eggs, separated • bread crumbs

Freshen fish according to directions (p. 335). Grind fish together with parsley, onion, garlic, Tabasco pepper, tomato sauce and Worcestershire sauce, or pass through a blender. Add relish, mix and let stand. Prepare a white sauce with the butter, flour and milk, and stir in codfish mixture. Beat egg whites until stiff, add beaten yolks and then the codfish mixture. Turn into a generously-buttered 3-quart cake tin, and sprinkle with bread crumbs. Set cake tin in a pan of hot water and bake like custard in a preheated 325° oven for 1 1/2 hours, or until a knife inserted in center comes out clean. Unmould and serve with Shrimp Sauce (p. 59), boiled potatoes and cauliflower. This pudding needs plenty of room, as it puffs up before it "settles down."

[MARIA LUIZA SALLES,* SÃO PAULO]

---

[13]This recipe was given to me by Doris Salles Beckmann and is a favorite from her grandmother's notebook.

Codfish with Vegetables
Bacalhau com Legumes

1 pound codfish • 2 1/2 cups water • 1 chopped onion • 1 bayleaf • a few grains garlic salt
1/2 cup tomato sauce, or 2 chopped tomatoes • 1/4 cup good olive oil • salt
cayenne pepper • 2 cups cut-up parboiled vegetables (okra, chayote, zucchini squash)
1/8 cup chopped olives • 2 tablespoons butter • 2 tablespoons chopped parsley

Freshen fish according to directions (p. 335). Next day, if you have soaked the fish overnight, cut into small pieces, remove to covered skillet with water and bring to a rolling boil, then reduce heat until fish is cooked. Remove from broth. To 1 1/2 cups of the broth, add 1/2 the onion, whole bayleaf, garlic salt and tomato sauce (or tomatoes). Boil 5 minutes, then simmer for 5 minutes and strain. Heat oil, add other half of onion and sauté the fish in the mixture. When fish begins to brown slightly, cover with the strained broth and add parboiled vegetables. Season with salt, if necessary, and a few grains of cayenne pepper. Cook over low heat. Before serving, add olives, butter and parsley and recheck seasonings, as this should be piquant. Cook 2 or 3 minutes more and serve with Corn Angu and Brazilian Rice.

VARIATION: Zorô, the famous Northern dish, is practically the same as above, but the fish is left in large pieces and palm oil is used. Serve Zorô with Rice Pirão.

[GLADYS MARIE SILVA, MATO GROSSO]

Codfish Scramble
Fritada de Bacalhau

1 pound dried codfish • 2 tablespoons oil or butter • 1 large thinly-sliced onion
1/4 cup chopped parsley • 5 medium-boiled potatoes, sliced
6 eggs, separated • seasoning

Freshen codfish according to directions (p. 335). Melt shortening in a skillet and sauté parsley and fish, then add the onion and sliced potatoes. Beat egg whites until stiff, then fold in the beaten yolks. Add one half the egg mixture to the fish, stir and heat for 5 minutes. Check seasoning. Transfer mixture to a casserole, cover with other half of egg mixture and place under the broiler to brown.

Codfish Soufflé
Soufflé de Bacalhau

1 pound dried codfish • 3 tablespoons butter or oil • 1/2 chopped onion
1/4 cup chopped parsley • 1/2 chopped tomato • 1/2 pound boiled potatoes
1/2 cup milk • 2 tablespoons grated cheese • 4 eggs, separated

Freshen codfish according to directions (p.335). Melt butter or oil in a skillet and sauté fish with onion, parsley and tomato. Add potatoes, mix well and mash or put through a meat grinder. Cool and check seasoning. Add milk, cheese and beaten egg yolks. Fold in beaten egg whites. Turn into a mould that has been buttered and sprinkled with bread crumbs. Sprinkle with grated cheese and bake in a preheated 350° oven until done (30-35 minutes). Unmould and serve with plain white sauce or tomato sauce.

[TRANSLATED FROM: **A ARTE DE COMER BEM** BY ROSA MARIA (MME. H. LEONARDOS)]

342

Codfish Supreme
Supremo de Bacalhau

1 pound codfish • 1/4 cup lemon juice • black pepper • 1/4 cup olive oil
1/8 teaspoon garlic salt • 2 thinly-sliced onions • 1/4 cup chopped green pepper
1 cup tomato sauce • 2 tablespoons butter • 1/4 cup chopped olives
2 tablespoons chopped parsley • seasoning • 1 cup good stock (fish or meat)
1 beaten egg • bread crumbs • oil for frying • 2 pounds cooked sweet potatoes, sliced in 1-inch
slices and browned in butter • 1 package frozen okra, cooked as directed
2 hard-boiled eggs • grated Parmesan cheese

Freshen fish according to directions (p. 335). Bring to a rapid boil, drain, cut in 2-inch strips and marinate for about 1 hour in lemon juice and black pepper. Meanwhile heat olive oil and sauté garlic salt, onions and green pepper. When onions are brown, add tomato sauce, butter, olives and parsley and season to taste. Bayleaf, nutmeg or coriander powder may be used with salt and pepper. Bring sauce to a rolling boil, add stock, reduce heat and simmer for 2 or 3 minutes. Remove from heat and set aside. Take fish from marinade, dip in egg, then in bread crumbs and again in the egg. Fry in hot oil to a golden brown and drain on absorbent paper. Place sweet potatoes in the bottom of a buttered casserole and cover with the fried fish. Top with cooked okra. Arrange sliced hard-boiled eggs over fish. Cover with the sauce. Sprinkle cheese on top and bake in a preheated 400° oven for 10 or 15 minutes.

Cold Codfish Plate
Bolo Frio de Bacalhau e Enchovas

1 pound codfish • 1 sliced onion • 1 sprig parsley • 1 bayleaf • garlic salt
1/4 cup lemon juice • 1 tablespoon olive oil • black pepper • 3 pounds small potatoes
1 small can drained anchovies • 1 tablespoon prepared mustard • 1/2 cup Indian relish
salt and pepper to taste • 1/4 cup chopped parsley • 1 1/2 cups good mayonnaise
shredded lettuce, hard-boiled eggs, black olives, tomatoes, radishes for garnishing

Freshen codfish according to directions on p. 335 and place in covered skillet with onion, parsley, bayleaf, garlic salt and enough water to cover. Cook over medium heat until tender, then remove fish from broth, wipe dry and marinate in lemon juice, black pepper and oil. Strain broth over the potatoes that have been pared and quartered, and add enough fresh water to boil the potatoes. When potatoes are boiled, drain and, while still warm, mash with the codfish and marinade. Mix in the anchovies, mustard, Indian relish, salt and pepper and parsley. Let stand to cool and for flavor to set, then refrigerate until thoroughly cold. Add mayonnaise, a little at a time. Press into a slightly oiled 2-quart mold and refrigerate until ready to serve. Unmould on a bed of shredded lettuce and garnish with any of the garnishes mentioned above. Decorate with mayonnaise or serve plain. Serves 8.

[TRANSLATED FROM: **A COZINHA DELICIOSA E MODERNA** BY MARIA THEREZA SENISE]

Fried Codfish
Bacalhau Frito

1 pound dried codfish • 2 tablespoons lemon juice • black pepper
2 stiffly-beaten egg whites • hot oil

Freshen codfish according to directions (p. 335), and cut into portion-size pieces. Let stand in lemon juice and pepper for 15 or 20 minutes. Dip into beaten egg whites and fry in hot oil until golden brown. Drain on absorbent paper. Serve on lettuce garnished with lemon wedges and stuffed olives.

Delicious Crabs
Caranguejos Deliciosos

2 tablespoons chopped green pepper • 2 tablespoons butter • 2 tablespoons all-purpose flour
1/2 teaspoon prepared mustard • 1/2 teaspoon Worcestershire sauce
Salt and black pepper • 1 cup chopped peeled tomatoes • 1 cup grated Muenster cheese
1 egg • 1 cup warm milk • 1 cup cooked or canned crabmeat

Sauté pepper in butter for 5 minutes. Add flour, mustard, Worcestershire sauce, salt, pepper and tomatoes and simmer for 5 minutes or until mixture is thoroughly blended. Add cheese and lightly-beaten egg and cook 2 minutes, stirring constantly, then add the warm milk and continue to cook another 3 or 4 minutes. Add crabmeat and cook gently over low heat stirring constantly until mixture thickens. Serve over buttered toast wedges or plain boiled rice or use as a filling for *empadinhas* or *pastéis*. Yields 2 1/2 to 3 cups.

VARIATION: Substitute cooked chicken or shrimp in place of crabmeat.

[IZAURA PINTO, MINAS GERAIS]

Crabmeat Scramble
Fritada de Caranguejo

1 pound cooked crabmeat • thick and thin milk from 1 coconut • 2 tablespoons olive oil
1 minced onion • 2 tablespoons chopped parsley • 1 chopped tomato
1/4 teaspoon crushed coriander seed • 1 small hot pepper, minced • 9 eggs
salt and pepper • 2 tablespoons all-purpose flour

Pick over crabmeat and add coconut milk. Heat oil and sauté onion, parsley, tomato, coriander seed and hot pepper. Add the crabmeat that has been mixed with the coconut milk and cook down over medium heat until mixture is almost dry, then remove from heat. Beat the eggs with salt, pepper and flour. Add a little of the egg mixture to the crabmeat (enough to bind the mixture) and cook. Transfer crab mixture to a buttered casserole and cover with the rest of the egg mixture. Bake in a 375° oven until brown and serve with slices of French bread.

[RENATA ARAGÃO SILVEIRA, SÃO PAULO]

Lobster Caruaru

Lagosta Caruaru [13]

Meat from 1 lobster • juice of 1 lemon • 2 tablespoons olive oil • 1 chopped onion
2 tablespoons chopped parsley • 2 peeled, cut-up, fresh tomatoes • salt
cayenne pepper • 1 cup coconut milk

Sprinkle lemon juice over lobster and let stand 30 minutes. Heat olive oil, add lobster, onion, parsley and tomato and sauté until lobster and vegetables are cooked. Season with salt and cayenne to taste and cook another 10 minutes over low heat. Add the coconut milk, continue cooking over low heat for 5 minutes, stirring constantly to prevent solidifying. Serve with Brazilian Rice, p. 131.

[THEREZINHA MARIZ, RIO GRANDE DO SUL]

---

[13] Caruaru is the name of a city in Pernambuco State.

Lobster Yolanda
Lagosta Yolanda

1 tablespoon butter or olive oil • 1 chopped onion • salt and pepper
1 pound cooked lobster meat • 2 cups milk • 3 tablespoons cornstarch
1 tablespoon butter • 1 cup grated Parmesan cheese • 1 cup thin cream
1 teaspoon prepared mustard, mixed with 1 tablespoon milk

Heat oil and sauté onion with salt, pepper and cooked lobster meat. Turn into a buttered baking dish. Scald 1 3/4 cups of milk and add cornstarch dissolved in the other 1/4 cup of cold milk. Cook over low flame, stirring to prevent lumps and, when mixture thickens, add the butter, cheese and cream, and continue to cook over low flame for 3 or 4 minutes. Add mustard and milk mixture, pour over lobster meat and bake in a preheated 375° oven until brown.

[SARITA BRANT, MINAS GERAIS]

Stuffed Crabs
Caranguejos Recheados

12 good-sized crabs • salt • black pepper • malagueta pepper (optional)
1/4 cup lemon juice • 3 slices of bread with crusts removed • milk
2 tablespoons butter • 1 finely-chopped onion • 1 tablespoon chopped parsley
4 tomatoes, peeled and chopped • 1 tablespoon all-purpose flour
3 yolks of hard-boiled eggs • 1 raw egg yolk • black olives • lettuce

Wash crabs well and drop into enough boiling water to cover, using 1 tablespoon of salt, 1/2 teaspoon lemon juice and 1 teaspoon cayenne pepper (optional) to each quart of water required. Boil crabs for 5 minutes and then simmer for 15 minutes. Cool crabs in cooking water then remove and reserve 1 cup of the strained cooking water. Pull off claws and legs and break the segment that folds under the body at rear. Hold crab in left hand with back toward you, slip fingers of the right hand under the top shell and pull the body downward so as not to break the shell, which is to be used later. Remove the digestive tract by holding crab under running cold water. Split the body along the central membrane covering the outside edge. Remove the tender sweet meat in each cavity with a nutpick, taking care not to break pieces of shell into the meat. Be careful to remove all shell particles, but do not wash crabmeat as it loses flavor.

Shred crab meat into small pieces and season with the salt, black pepper (also malagueta, if desired) and lemon juice. Let stand 15 minutes. Soak the bread in just enough milk to make a heavy mush. Melt butter and sauté onion, parsley and tomatoes, then add the crabmeat and the bread mush. Simmer 3 or 4 minutes so that the flavor permeates the mixture. Add the cup of strained cooking water and bring to a slow boil over medium heat. Thicken with the flour, which has been mixed in a little cold water, and cook until mixture holds its shape. Add the chopped hard-boiled egg yolks. Taste to check seasoning. Spoon the mixture into reserved crab shells, brush with the raw egg yolk and place a black olive in the center of each. Bake in a preheated 375° oven until golden brown on top (about 35 minutes). Serve on a bed of shredded lettuce.

N O T E : If frozen crabmeat is used, 3 cups are required plus the cup of fish stock. Fashion your own shells from aluminum foil or buy them ready-made.

[IGNÊZ SANTOS NEVES CERQUEIRA LIMA, ESPÍRITO SANTO]

Creamed Oysters with Palm Hearts
Creme de Ostras com Palmito

*1 cup thick white sauce • 24 shucked oysters and juice • 2 beaten egg yolks
salt and pepper • 2 tablespoons butter • 1 small can palm hearts, drained
3 hard-boiled eggs • paprika • wedges of buttered toast*

Heat white sauce over medium heat and, when hot, add oysters and their juice and cook for 3 or 4 minutes. Add egg yolks and 1 tablespoon butter and stir until yolks have been cooked. Season. Shred palm hearts and sauté in the other tablespoon of butter. Spoon into shallow Pyrex dish and cover with the creamed oysters. Garnish with sliced hard-boiled eggs. Brown under broiler. Insert wedges of toast and serve.

Oyster Croquettes
Croquetes de Ostras

36 oysters in their juice • 2 tablespoons lemon juice • 2 tablespoons olive oil
1/2 finely-chopped onion • 1 tablespoon tomato paste • salt and pepper
2 tablespoons all-purpose flour • 1/3 cup bread crumbs • 3 egg yolks
beaten eggs • bread crumbs • oil for frying

Poach oysters over low heat in their own juice, until edges curl. Remove, strain out the juice and mince the oysters. Sprinkle lemon juice on oysters and set aside. Heat oil and sauté onion, tomato paste, salt and pepper. Add all the juice from the oysters and thicken with flour mixed with bread crumbs. Remove from heat, add the egg yolks, return to heat and cook slowly until mixture holds its shape. Add the minced oysters and check seasoning. Cook for 3 or 4 minutes, then turn onto a platter to cool. When cool enough to handle, shape into croquettes, roll in bread crumbs, then in lightly-beaten egg and back in the crumbs. Fry in oil at 375° until golden brown.

Oyster Soufflé

Soufflé de Ostras

1 tablespoon butter • 1/4 cup minced onion • 1 peeled, chopped tomatoes
1 1/2 cups shucked oysters in their liquor • salt and black pepper
1 cup heavy white sauce • 3 eggs, separated • 3 tablespoons grated Parmesan cheese

Melt butter in a skillet and gently sauté onion and tomatoes. Add drained oysters and cook with sautéed vegetables over medium heat for 5 minutes, then pour in the oyster liquor and simmer 3 or 4 minutes. Season with salt and black pepper and arrange in a baking dish. Add the white sauce to the beaten egg yolks and fold into stiffly-beaten whites. Add the cheese and pour over oysters. Bake in a preheated 375° oven from 60 to 70 minutes until brown.

[TRANSLATED FROM: **NOÇÕES DE ARTE CULINÁRIA** BY MARIA THEREZA A. COSTA]

Oyster Fry
Fritada de Ostras

1 1/2 cups shucked oysters, in their liquor • 1 tablespoon lemon juice
salt and black pepper • 1/4 cup olive oil • 1/2 cup minced onion
2 tablespoons tomato sauce • 2 tablespoons chopped parsley
1 cup stale bread with enough milk to make a mush • 3 beaten eggs • paprika

Separate oysters from their liquor and sprinkle with lemon juice, salt and pepper and let stand 10 or 15 minutes. Heat oil and gently sauté onion, tomato sauce and parsley, adding garlic salt, if desired. When vegetables are cooked, stir in the oysters and continue to sauté over low heat for 2 or 3 minutes. Add the oyster liquor. Force bread through a coarse strainer, add it to the oysters and stir over medium heat for 5 minutes. Remove from heat, add 1/2 the beaten eggs. Taste and correct seasoning. Turn into a well-buttered Pyrex dish and cover with the other half of the beaten eggs. Sprinkle paprika on top. Bake in a 350° preheated oven until golden brown (20 to 25 minutes). Serve immediately in same dish. Yields 4 good-sized portions.

Baked Avocado with Shrimp
Abacate Recheado com Camarão

4 large avocados • Shrimp Cream recipe, p. 60 • grated Parmesan cheese

Cut avocados lengthwise and remove the stone. Fill with Shrimp Cream, pile meringue on top and sprinkle with grated cheese. Bake in a 400° preheated oven for about 15 minutes.

Chayote with Shrimp
Soufflé de Camarão[14]

1 pound fresh shrimp • 1 tablespoon butter or oil • 1 tablespoon chopped onion
1 tablespoon chopped parsley • 2 peeled, chopped tomatoes • 2 or 3 drops Tabasco sauce
2 cups heavy white sauce • 2 egg whites • grated Parmesan cheese

Shell, devein and clean the raw shrimp. Sauté in butter or oil with the onion parsley and tomatoes until cooked. Add the Tabasco sauce and check seasoning. Turn sautéed shrimp into a buttered baking dish, then cover with the white sauce. Top with the stiffly-beaten egg whites, sprinkle cheese over top and bake in a preheated 375° oven for about 15 minutes. Serve in same dish garnished with thinly-sliced raw onion rings and olives.

---

[14] This recipe was served at a dinner party at the Brazilian Embassy in Washington to a group including several Cabinet members of the United States Government and was prepared by Mrs. Emerita Pires de Souza from Rio de Janeiro. The following day, one of the Cabinet members asked the Ambassador for a copy of the recipe and I was requested to do the translation. That is how I came by the recipe. Although the Brazilian name uses "soufflé," to conform to the American conception of a soufflé, the whites would have to be mixed with the minced shrimp and it would also have to contain the egg yolks.

Corn and Shrimp Casserole
Caçarola de Milho com Camarão

1 pound fresh shrimp • 2 tablespoons olive oil or butter • 1/2 cup chopped onions
2 tablespoons chopped parsley • 1/4 cup chopped green pepper
1/4 cup tomato sauce • salt and black pepper • 2 tablespoons all-purpose flour
1 cup milk • 2 cups canned corn, cream style • grated Parmesan cheese

Shell, devein and clean shrimp and dry on absorbent paper. Heat oil, add onions, parsley, green pepper and tomato sauce. Sauté vegetables in oil and then add the shrimp and continue cooking until shrimp begins to turn pink. Season well with salt and pepper, mix thoroughly, cover skillet, reduce heat, and simmer 2 or 3 minutes. Sprinkle flour over the shrimp, combine well, gradually adding the milk. Cook over medium heat until mixture thickens, then allow to cool. Spoon into a buttered baking dish. Pour the corn on top without stirring and sprinkle with Parmesan cheese. Bake in a preheated 375° oven until brown (about 30 minutes).

[HILDA LEITE QUEIROGA, MINAS GERAIS]

E g g s   S t u f f e d   w i t h   S h r i m p
Ovos Recheados com Camarão

12 hard-boiled eggs • 1 tablespoon butter
1 tablespoon minced onion • 1 tablespoon chopped parsley • 1 finely-chopped tomato
1/2 cup cooked minced shrimp • garlic salt • salt and pepper
1 egg mixed with 1 tablespoon all-purpose flour • bread crumbs

Cut eggs in half lengthwise, as for deviled eggs, and remove yolks. Melt butter and
sauté onion, parsley and tomato. Add minced shrimp and seasoning, and simmer
gently until well blended. Stir in the egg yolks, breaking them up against the side
of the saucepan as you mix them into the shrimp and sautéed vegetables. Check
seasoning. Fill the egg whites with the mixture, covering each one with the other
half of the filled hard-boiled white. Roll each one in the flour-and-egg mixture and
then in bread crumbs, taking care not to have the covers come off. Place each
whole stuffed egg in a buttered baking dish and brown in the oven, at 375°. Serve
with your favorite sauce or plain on lettuce leaves garnished with olives.

V A R I A T I O N : Substitute chopped, cooked mushrooms for the shrimp.

[TRANSLATED FROM: **NOÇÕES DE ARTE CULINÁRIA** BY MARIA THEREZA A. COSTA]

357

Shrimp in Cognac
Camarão em Conhaque

1 pound fresh shrimp • 1 tablespoon butter • 1/2 cup cognac • 2 tablespoons ketchup
1/2 cup heavy cream • seasoning • parsley

Shell, devein and clean shrimp. Place in a covered saucepan and gently steam. Allow to cool in the broth. Drain. Melt butter in a skillet, add cognac and ketchup and blend in the cream. Mix in the shrimp and check seasoning. Heat and serve on a bed of parsley.

[DAURA ALVES DA COSTA, RIO DE JANEIRO]

Shrimp Cream
Creme de Camarão

1 pound fresh shrimp • 1 tablespoon oil • 1 tablespoon chopped onion
1 tablespoon chopped parsley • 2 peeled, chopped tomatoes
1/2 cup bread, without crusts • 1/2 cup milk • 4 eggs, separated
salt and pepper • grated cheese

Shell, devein and clean shrimp. Sauté in oil with onion, parsley and tomatoes. Soak bread in milk and then add to lightly-beaten egg yolks. Remove 5 or 6 of the better looking shrimp and reserve as garnish. Combine bread and milk-egg mixture with the shrimp in the skillet, which should be cold. Mix and return to heat, cooking gently, until thoroughly cooked. Season to taste. Turn into a buttered casserole and sprinkle with grated cheese. Spoon stiffly-beaten egg whites on top of shrimp mixture, shaping into pyramids. Place a reserved shrimp on top of each pyramid. Bake in preheated 400° oven around 10 minutes until meringue is delicately brown.

[TRANSLATED FROM: **AS RECEITAS PARA VOCÊ DE TIA EVELINA, 4TH ED.**]

Shrimp with Creamed Corn
Creme de Milho com Camarão [15]

4 pounds shrimp, cleaned and deveined • 1 teaspoon garlic salt • 1 tablespoon salt
1/4 teaspoon black pepper • 1 bayleaf • 1/4 cup lemon juice • 1/4 cup olive oil
2 tablespoons grated onion • 1 cup tomato sauce • 1 teaspoon oregano
juice of 1/2 lemon • 1 cup light cream • 1 coconut • 1/2 cup ground roasted peanuts
1 1/2 cups milk • 1 1/2 tablespoons cornstarch • 1 No. 2 can creamed corn (2 cups)

Season shrimp with garlic salt, salt, black pepper, bayleaf and lemon juice and marinate 2 hours. Heat olive oil in a skillet and, when it is hot, add shrimp and sauté over high heat, stirring constantly so that shrimp does not steam. When almost cooked, add onion, tomato sauce and oregano, stir and cook until done. Mix the juice of 1/2 lemon with the cream and add to shrimp. Remove *thick* milk from coconut and extract the *thin* milk with the 1 1/2 cups cow's milk. Add *thick* milk to shrimp together with peanuts. Check seasoning. Mix thin coconut milk with cornstarch. Heat with the corn until sauce thickens. Liquify and strain or press through a coarse sieve. Season to taste and reheat. Pour the sauce onto a very large platter. Spoon shrimp in center and serve accompanied by a Pepper and Lemon Sauce, p. 91. Serves 12.

---

[15] This recipe was lent to me by Mrs. Flávia Chermont Ararigboia — wife of Brigadier Armando de Souza e Mello Ararigboia — who in turn had received it from Mrs. Marina Hartz of Rio de Janeiro. It was created in honor of Mrs. Hartz by her mother.

Shrimp Meringue
Chuchu com Camarão

1 pound fresh shrimp • 1 tablespoon lemon juice • salt and black pepper
1/8 cup olive oil • 1/4 cup minced onion • 1/2 cup chopped, peeled tomatoes
4 cups peeled and cubed chayote

Shell, devein and clean shrimp. Marinate in lemon juice, salt and pepper for 15 minutes. Heat oil and gently sauté onion and chopped tomatoes, adding parsley, if desired. Then add the shrimp and simmer 2 or 3 minutes. Add the chayote to the shrimp mixture, cover the skillet or saucepan, bring to boil, then simmer about 30 minutes or until chayote is cooked. Do not add water. Adjust seasoning and serve with Brazilian Rice, p. 131.

VARIATIONS: Sometimes, in place of the chayote, this dish is prepared with okra (quiabo) or green papaya (mamão verde). It is also delicious prepared with round summer squash.

Shrimp Pudding
Pudim de Camarão

1 pound fresh shrimp • 2 tablespoons butter • 1 tablespoon chopped parsley
1 tablespoon chopped onion • salt and pepper • 2 tablespoons tomato paste
1 14-ounce can palm hearts • 4 slices bread • milk or thin coconut milk
3 egg yolks • olive oil • bread crumbs

Shell, devein and clean shrimp. Sauté in 1 tablespoon butter with parsley and onion and seasoning. Add the water and steam for about 5 minutes. In another saucepan melt the other tablespoon of butter with tomato paste and the palm hearts, which have been drained and sliced. Soak bread in enough milk (or thin coconut milk) to make a mush, then press through a coarse sieve and add the beaten egg yolks. Taste and season. Coat a 1 1/2-quart Pyrex baking dish with oil and sprinkle with bread crumbs. On bottom, place a layer of the palm hearts, cover with bread-and-egg mixture, then the shrimp. Repeat until all mixtures are used, reserving enough bread misture for the top. Set the dish in a pan of hot water and bake in preheated 350° oven until mixture is solid (about 1 hour). Turn baking dish over on a serving plate on a bed of shredded lettuce and garnish with tomato wedges. Serve plain or with a sauce.

Shrimp Croquettes
Croquetes de Camarão

12 fresh jumbo shrimp • 2 tablespoons butter • 1/4 cup chopped onions
1/2 clove garlic, minced • 1 tablespoon chopped parsley • 2 tablespoons milk
1 slice dry dread, crusts, removed • 2 eggs • seasoning
1/2 cup all-purpose flour • bread crumbs

Shell, devein and clean shrimp, then chop into small pieces. Melt butter in a skillet, add onion, garlic, parsley and the shrimp and sauté all together until shrimp are cooked. Moisten bread in milk, add one of the beaten eggs, then pour into the shrimp mixture. Season to taste. Gradually sift in the flour, enough to blend and hold the mixture. It may not be necessary to use the entire quantity of flour. Mould into oval shapes and allow to cool thoroughly. Dip in the other beaten egg, roll in bread crumbs and fry until golden brown in deep fat at 375°. Drain on absorbent paper. Yields 12.

Shrimp Fry
Fritada de Camarão

2 1/2 pounds fresh shrimp • 1/2 cup fine olive oil • 1 minced onion • 1 minced hot pepper
1 cup thin coconut milk • Salt and pepper • 3 eggs, separated

Shell, devein and clean the shrimp. Heat, oil, add shrimp, onion and hot pepper, and cook over medium heat until shrimp is done. Add the coconut milk. Beat egg whites and yolks separately, then combine. Spoon shrimp mixture into a casserole, pour egg mixture over the shrimp and bake in a preheated 375° oven until done. If desired, garnish with large onion rings before placing in oven.

[LIA MAGRO, PERNAMBUCO]

Anna Pereira's Shrimp Pudding
Pudim de Camarão à Moda de Anna Pereira

1 pound fresh shrimp, shelled, deveined and cleaned • 1/2 pound fresh jumbo shrimp, shelled deveined and cleaned • 1 1/4 tablespoons margarine or olive oil
1 finely-minced onion • 1 cup warm fish or meal stock • 1 tablespoon chopped parsley
1 large chopped tomato • 1 tablespoon chopped green pepper • salt and pepper to taste
3 tablespoons all-purpose flour • 1 2/3 cups milk • 2 tablespoons butter
1/3 of a 1-pound loaf of bread • 5 eggs, separated • 1 tablespoon lemon juice

SAUCE:

2 tablespoons lemon juice • 2 egg yolks

Melt margarine or heat olive oil, and cook onion. Do not fry. Add parsley, tomato and green pepper and 1/2 the stock, and continue to cook for about 15 minutes. Strain and use any of the leftover stock to press out as much of the vegetable sauce as possible. Chop the smaller shrimp and leave jumbo shrimp whole. Simmer in the sauce with salt and pepper (and cayenne or other seasonings, if desired) until shrimp is pink and tender. This takes about 10 minutes. Remove jumbo shrimp with about 1/2 cup of the sauce and reserve. Allow chopped milk until it is of the consistency of a medium batter or porridge. Add butter. Remove crusts from bread and soak in the other 2/3 cup of milk. Combine chopped shrimp in sauce with the flour mixture, then add the bread and milk. Stir in the lemon juice and the egg yolks, then the stiffly-beaten whites. Taste to check seasoning. Spoon into a well-buttered 2-quart Pyrex baking dish and bake in a 325° oven for about 65 minutes or until a knife comes out clean when inserted in center. Meanwhile, heat the reserved jumbo shrimp in the sauce with the 2 egg yolks, which have been beaten with the 2 tablespoons lemon juice. Unmould the pudding, garnish with the jumbo shrimp and sliced olives and pour sauce over the pudding.

N O T E : It is possible to use only one size of shrimp, preparing recipe with 1 1/2 pounds and reserving 8 or 9 of the largest for garnish.

Shrimp Tempura[16]

1 pound fresh jumbo shrimp • 2 tablespoons lemon juice
salt and freshly-ground black pepper • 3/4 cup sifted all-purpose flour
1/2 teaspoon salt • 1 egg • 2 tablespoons melted butter • milk

Shell, devein and clean shrimp. Partially split down outer side, spread out like a butterfly and sprinkle with lemon juice, salt and pepper. Let stand 3 hours, turning shrimp so that both sides are coated with the marinade. Make a batter with the flour, salt, egg and melted butter, adding enough milk to make it thin. Beat until smooth. Dip each shrimp in the batter and fry in deep fat at 370° until done. Serve with wedges of lemon.

VARIATION: Clams may also be prepared in the above manner.

---

[16] Tempura was introduced to Japan about 200 years ago by Portuguese traders and has since become one of Japan's most popular dishes, the Japanese using this method to prepare a great variety of sea foods and vegetables. The word *tempura* refers to the deep fat frying of foodsstuffs coated with a batter.

Shrimp Rosita Sá
Camarão à Moda de Rosita Sá

8 slices buttered toast • 1 pound fresh shrimp • 1/4 cup olive oil
2 tablespoons minced onion • 2 tablespoons chopped tomato
2 tablespoons chopped green pepper • salt and pepper • mozarella cheese

Place toast in the bottom of a baking dish that has been well-buttered and cover with just enough milk to wet the toast. Shell, devein and clean shrimp and sauté in hot oil with onions, tomato and green pepper. Season with salt and pepper. When shrimp is cooked (about 10 minutes), place a layer over the toast and cover with the cheese. Bake in 375° preheated oven until cheese melts.

[MARIA ROSA BARBOSA DA SILVA DE SÁ, MINAS GERAIS]

Shrimp Soufflé
Soufflé de Camarão

1 pound cooked ground shrimp • 1 tablespoon lemon juice • 1 teaspoon onion juice
1 1/2 teaspoon salt • 3/4 cups sifted all-purpose flour • 3 cups milk
2 tablespoons grated Parmesan cheese • 1 tablespoon butter
6 eggs, separated • breads crumbs

Mix shrimp with lemon and onion juices and half the salt, and let stand. Make a smooth paste with the sifted flour and some of the milk. When smooth, add rest of milk and salt. Heat, stirring constantly until mixture thickens. If there are any lumps, strain. Cool slightly, add cheese, butter and beaten egg yolks, then the shrimp mixture. Fold in stiffly beaten egg whites and pour into a 3-quart casserole or soufflé dish, which has been well-buttered and sprinkled with bread crumbs. Bake in a preheated 350° oven for 1 hour. Serve immediately, garnished with sliced tomatoes and hard-boiled eggs.

[NINI MACHADO, SÃO PAULO]

366

Turtle Sarapatel
Sarapatel de Tartatuga

Turtle liver • large intestine • lemon juice • turtle paws • turtle fat • chopped onion
1/4 teaspoon coriander powder • 1/4 teaspoon garlic salt • 1/2 teaspoon salt
cayenne pepper • some of the turtle blood

Scald the liver and intestine in hot water to remove membranes and then sprinkle with lemon juice. Cut the liver and intestine, add the paws and some of the turtle meat. Render enough turtle fat to sauté the cut-up meats. While the meats are frying, add minced onion, coriander powder, garlic salt, salt and cayenne pepper. Sauté for 15 minutes, then add enough water to cover. Simmer until meats are tender. Correct seasoning. When cooked, add a little of the turtle blood, heat and serve.

VARIATION: Intead of using the blood, thicken the stew with 3 or 4 tablespoons of all-purpose flour dissolved in a little cold water. This stew may be ladled into the turtle shell and baked, and then served at the table directly from the shell.

Minced Turtle Meat with Farofa
Picadinho de Tartaruga com Farofa

Grind the turtle meat and season with salt, pepper, garlic salt, minced onion, lemon juice and coriander powder. Let stand 30 minutes. Season the turtle shell with salt and lemon juice. Prepare the ground turtle meat as for *Picadinho,* p. 378. Make a butter *Farofa.* Turn turtle meat into the shell, cover with the *Farofa* and garnish with cooked turtle eggs or hardboiled eggs. Serve immediately.

Turtle Steaks
Bifes de Tartaruga

Cut breast of turtle into steaks. Season with garlic, salt and lemon juice and let stand 1 hour. Fry in hot oil, and, when done, remove from oil and drain. Cover with onion rings, sliced tomatoes and parsley, and simmer with a jigger of white wine until tender.

Turtle Legs
Perninhas de Tartaruga

Remove the 4 legs from the turtle and reserve the paws for another recipe *(Sarapatel)*. Marinate the legs overnight in the marinade used for Brazilian Turkey, p. 470. Next day, bake and baste with the marinade until legs are tender.

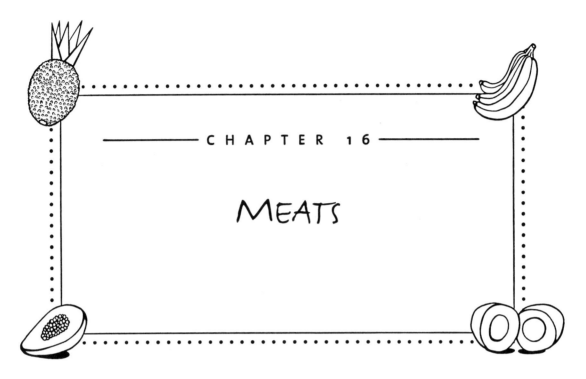

CHAPTER 16

MEATS

Some have meat but cannot eat;
Some could eat but have no meat;
We have meat and can all eat;
Blest, therefore, be God for our meat.

UNKNOWN, THE SELKIRK GRACE

The principal meats used in Brazil are beef, veal and pork. While lamb is raised and consumed in the South, where it is very popular barbequed, other areas of Brazil use very little of this meat. As a matter of fact, the three lamb recipes included in this chapter were very hard to come by.

Generally, meat is not consumed in Brazil to the extent that it is in the United States, the per capita consumption of beef in Brazil amounting to about 44 pounds[1] as compared to 88 pounds in the United States.[2]

Jerked beef is very popular and is one of the staples of the laboring class. The jerked beef is also one of the principal ingredients of the Brazilian national dish, *Feijoada* as well as such noted Afro-Brazilian specialities as *Escaladas de Peru* and *Quibebe*. Known as *carne seca* (dried beef), also as *charque*, it is prepared by sun-drying beef which has been brushed with a salt solution.

The Brazilian laborer and the *sertanejo* (inhabitant of Northeastern Brazil) prefer a diet of rice, beans, manioc meal and the *carne seca* or dried beef. His brother to the South or *gaucho* (cowboy) swings the pendulum to the other extreme, subsisting mainly on barbequed fresh meat, manioc and maté, the Brazilian tea.

Even though the majority of Brazil's population consumes little fresh meat, Brazil is one of the important cattle-producing countries of the world, producing the number of head being about 3/4 of that in the USA.[3]

---

[1] U.S. Dept. of Agriculture, Foreign Agricultural Service, *Foreign Agriculture Circular, FLM 17-62*, October 1962.

[2] U.S. Dept. of Agriculture, *Livestock and Meat Situation* (Pub. No. LMS 127), November 1962, p. 3.

[3] According to the *Anuário Estatístico do Brasil*, 1962, p. 67, there were 76,176,000 head of cattle in Brazil in 1961. In 1962 the U.S. count was 99,782,000 according to the U.S. Dept. of Agriculture's *Livestock and Meat Situation* (Pub. No. LMS-129), March 1963, p. 6.

The two leading cattle-raising areas in Brazil are in the central plateau, embracing the States of Minas Gerais, Mato Grosso, Goiás, São Paulo and Rio Grande do Sul. The island of Marajó, situated at the mouth of the Amazon River, and 400 square miles short of being twice the size of the State of New Jersey, has been pointed out as being a logical region for expansion of the cattle industry.[4]

In general, Brazilian cooking processes for meats, fish or poultry begin with the making of a *refogado* for the meat or marinating it in *vinha d'alho. Refogar* means to sauté the meat. *Refogar com todos os temperos* appearing in a recipe means to sauté with all seasonings, in which case onions, parsley, tomatoes, garlic and condiments may be used.

The other process, marinating in a preparation known as *vinha d'alho,* involves a tenderization and flavoring of the meat by soaking in a seasoned vinegar solution. Other ingredients in the marinade or *vinha d'alho* are sometimes lemon juice, wine, grated carrots, herbs and seasonings.

Still another way, one of which the Southern Brazilian is very fond, is the *churrasco* or barbeque described by Dona Maria Alencastro Guimarães. Both Ambassador and Mrs. Alencastro Guimarães were born in the cattle-raising state of Rio Grande do Sul, where *churrascos* are part of the way of life. When I requested a recipe for *churrasco* from Dona Maria, I was rewarded with the following complete account of how she and the Ambassador prepare it.

---

[4] Marajó Island measures 16,000 square miles while the State of New Jersey comprises an area of 8,208 square miles.

CHURRASCO OF RIO GRANDE DO SUL

Described by Maria Alencastro Guimarães

This is not a recipe in the strict sense of the word because the necessary ingredients are only meat, water and salt. The most important is the fire which is made with charcoal, and, in order to light it, one should not, under any circumstances, use inflammables such as gasoline, kerosene, alcohol, etc.

Arrange the fuel on the ground, preferably in a pit dug in the earth or surrounded by a few bricks to avoid the heat being disturbed by the wind. Underneath the charcoal, lay a few pieces of kindling wood and paper which, when lit, make the charcoal start to glow. Generally, the fire is started about an hour before the barbequing of the meat, so that only the live embers are left and no flame.

While you are waiting for the fire to get a good start, begin to prepare the meat. Trim and cut it in strips 6 or 7 inches long. Take a handful of coarse salt and mix with a little water to make a brine solution. Brush the brine on the strips of meat and then thread the meat onto skewers in accordance with the amount you plan to barbeque.

The spit may be of iron, but in Rio Grande do Sul it is made from sturdy tree branches, which serve as the skewers and hold the meat. They vary in length from 2 1/2 to 4 feet, depending upon the size of the fire. They are assembled over the fire by inserting two verticle branches, forked on one end and sharpened on the other, into the ground deep enough to support the weight of the horizontal branch

These forked branches should extend from 12 to 16 inches above the fire so that when the spit is placed in the forked supports, the meat will cook slowly. If the spit is too close to the fire, the meat will cook quickly on the outside and remain raw inside. The spit is made by sharpening one end of a branch, which is long enough to reach between the two forked supports, with a little to spare on each end. The meat is then speared onto the spit, which is placed in position between the forks.

An alternative method is to eliminate the verticle forked branches and thrust the skewer into the ground to one side of the fire, allowing it to incline obliquely over the glowing embers, remembering to keep the meat 12 to 16 inches above the embers.

If the spit is resting between the two forked branches, it should be turned once in a while to cook the meat evenly on all sides. If the alternative method is used, the spit should likewise be rotated for the same purpose. Whenever the skewered meat is turned, some of the salt solution should be brushed on, taking care not to let any drop on the fire, as it might extinguish it. Brushing with the brine solution keeps the meat from drying out.

When preparing meat for the *churrasco* the bones are not removed. It is therefore necessary to allow a minimum portion for each person of at least 1 1/2 pounds. Or, better still, figure on 2 pounds because the meat is usually ribs and these have little meat and much bone. The *churrasco* is tastier when made with meat that has some fat on it.

The Gaucho eats the meat dipped in manioc meal and accompanies it with maté tea, which he drinks from a gourd.

Beef Rolls
Bifes Enrolados

2 pounds round steak, sliced as thinly as possible • garlic, salt and pepper
1 cup port wine • 1/2 pound thinly-sliced boiled ham • 8 hard-boiled eggs
1 tablespoon prepared mustard • seasoning • 1/2 cup chopped black olives
6 tablespoons butter (3 plus 3)

Have the butcher cut the steaks as thinly as possible and then pound them with a mallet. Rub garlic on both sides and sprinkle with salt and pepper. Cover with wine and marinate overnight. Next day, remove meat from the marinade and cover with the sliced ham. Save the marinade. Mash egg yolks[5] with 3 tablespoons of the butter and the mustard, and season to taste. Spread mixture over ham and sprinkle the olives on top. Roll steaks up lengthwise, cut in thirds and tie each roll securely at both ends. Sauté meat rolls in the remaining 3 tablespoons butter until well browned on all sides. Add the reserved marinade. Cover and cook over medium heat 5 minutes, lower heat and cook until steak rolls are very tender. Add small amounts of water if too much of the marinade evaporates. This takes almost 2 hours. Remove string and serve hot with the pan gravy, and a border of mashed potatoes with buttered peas separating the rolls. May also be served cold with a salad.

[TRANSLATED FROM: **AS RECEITAS PARA VOCÊ DA TIA EVELINA, 4TH EDITION**]

---

[5] Leftover hard-boiled egg whites may be used for Egg White and Pickle Sandwich Filling, p. 106.

Brazilian Stew

Cozido [6]

THE DAY BEFORE: Make a marinade with

2 pounded garlic cloves • 1 teaspoon pounded coriander seed • 3/4 cup chopped parsley
3 thinly-sliced onions • 1 cup vinegar • 2 teaspoons salt • 3 bayleaves

Divide the marinade in half. In one portion, marinate 1 whole cleaned stewing chicken, and in the other, 2 pounds rump of beef and 2 pounds lean chuck.

THE NEXT MORNING: Brown the chicken in a skillet with a small amount of fat, just enough to fry. In another larger saucepan, brown the meats, also in a small amount of fat. When chicken and meats are brown, add 1 1/2 cups water to each, cover and simmer for 1 hour. When the hour is up, remove chicken and meats to a large kettle, together with their broths, and, if necessary, add more water to cover. Then add:

1 large can plum tomatoes • 2 whole peeled onions

and cook slowly over medium heat until meats are tender. Then, if available, add a ham bone with a little ham on it and also:

---

[6] As can readily be seen, this is a dish for a large group, a glorified Brazilian version of a boiled dinner. Do not attempt it unless you are well-stocked with extra-large pots. But if you can beg or borrow pots, plan to serve this excellent Brazilian Stew at your next big get-together. Mrs. Aragão, a noted Brazilian gourmet cook, recommends that a hot pepper sauce, like the Pepper and Lemon Sauce described on p. 91, be served with the meats.

2 pounds smoked seasoned sausage (Polish bologna or Kohlbasi will do)
2 pounds fresh loin of pork • 1/2 pound fresh pork sausages
3 pieces peeled cassava or manioc root • 3 peeled yams • 4 peeled sweet potatoes
9 medium-sized, peeled white potatoes • 1 small head of cabbage, quartered with core removed
4 small white turnips • 1 pound whole string beans, with strings removed
1 pound yellow pumpkin cut in large pieces

Taste and add necessary seasoning and water to cover. Cook over low heat in covered kettle, and as the vegetables become cooked, remove them and set aside, keeping them warm. When nearly all have been removed, add:

A small peeled squash, cut in rounds, with seeds removed • 4 corn cobs cut in halves
1 pound fresh whole okra • 6 plantains

Cook all together. Remove each vegetable from the broth as it is cooked, taking care not to break them, especially the plantains. When all the vegetable have been removed, arrange everything on a very large platter or a tray covered with foil paper. The chicken and cut meat should go in the center surrounded by all the vegetables. The sliced bologna and other sausages are arranged around the outer edge of the tray. Make a gravy with part of the broth, pouring over a sautéed, chopped onion and thickening by mashing in some of the cooked pumpkin. Pour over the platter. With the rest of the broth, make a *Pirão* (p. 50) by thickening with manioc meal, and serve on a separate platter.

[RENATA SILVEIRA ARAGÃO, SÃO PAULO]

Chopped Beef Brazilian Style
Picadinho

1 pound lean chopped beef • 1 tablespoon shortening • 1 chopped onion
2 chopped fresh tomatoes • black pepper • salt and herbs to taste
1/2 cup meat stock • olives • 2 hard-boiled eggs

The meat, preferably top round, is finely chopped by hand or machine-ground as coarsely as possible. Heat shortening and sauté meat with onion, tomatoes, black pepper, salt and herbs. After the meat is well-browned, add enough meat stock or bouillon to moisten, then cover the saucepan and reduce heat to medium. The cooking is completed through evaporation. Just before removing from heat to serve, add a few olives and chopped hard-boiled eggs.

N O T E : Because *Picadinho* is simple and easy to make, yet very tasty when properly prepared, it has won great popularity in Brazil. It belongs to the hamburger or Salisbury steak family, but it is greatly superior in taste. It is served in loose form, usually accompanied by Brazilian Rice (p. 131), mashed potatoes, or *Angu* (p. 53). *Picadinho* is also prepared with okra *(quiabo)* or chayote *(chuchu)* using the same recipe and adding the chopped-up vegetable. The olives and eggs are omitted when the *Picadinho* is made with these vegetables, and no water is added, as the vegetables steam with the meat.

[REPRINTED FROM AUTHOR'S ARTICLE IN JULY 1963 ISSUE OF **GOURMET MAGAZINE**)

Chopped Beef Rio Grande Style
Picadinho do Rio Grande

The full recipe for Chopped Beef Brazilian Style, above • 3 tablespoons raisins
1 tablespoons butter • 1 cup manioc meal • 1 teaspoon sugar

Prepare the full recipe for Chopped Beef Brazilian and add the raisins. Melt butter in a skillet and gradually pour in the manioc meal, stirring constantly. (This is called *Farofa*). Add sugar and mix. Butter a baking dish and place a layer of the *Farofa* in the bottom. Pile the Chopped Beef Brazilian on top and sprinkle the rest of the *Farofa* over the meat. Dot with butter and bake in a 375° oven a few minutes to brown topping.

[TRANSLATED FROM: **AS RECEITAS PARA VOCÊ DA TIA EVELINA, 4TH ED.**]

Fried Beef Steaks
Bifes Fritos

2 pounds tender beef, cut into steaks • salt and pepper • lemon juice
2 tablespoons shortening

Shake salt and pepper on both sides of steaks and cover with lemon juice. Let stand a few hours or over night. Heat shortening in a skillet and, when hot, add the steaks. Brown on both sides and then pour on the marinade in which meat was soaked. Cover, reduce heat and cook until tender.

Chopped Beef Cearense Style
Carne Picadinha à Moda do Ceará

2 cans tomato paste • 1 cup water • 3 large green peppers, chopped
2 large onions, chopped • 1/2 cup corn oil • 1/2 cup whiskey or Scotch
4 pounds extra-lean ground beef • salt, to taste
finely-chopped hot red peppers to taste, or cayenne, or black pepper

Dissolve tomato paste in water in a large saucepan and add peppers, onions and oil. Cook over medium heat for about 15 minutes and then add whiskey and the meat, which must be as lean as possible. Mix well and continue cooking, stirring constantly to prevent sticking. Cook in this manner until most of the liquid has evaporated. This will take about 1 hour. Add the salt and pepper to taste and continue cooking until mixture is almost dry. Then transfer to a casserole and bake in a 250° oven, allowing most of the moisture to evaporate. When a tender crust begins to form on top, remove from oven and serve with Brazilian Rice (p. 131), a green vegetable or salad, and Cearense Omelet (p. 66).

N O T E : When properly prepared, the beef has the consistency of a coarse meal.

[WILSON AGUIAR, CEARÁ]

Meat Balls No. 1
Almôndegas[7] Nº 1

1 pound lean ground beef • 1/4 pound chopped smoked tongue
1 grated onion • 2 tablespoons chopped parsley • salt and pepper
1 cup stale bread, covered with enough milk to make a mush • 1 egg yolk
all-purpose flour • 1 beaten egg • oil or fat for frying

Mix beef with next six ingredients and shape into balls the size of an egg. Roll each ball in flour, then in the beaten egg. Fry in deep fat. Drain on absorbent paper and serve plain or with a sauce. Yields approximately 33 balls.

---

[7] *Almôndegas*, very popular in Brazil, were inherited from the Mother Country, Portugal and brought to Brazil by Portuguese colonizers. As early as 1692, several recipes for *almôndegas* appeared in a Portuguese cookbook by Domingos Rodrigues, Master Cook to His Majesty.

Meat Balls No. 2

Almôndegas Nº 2

1 small chopped onion • 1 tablespoon chopped parsley • 2 chopped tomatoes
2 tablespoons butter • 1 cup beef stock or bouillon • 1 pound lean ground beef
2 eggs • 2 tablespoons all-purpose flour (optional) • bread crumbs • fat or oil for frying

Prepare a gravy by sautéing the onion, parsley and tomatoes in butter, then add stock and simmer. Strain and season to taste. Mix meat with eggs and 2 tablespoons of the gravy. Check seasoning, add the flour (optional) and shape into small balls, the size of an egg. Roll in bread crumbs, then fry in hot fat until delicately browned. Remove to absorbent paper to drain excess fat. Return to the gravy and simmer. Yields approximately 28 small balls.

[TRANSLATED FROM: **NOÇÕES DE ARTE CULINÁRIA** BY MARIA THEREZA A. COSTA, SÃO

PAULO]

Pot Roast
Carne Ensopada

*4 pounds rump roast of beef • 2 ounces chopped ham mixed with
2 ounces chopped bacon • 1/2 cup vinegar • 1 teaspoon salt pounded with
1 garlic clove • 1 grated onion • 2 tablespoons margarine (optional)*

Trim all excess fat from meat and lard it by making several small incisions and stuffing with the mixture of ham and bacon. Make a marinade with the vinegar, salt, garlic and onion. Soak the meat about 2 hours in this marinade, then wipe dry with a piece of absorbent paper. If meat has a fatty surface, place the fatty side down in a heavy aluminium saucepan and render enough fat to sear the meat on all sides. Pour off excess fat. If the meat has no fat, use the margarine and sear on all sides. When meat is richly browned on all sides, add the marinade. Cover the saucepan and cook over low heat, turning meat to cook evenly on all sides. It should take from 1 1/2 to 2 hours to cook.

[MARIA BARBOZA NUNES, RIO DE JANEIRO]

Roast Beef
Rosbife

6 pounds rump roast of beef • 4 or 5 whole cloves • 1 garlic clove • 1 teaspoon salt
1/2 cup chopped green pepper • 1/2 cup minced onion • 1/4 teaspoon black pepper
1/4 teaspoon ground coriander seed • 1 tablespoon chopped parsley
1 tablespoon lemon juice • 1 tablespoon vinegar • 3/4 cup stout beer
1/4 cup melted butter or margarine

Wash and pat meat dry. Make 4 or 5 incisions and insert 1 whole clove in each. Prepare a marinade by crushing garlic with salt and mixing in green pepper, onion, black pepper, coriander and parsley. Add the lemon juice, vinegar and beer. Mix well and marinate the meat 8 or 9 hours, turning once or twice. Remove from marinade, pat dry with absorbent paper and place in a baking pan. Cover with the melted butter and sear on all sides in a 400° preheated oven. Reduce heat to 350° and baste often with the strained marinade, allowing about 20 minutes cooking time per pound of meat for well done. Remove meat to a platter and prepare a pan gravy with the drippings.

[GLADYS MARIE SILVA, MATO GROSSO]

Roast Beef with Vegetables
Rosbife com Legumes

6 pound rump roast of beef • 1/2 teaspoon garlic salt • salt and pepper • 1/2 cup red wine
1/2 cup butter • 1 sliced onion • assorted hot, cooked vegetables
1 cup beef bouillon • 1 tablespoon potato flour

Soak meat for at least 2 hours in a marinade made with garlic salt, salt, pepper and 1/4 cup of the wine. Remove from marinade and wipe dry. Two hours before serving time, melt butter in a roasting pan and brown meat on all sides. Bake in a 375° oven, basting from time to time with the marinade and allowing about 20 minutes cooking time for each pound for well-done beef. For rare, reduce cooking time by half. When beef is roasted to your taste, remove from roasting pan, slice and arrrange on a platter with an assortment of hot buttered vegetables. Make a pan gravy by browning onion in the drippings and adding bouillon and the rest of the wine. Bring to boil and thicken, if desired, with potato flour. Check seasoning and serve in a gravy boat accompanying the meat.

VARIATIONS: Add lemon juice, parsley, and sweet marjoram to marinade or make small incisions with a sharp knife (not deep enough to break the slices when cut) and stuff small pieces of bacon in the cavities, then follow recipe.

Steaks Cooked in Beer
Bifes com Cerveja

1 pound sirloin steak, sliced 1/2 inch thick and cut in strips as for Stroganoff
1 tablespoon butter • seasoning • 1 cup light beer • 1/2 cup sliced onions
1 tablespoon tomato paste • 1/2 tablespoon all-purpose flour

Sauté meat in butter and add salt and pepper to taste. Let stand. Mix beer, onions, tomato paste and flour and let stand 2 hours. Place beef in a buttered casserole and pour beer mixture on top. Cover and bake in a 375° oven for 30 minutes, then remove cover and continue baking for another 15 or 20 minutes to thicken the gravy.

[TRANSLATED FROM: **AS RECEITAS PARA VOCÊ DA TIA EVELINA, 4TH EDITION**]

Steaks in Milk Gravy
Bifes com Molho de Leite

8 or 9 tender steaks • salt • 1 tablespoon butter • 1/4 cup port wine • 1/2 cup water
1/4 teaspoon dry mustard • 1/2 cup milk • cornstarch

Sprinkle steaks with salt on both sides. Melt butter in frying pan and brown steaks on both slides. Add the wine, water, mustard and milk. Reduce heat and simmer until steaks are very tender. Remove steaks and thicken the gravy with a little cornstarch.

[LAURITA PIRES, MINAS GERAIS]

Roast Meat for Salad
Carne Assada em Salada

1 teaspoon salt • 2 chopped onions • 3 chopped tomatoes • 1 chopped spring onion
1/4 cup chopped parsley • 1 stick of cinnamon • 1 cup rosé wine • 1 cup dry white wine
juice of 1 lemon • 2 tablespoons olive oil • 1 tablespoon butter • 1/2 teaspoon sugar
4 pound rump of beef • about 2 cups consommé

Make a marinade with salt, onions, tomatoes, spring onion, parsley, cinnamon, the 2 wines, lemon juice and oil. Marinate the meat for at least 2 hours, turning occasionally. Melt butter in a large skillet with the sugar. Remove meat from the marinade and sauté on all sides. Add the marinade, cover the skillet and cook over low heat, adding consommé as required. When meat is cooked, allow to cool in the uncovered skillet until it is cold. Then, remove from the sauce and wrap in aluminum foil. Refrigerate. Serve thinly sliced with a salad of grated carrots and apples and mayonnaise, which has been laced with a few drops of Tabasco sauce. The leftover gravy may be strained and thickened for use over vegetables or plain meats.

[TRANSLATED FROM: **RECEITAS CULINÁRIAS** BY MYRTHES PARANHOS]

Steak — Portuguese Style
Bifes à Portuguesa

6 tender portions of beef fillet or sirloin • pounded garlic clove mixed with salt
1/4 cup olive oil • 1 chopped tomato • 1 chopped onion • 1 chopped green pepper
6 boiled potatoes, sliced • 6 olives • toast

Season steaks with the pounded garlic and salt by rubbing both sides. Let stand 10 minutes. In a skillet, heat olive oil, add the tomato, onion and green pepper and sauté all together. When vegetables are cooked, add the steaks. Brown lightly on both sides, cover the skillet and cook over low heat until steaks are done. Remove steaks and keep warm. Add the potatoes and olives to the sautéed vegetables and heat. Serve the steaks on pieces of buttered toast or rounds of French bread that have been fried in oil. Surround with the vegetables.

[TRANSLATED FROM: **AS RECEITAS PARA VOCÊ DA TIA EVELINA, 4TH EDITION**]

Steaks with Vegetables
Bifes Empanados

1 pound of steaks cut from eye of the round or rump • 2 tablespoons lemon juice
1/2 teaspoon garlic salt • salt and pepper • bread crumbs • 1 lightly-beaten egg
olive oil • buttered cooked vegetables

Pound the steaks with a mallet and let stand 1 hour in a marinade made from lemon juice, garlic salt, salt and pepper. Turn steaks over from time to time. When ready to serve, bread each steak with the breadcrumbs, dip in the egg and again in the crumbs. Fry in the hot oil. Remove to serving platter and border with buttered vegetables. Garnish with thin slices of lemon topped with chopped parsley.

[TRANSLATION FROM: **NOÇÕES DE ARTE CULINÁRIA** BY MARIA THEREZA A. COSTA, SÃO PAULO]

Stewed Steaks
Bifes Ensopados

6 slices eye of the round, sliced 1/2 inch thick • salt • garlic • 1 sliced onion
4 sprigs of parsley • 1/4 cup vinegar • 2 tablespoons shortening
1/3 cup port wine • 1/2 cup water

Sprinkle both sides of the sliced meat with salt and rub with garlic. Let stand 30 minutes. Make a marinade of onion, parsley and vinegar, and soak meat about 2 hours, turning at least once so that both sides absorb the marinade evenly. Melt fat and fry meat on both sides. Remove onions and parsley from the marinade and fry with the meat, then pour on the marinade and wine. Cook in a covered skillet over medium heat for about 2 hours, adding water as necessary.

[NOEMI PRATES, MINAS GERAIS]

Stuffed Beef
Bifes Recheados

2 pounds round steak • garlic • salt • 1 package smoked sausages (12 ounces)
1 onion • 1 egg • 2 tablespoons shortening • 1/2 cup chopped onion
1 cup red wine • 2 tablespoons all-purpose flour • 1/4 cup water • seasoning

Have the butcher cut round steak as thinly as possible and then pound with a mallet. There should be at least 4 slices of steak. Rub with garlic and salt on both sides and cut in halves. Let stand. Grind sausage and onion in meat grinder or blender and add egg. Mix and pat on steaks. Roll up steaks (you now have 8) and tie each end and center. Melt shortening in a large skillet. Brown steak rolls on all sides. Add chopped onion, cover skillet and simmer 30 minutes turning steaks frequently. Add the wine, cover and cook over low heat until steaks are tender (about 40 minutes). Check seasoning. Mix flour and water and thicken gravy.

[TRANSLATED FROM: **NOÇÕES DE ARTE CULINÁRIA** BY MARIA THEREZA A. COSTA, SÃO PAULO]

Paçoca of Jerked Beef
Paçoca de Carne Seca

1 pound jerked beef • 2 tablespoons bacon fat • 1 tablespoon butter • 1 grated onion

salt • malagueta pepper • 1 1/2 cups toasted manioc meal or corn meal

Cut meat in regular-size pieces, trim off excess fat and wash well. Soak overnight in cold water. Next morning, hold under running cold water and dry on absorbent paper. Heat bacon fat and butter and sauté onion. When onion starts to brown, add pieces of meat and seasoning and cook over low flame. Stir with a fork, adding a few drops of boiling water from time to time, as liquid evaporates. When meat is brown and tender and almost dry, add salt and chopped pepper, and turn into a heavy mortar to be pounded until meat is shredded. (This may also be accomplished by grinding twice through the food chopper.) Add the manioc or corn meal, a little at a time, until mixture is of the consistency of bread crumbs. Serve immediately.

Ragout of Jerked Beef
Guisado de Carne Seca

1 pound lean jerked beef • 1 garlic clove • 1/2 bayleaf • 2 sprigs parsley
2 spring onions • 1 tablespoon butter • 1 large thinly-sliced onion
4 peeled, chopped tomatoes • 1 sliced green pepper • soup stock
salt and malagueta pepper • a few drops lemon juice

Trim excess fat and membrane from meat and scald in boiling water. Drain, cool and then soak in cold water until the following day. Change water and boil with garlic clove, bayleaf, parsley and spring onions until tender. Remove beef from the liquid and shred it or cut into small pieces. Discard the pot liquor. Melt butter in a skillet, add jerked beef and sauté until browned, and then add the sliced onion, tomatoes and the rounds of green pepper. Season with salt and pepper, and cook over low heat, adding a few drops of water or soup stock from time to time for the gravy. Cook until gravy is thick and meat is very tender. When ready to serve check seasoning and add a few drops of lemon juice. Serve hot with a vegetable purée.

VARIATION: Proceed as above, using only 2 tomatoes to have less gravy. Omit soup stock and lemon juice. When beef is tender, cover with 5 beaten eggs. Stir with a fork, as for scrambled eggs, until eggs are set. Correct seasoning and serve immediately with plain boiled rice.

Viennese Meat Torte
Torta de Viena

3 tablespoons butter • 2 peeled chopped tomatoes • 2 chopped onions
1/4 cup chopped parsley • 1/2 teaspoon salt • 1/4 teaspoon pepper
1 pound lean beefsteaks, cubed • 1/4 cup port wine • 1/2 pounds smoked link sausage
1 loaf French bread, small type used for Hero sandwiches • 1/2 cup milk
1 tablespoon sifted all-purpose flour • 1 cup consommé • 1/4 cup raisins
1/2 teaspoon grated nutmeg • 2 beaten eggs • grated Parmesan cheese

Melt butter and sauté tomatoes, onions, parsley, salt and pepper. Add the steaks and brown on both sides. Add wine, cover and stew the meat for about 1 hour, adding small amounts of water as the wine evaporates. When meat is tender, add the sliced sausages and put the mixture through a food chopper (meat, gravy and sausages). Soak the inside of the bread in milk and mash with a fork to make a mush. Dissolve flour in the consommé. Stir together ground meats, bread mush, raisins, nutmeg and consommé-flour mixture. Taste to check seasoning. Spoon into a 2-quart buttered Pyrex baking dish. Cover with the beaten eggs, sprinkle with cheese and bake in a 375° preheated oven 45 to 50 minutes. Serve immediately with Brazilian Rice and a good *Farofa*.

[TRANSLATED FROM: **RECEITAS CULINÁRIAS** BY MYRTHES PARANHOS]

VEAL
VITELA

Veal Cutlets No. 1
Costeletas de Vitela N° 1

6 portions veal cutlet • 1 tablespoon butter
1/2 cup meat broth or bouillon mixed with 1 teaspoon all-purpose flour
2 tablespoons lemon juice • 1 egg yolk

Fry cutlets in butter until brown on both sides and then add broth mixture and cook slowly for 5 minutes. Mix lemon juice with egg yolk and pour over meat. Stir and remove from heat.

Veal Cutlets No. 2
Costeletas de Vitela Nº 2

6 portions veal cutlets • 1/2 lemon • 1 garlic clove • salt • 1 tablespoon hot fat
2 chopped onions • 1 teaspoon all-purpose flour • 1 tablespoon tomato paste
1/2 cup Madeira wine

Rub both sides of cutlets with lemon juice and garlic and sprinkle with salt. Let stand 10 minutes then sauté in hot fat. When both sides of the cutlets are brown add the onions and sprinkle with flour. Mix tomato paste and wine, and pour over the meat. Cover skillet and cook over low heat. When veal is done, add a few stuffed olives and serve on toast with the gravy poured over the cutlets.

Veal Cutlets No. 3
Costeletas de Vitela Nº 3

8 portions veal cutlets • 4 tablespoons butter • 1/4 pound smoked sausage
1/4 pound liverwurst • 1/2 cup minced onions
1 cup stale cubed bread soaked in enough milk to make a mush
2 eggs • salt and pepper • grated Parmesan cheese

Fry cutlets on both sides in 1/2 the butter and keep warm over hot water. Make a dressing by chopping the sausage finely and mixing with the liverwurst. Fry in the other half of the butter with the minced onion. When mixture is cooked, remove from heat and cool. Add the soaked bread, eggs, salt and pepper to taste and heat over medium heat. Cook until mixture is thick enough to hold its shape. Arrange cutlets in a baking dish, cover each with a thick layer of dressing and grated cheese. Dot with butter and bake in a hot oven to brown the dressing. Serves 8.

[LAURITA PIRES, MINAS GERAIS]

Veal Loaf No. 1
Bolo de Vitela N° 1

3 ounces salt pork, diced • 2 pounds lean veal, ground
1 thick slice of bread, soaked in enough milk to make a mush • 4 eggs
1 tablespoon butter • salt • 1 or 2 crushed Tabasco peppers, or powdered cayenne pepper

Spread diced salt pork in the bottom of a roasting pan. Mix veal, bread, lightly beaten eggs, butter and seasoning. Shape like a French loaf of bread and place in roasting pan on top of the salt pork. Bake in a 350° oven for 1 hour. Serve cold, sliced on lettuce leaves.

[TRANSLATED FROM: **A ARTE DE COMER BEM** BY ROSA MARIA (MME. H. LEONARDOS)]

Veal Loaf No. 2
Bolo de Vitela N° 2

1 pound lean veal, ground • 6 ounces lean, smoked ham, ground
4 ounces liverwurst or paté de foie gras • 1 tablespoon bread crumbs
4 eggs, slightly beaten • 1 1/2 cups milk • 1/2 teaspoon powdered mustard
1 tablespoon Worcestershire sauce • 1 tablespoon butter
2 tablespoons drained Indian relish or chopped pickles • 1 tablespoon chopped parsley
6 or 7 stuffed olives • salt and pepper

Mix ground veal, ham and liverwurst with the bread crumbs. Add milk, mustard, Worcestershire sauce and butter to eggs, then combine with the meat mixture. Stir in Indian relish or pickles, parsley, and olives, then salt and pepper to taste. Turn into a buttered mould and bake in 375° oven for 1 hour, then raise heat to 400° for 15 or 20 minutes. Pour off all the liquid. Unmould and serve with hollandaise sauce or mayonnaise and garnished with sliced apples or grapes and raisins.

[SARITA BRANT, MINAS GERAIS]

Veal Steak with Orange Sauce
Vitela com Molho de Laranja

*1 large veal cuttlet, about 2 inches thick • salt and pepper • 1 tablespoon butter
1 minced onion • 1 peeled and chopped tomato or 2 tablespoons tomato sauce
1 chopped green pepper • 1 cup orange juice*

Rub salt and pepper on veal and brown in hot butter. Add onion, tomato or tomato sauce and chopped pepper and sauté. Cover with orange juice and cook over low heat in a covered skillet or saucepan, adding more orange juice, if necessary, until meat is cooked. Remove meat, thicken sauce and strain over meat and serve.

[REPRINTED FROM AUTHOR'S ARTICLE IN JULY 1963 ISSUE OF **GOURMET MAGAZINE**]

Stuffed Veal
Vitela Recheada

*5 pound veal roast, rump or leg • uncooked prunes • 1 tablespoon butter
1 grated onion • 1/2 teaspoon salt • 1 tablespoon tomato paste • 1 cup wine, red or white*

Make several small incisions in meat and stuff with prunes, reserving pits and fibers clinging to them. Melt butter in a large saucepan and sear the meat, turning several times. Mix grated onion, salt, tomato paste and wine, and add to browned meat. Also add the prune pits and 3 or 4 whole prunes. Cover and cook over low heat until meat is done. When cooked, remove from saucepan and strain the gravy.

[LAURITA PIRES, MINAS GERAIS]

Pot Roast of Veal
Vitela Assada

5 or 6 pounds rump or leg of veal • 1 minced garlic clove • 1 minced onion
2 tablespoons chopped parsley • salt and pepper • 1/4 cup cider or tarragon vinegar
1/2 cup white wine • 1 tablespoon shortening • 1 grated carrot • 2 chopped onions
2 egg yolks • 1 tablespoon butter

Make a marinade of garlic, onion, parsley, salt and pepper, vinegar and wine, and soak meat overnight, turning at least once. Next day, brown meat in the shortening and, when brown, add the carrot and onions and leftover marinade. Cover and cook over low heat. When meat is tender, remove from pot and strain the gravy. If there is not enough liquid to make a gravy, add a chicken bouillon cube dissolved in 1 cup hot water. Add egg yolks and the butter, and heat. Slice the meat and serve with hot gravy poured over it.

LAMB

CARNEIRO

Roast Leg of Lamb
Perna de Carneiro Assada

1 8-pound leg of lamb • salt and black pepper • 2 cups dry white wine
1 crushed malagueta pepper • garlic salt • chopped mint • 1/4 cup chopped parsley
1 grated onion • 4 slices bacon

Clean and trim lamb and remove the fell or have the butcher do it. Make several incisions with a sharp knife and rub with salt and black pepper. Let stand overnight in a marinade made with half the wine (1 cup), malagueta pepper, garlic salt, mint, parsley and grated onion. Turn 2 or 3 times. Next day, strain the marinade and remove lamb to a buttered roasting pan. Cover with the bacon strips and bake in a preheated 375° oven until brown. Reduce temperature to 325°, cover with the marinade and roast, allowing 30 minutes per pound, basting frequently with the drippings and remaining cup of wine. Serve with cooked white beans, a vegetable, and the thickened pan gravy.

V A R I A T I O N : When lamb has been completely roasted, brush with lightly-beaten egg yolk, sprinkle generously with bread crumbs and return to oven to brown.

Shoulder Lamb Chops
Costeletas de Carneiro

6 shoulder lamb chops • 1/2 pounded garlic clove • 1/4 teaspoon salt • black pepper
1/2 cup vinegar • 2 tablespoons chopped parsley • 1 bayleaf • 1/2 chopped onion
1 cup white wine • butter for frying chops • 3 tablespoons cream

Make a marinade of the garlic, salt, pepper, parsley, bayleaf, onion, wine and vinegar, and let the chops marinate for 2 hours. Remove from marinade, brown both sides in butter. Strain marinade on top of chops, reduce heat and simmer until part of the liquid evaporates. Remove chops to serving platter, add cream and prepare a pan gravy. Pour over the chops.

Stuffed Leg of Lamb
Perna de Carneiro Recheada

1 leg of lamb with bone and fell removed • 1/2 recipe for vinha d'alho
2 tablespoons butter • 1 minced onion • 3 cups leftover cooked pork, chicken or veal, chopped
3 chopped truffles • 2 hard-boiled eggs • 3 chopped pitted olives • salt and pepper
3 or 4 slices bacon • 1 peeled onion with a garlic clove inserted in the center
1 cup chicken stock

Wash lamb and wipe dry. Marinate overnight in the *vinha d'alho*. Prepare stuffing by melting butter and sautéing minced onion, chopped meat and truffles. Add chopped eggs, olives and season to taste. Remove lamb from marinate and reserve marinade. Stuff the leg cavity, and sew or truss. Place in a roasting pan, cover with bacon and set the stuffed onion in the pan. Roast in a slow oven (300°-325°F), allowing 30-35 minutes per pound, or until a roasting thermometer registers 175°-180°. Baste with a mixture of the strained marinade added to the stock. When lamb is baked, remove stuffed onion, discard and make a pan gravy with the drippings.

[TRANSLATED FROM: **NOÇÕES DE ARTE CULINÁRIA** BY MARIA THEREZA A. COSTA]

Roast Fresh Ham No. 1
Pernil de Porco Nº 1

1 small fresh ham • 2 large spring onions • 1 small hot pepper
3 tablespoons chopped parsley • 1 teaspoon salt • 1/2 cup vinegar
1 cup wine, red or white • 2 tablespoons fat

Remove rind from ham and make small incisions about 2 inches deep all over the ham. Grind spring onions, using heads and some of the tender green stems, together with the hot pepper and add the parsley. Add salt, vinegar and wine and let stand about 10 minutes. Strain the marinade and stuff the vegetables in the incisions. Let the ham soak in the marinade for about 4 hours, turning occasionally. Remove from liquid, place in a roasting pan with the melted fat and sear in a 400° oven turning until the ham is delicately browned on both sides. Reduce heat to 375° and baste with the marinade, until pork is roasted, allowing 25 minutes per pound. Serve with slices of lemon and a *Farofa*.

[LAURITA PIRES, MINAS GERAIS]

Roast Fresh Ham No. 2
Pernil de Porco N° 2 [8]

1 fresh ham (10 to 12 pounds) • 3 cups muscatel wine • 2 tablespoons salt
1/2 teaspoon oregano • 1/2 teaspoon black pepper • 1 bayleaf • 1/4 cup olive oil
1 can (2 or 3 ounces) paté de foie gras • 1 1/2 cups apple sauce, seasoned to taste with
sugar, ground cloves and cinnamon • sliced mozzarella cheese • 1 cup cream
1 tablespoon lemon juice

Marinate ham overnight in a mixture of wine, salt, oregano, pepper and bayleaf. Next day, wipe and rub with oil. Bake in a 350° oven, allowing 30 minutes to the pound or until meat thermometer reaches 185°. Baste frequently with drippings. When ham is cooked, drain off excess fat and cut thick slices across the bone, but do not remove them. Spread each slice with a layer of paté, some of the apple sauce and a slice of cheese. Return to a 375° oven for 5-10 minutes, then pour over the cream, which has been mixed with the lemon juice, and bake another 10 minutes, basting frequently. Serve accompanied by rice, a *Farofa* and bean salad.

---

[8] This recipe was given to me by Senhora Flavia Chermont Ararigboia, wife of Brigadier Armando de Souza e Mello Ararigboia, who served twice as Air Attache of Brazil in Washington. Sra. Ararigboia, in turn, received the recipe from Senhora Marina Hartz of Rio de Janeiro.

Pork Chops
Costeletas de Porco

6 lean pork chops • 1/4 cup lemon juice • 1 bayleaf • 1/4 teaspoon garlic salt
1 chopped onion • 1/4 cup chopped parsley • 2 chopped tomatoes • 2 tablespoons olive oil
salt and black pepper • 1/4 of a malagueta pepper • 3 tablespoons butter

Trim chops and wipe with absorbent paper. Liquify next 9 ingredients, pour over chops, and marinate them for 1 hour, turning the chops occasionally. Melt butter and fry chops on both sides. Remove to serving platter and make a pan gravy by mixing rest of the marinade with drippings and adding a little water. Boil, pour over chops and serve with Butter Farofa, p. 50.

Brazilian Roat Stuffed Suckling Pig
Leitão Recheado

1 1/2 cloves garlic, pounded into a paste • 1 1/2 tablespoons salt
1 1/2 teaspoons black pepper • 1 tablespoon whole cloves • 2 bayleaves • 2 cups vinegar
2 cups red wine • 1 teaspoon cumin seeds • 1 suckling pig (reserve and chop heart,
kidneys and liver) • 1/2 pound sliced bacon (reserve 6 or 7 slices, chop up the rest)
1 cup smoked sausages, chopped • 1 onion, chopped • 1 tablespoon chopped parsley
2 tablespoons chopped scallions • 3 cups manioc meal (or Farina or Cream of Wheat)
2 hard-boiled eggs, chopped • 1 cup whole pitted or stuffed olives

Remove 1/3 of the garlic paste and reserve. With the other 2/3 make a marinade by adding salt, pepper, cloves, bayleaves, vinegar and wine. Pour over the pig and marinate for 24 hours, turning it over occasionally in order to thoroughly soak in the marinade.

Make the stuffing by frying chopped bacon, ham and sausages with reserved garlic paste and the piglet's liver, kidneys and heart all very well chopped. Brown, stirring continuously and adding small amounts of water until all meats are cooked and tender. Add onion and parsley and scallions, and continue to fry until well-browned. Gradually add the manioc meal, stirring constantly until mixture is thoroughly blended. Remove from heat and add the eggs and olives. Taste and season accordingly. Stuff the piglet with this mixture and lace it up. Place in roaster, cover with the bacon strips and bake in preheated 400° oven for 20 minutes, then lower to 350° and bake 35 minutes for each pound. Baste several times with the strained marinade.

When nearly done, slide from oven and puncture skin with a fork, especially under the legs, in order to produce a crisp and crackling overall effect.

N O T E : Roasting on a spit is always preferable to the oven. If this method is available, omit the bacon strips and baste with cooking oil, the latter being used in preference to any other fat, owing to the greater crispness it gives to the skin of the suckling pig.

Pork Madrilena
Carne de Porco Madrilena

1 pound coarsely-ground or chopped lean pork • 1/2 tablespoon shortening
1/2 cup minced onion • 1/4 cup chopped parsley • 1/2 cup tomato sauce
1 cup water • salt, black pepper, cayenne pepper
rosemary or sage (optional) • 6 sliced olives or 12 to 15 seedless raisins

Brown pork in shortening with onion. Add parsley, tomato sauce, water and seasoning to taste. Bring to boil, reduce heat to low and cook until pork is done and most of the liquid has evaporated. This takes about 25 minutes. Check seasoning, add raisins or olives. At this stage, the meat should be just moist as most of the liquid has evaporated. Let stand while you prepare the white sauce.

WHITE SAUCE *(Molho Branco)*:

1 tablespoon grated onion • 1 tablespoon butter • 1 1/2 tablespoons all-purpose flour
2 cups milk • salt and pepper

Sauté onion in butter and flour. When flour is browned, gradually add the milk to make a medium white sauce. This takes about 20 minutes. Season to taste. Turn the meat into a 9-inch Pyrex pie plate, cover with the sauce and bake in a preheated 375° oven 40 to 45 minutes or until top browns.

[OTTILIA JANSEN DE MELLO, MINAS GERAIS]

Roast Loin of Pork with Prunes
Lombo de Porco com Ameixas

6 pound loin of pork, boned and rolled • 1 cup white wine • 1 tablespoon lemon juice
salt • black pepper • 1 pounded garlic clove • 1 bay leaf • sliced onions
1 pound extra large prunes, semi-cooked, with pits removed

Make a marinade of 1/2 cup of wine, lemon juice, salt, pepper, pounded garlic clove and bayleaf and marinate pork overnight. Next day, remove from marinade and set in roasting pan over a layer of sliced onions. Bake in 375° oven, allowing 20 minutes per pound and basting with some of the marinade. When meat is done, remove from baking pan, drain off all the grease and to the remaining drippings add 1/2 cup water, the rest of the marinade and 1/2 cup wine. Cook gravy and thicken if desired. Pile prunes in the center of the dish. Slice the pork and arrange around the prunes. Serve gravy separately.

[OTTILIA JANSEN DE MELLO, MINAS GERAIS]

Stuffed Loin of Pork
Lombo de Porco Recheado

6 pounds boned loin of pork • 1/2 recipe for Vinha d'Alho (see Brazilian Turkey recipe p. 470)
5 eggs • 3 tablespoons butter • 1 can deviled ham • 1 cup bread soaked with milk
3 or 4 chopped olives • 1/3 teaspoon rosemary • salt and pepper • white wine

Marinate the pork overnight in the *vinha d'alho* and, next day, cut meat lengthwise through the center. Make a cavity in the centers of each half by removing some of the meat. Grind and sauté the meat that was removed. Make an omelet with eggs and butter, and cut into small pieces. Add deviled ham, sautéed meat, milk-moistened bread, chopped olives, rosemary and season to taste. Fill the cavities of the pork with the dressing and tie together tightly so that none of the dressing can escape. Place roast in a baking dish, bake in 350° oven, basting with leftover *vinha d'alho* or white wine until done. Excellent when served cold, in slices, but may also be served hot.

[TRANSLATED FROM: **NOÇÕES DE ARTE CULINÁRIA** BY MARIA THEREZA A. COSTA]

Fresh Tongue
Língua Fresca

1 fresh tongue, large • 2 or 3 slices bacon • 1 tablespoon butter • 1 chopped onion
2 tablespoons chopped parsley • garlic salt • 3 chopped tomatoes
1 1/2 cups white wine • Salt and pepper

Wash tongue, cover with cold water and 1 tablespoon salt. Bring to a boil, then reduce heat to simmer and cover. Simmer until tongue is so tender that skin can easily be removed (from 2 to 4 hours, according to size of tongue). When tongue is cooked, place in cold water for a few minutes, drain and remove skin and bones at base of the tongue. Make small incisions in tongue and stuff with bits of bacon. Melt butter, sauté onion, parsley and garlic salt, then add the tomatoes. When tomatoes are cooked, add the wine and salt and pepper to taste and bring to boil. Place tongue in a buttered baking pan, cover with the sauce and bake at 375° for 1 hour, basting frequently with the drippings and adding more wine, if necessary. Remove tongue, slice and arrange on serving platter. Bring the drippings to a boil, correct seasoning and strain over tongue. Serve with mashed potatoes and asparagus.

VARIATIONS: **1.** Slice boiled tongue, dip in lightly beaten egg, then in bread crumbs and again in egg. Fry in hot oil. **2.** Serve chilled with a sharp mayonnaise.

Leftovers
Sobras

1 pound leftover cooked roast • 1 tablespoon butter • 1 large onion, thinly sliced
1 tablespoon all-purpose flour • 1/2 cup port wine • 1/2 cup meat broth • seasoning

Shred the cooked meat. Melt butter and brown onion. When onion is brown, add the flour and stir until flour browns. Gradually pour in the wine and stir, then add the broth. Add the shredded meat, season to taste and heat very well. Serve with Brazilian Rice (p. 131) or Angu (p. 53).

Liver No. 1
Fígado Nº 1

4 slices beef liver, from which membranes have been removed
juice of 1 lemon (less 1/2 teaspoonful) • 1/2 teaspoon salt • black pepper
3/4 cup water • 2 tablespoons hot bacon fat or butter • 2 or 3 sliced onions
1/4 cup chopped parsley • the reserved 1/2 teaspoon of lemon juice
4 boiled potatoes, cut in quarters

After membranes and tubes have been removed from liver, wipe with a damp cloth and marinate for 1 hour in the lemon juice, salt and pepper, turning after 30 minutes so that both sides of the liver are equally seasoned. Fry both sides in the hot fat and, when brown, remove to a platter to keep warm. Add onions and parsley and the reserved 1/2 teaspoon of lemon juice to the fat. When onions are fried, add the water and bring to a boil. Mix in the potatoes, heat thoroughly and season to taste with salt and pepper. Spoon the potatoes around the liver on the platter. Garnish with sliced tomatoes and olives. Serves 4.

Liver No. 2
Fígado Nº 2

5 slices beef or calf's liver • 1 tablespoon oil • 1/4 teaspoon salt • 1 sliced onion
2 tablespoons tomato sauce • 1 chopped green pepper • 1/4 cup Madeira wine

Coat liver in a mixture of the oil and salt. Pour the rest of the oil and salt mixture in the skillet, heat and brown liver on both sides, add onion, tomato sauce and green pepper, and cook over low flame until vegetables and liver are done. When ready to serve, add the wine. Check seasoning and serve with boiled potatoes. If gravy is to be strained, do not strain the green pepper, but leave it in the gravy. Serves 5.

[SARITA BRANT, MINAS GERAIS]

Liver and Ham Croquettes
Croquetes de Fígado e Presunto

1 pound calves' liver • 1 pounded garlic clove • 1/2 cup parsley • 1/2 teaspoon salt
1 cup chopped onion • 1 1/2 cups water • 1/2 pound cooked ham
1 ounce cut-up bacon • 1/2 chopped Tabasco pepper • 1 teaspoon cornstarch
1/2 cup milk • 1/2 teaspoon vinegar • 1 egg yolk • bread crumbs
1 beaten egg • oil for frying

Remove membranes and tubes from liver and wipe dry with a damp cloth. Cut into small pieces, and pounded garlic, parsley, salt and pepper, 1/2 cup of the onion, and the water. Bring to a boil, cover and stew the liver until it is tender and most of the gravy has evaporated, removing the cover towards the end of the cooking. Grind the stewed liver with the gravy and ham in a meat grinder. Fry bacon in a skillet and, when rendered, remove and sauté the other 1/2 cup chopped onion and the pepper in the drippings. Add the ground mixture to the skillet and combine thoroughly. Stir the cornstarch into the milk and pour into the skillet, cooking over low heat and stirring for about 5 minutes. Add vinegar to the egg yolk and stir into the mixture, then remove from heat and adjust seasoning. Turn onto a shallow platter to cool, then chill in refrigerator. Shape into croquettes, roll in bread crumbs, then in beaten egg and again in crumbs. Fry in deep fat or oil at 375°. Serve with a mustard sauce made by adding prepared mustard to 1 cup of heavy white sauce. Yields 12 croquettes.

Carioca Meat Loaf
Bolo de Carne Carioca

1 pound lean beef, ground • 1/2 pound lean veal, ground • 1/2 cup chopped onion
1/2 teaspoon ground coriander seed • 1 1/2 teaspoons salt • 1/2 teaspoon cayenne pepper
1/4 cup chopped olives • 2 slightly-beaten eggs • 1/2 teaspoon Angostura bitters
1 teaspoon Worcestershire sauce • 3/4 cup stout beer • 1/2 cup bread crumbs
2 sliced hardboiled eggs • 1 thin slice bacon • the full recipe for Madeira Wine Sauce, p. 57

Combine first 7 ingredients. Mix lightly-beaten eggs with bitters, Worcestershire sauce and beer, and stir into meat mixture. Knead in the bread crumbs and hard-boiled eggs. Cover and refrigerate about 1 hour. Taste to check seasonings. Press into a slightly-buttered loaf pan. Cut the strip of bacon into 4 or 5 pieces and place on top of loaf. Bake in a preheated 375° oven for 15 minutes, then reduce heat to 350° and bake 1 more hour. Unmould onto serving plate, cut into 6 slices and cover with the Madeira Wine Sauce. Serve accompanied with French fried onion rings and grilled tomatoes.

[GLADYS MARIE SILVA, MATO GROSSO]

Tripe
Dobradinha

1 pound tripe • 3 tablespoons butter • 1 grated onion • 1 crushed garlic clove
1 cup tomato sauce • 1 bay leaf • 2 tablespoons minced parsley
1 chopped sweet red pepper • salt and black pepper • 2 cups beef broth
6-8 slices buttered toast • 6-8 slices Swiss cheese
grated Parmesan cheese • black olives

Thoroughly wash tripe, then simmer in salted water for 2 hours or until very tender. Drain and wipe dry. Melt butter in a skillet, add onion and garlic and, when slightly yellow, pour in the tomato sauce with bayleaf and parsley. Cook well and then add the cut-up tripe and chopped red pepper. Continue cooking, add salt and pepper to taste, and the broth. Cover skillet and simmer until sauce thickens and tripe is cooked. Arrange pieces of toast in a shallow baking dish and cover each with a piece of cheese. Spoon tripe over the cheese. Dot with butter, sprinkle with Parmesan cheese and brown in oven. Garnish with olives.

VARIATION: Add 2 cups uncooked okra with the broth and continue to cook.

Stuffed Beef or Calf Heart
Coração Recheado

1 calf or beef heart with a pocket for dressing • 1/2 teaspoon garlic salt • 1 teaspoon salt
1/3 cup Burgundy wine • black pepper • 1 tablespoon chopped parsley
1 tablespoon lemon juice • 1/2 recipe for Corn Bread Stuffing, p. 61
1/4 cup melted butter • 1 very thinly-sliced onion • 1 cup Madeira wine
1/2 cup beef stock • seasoning

Remove fat, arteries and veins from the heart. Rinse in cold water and pat dry with absorbent paper. Mix garlic salt and salt, and rub surface of the heart. Make a marinade from the Burgundy, black pepper, parsley and lemon juice and marinate the heart for 2 or 3 hours, turning once. Remove heart from marinade and reserve marinade for basting. Fill the cavity of the heart with stuffing and sew edges together or fasten securely with skewers. Place stuffed heart into a casserole baking dish that can be covered and pour melted butter on top. Brown in oven, uncovered, on all sides. Cover and bake in a 350° oven for about 3 hours, basting frequently with the leftover marinade until it is all used. About 1 hour before cooking time is up, add onion, Madeira and beef stock. Cover and continue to bake until fork tender. To serve, remove stitches from heart and slice crosswise to include dressing. Taste gravy and correct seasoning. Heat, pour into gravy boat to accompany sliced heart.

Meat Loaf
Bolo de Carne

1 pound leftover pork roast • 1/4 pound boiled ham or smoked sausage
1 cup cubed stale bread • 1/2 cup gravy or stock • 1/3 cup grated Parmesan cheese
3/4 cup cream or evaporated milk • 1 tablespoon Worcestershire sauce
1/4 cup port wine • 1/4 cup seedless raisins • salt and pepper to taste • 3 eggs, well beaten

Grind the pork and ham in meat grinder and soak the bread in the gravy. Press the gravy bread through a coarse sieve and add cheese, cream or evaporated milk, Worcestershire sauce, wine and raisins. Then add to the meat. Season to taste. Add beaten eggs and pour into a well-buttered casserole. Bake in a preheated 375° oven for 1 hour. Let cool slightly, loosen edges and turn onto serving plate. If desired, sprinkle top with a mixture of bread crumbs and cheese and serve with tomato sauce. May also be served cold with a salad. Serves 5.

Veal Kidneys
Rim de Vitela

2 veal kidneys • 2 tablespoons olive oil • 1/4 teaspoon salt • garlic salt • 1 chopped onion
2 tablespoon tomato sauce • pepper • 1/4 cup sherry wine

Open kidneys, remove membranes and fat. Wash well and soak in cold, salted water for 30 minutes. Remove from water, drain on absorbent paper and moisten each side with oil and salt mixed together. Scrape remaining oil mixture into skillet and heat. Slice the kidneys and sauté in the hot oil, browning on both sides. When brown, reduce heat and sprinkle with garlic salt. Remove skillet from heat, add onion, tomato sauce and pepper. Cook over low heat with a cover until vegetables are done. Add salt and pepper to taste and, just before serving, mix in the sherry wine.

Stewed Lamb Kidneys
Rins de Carneiro Ensopados

8 lamb kidneys • garlic salt • 1 tablespoon lemon juice • 2 strips bacon
1/4 cup chopped onions • 1/4 cup chopped parsley • 2 tablespoons chopped green pepper
1 peeled and chopped tomato • Tabasco sauce • 1 cup water
1 large potato, grated • salt and pepper

Open kidneys, remove membranes, wash and soak in cold, salted water for 15 minutes. Drain, wipe dry, cut in halves and season with garlic salt and lemon juice. Gently render bacon, add onions, parsley, kidneys and green pepper. Sauté, and when kidneys are browned, add chopped tomato and a few drops of the Tabasco. Mix, add water and grated potato, cover and simmer for about 20 minutes. As liquid begins to evaporate, add another 1/2 cup of water. Season to taste with salt and pepper.

[NINI MACHADO, SÃO PAULO]

Oxtails
Rabada

2 oxtails • 1 garlic clove crushed with salt • 1/4 cup lemon juice • 1 cup red wine
1/2 cup olive oil • 1 cup sliced onions • 3 peeled, chopped tomatoes
2 tablespoons chopped parsley • 1/8 teaspoon black pepper • beef broth

Have the butcher cut oxtails at the joints. Wash, cover with cold water and bring to a rapid boil. After 10 minutes, remove from water, dry and cover with a marinade made from garlic, lemon juice and wine. Let stand 3 or 4 hours, turning several times. Remove from marinade and brown in the hot olive oil with the onions. When onions begin to fry, add tomatoes, parsley and pepper and gently fry mixture for 20 minutes, stirring and turning over the pieces of oxtail. Remove excess fat. Pour leftover marinade on the mixture of oxtail and vegetables, and cover the skillet. Simmer for around 4 hours or until meat is tender. As liquid evaporates, replace it with canned consommé or a bouillon cube dissolved in 1 cup of hot water, so that the oxtails will always be cooking in a sauce. Check seasoning. Serve with Cornmeal Mush (p. 53) and plain white rice.

N O T E : If a pressure cooker is used, cooking time can be cut in half and no extra liquid need be added.

Sarapatel from the Northeast

Tripe, liver and heart from a pig • 1 lemon, cut in half • pounded garlic mixed with salt
coriander powder • chopped onion • chopped parsley • Bayleaf • black pepper
cumin powder • pinch of ground cloves • fresh pig blood • malagueta pepper

Rinse tripe and giblets very well several times then rub surfaces with the lemon. Boil in salted water until tender, about 2 hours. Remove from water and chop or mince. Pound the garlic in a mortar with salt, coriander, onion, parsley, bayleaf, black pepper, cumin and ground cloves and mix thoroughly with the tripe and giblets and about 1/4 cup of the blood. Simmer over low heat, adding small quantities of hot water when necessary until well cooked. Before removing from heat, add pounded malagueta pepper. Serve with Brazilian Rice (p. 131) and Pepper and Lemon Sauce (p. 91).

[TRANSCRIBED FROM: **CADERNO DE ZANGÔ** BY SODRÉ VIANNA]

Old Clothes
Roupa-velha

5 cups leftover cooked meat, preferably beef • 1 tablespoon fat or oil • 1 thinly-sliced onion
1 sliced fresh tomato • 1 tablespoon chopped parsley • 2 tablespoons vinegar
salt and pepper • Tabasco (optional)

Only meat that is grainy should be used. Pull the cooked meat apart and shred it. Fry in the fat with the onion, tomato and parsley. When brown, add the vinegar. Cover, cook 5 or 6 minutes, then season to taste with salt and pepper and Tabasco, if desired. It may be necessary to add water and steam the mixture, but the water should only be enough to moisten.

N O T E : In order to prepare this dish, it is necessary that the meat be stringy enough to pull into shreds.

[TRANSLATED FROM: **NOÇÕES DE ARTE CULINÁRIA** BY MARIA THEREZA A. COSTA, SÃO PAULO]

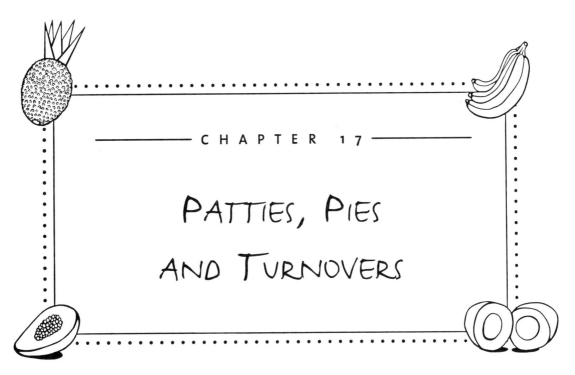

CHAPTER 17

PATTIES, PIES AND TURNOVERS

The discovery of a new dish does more for the happiness
of Man than the discovery of a new star.

BRILLAT-SAVARIN, THE PHYSIOLOGY OF TASTE

he great French philosopher and gourmet must have been thinking of something like empadas and pastéis when he penned these words. Certainly, being alive when a new star is discovered can be very exciting to an accomplished epicure, but the discovery of a new dish gives much more pleasure, especially if that "new" dish is one of the delicious patties node of meat, fish, fowl or chesse that have been a part of Brazilian fare for many years.

Pastéis and *Empadas* form part of that tasty and ofttimes ingenious group of Brazilian foodstuffs known as *salgadinhos.*[1] Today, they are as indigenous to Brazil as coffee, but it was the Portuguese who first brought them to Brazil. An old Portuguese cookbook, printed in 1692, gives recipes for 48 different *Empadas,* 26 *Pastéis* and 14 *Pasteizinhos.*[2] They have now been adapted to use the more abundant raw materials found in Brazil, and have attained great prominence in the foodfare of that country. Every visitor who leaves this great neighbor to the South remembers with a nostalgic longing or *saudades* the piquant taste of these delectable adjuncts to a culinary life worth living.

The finest assortment to be found anywhere in Brazil is at the Confeitaria Colombo in Rio de Janeiro. There, you may walk in from the street and hurriedly eat two or three standing. If time is not of the essence, one may take a table in the tearoom, order a pot of tea or a beer and an assortment of *Salgadinhos* and leisurely take a gourmet's delight in sampling these tasty concoctions, which one would do well to duplicate.

---

[1] Literally, the word means "little salties" and it is used to define appetizers or foods made into small shapes that can be eaten with the fingers.
[2] The book, written by Rodrigues Domingos, Master Cook to His Majesty, was printed in Lisbon in 1692.

The evolution of the *Salgadinho* — especially that of the *pastel* — has been masterfully developed and perfected by the cooks of Brazil. Thirty years ago, the dough for the *Pastel* was made of flour, shortening, water and eggs, while the fillings were meat or shrimp and, on rare occasions, chicken. The *Pastel* was always fried. Today, the dough may have cheese incorporated into it, or mashed potatoes, and the flours used are of a great variety. The *Pastel* may be baked or fried and some are boiled, like ravioli and served with a sauce. A variety of fillings have been devised to make them more tasty. In short, the *pastel* has come of age!

This makes me very happy because I *like Pastéis*, and in using the word *like* I mean that I really entertain great concern for their fate. *Pastéis* and *Empadinhas* were one of my first loves of the Brazilian table. I would be sad indeed, were they to disappear, as sometimes certain dishes do go out of style.

But I am confident this will never come about, for they are just as popular now as when Rodrigues handed down his first recipes in 1692. Certainly, as long as the Portuguese language and heritage prevail in Brazil, and as long as a Confeitaria Colombo exists in Rio de Janeiro, and its counterparts in other Brazilian cities, the appreciation and demand for these — my first loves of the Brazilian cuisine — will continue to be felt.

The Brazilian housewife also makes constant use of puff pastery and *vol-au-vent* dough. These recipes are not included in this book because, due to their international use, they are available in any good general cookbook.

The dough for *Empadas* is rich in shortening and eggs, while that of the *pastel* is more like a pie dough containing an egg or two. The same succulent filling may be used in both, but *Empadas* are always baked, while the *pastel* may be cooked by other processes.

Fillings are interchangeable, according to taste and they run the gamut from seafood, fowl, meat, cheese and vegetables to sweets. Often the filling is a combination of two or more of these items. Vegetables are used to great advantage, especially palm hearts, which in taste and appearance resemble white asparagus. Leftovers are also very well employed in preparing the fillings.

The convenient asset of these two formidable bulwarks of the Brazilian housewife is their versatility. They may be prepared bite size as appetizers for cocktail parties, in which case they are called *Empadinhas* and *Pasteizinhos*, or they may be made into individual servings to be passed around at meals. These are called *empadas* or *pastéis*.

Again, they may be made into family-sized dishes called *Empadão* or *Pastelão*. The *torta* resembles the turnover or pie because of the consistency of the dough used.

The recipes that follow, both for the dough or crust, as well as for the fillings, represent only a few used in Brazil.

THE PREPARATION OF "EMPADAS" AND "PASTÉIS" AND THEIR FILLINGS

1. As both may be eaten with the fingers, it is important that the fillings be thick enough to hold their shape.

2. Dough mixtures are always improved if they are allowed to stand an hour or so before rolling out or pressing into shape.

3. There are several sizes for the *Empadas* and special tins are made for the small ones. These are like muffin or cupcake tins, but each one is separate. If you are unable to obtain the special tins, try preparing them in ramekins, custard cups or timbale forms.

4. Round glass baking dishes may be used for the *Empadão*, but whenever glass is used, it is necessary to reduce the heat 25°.

5. *Empadas* are baked in a 375° oven, unless recipe states otherwise.

6. The process for making *Empadas* is to roll out the dough or press it into rounds in the palms of the hands and fit into the little tins. Press well against the sides of the tins, leaving a little dough hanging over the edges, and make several perforations with a fork to ensure smooth baking. Introduce the filling and make a cover to fit the top. Pinch under layer and cover together with the thumb and forefinger, and then dip fork into cold water and seal edges with the tines. Brush with egg yolk and bake in 375° oven, unless otherwise stated.

7. Allow to cool partially before attempting to remove from the tins, as the pastry is rich and crumbles easily. *Empadões* may be served from the dish in which they were baked.

8. *Pastel* dough is easier to work with since the pastry is not as rich as that used for *empadas*. After it has stood an hour or so, roll out on a floured board as thinly as possible and cut with round cookie cutter to size desired. Introduce filling to one side of the center. Fold over other side, press together with fingers, seal with tines of a fork dipped in cold water and proceed with the cooking as directed.

If a pastry cutter is used, roll the dough into larger rounds. Place the filling in three different mounds fold over edges to make three triangles and cut evenly with pastry cutter. Proceed with cooking as directed.

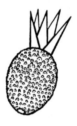

EMPADINHAS E EMPADAS

Cheese Patties
Empadinhas de Queijo

PASTRY (Massa)

2 tablespoons lard • 2 tablespoons butter • 1 cup sifted all-purpose flour
2 egg yolks • 1/2 teaspoon salt

Blend lard and butter with sifted flour, add egg yolks and salt, knead well and let stand 1 hour. Press dough out as thinly as possible and fit into individual tins that have been well buttered. Prick with the tines of a fork. Pour in the filling, but do not cover. Bake in a 400° oven for 20 minutes, then reduce heat to 350° and bake another 30 minutes. Yields approximately 1 dozen.

NOTE: These patties puff up during the baking and should be served at once, like a soufflé, otherwise they droop.

FILLING (Recheio)

1 cup Muenster cheese at room temperature, then slivered or mashed • 1 cup milk
1 tablespoon butter • 2 eggs • chopped ham, if desired • seasoning

Mix all ingredients very well and season.

[OLIVIA LODER, MINAS GERAIS]

427

Chicken Patties
Empadinhas de Galinha

PASTRY *(Massa)*

2 1/2 cups sifted all-purpose flour • 1/4 cup butter • 1/4 cup lard • 1/2 teaspoon salt
1/2 tablespoon water • 3 eggs yolks • approximately 1/4 cup milk

Place flour in a mixing bowl and add butter and lard that have been melted together. Into another bowl, dissolve the salt and water, then add egg yolks, saving a small amount of the yolk to brush on top of each patty before baking. Combine egg mixture with the flour mixture and blend in the milk — enough to make a pastry. Let stand 1 hour. Roll out as thinly as possible and cut with a cutter 1 inch larger than the tins. As this pastry is crumbly, it may be easier to shape each round in the palm of the hand. Press into small size individual muffin tins (or *empadinha* tins) and shape firmly around sides of tins and the bottoms. Fill 3/4 full with the filling. Add a piece of sliced hard-boiled egg and olive to each. Cover with a topping made of the pastry by cutting or by flattening pastry in the palm of the hand. Press sides and tops together and seal firmly by using the thumb and forefinger or with tines of a fork dipped in water. Brush each patty lightly with the reserved egg yolk and bake in 375° oven for 20 to 30 minutes. Yields approximately 12 small sized patties or 1 10-inch *empadão*.

CHICKEN FILLING *(Recheio de Galinha)*

4 medium chicken breasts • 1/2 the marinade used in Stewed Chicken (p. 468)
1 tablespoon margarine • 1/4 cup tomato sauce • 1/2 cup water
2 tablespoons all-purpose flour or cornstarch • 3 cups milk • 2 egg yolks • seasoning

Marinate chicken breasts overnight in the marinade prepared from first 10 items of the recipe for Stewed Chicken (p. 468) turning once. Next day, melt margarine in a large skillet and brown chicken on both sides. Cover and cook over medium heat for 10 minutes, then add the marinade and cook covered for 2 minutes. Add tomato sauce and water, recover and cook over medium heat until chicken is fork tender. This takes about 1 hour. Remove skin and bones, cut chicken into small cubes and put aside. Strain the sauce (which should be about 1/2 cup). Return sauce to the skillet and heat. Mix the flour or cornstarch with 1/2 cup of the milk and stir until smooth, then add to hot sauce and cook over low heat until sauce begins to thicken. Gradually, add the remaining 2 1/2 cups milk and continue to cook until mixture is of the consistency of a medium white sauce. Remove from heat. Stir egg yolks with a fork and mix with a little of the hot sauce, then pour back into saucepan and return to low heat. Cook, stirring for 4 or 5 minutes. Stir in the diced chicken, taste and correct seasonings. Yields 4 cups.

Cheese Pie
Empada de Queijo

PASTRY *(Massa)*

2 tablespoons lard • 2 tablespoons butter • 3 cups sifted all-purpose flour
2 egg yolks • 1/2 teaspoon salt • 1/2 cup milk

Blend lard and butter with sifted flour, add yolks, salt and milk, knead well and let stand 1 hour. Roll out and line a 10-inch Pyrex pie dish, leaving enough pastry on sides to flute edges. Pour in the filling and bake in a 400° oven for approximately 30 minutes. Serve in same dish.

FILLING *(Recheio)*

4 eggs • 2 cups grated Parmesan cheese • 1 cup milk • 2 tablespoons melted butter

Beat the eggs, add cheese, milk and butter. Season to taste.

[DAURA ALVES DA COSTA, RIO DE JANEIRO]

430

Shrimp Patties
Empadinhas de Camarão

PASTRY *(Massa):* Same as for Chicken Patties.

SHRIMP FILLING *(Recheio de Camarão)*

1 pound fresh shrimp • 1 1/2 tablespoons butter • 1 minced onion
2 tablespoons all-purpose flour • 1 cup milk • 2 eggs • 1 teaspoon tomato paste
salt and black pepper • cayenne pepper • sliced palm hearts (2 or 3)
5 or 6 stuffed olives • sliced hard-boiled eggs

Wash fresh shrimp very well and cook in a covered saucepan with 1 cup of cold water until water boils. Lower heat to medium and cook 5 minutes. Drain and reserve the liquor from the shrimp, which should be a scant cupful. Shell shrimp, devein and wash. Melt butter, brown the onion, and add shrimp liquor. Simmer for 10 minutes. Make a paste of the flour and some of the milk and gradually add rest of the milk. Mix shrimp liquor with the milk and heat over a low flame, stirring constantly. Beat eggs and pour in a little of the hot mixture, then add the rest of the hot liquid and cook about 3 minutes. Add tomato paste, strain into another saucepan. Mix in the cut up shrimp and slices of palm hearts and cook from 5 to 10 minutes longer until the mixture is thick enough to hold its shape. Season and remove from heat and cool. While the filling is cooling, line the *Empadinha* tins as for Chicken Patties. Fill 3/4 full with the cold filling, add a piece of sliced olive and hard-boiled egg and fit with a top made from the pastry. Seal edges by pressing with the tines of a fork dipped into cold water. Brush with egg yolk and bake like Chicken Patties.

Shrimp Pie No. 1
Tortão de Camarão

PASTRY (Massa)

2 egg yolks • 1/2 teaspoon salt • 2 tablespoons olive oil • 1 tablespoon butter
1 tablespoon lard • 2 tablespoons milk • sifted all-purpose flour (about 1 cup)

Mix the above ingredients well, then add the flour, enough to make a stiff dough that does not stick to the hands. Cover with a towel and let stand for 1 hour.

FILLING (Recheio)

1 pound fresh shrimp • 2 tablespoons lemon juice • salt and black pepper
2 white squashes • 4 tablespoons olive oil • 2 tablespoons butter • garlic salt
1 grated onion • 1/2 cup tomato sauce • 1 no. 2 can peas, drained
1/4 cup chopped olives • 1/2 cup chopped parsley
3 tablespoons all-purpose flour • 1 cup milk

Remove shells from shrimp, devein and clean. Cover with lemon juice, salt and pepper. Peel squash and cut into cubes. Heat oil and butter and sauté the garlic salt, onion and tomato sauce. Add shrimp and squash and fry all together. Cover and cook over a low flame, adding water only when necessary, just enough to make a little gravy. When cooked, add the peas, chopped olives and parsley and cook about 5 minutes more. Taste and correct seasonings. Mix flour and milk and strain into the shrimp. When mixture is as thick as heavy cream, remove from heat. Press out pastry dough with the hands and line a 2-quart glass baking dish. Save any scraps to garnish the top. Even off the edges of the pie shell by turning a little of the pastry back and fluting with the tines of a fork. Pour in the filling and cover with the following topping.

TOPPING

2 eggs • 2 tablespoons grated Parmesan cheese

Beat the eggs, add cheese and pour over the shrimp mixture. If any pastry is left, fashion a pinwheel from small strips or cut into fancy shapes. Arrange on top of the pie and bake in 375° oven for 30 minutes.

[HILDA LEITE QUEIROGA, MINAS GERAIS]

Shrimp Pie No. 2
Empadão de Camarão

PASTRY *(Massa)*

3 cups sifted all-purpose flour • 4 egg yolks • 1/2 teaspoon salt • 2 tablespoons lard
2 tablespoons butter • 3/4 cup milk

Sift flour into a bowl and make a well in the center. Add other ingredients and mix with fingers. Let stand 1 hour.

FILLING *(Recheio)*

1 pound fresh shrimp • 1 tablespoon olive oil • 1 chopped onion
1 tablespoon chopped parsley • 1 small can palm hearts • 3 tablespoons all-purpose flour
1 cup milk • 2 tablespoons tomato paste or ketchup
seasoning (salt, black pepper and Tabasco)

Remove shells from shrimp, devein and clean. Fry in oil with onion and parsley, then add the liquid from the can of palm hearts. Mix flour and milk and pour over the shrimp. Cook until mixture thickens, then add the tomato paste or ketchup and sliced palm hearts. Season with salt, black pepper and Tabasco. Line sides and bottom of a baking dish with the pressed out pastry. A round 10-inch casserole dish will do. Smooth out the pastry with finger tips, prick with a fork to ensure even baking and add the filling. If any pastry is left over, use to make fancy garnishes for the top of the pie. Sliced hard-boiled eggs may also be used. Bake in a 375° to 400° oven until crust is baked. Serve in the baking dish.

[ILKA RODRIGUES, RIO DE JANEIRO]

Manioc Pastry
Massa de Mandioca

1 pound manioc root (cassava root) • 2 tablespoons butter • 3/4 cup grated Muenster cheese
1 teaspoon salt • 3 beaten egg yolks • 2 tablespoons cornstarch
1 1/2 cups all-purpose flour plus 3/4 cup • 2 teaspoons baking powder

Peel manioc root, cut into small pieces and boil vigorously in salted water until tender. Drain and mash very thoroughly. Cool, knead in butter, cheese and salt. Add beaten egg yolks. Sift cornstarch, flour and baking powder together, then knead into mixture. Cover and let stand 1/2 hour. Knead in other 3/4 cup of sifted flour or a sufficient quantity of the 3/4 cup to render the dough pliable. Cover and let stand another 1/2 hour. Follow general principles for preparing *Empadinhas* and bake in a preheated 400° oven from 15 to 20 minutes for an *Empadão*. Yields 16 *Empadinhas* and 1 10-inch *Empadão*.

Potato Pastry
Massa de Batatas

1 pound potatoes • 2 egg yolks • 3 tablespoons Parmesan or Muenster cheese
3 tablespoons cornstarch • 1 tablespoon butter • salt to taste

Boil potatoes and drain well. Press through a ricer or mash very well and cool. Add egg yolks, grated cheese, cornstarch, butter and salt. Let stand 1 hour. Press with the finger tips into buttered moulds and spoon in the filling. Shape tops from the pastry and cover the moulds. Bake in a 425° oven 40 minutes. Yields 16 *Empadinhas* or 1 8-inch *Empadão*.

[HILDA LEITE QUEIROGA, MINAS GERAIS]

Rich Pastry
Massa Podre

4 cups sifted all-purpose flour • 1 teaspoon salt • 2/3 cup butter • 3 tablespoons lard
3 egg yolks • 1-2 tablespoons water

Make a mound of the flour and salt and scoop out a well. Pour melted shortening and egg yolks into the well and work with the finger tips. Add 1 or 2 tablespoons cold water to make a pastry. Handle only enough to mix. Cover and let stand 1 hour before shaping and pressing into *empadinha* tins. Yields approximately 28 *Empadinhas*.

[MARIA MUNIZ RONDON, MATO GROSSO]

Mrs. Lima's Empadinha Pastry
Massa para Empadinhas[3]

3 cups all-purpose flour • 1 cup butter • 1 tablespoon lard
4 egg yolks • 1/2 teaspoon salt

Sift flour and make a well in the center. Add rest of ingredients. Mix well with finger tips. Let stand 1 hour then shape into *Empadinha* tins. Yields approximately 20 *Empadinhas* or 1 9-inch *Empadão*.

N O T E : This is a rich, crumbly pastry and must be worked with the finger tips. The *empadão* takes 30 to 40 minutes to bake in a preheated 375° oven. *Empadinhas* will require much less time to bake.

---

[3] While researching at the Oliveira Lima Library in Washington, D.C., I had occasion to use an old Portuguese cookbook by Lucas Regaud (Portugal, MDCCXCCIII). Tucked between the pages was a piece of note paper with the above recipe in Mrs. Oliveira Lima's handwriting. I tried the recipe, found it very good, and I am happy to pass it on to you.

Pastry for Fried Turnovers
Massa para Pastéis Fritos

2 cups all-purpose flour • 1 egg yolk • 2 tablespoons butter
1/3 cup water combined with • 1 teaspoon salt

Sift flour on a pastry board and make a well in the center. Drop egg yolk and butter into the well and knead. Add salted water and continue to knead until pastry is elastic to the touch. Let stand 1 hour. Roll out very thin, cut with a round cookie cutter or glass 3 or 4 inches in diameter. Place a small amount of filling in each, to one side of center and add slices of hard-boiled egg and stuffed olives to each. Do not overfill. Moisten edges with cold water, fold over, pressing edges together with tips and then with the tines of a fork dipped into cold water. Fry in hot fat, 360° to 375° until golden brown and drain on absorbent paper. Yields approximately 30.

Milk Pastry

Massa de Leite para Pastéis Fritos

1 cup milk • 1 tablespoon butter • 1 teaspoon salt • 1 cup all-purpose flour
2 beaten eggs • bread crumbs

Boil milk, butter and salt. Gradually sift in the flour, beating constantly so that no lumps form. Remove from heat and let stand until cool. Knead well. Let stand 1 hour and then follow procedure for Fried Turnovers (above), cutting with a 4-inch cutter. Fill, dip in beaten eggs, coat with bread crumbs and fry in hot fat or oil. Yields 16.

[OTTILIA JANSEN DE MELLO, MINAS GERAIS]

Cream Pastry

Massa de Creme para Empadas ou Pastéis Assados

4 tablespoons butter • 1 1/2 teaspoons salt • 3 egg yolks
1/2 cup light cream • 2 1/2 cups sifted all-purpose flour

Cream butter, and salt, yolks and cream. Gradually add the flour until you have a light pastry that does not stick to your hands. Knead. Cover and let stand 2 or 3 hours. Roll out or shape with hands and line *Empadinha* tins. Spoon in the filling, add pieces of hard-boiled egg and stuffed olives and fit pastry tops over the tins. Flute edges, brush with egg yolk, melted butter or cream and bake in a 375° preheated oven for 30-35 minutes. Yields approximately 20 *Empadinhas*.

Cheese Pastry
Massa de Queijo para Pastéis Assados

1/4 pound cream cheese or ricotta cheese • 1/4 pound butter
1 1/2 cup sifted all-purpose flour • 1 teaspoon salt

Let butter and cheese stand at room temperature for an hour, then cream together until smooth. Add flour and salt and knead until mixture is pliable and spongy like rich pastry dough. Cover and refrigerate overnight or let rest 1 hour. Roll out thin and cut with a 3-inch cookie cutter. (A glass or teacup will do). Place a small amount of filling in each round, add slices of hardboiled egg and stuffed olives and fold over. Press edges together and seal with tines of a fork dipped into cold water. Place on ungreased cookie sheet and bake in 400° oven 25-30 minutes. Yields 26.

[DAURA ALVES DA COSTA, RIO DE JANEIRO]

Corn Meal and Manioc Pastry
Massa de Milho e Farinha de Mandioca

3/4 cup fine white corn meal • 3/4 cup manioc meal • 1/2 cup boiling water
2 egg yolks • 1 teaspoon salt • 2/3 cup milk

Sift meals together and pour enough boiling water on them (about 1/2 cup) to form a crumbly mixture. Work mixture between finger tips to make as smooth as possible. When cool, add egg yolks and salt. Work in the milk and knead. Let stand at least 1 hour. Dredge a rolling pin with flour, break off egg-size pieces of the dough and carefully flatten them with the pin. Cut in 5-inch circles. Follow general directions for *pastéis* filling, sealing, etc. and frying in oil. Yields 18 large *pastéis*.

Wine Pastry
Massa de Vinho para Pastéis Fritos

2 cups all-purpose flour • 1 teaspoon salt • 2 tablespoons butter • 2 tablespoons lard
1 egg yolk • 1/4 cup port wine • approximately 1 ounce water

Sift flour with salt. Knead in butter and lard. Make a well in center, add egg yolk mixed with wine and water. Knead very well, cover and let stand 1 hour, then follow procedure for Pastry for Fried Turnovers (p. 438). Yields approximately 40.

FILLINGS
RECHEIOS

Carrot Filling
Recheio de Cenouras

1 cup coarsely-grated carrots • 1 tablespoon butter • 1 teaspoon chopped parsley
salt and pepper • 1 teaspoon cornstarch • 3/4 cup milk
1/2 cup grated Parmesan cheese • 4 or 5 stuffed olives, sliced

Steam carrots, butter and parsley in a covered skillet over low heat until carrots are tender. Season to taste with salt and pepper. Add cornstarch dissolved in milk. Stir over medium heat until mixture thickens. Remove from heat, beat in the cheese and cool. Correct seasoning. Add olives. Yields 1 1/4 cups.

Bahian Shrimp Filling
Recheio de Camarão Baiano

1 pound fresh shrimp • 1/4 cup olive oil • 1/4 cup finely-chopped green pepper
1 large minced onion • 1 1/2 cups coconut milk • 3 tablespoons grated cheese
2 egg yolks • seasoning

Shell, devein and clean shrimp. Cut up fine, then sauté in the olive oil with green pepper and onion. When shrimp are cooked, add the coconut milk, cheese and egg yolks. Cook until mixture has a thick, creamy consistency. Season with salt and black pepper (and cayenne, if desired). Yields 3 cups.

Crabmeat or Lobster Filling
Recheio de Caranguejo ou Lagosta

1/2 cup chopped onion • 1 tablespoon chopped parsley • 1 tablespoon olive oil or butter
garlic salt, salt, black pepper • 1/4 teaspoon ground coriander seed
a few grains cayenne pepper • 4 tablespoons tomato sauce • 2 tablespoons cornstarch
2 cups thin coconut milk or cow's milk • 1 egg yolk • 1 1/2 cups cooked crabmeat
(or lobster meat) • 1/4 cup cooked green peas • capers (optional)

Sauté onion and parsley in oil or butter. Add seasonings, then stir in the tomato sauce. Make a smooth paste with the cornstarch and some of the milk and, when well blended, add to the onions and seasonings. Heat slowly, then add the rest of the milk and stir until mixture thickens. Mix in the egg yolk and cook 1 minute then add crabmeat (or lobster meat) which has been thoroughly picked over for shells. Stir in the peas and continue to cook until mixture is thick enough to hold its shape. Add a few capers, if desired. Taste to check seasoning. Yields 3 1/2 to 4 cups.

443

Sardine Filling
Recheio de Sardinhas

2 cans sardines • 1/2 tablespoon lemon juice • 1 tablespoon oil • 1 minced onion
2 tablespoons chopped parsley • 1 tablespoon tomato paste • 3/4 cup water • seasoning
1/2 cup sliced palm hearts • 3 stuffed olives • 2 sliced hard-boiled eggs

Drain oil from sardines. Mash and add lemon juice. Fry onion and parsley in oil in a skillet, and, when onion begins to brown, add the tomato paste and water and simmer until most of liquid has evaporated. Season with salt, black pepper and cayenne or Tabaco sauce and allow to cool. When mixture is cold, add the palm hearts, sliced olives, eggs, and mashed sardines. Yields 2 1/2 cups.

Oyster Filling
Recheio de Ostras

1 1/2 cups shucked oysters in their liquor • 1 tablespoon olive oil
4 tablespoons minced onion • 1 tablespoon minced parsley • few grains garlic salt
1/4 teaspoon sweet marjoram • 2 tablespoons tomato sauce • 1 tablespoon butter
salt, black pepper to taste • 4 tablespoons bread crumbs
1/2 teaspoon lemon juice • 2 egg yolks

Gently parboil oysters in their liquor and strain, reserving 3/4 cup of the liquor. Sauté onion in oil and add parsley, garlic salt and sweet marjoram. Mix in the tomato sauce. When vegetables are cooked, add the butter and the oysters and slightly sauté, stirring so that the oysters become coated with the vegetables and seasoning. Add salt and pepper to taste, then the reserved oyster liquor and bring to a slow simmer. Stir in the bread crumbs. Remove from heat, add the lemon juice and the egg yolks. Yields 1 1/2 cups.

Cheese Filling
Recheio de Queijo

1/2 pound cottage cheese • 2 egg yolks • salt and black pepper
1 teaspoon chopped parsley • 2 tablespoons melted butter • 1/2 teaspoon marjoram
1/2 teaspoon celery sal (optional, but desirable)

Mix all ingredients and beat well. Allow to set for at least 1 hour before using. Yields approximately 1 cup.

Chicken and Ham Filling
Recheio de Galinha com Presunto

Mix equal amounts of chopped chicken and chopped ham with enough highly-seasoned white sauce to make a stiff filling.

Chicken and Mushroom Filling
Recheio de Galinha com Cogumelos

1/4 cup slivered, cooked or canned mushrooms • 1 cup shredded cooked chicken
2 tablespoons butter • 1 cup thick white sauce, well-seasoned
1 tablespoon grated Parmesan cheese

Sauté mushrooms and chicken in melted butter and add well-seasoned white sauce, which may be seasoned with 1/4 teaspoon of nutmeg, if desired. Mix well, add the grated cheese and cool. Yields 2 cups.

Meat Filling
Recheio de Carne

1/2 pound lean, ground beef • 1 tablespoon oil • 1/2 cup minced onion
2 tablespoons chopped parsley • 2 tablespoons tomato sauce • salt and black pepper
Tabasco sauce (optional) • sliced olives and hard-boiled eggs

Sauté meat in hot oil with onion and parsley. Add tomato paste, salt, pepper and Tabasco sauce, cover skillet and simmer, stirring often, until mixture is almost dry. It may be necessary to add a few tablespoons of hot water. Taste and check seasoning and add a few sliced olives and sliced hard-boiled eggs. (Or put the latter 2 ingredients into each patty or turnover, when you add the filling). Yields approximately 1 1/2 cups.

Palm Heart Filling No. 1
Recheio de Palmito Nº 1

1 tablespoon butter • 1 cup palm hearts, slivered • 1 tablespoon all-purpose flour
1 cup milk • salt and pepper • 1 tablespoon chopped parsley • 2 hard-boiled eggs, chopped

Melt butter and sauté the palm hearts over low flame. Add the flour and the milk gradually to make a thick sauce. When the mixture is thick, remove from heat and season to taste with salt and pepper. Add the parsley and eggs. Yields 1 1/2 cups.

Palm Heart Filling No. 2
Recheio de Palmito Nº 2

1 cup palm hearts, slivered • 2 tablespoons butter or oil • 2 tablespoons minced onion
salt and pepper • 2 egg yolks • 1 tablespoon chopped parsley

Melt butter and sauté onion, without browning. Add palm hearts and cook over low flame another 3 minutes. Season with salt and pepper, add beaten egg yolks, and parsley. Mix well and cook over low flame, stirring with a fork until eggs set. Yields 1 cup.

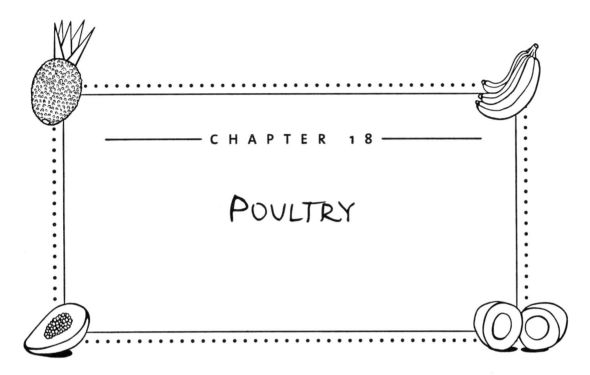

CHAPTER 18

POULTRY

Alas! my child, where is the Pen
That can do justice to the Hen?
Like Royalty she goes her way,
Laying foundations every day,
Though not for Public Buildings, yet
For Custard, Cake and Omelette.

OLIVER HERFORD, THE HEN

A s in this country, the most common member of the poultry family served in Brazil is the chicken. Ducks, guinea fowls, geese and turkeys, while highly appreciated, are expensive and are therefore reserved for special occasions. Turkey, especially, is a festive dish and, at Christmas time, it occupies the place of honor on the table. Generally, it is carved in the kitchen and brought to the table on a platter, the meat, thinly sliced, arranged with the dark on one side and the light on the other. One or two varieties of *Farofa* (p. 39) and thin slices of rolled boiled ham sometimes serve as a garnish.

At very elegant and formal affairs, the turkey is accompanied by *Fios de Ovos* (p. 48) — those delicate strands of egg yolks that have been solidified in hot syrup and piled into miniature beehives. The turkey skin is pulled back and the meat sliced from both sides of the breast bone. The skin is then replaced over the turkey and it is brought to the table whole, garnished with bunches of grapes, canned pears or apricots and the *Fios de Ovos* to highlight the dish.

Peru Brasileiro is one of the most delicious ways of preparing turkey, and, along with *Feijoada* (p. 124) and some of the Afro-Brazilian dishes, it is considered to be one of Brazil's outstanding contributions to the culinary art. In presentation and taste, *Peru Brasileiro* has all the requisites to make it a gourmet's delight.

To prepare turkey in this manner, it is necessary to stuff the breast cavity as well as the crop. Usually, the stuffing for the latter is one of the *Farofa* dressings that would become too moist if used in the breast cavity. One of the principal qualities of *Farofa* is that it should be dry.

There are several excellent ways of preparing chicken in the Brazilian manner. Here again, as in the cooking process for meat and fish, many recipes call for marination in *vinha d'alho* or for sautéeing with seasoning and vegetables, known as to *refogar*.

There is also a *Vatapá* (p. 88) and a *Cuscuz* (p. 281) made from chicken. These are excellent and may be considered as gourmet recipes. However, one of the tastiest ways of cooking chicken is with the *Molho Pardo* or brown gravy. This requires a freshly-killed chicken, which may be difficult to obtain in large cities, unless arrangements can be made with a Kosher butcher or a farmer who will butcher the chicken and reserve some of the fresh blood in vinegar. *Frango Molho Pardo* is one of the traditional dishes of Brazil, therefore, notwithstanding the difficulty of obtaining freshly-butchered chickens, it would be a grave omission not to include it in any book on Brazilian cuisine.

Chickens, especially hens, do not always find their way to the stew pan in this picturesque land of modern cities, samba schools and coffee. They figure prominently in many of the *Macumba*[1] ceremonies in Brazil. The latter are described by Lima and Barroso as "a fetishistic ceremony with a Negro base and showing Christian influence, accompanied by dancing and singing to the sound of a drum."[2]

There appears to be a distinct predilection for the hen in these ceremonies, which is pointed out by Freyre, who states: "The hen, moreover, figures in a number of African religious ceremonies and aphrodisiac potions in Brazil. Dampier had noted this in the Seventeenth Century, alluding in particular to a form of grill known as *Macker*, employed in the making of love-philters. Certain Afro-Brazilian dishes still keep something of a religious or liturgical character as regards the manner of their preparation. In order to prepare them as they should be prepared, in all their fine points, the Negroes for a long time brought over from Africa, in addition to the oil of the dendê palm, a number of exquisite condiments: *Bejerecum, Ierê, Uru, Atarè*. Manuel Querino speaks of certain rice-cakes made with the dendê oil or with honey which the black Mussulmans at Bahia were accustomed to consuming at religious ceremonies."[3]

The same author tells of his observation of the rites of African sects in Pernambuco, where "there was an earthen vessel with the sacred food — swimming in the blood of a black hen."[4]

---

[1] The macumba is a Brazilian variant of voodooism.

[2] Gilberto Freyre, The Masters and the Slave (New York: Alfred A. Knopf, 1946), p. 335, footnote by the translator, Samuel Putnam.

[3] Freyre, *op. cit.*, p. 165.

[4] *Ibid.*, p. 316.

The chicken, savory as it may be on the table, is also the source of several Brazilian superstitions, largely evolved by the Afro-Brazilian who maintain many beliefs concerning it. Among these are the beliefs: lucky in raising chickens, unlucky in love and marriage; labor pains may be alleviated by sipping the broth made from a black chicken; if an expectant mother passes near a sitting hen, or disturbs its nest, she may lose her child; a man or woman disturbing a sitting hen will suffer business reverses; chicken's feet have not been blessed because they trampled the straw of the Manger; when chickens are frightened without any apparent reason, it is an omen of good news or a visit.[5]

The chicken, or more specifically, the hen, rises above a food item in Brazil. Although it lends itself well to the preparation of many excellent dishes, the African element has surrounded this barnyard fowl with a mystical aura. Thus, by ethnological association, it takes its place in Brazilian folklore and, at the same time, provides many culinary treats not found in other countries.

[5] Cascudo, Luís da Câmara, *Dicionário do Folclore Brasileiro*, p. 283.

Boneless Stuffed Chicken
Galinha Dessossada com Recheio

TO BONE A CHICKEN: Select a chicken that has been freshly killed, dry picked and not drawn. Tough-skinned fowl, such as chickens, turkeys, roosters, etc. are the best to use for removing the bones; tender fowls, such as young chicks, will not suit the purpose. Singe, remove pinfeathers (but not by placing in boiling water, as this tends to weaken the skin), then cut off head and feet and the wings, close to the body in small birds. Lay bird on a board, breast down. Begin at neck with a sharp knife and cut through the skin and bone to the body cavity along the length of the fowl. Scrape flesh from the backbone until one shoulder blade is reached. Scrape flesh from shoulder blade and continue around wing joint; then bone the other side. Scrape skin from backbone the entire length of the body, working across the ribs. Free wishbone and collar bones, at same time removing crop and windpipe; continue down breast bone, taking particular care not to break the skin as it is very near the bone, or to cut the delicate membranes which enclose entrails. Scrape flesh from second joints and drum sticks, and draw it back. Withdraw carcass and put flesh back in its original shape. Wash, pat dry and stuff with the following:

1 pound lean raw pork • chicken liver and gizzard • 1/4 pound boiled ham
2 hard-boiled eggs • 3 raw egg yolks • 1 tablespoon butter • 1/4 cup white wine
2 tablespoons chopped parsley • garlic salt • salt and pepper • 4 or 5 chopped truffles

Grind pork, liver, gizzard and ham, then mix in the chopped eggs, raw egg yolks, butter, wine and parsley. Season to taste with garlic salt, salt and pepper. Add the chopped truffles and mix well. Stuff chicken and sew together with a needle and twine or heavy thread so that the stuffing cannot come out. Sauté the chicken in butter, turning gently so as not to pierce the skin and cook slowly in an uncovered skillet, basting with chicken consommé in small quantities. It should take about 1 1/2 hours to cook. Remove to a platter and place a weight on top so that it will not fall apart and will stay dry inside. Slice when cold and serve with a highly-seasoned vegetable salad.

[ABILIO CORREA, CHEF IN THE HOME OF THE PALHA BLANCO FAMILY, PORTUGAL]

Chicken

Frango

1 small whole chicken • juice of 1 lemon • 2 tablespoons butter • 2 chopped onions
1/4 cup chopped parsley • 4 peeled, chopped tomatoes • 1/4 teaspoon sugar
1 small can paté de foie gras • 1 8-ounce can cooked, sliced mushrooms
1 cup white wine • 3/4 tablespoon prepared mustard • salt • grated Parmesan cheese

Wash inside and outside of chicken and wipe dry with absorbent paper. Sprinkle lemon juice inside and outside chicken and let stand 20 or 30 minutes. Melt butter in a large skillet and sauté onions, parsley and tomatoes for 5 minutes. Add the chicken and sugar, and brown on all sides with the vegetables, adding small amounts of water, just enough to prevent chicken from sticking to the bottom of the saucepan. Cover the skillet, reduce heat and steam for about 20 minutes or until chicken is fork tender. Remove from heat and with a sharp knife cut breast in two full slices, removing bones. Separate rest of chicken meat from the bones. Butter a baking dish and place a layer of chicken meat on the bottom. Reserve breast pieces for the top. Dot layer with paté and sliced mushrooms. Place the pieces of breast on top. Add the wine and mustard to the drippings in the skillet. Season with salt to taste and make a sauce. Pour over the chicken. Sprinkle cheese on top and bake in a preheated 375° oven for 20 minutes.

[TRANSLATED FROM: **RECEITAS CULINÁRIAS** BY MYRTHES PARANHOS]

455

Chicken Ignez

Galinha Ignez

1 large roasting chicken • 1 garlic clove, pounded with 1 teaspoon salt
1 medium onion, grated • salt and pepper • 1 cup white wine • 1 teaspoon marjoram
1/4 cup lemon juice • 1/2 teaspoon ground coriander seed

After cleaning and patting chicken dry, rub inside and outside with the garlic salt mixture then place in a marinade made with onion, salt and pepper, wine, marjoram, lemon juice and coriander. Marinate overnight, turning chicken 2 or 3 times. While chicken is marinating, cook the giblets in a small amount of seasoned water. When done, drain off the liquid and chop the giblets to be used in the following dressing:

2 tablespoons butter • 1/2 grated onion • 1 peeled, chopped tomato
1 tablespoon chopped parsley • chopped giblets • 1/2 cup chopped, cooked chestnuts
2 cups plain boiled rice • seasoning • giblet liquor

Melt butter, sauté onion, tomato, parsley and chopped giblets, stirring until vegetables are cooked. Mix in the chestnuts and rice. Season well with salt and pepper and moisten with some of the giblet liquor. Remove chicken from the marinade, pat dry with absorbent paper and stuff with the dressing. Close the chicken with skewers or by sewing. Rub outside surface with butter and place in a buttered baking tin. Strain the marinade. Bake in a preheated 325° oven, according to the Roasting Guide (p. 477). Baste several times with some of the marinade and the pan drippings. Serve with Banana Scallops (p. 64).

Chicken and Bacon
Galinha com Toucinho

1 chicken, cut for frying • 1 chopped onion • 1 tablespoon chopped parsley
salt and pepper • 1/4 cup vinegar • 1/4 cup water • 1 beaten egg • oil for frying
5 or 6 strips of bacon • shredded lettuce • 2 cups canned peas • 2 cups cooked carrots, cubed
few olives • 2 hard-boiled eggs

Wash chicken and marinate overnight in a marinade made with the onion, parsley, salt, pepper, vinegar and water. Next day, dip each piece of chicken in beaten egg and fry in the oil. Reserve the marinade. Drain fried chicken on absorbent paper. Arrange a layer of the chicken in a saucepan and cover with the strips of bacon. Add the marinade, cover and allow to simmer. Lift pieces of chicken once in a while not to let them stick to bottom of saucepan, adding a few drops of water occasionally, so that bottom of saucepan always contains a layer of liquid. When chicken is done, remove to serving platter and surround with the lettuce. Add the peas and carrots and olives to the gravy. Pour over the lettuce and garnish with the sliced eggs.

[IZAURA PINTO, MINAS GERAIS]

457

Chicken with Dark Brown Gravy
Galinha ao Molho Pardo[6]

*1 chicken • 1/2 cup vinegar • 1 teaspoon salt • 1 chopped onion • 1 tablespoon vinegar
1/4 cup fat • 1 tablespoon chopped parsley • 1 bayleaf • 1 chopped tomato
1 thinly-sliced onion • 1 1/2 cups water • salt and pepper • 1 tablespoon sugar
1 tablespoon all-purpose flour*

This requires a freshly-killed chicken from which some of the blood has been drained into a soup plate or shallow dish containing the 1/2 cup of vinegar. The mixture should be stirred once in a while to prevent coagulation. Dress chicken, cut into serving-size pieces and marinate for 1 hour in the salt, chopped onion and vinegar. Melt the fat and fry the chicken. When the chicken is brown, add the leftover marinade with parsley, bayleaf, tomato and sliced onion. Simmer 5 minutes and add the water. Cook slowly until chicken is done, add salt and pepper to taste and the sugar. Just before serving, add the blood and vinegar mixture and gently simmer until smooth and thick. Thicken with flour, if necessary. Place chicken on a platter, cover with the gravy and serve with Cornmeal Mush (p. 53) and Brazilian Rice (p. 131).

N O T E : Sweet marjoram and garlic are sometimes used as seasoning.

[FLORINDA K. MACHADO, RIO GRANDE DO SUL]

---

[6] Also called *cabidela* in some regions of Brazil.

Chicken in Peanut Sauce

Galinha com Molho de Amendoim

1 frying chicken, cut up • garlic powder • 3 tablespoons butter • 1 chopped onion
1/2 cup green pepper • 1 1/2 cups chicken broth • 1/2 teaspoon pounded coriander seeds
1/2 teaspoon powdered ginger • 1/2 cup ground peanuts (or 3 tablespoons peanut butter)
salt and black pepper

Wash and dry chicken and sprinkle with garlic powder. Melt butter in an uncovered skillet, add onion, green pepper and sauté chicken. When chicken is done on both sides, add broth or bouillon, coriander, ginger and peanuts or peanut butter. Cover and simmer until chicken begins to fall away from bones. Remove skin and bones, and return chicken to the gravy. Season with salt and black pepper. Serve garnished with large black olives and fried bananas, accompanied by Brazilian Rice (p. 131).

C h i c k e n   i n   M i l k
Frango no Leite

1 whole chicken • 1 garlic clove • 1 tablespoon salt • 1/4 cup vinegar • black pepper
cayenne pepper (optional) • 1/4 cup bacon fat or vegetable shortening
2 chopped onions • 2 small tomatoes, peeled and chopped • 1/4 cup chopped parsley
1 quart milk at room temperature

Make a marinade by pounding garlic with salt, then adding vinegar and the peppers. Pierce the chicken in several places with a long-tined fork and place in the marinade overnight, turning once or twice. The next day, melt the bacon fat or shortening in a large uncovered saucepan. Brown the chicken on all sides and when it is browned, remove to a platter and reserve. Fry the onions, parsley and tomatoes in the drippings remaining in the saucepan until they are well sautéed, then pour in the leftover marinade. Add the milk (which should not be chilled) and gently heat the mixture until it begins to curdle. If it does not curdle, add a few drops of lemon juice. Replace the chicken in this sauce, cover the pan and cook the chicken over medium heat until it is fork tender. When the chicken is cooked, remove it again to the platter and boil down the sauce in the uncovered saucepan until all liquid has evaporated and large curds form, similar in appearance to cottage cheese. There should be enough shortening in the saucepan to fry these curds after all the liquid has evaporated. Once in a while, scrape down the sides and bottom of the saucepan. The chicken, which has lost some of its brownness from cooking in the milk, should be returned to the saucepan and browned from cooking in the curds. Chicken prepared in this manner is simply delicious. Serve it with rice and a good vegetable salad and you have a gourmet creation to please the most exacting taste.

[IRIS FERNAL,[7] MINAS GERAIS]

---

[7] This recipe came from the Minas Gerais branch of the Junqueira family and was handed down to Dr. Iris by her mother, Mrs. Maria Verônica Junqueira, who probably originated the recipe.

Mock Chicken Legs
Coxinhas de Galinha

Full recipe for Stewed Chicken (p. 468), omitting vinegar • 1 cup rice flour
2 cups milk • 1 tablespoon butter • 3 egg yolks • beaten egg for breading
salt, pepper, Tabasco sauce • bread crumbs • oil for frying

After the stewed chicken is ready, take chicken from the gravy and remove skin
and bones. Reserve long bones, like leg and thigh. Keep as many finger length pieces
of chicken as there are bones, and chop the rest. Measure 1 cup of strained gravy
from the stewed chicken (which should be highly seasoned) and heat with rice
flour and milk, stirring constantly to prevent formation of lumps. When the mixture
is thick enough to hold its shape, add the butter and egg yolks and beat well. The
mixture should be thick enough to handle. Allow to cool thoroughly and then add
the chopped chicken. Taste to check seasoning by adding salt, pepper and 2 or 3
drops of Tabasco sauce. Do not try to work the mixture until it is entirely cooled.
Shape the mixture around one of the long pieces of chicken to simulate a chicken
leg. Insert one of the bones saved for this purpose in the small end. Roll in fine bread
crumbs then in beaten egg and in crumbs again. Fry in hot oil until golden brown and
remove to absorbent paper to drain. Makes approximately 8 good-sized "legs."

Anna Pereira's Chicken
Galinha à Moda de Anna Pereira

6 chicken thighs • 6 chicken drum sticks • 2 tablespoons margarine or butter
1 finely-minced onion • 2 tablespoons chopped parsley • 1 tablespoon chopped green pepper
2 chopped tomatoes or 1/4 cup tomato sauce • 1 1/2 cups stock or water
salt and pepper • cayenne pepper (optional) • 3 egg yolks • juice of 1 lemon, or more, if desired

Melt margarine or butter and sauté onions 5 minutes, then add other vegetables and continue sautéing, adding small amounts of the stock or water, for another 5 minutes. Season, add the chicken, recover and steam the chicken in this sauce. Turn the chicken over once in a while and add the stock or water as necessary so that there will always be at least 1 cup of sauce. When chicken is fork tender and falls away from bones, after cooking over medium heat for at least 1 hour, remove to a platter and strain the sauce, forcing through as much of the vegetables as possible. Mix the egg yolks with the lemon juice and thicken the sauce. Taste to check seasoning. Return chicken to the sauce and simmer gently for 10 minutes. Serve with rice or mashed potatoes.

N O T E : While whole cut-up chickens can be prepared this way, the darker parts of the chicken are tastier. Mrs. Pereira prepares shrimp in this sauce, which is also very delicious. Use 1 1/2 pounds cleaned shrimp to the same strained sauce as above. Cook shrimp in the sauce until tender, then thicken with lemon juice and egg yolks.

[ANNA PEREIRA, LISBON, PORTUGAL]

Chicken with Wine
Galinha com Vinho

1 cut-up frying chicken • 1/2 recipe for vinha d'alho, *p. 470 • 2 ounces shortening*
1 chopped onion • 1/4 cup tomato sauce • 2 tablespoons rice flour

Soak chicken overnight in the *vinha d'alho*. Next day, remove from the marinade, fry in hot shortening with onion and tomato sauce, and when chicken is delicately browned, add 1/2 the *vinha d'alho* and simmer until it is reduced by half. Then add the remaining *vinha d'alho*, turn each piece of chicken, cover skillet and cook until chicken is tender. Taste gravy and check seasoning and thicken with rice flour that has been mixed with a little water. Cook over low heat until gravy thickens.

Chicken Pudding
Pudim de Galinha

2 cups minced chicken (leftover will do) • 2 tablespoons butter • 1 tablespoon minced onion
black pepper and salt • 2 tablespoons all-purpose flour • 1 cup milk
1 cup strong chicken stock[8] • 3 tablespoons grated Parmesan cheese • 3 eggs, separated

Melt 1/2 of the butter in a skillet and sauté the onion, then add the chicken and season well with black pepper and salt. Set aside. Make a white sauce with the rest of the butter, flour and milk, stirring constantly until thick. Thin down with the rich chicken stock and strain, if necessary. Add cheese and stir until well-blended with the sauce. Add chicken and check seasoning. Beat in the egg yolks and mix well, then remove from heat. Fold in the beaten egg whites, pour into a buttered 2-quart casserole and sprinkle with fine bread crumbs and cheese. Bake in preheated 350° oven from 50 to 60 minutes, then serve at once, otherwise the pudding will drop.

[8] If canned chicken consommé is used for the stock, add only 1/2 can of water, instead of the can called for on label.

Chicken Livers in Madeira Wine

Fígados de Galinha com Vinho Madeira

1 pound chicken livers • 3 tablespoons butter or oil • 1/4 cup chopped onion
1/4 cup chopped parsley • 1 peeled tomato, chopped
3 ounces Madeira wine • seasoning

Cut livers in halves. Melt shortening, sauté onion, parsley and chicken livers. When brown, add the tomato and cook until livers are almost done. Add wine and complete the cooking. Season to taste. Serve with young green peas and shoestring potatoes. Serves two.

[TRANSLATED FROM: **AS RECEITAS PARA VOCÊ DA TIA EVELINA, 4TH EDITION**]

Chicken with Palm Hearts
Galinha com Palmito

1 stewed chicken, cut into serving-size pieces • 3 slices of bread with crusts removed,
toasted or fried in butter • 1 14-ounce can of palm hearts

Arrange hot pieces of chicken on the toast, which has been cut into wedges, and cover with the following sauce. Surround with the sliced palm hearts.

2 tablespoons butter • 2 tablespoons cornstarch • 1/4 cup minced spring onions
1/2 cup port wine • 2 egg yolks • 1 tablespoon tomato paste • 3/4 cup chicken broth

Melt butter, stir in the cornstarch and onions, and cook over low flame 2 or 3 minutes. Add port wine which has been mixed with the egg yolks. Stir tomato paste into broth and pour over the mixture. Cook, stirring constantly, until sauce thickens. Strain and pour over the chicken.

[TRANSLATED FROM: **AS RECEITAS PARA VOCÊ DA TIA EVELINA, 4TH ED.**]

Roast Chicken
Frango Assado

1 2 1/2-pound chicken • juice of 1 lemon • 1 1/2 cups stout beer • 1/2 bayleaf
1/4 cup chopped parsley • 1 teaspoon salt • 1 chopped onion • butter

Rinse chicken under running cold water and dry inside and outside with absorbent paper towel. Sprinkle lemon juice in the cavity of the chicken and on outisde, and let stand. Make a marinade with the beer, bayleaf, parsley, salt and onion. Marinate chicken for 8 hours in this liquid. Remove chicken from marinade, stuff with Prune *Farofa* (p. 52) and rub with butter. Bake in a preheated 325° oven, according to the Roasting Guide (p. 477) and baste from time to time with the marinade. When chicken is fork tender, remove to serving platter. Garnish with sliced onions and tomatoes. Prepare a gravy from the drippings in baking tin and some of the marinade. Serve gravy separately.

[TRANSLATED FROM: **RECEITAS CULINÁRIAS** BY MYRTHES PARANHOS]

467

Stewed Chicken
Galinha Ensopada

Juice of 1 lemon • 1/4 cup chopped parsley • 1 medium chopped onion
1/4 cup olive oil • 1/4 cup vinegar • 1 teaspoon dried savory • 1/4 teaspoon garlic powder
salt and black pepper • 2 or 3 mint leaves (optional) • 1 teaspoon coriander seeds
1 cut-up chicken • 1 tablespoon margarine • 1/2 cup tomato sauce • 1/2 cup water

Make a marinade of first 10 items and marinate chicken overnight, turning once or twice, if possible. Heat margarine in a large skillet and sauté chicken until brown, add the marinade, cover and simmer about 10 minutes. Add tomato sauce and water, replace the cover and cook until chicken is tender, turning each piece over once in a while. Cooking should take 1 1/4 to 1 1/2 hours. Remove chicken to serving platter. Taste the gravy and check seasoning, then strain over the chicken. Serve with Corn Meal Mush (p. 53).

Chicken in Fruit Sauce
Galinha com Molho de Frutas

1 stewing chicken, cut up for frying • *1/2 recipe for* vinha d'alho, *p. 470*
2 tablespoons butter • *1/4 cup tomato sauce* • *1/2 cup orange juice*
1 cup pitted dates, or prunes, soaked in water 4 hours or cooked to a pulp
1/4 cup heavy cream • *seasonings*

Soak chicken overnight in the *vinha d'alho*. Next day, fry in the butter and brown evenly. When chicken is brown, add some of the *vinha d'alho*, turning from time to time and adding more marinade until all has been used. Add the tomato sauce, orange juice and the cut-up dates (or prunes). Cover and simmer until chicken is tender, adding more orange juice if skillet becomes too dry. Once in a while, remove cover allowing some of the liquid to evaporate. When chicken is done, remove from gravy and strain gravy into a double boiler and add cream, stirring for 4 or 5 minutes to prevent curdling. Season.

Boil 1 pound carrots and 1 pound potatoes together and mash with a little butter and seasonings. Place in center of a large round serving dish and cover with pieces of chicken. Pour gravy over chicken. Surround with green peas flavored with butter and fresh mint.

[TRANSLATED FROM: **AS RECEITAS PARA VOCÊ DA TIA EVELINA**, 4TH EDITION]

Brazilian Roast Duck with Orange
Pato Assado à Moda Brasileira

1 large duck • butter and salt • 1 cup orange juice • 1/4 cup raisins • cornstarch

Marinate overnight as for Tropical Duck, p. 474. Next day, wipe dry, rub with butter and salt and bake in a pre-heated oven according to Roasting Guide, p. 477, basting with strained marinade. When duck is tender and brown, remove to serving platter and surround with watercress and Baked Oranges, p.65. Add orange juice to drippings, bring to boil, stirring with a fork, then add the raisins, simmer and thicken with cornstarch, if necessary. Pour sauce into a gravy boat and pass with the duck.

Roast Turkey — Brazilian Style
Peru à Brasileira

The day before, clean the turkey of entrails (if not already dressed) and remove gizzard, heart and liver. Rub the inside of turkey with salt and rinse clean with cold water once or twice to be sure all entrails have been removed. Dry out cavity with paper towels. Pull the neck out of the skin, keeping skin intact to hold the neck dressing. Reserve the giblets.

Soak the turkey overnight in a marinade called *vinha d'alho* which is made by mixing the following. For a small turkey use only half the recipe. Turn the turkey once in a while, but see that the breast lies longer in the marinade than the back.

3 garlic cloves, pounded into a paste • 1/4 teaspoon black pepper • 1/2 teaspoon salt
1 clove • 1/2 cup chopped celery • 1 chopped onion • 1/2 cup chopped parsley
1 grated carrot • 2 cups white wine • 1 cup vinegar

The next day, cut gizzard in half and rinse under cold water to remove all the stones. Wash rest of giblets and cover with 4 cups of water, 1/2 teaspoon salt, celery and parsley and simmer gently until the giblets are thoroughly cooked. A pressure cooker may be used. When completely cooked, remove from broth, chop fine and reserve the liquid. Divide giblets into two portions. Stuff the neck or crop with the following:

NECK STUFFING *(Farofa)*

2 tablespoons butter • 1 chopped onion • 1/2 cup chopped tomatoes (optional)
1/4 cup chopped parsley • 1 portion of the giblets • 4 or 5 drops Tabasco sauce
3 tablespoons butter • 4 cups manioc meal[9] • 1/2 cup stuffed olives
3 chopped hard-boiled eggs

Melt butter in a large skillet and sauté onion, tomatoes and parsley. Add giblets, Tabasco sauce and the other three tablespoons of butter, and when butter is melted, remove from heat and gradually stir in the manioc meal, which has been delicately browned in the oven. Mix well until all the meal has been blended, then return to low heat, stirring constantly until mixture is loose. Add olives and chopped eggs and taste to check seasoning. Stuff neck and close by sewing the skin together over the *Farofa* and save any leftover *Farofa* to serve with the sliced turkey. Stuff the breast as follows:

---

[9] If manioc is not available, substitute Cream of Wheat or Farina.

BREAST STUFFING

1/4 cup chopped bacon • 1/2 cup chopped onion • 1/4 cup minced parsley
1/2 cup chopped tomatoes • 1 cup giblet broth • 1 portion of the giblets
6 cups of bread soaked in 3/4 cup of milk

Fry bacon in skillet and remove the fat. Add onion, parsley and tomato. When brown cover with the broth and bring to boil. Press through a sieve and add the giblets and bread. Mix well with a fork. Season to taste. Cool and then stuff the breast cavity. Close and truss the turkey. Brush well with melted butter and baste with some of the strained marinade, also the drippings in the roasting pan, or with a mixture of white wine and giblet broth. Bake in accordance with the Roasting Guide (p. 477).

Cold Turkey Platter
Travessa de Peru Frio

1 young turkey, about 6 pounds • 4 long slices of boiled ham • 2 bayleaves • 1 sliced lemon
1 teaspoon rosemary • 1 teaspoon salt • 1 sliced onion • 3 sprigs parsley
1/2 cup chopped celery • 1 cup chopped carrots • 1 cup water • 2 cups white wine

Clean and dress turkey and cover both sides with the ham, bayleaves and lemon. Sprinkle rosemary on top. Wrap turkey in a double fold of cheese cloth and sew ends together. Place in a large stewing pot or a roasting tin with cover and add salt, onion, parsley celery, carrots, water, giblets and wine. Bring to boil, cover the saucepan and stew turkey over low heat until it is fork tender, adding water as needed. When turkey is cooked, remove from broth and allow to cool in the cheesecloth. Cool and chop the giblets. Strain the broth and measure 3 cups. If you do not have this amount, add enough chicken consommé to equal 3 cups.

GELATIN FOR GARNISH

*3 cups of strained broth • 2 envelopes unsweetened gelatin • 1/2 teaspoon Worcestershire sauce
chopped giblets • 1/4 cup chopped green and black olives
1 tablespoon chopped pimiento • 1 tablespoon minced parsley • 1 tablespoon minced onion
salt and pepper to taste • Sliced tomatoes and hard-boiled eggs*

Dissolve gelatin in 1 cup of cold broth. Heat other 2 cups and pour over gelatin mixture, stirring until it is clear. Add Worcestershire sauce, giblets, olives, pimiento, parsley and onion. Season with salt and pepper. Pour small amounts into individual moulds containing a slice of hard-boiled egg topped with a slice of tomato. Refrigerate until firm and when the tomato is set, fill the moulds and chill in the refrigerator.

Remove cheese cloth from the turkey, which has also been chilled, and arrange turkey on a large platter. Remove the bayleaves and lemon and discard. Use the ham as part of the garnish. Make a bed of shredded lettuce around the turkey and unmould the gelatin on the lettuce. Garnish with a piquant mayonnaise and black olives.

[TRANSLATED FROM: **A BOA COZINHEIRA NO. 7-150 RECEITAS DE AVES** BY LÍGIA JUNQUEIRA]

Tropical Duck
Pato Tropical

1 cut-up duck, marinated overnight in • 2 tablespoons minced parsley • 1 chopped onion
1 bay leaf • 1/2 grated carrot • 1 cup red wine • 1 teaspoon salt • black pepper

Next day, dip each piece of duck in flour and fry in butter, then add:

Leftover marinade • 1/2 cup dried pitted dates • 1/2 cup dried pears
1/2 cup pitted prunes • 3/4 cup orange juice • 1 teaspoon corn starch
1/4 pound chopped cooked ham • seedless grapes

Cook over low heat until duck is tender, then remove it from the saucepan and check to see if fruits are cooked. If they are not cooked, simmer until they are done, then strain and purée fruits into the sauce. Thicken sauce with 1 teaspoon cornstarch, add 1/4 pound chopped cooked ham and return to low heat until sauce thickens. Taste and correct seasoning. Just before serving add a few seedless grapes. Arrange duck on a platter, cover with the sauce and serve with sliced oranges accompanied by a mould of white rice.

Guinea Fowl in Yoghurt
Galinha D'Angola em logurte

2 cut-up guinea fowls • 1/2 recipe for marinade used in Roast Turkey, p. 470
4 tablespoons bacon fat • 3 peeled, chopped tomatoes • 1 grated onion
1 cup plain yoghurt • seasoning

Wash and wipe dry pieces of guinea fowls. Cover with the marinade and let stand overnight, turning once or twice. Next day, sauté in the bacon fat with tomatoes and onion, adding some of the strained marinade from time to time and cooking over low heat for about 1 hour. Turn the pieces several times so that they will be evenly cooked. When the hour is up, remove the pieces of guinea fowl to a platter and add yoghurt to the dripping in the tin. Heat and blend thoroughly and correct seasoning. Return the guinea fowl to the sauce and simmer until they are fork tender. While they are cooking, spoon some of the sauce over the top pieces. Serve around a mould of plain boiled rice and garnish with palm or artichoke hearts and black and green olives.

Roast Guinea Fowl
Galinha d'Angola Assada

1 young dressed guinea fowl • 1/3 recipe for Roast Turkey marinade (p. 470)
2 tablespoons butter • 1/2 grated onion • 1 chopped, peeled tomato

Marinate guinea fowl overnight, turning at least once. Next day, remove from marinade and pat dry with absorbent paper. Rub with the butter and place in a buttered baking pan with onion and tomato. Bake in preheated 325° oven, according to the Roasting Guide (p. 477) for chicken. Baste with the strained marinade and the tin drippings. Serve with Stuffed Apples (p. 65).

Stewed Guinea Fowl
Galinha d'Angola Ensopada

1 large guinea fowl • 1/2 cup dry white wine • 1/2 cup wine vinegar • 1 sliced onion
1 garlic clove crushed with • 1 teaspoon salt • 1 tablespoon chopped parsley
1/4 teaspoon black pepper • 2 tablespoons olive oil • 1 tablespoon butter
1 teaspoon cornstarch • 1/3 cup Madeira wine • seasoning

Clean and dress fowl as you would a chicken. Marinate 24 hours in marinade made with wine, vinegar, onion, garlic and salt, parsley and pepper. Turn fowl occasionally. Next day, remove from marinade and pat dry. Strain the marinade. Heat oil in a large saucepan (with cover) and brown hen on all sides in uncovered saucepan. When fowl is brown, add 1/2 cup of the strained marinade. Cover the saucepan and simmer until meat is fork tender. Remove the fowl to a platter and add any leftover marinade to the drippings. Cool and skim off all the fat. Reheat and thicken the sauce with the butter that has been blended with the cornstarch. Add the Madeira wine and check seasoning. Place the fowl in a glass baking dish and cover with the sauce. Bake in a preheated 350° oven 25-30 minutes, basting several times with the sauce. Serve with noodles or dumplings.

476

ROASTING GUIDE [10]			
KIND OF FOWL	READY-TO-COOK WEIGHT (POUNDS)	LARGE BREAD-CRUMBS FOR STUFFING (QUARTS)	APPROXIMATE ROASTING TIME AT 325°F FOR A STUFFED CHILLED BIRD (HOURS)
TURKEY Fryers or roasters (very young birds)	4 to 8	1 to 2	3 to 4 1/2
Roasters (fully grown young birds)	6 to 12	2 to 3	3 1/2 to 5
	12 to 16	3 to 4	5 to 6
	16 to 20	4 to 5	6 to 7 1/2
	20 to 24	5 to 6	7 1/2 to 9
CHICKEN Broilers or Fryers	1 1/2 to 2 2 1/2	1/4 to 1/2	1 1/4 to 2
Roasters	2 1/2 to 4 1/2	1/2 to 1/4	2 to 3 1/2
Duck	3 to 5	1/2 to 1	2 1/2 to 3
Goose	4 to 8	3/4 to 1 1/2	2 3/4 to 3 1/2
	8 to 14	1 1/2 to 2 1/2	3 1/2 to 5

[10] U.S. Dept. of Agriculture, *Yearbook*, 1959, p. 533.

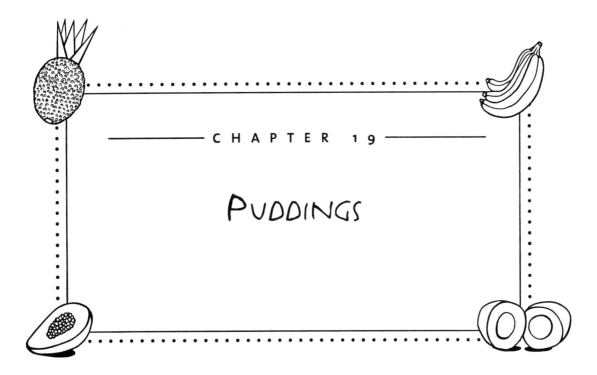

CHAPTER 19

PUDDINGS

Better some of a pudding, than none of a pie.

JOHN RAY, **ENGLISH PROVERBS**, P. 135

f you have lived in Brazil, you would undoubtedly take "some of a pudding" principally because there are no pies to speak of, other than the salted ones or *Empadas* and *Pastéis*. There are many tortes made of fruit, but because they are so rich and sweet, they cannot compare with the American pies, which can be served in generous wedges after a hearty meal. The Brazilian "pie counterpart" has to be served in small portions because it is so sweet.

But after a substantial Brazilian meal, puddings make a good dessert. Generally, they are light and fluffy, and are brought to the table attractively garnished with cooked fruits or a sauce, and sometimes they are moulded into fancy shapes.

One of the types of puddings most frequently served in Brazil is a variation of custard that is baked in a caramel sauce. This pudding may be made with fruit juices, cheese, dried or crystalized fruits, condensed milk, coconut, bread, nuts and many other ingredients, including corn and cornstarch.

The mould is lined with caramelized sugar, which is prepared by burning 3 tablespoons of sugar in a heavy skillet and then adding about 3/4 cup of water and cooking down for about 10 minutes, stirring until sugar is thoroughly dissolved in the liquid. If a large mould is to be used, the caramel syrup should be increased. The syrup is then poured into the mould, which is tilted until bottom and sides are coated. Then the pudding mixture is poured or spooned into the mould, the pudding is baked in a bain-marie and removed from the oven when it responds to the custard test.[1]

It is not difficult to unmould these puddings. After they have been removed from the oven and the bain-marie, they should be allowed to cool for 15 or 20 minutes

---

[1] The custard test for "doneness" is accomplished by inserting a sharp pointed knife in the custard midway between the rim and the center. The knife should come out clean when drawn toward the rim and retain some of the semi-liquid when drawn toward the center. The custard will continue to solidify as it cools.

and then the edges are loosened with a small paring knife, as one would with a gelatin dessert. Shake mould from side to side and turn onto the serving plate. A sauce may accompany the pudding or it may be served plain.

Blancmange prepared from cornstarch, eggs and coconut milk is another type of pudding very much used in Brazil. These should always be creamy and of a satiny texture. A consistent favorite in this class is the *Manjar Branco* — a blancmange made from coconut milk and served garnished with large juicy prunes.

One of the best-liked puddings is coconut pudding made from freshly-grated coconut. Although this is called a pudding, it usually has more of the consistency of a cake. The egg content separates slightly in baking so that, when it is served, a gelatin-like layer of eggs appears, which could account for its being called a pudding. Coconut pudding finds acceptance not only as a delicious dessert, but also as a tea-table attraction. It may be sliced like a cake and served with a wedge of cheese or eaten plain. Because *Pudim de Coco* is such a favorite, every cook has her own special recipe. Four are included here.

Apple Pudding
Pudim de Maçã

1 20-ounce can sliced apples for pie with the liquid or
2 1/4 cups sliced raw apples with 1/4 cup water • 1 cup sugar • 1 tablespoon cornstarch
1 tablespoon butter • 1/2 teaspoon vanilla • 1/4 cup crème de cacao • 6 eggs, separated
whipped cream • maraschino cherries

Cook apples (either canned with their liquid or raw with the water) with sugar in a covered saucepan until they are very well done, then mash and remove from heat. Cream cornstarch and butter and stir into apple mixture. Allow mixture to cool, then add the vanilla, crème de cacaó and beaten egg yolks. Mix and fold in stiffly-beaten egg whites. Turn mixture into a 2 1/2-quart pudding mould which has been caramelized (see p. 481). Set mould in a pan of hot water and bake in 375° oven about 50 minutes or until pudding responds to custard test. Remove from oven, allow to partially cool, then loosen sides of mould and turn into a pudding dish. Garnish with cherries and serve with whipped cream that has been sweetened with sugar and vanilla or with your favorite pudding sauce. If recipe is doubled, bake 1 1/4 hours.

[HILDA LEITE QUEIROGA, MINAS GERAIS]

VARIATION: For a Mocha flavor, mix 1/8 cup strongly-brewed instant coffee with 1/8 cup crème de cacaó and substitute for the 1/4 cup crème de cacao. Other substitutions are rum, port wine, brandy, a liqueur, or strong coffee.

Brazilian Bread Pudding
Pudim de Pão

1/2 freshly-grated coconut • 8 slices Italian bread
3 cups sugar boiled with 1 cup of water until it spins a thread • 3 eggs, separated
2/3 cup raisins • 1 teaspoon ground nutmeg • 1 tablespoon all-purpose flour
2 tablespoons butter

Mix 1/2 cup warm water with the coconut and extract the thick milk and reserve. Add another cup of water to the residue and extract the thin milk. Soak bread in the thin milk. Cool syrup and add little by little to the bread, then beat. Add egg yolks one by one and then the thick milk of the coconut. Stir in raisins and nutmeg. Beat in the flour with the butter and fold in stiffly-beaten egg whites. Turn into a caramelized mould (see p. 481) and bake in bain-marie in 375° oven until done — 1 to 1 1/2 hours.

N O T E : Port wine may be used in this recipe.

[LIA MAGRO, PERNAMBUCO]

Avocado Pudding
Pudim de Abacate

Prepare the full recipe for Avocado Cream (p. 291). Make a meringue with 2 egg whites, 2 tablespoons sugar and 1/4 teaspoon salt. Turn Avocado Cream into a baking dish. Cover with the meringue and bake in preheated 350° oven until meringue is delicately brown (10-15 minutes). Serve chilled.

Brazilian Pudding
Pudim Brasileiro

1 cup cooked, puréed pumpkin • 3/4 cup sugar • 2 ounces butter • 6 egg yolks
1/4 cup sifted all-purpose flour • 1/4 cup port wine • 1/2 teaspoon nutmeg
1/2 teaspoon cinnamon • 1 cup milk • 1/4 cup candied citrom

Cream sugar and butter and add to the pumpkin and well-beaten egg yolks. Stir in the flour, wine, nutmeg, cinnamon, milk and the citron, which has been cut into small pieces. Turn into a 2-quart caramelized mould (see p. 481) and bake in bain-marie in a preheated 375° oven until pudding responds to the custard test.

[TRANSLATED FROM: **NOÇÕES DE ARTE CULINÁRIA** BY MARIA THEREZA A. COSTA, SÃO PAULO]

Cassava Pudding
Pudim de Mandioca

2 cups grated raw cassava root (about 1 1/2 pounds of roots) • 1 cup milk
3/4 cup melted butter • 1/4 cup grated Muenster cheese • 12 egg yolks
6 egg whites • 1 1/4 cups sugar • 1 teaspoon salt • cinnamon

Squeeze or press any liquid from the cassava root and discard root. To the residue add milk, butter, cheese, beaten egg yolks, sugar and salt. Fold in the beaten egg whites. Turn into a well-buttered 2-quart Pyrex baking dish and bake in a preheated 375° oven for 15 minutes. Reduce heat to 350° and bake 35 to 40 minutes more or until a steel knife emerges clean when inserted in center of pudding. Cool slightly, then turn out onto a serving dish and sprinkle generously with powdered cinnamon.

N O T E : This pudding should be served the same day as it is prepared.

[MARIA LUIZA NARDON, SÃO PAULO]

Cheese Pudding
Pudim de Queijo

4 eggs, separated • 1/4 cup sugar • 1/2 cup grated Parmesan cheese
2 tablespoons butter • 1 tablespoon all-purpose flour • 2 1/2 cups milk

Beat egg whites until stiff, then add yolks and continue to beat well. Add sugar, cheese, butter, flour and beat until smooth, then add the milk. Pour into a caramelized mould (p. 481) and bake in a bain-marie in a preheated 350° oven for about 45 minutes or until pudding responds to the custard test.

[OTTILIA JANSEN DE MELLO, MINAS GERAIS]

Chestnut Pudding
Pudim de Castanhas

1/2 pound shelled, cooked chestnuts • 4 eggs, separated • 3 tablespoons sugar
2 tablespoons butter • 1/4 teaspoon salt • 1/2 teaspoon vanilla

Grind cooked nuts in the blender. Beat egg yolks with sugar and salt and add butter and vanilla, beating until light and fluffy. Add the chestnuts and fold in the stiffly-beaten egg whites. Bake in a well-buttered pudding mould in a preheated 350° oven for 30 or 40 minutes. Allow the pudding to cool slightly, then remove from the mold. Serve cold, covered with a rich chocolate sauce and garnished with some of the whole chestnuts, which have been soaked in a vanilla syrup or cognac.

[LAURITA PIRES, MINAS GERAIS]

Chestnut and Sponge Cake Pudding
Pudim de Pão-de-ló e Castanhas

1/4 pound sponge cake in pieces • 1/4 cup cognac • 6 cooked chestnuts, finely chopped
2 tablespoons melted butter • 1 cup sugar • 1/4 teaspoon salt • 6 egg yolks
3 egg whites, stiffly beaten

Mix all ingredients in the order given and fold in stiffly-beaten egg whites. Pour into a well-buttered 1 quart pudding mould and bake in a preheated 350° oven for 30 minutes. Serve plain or with a sauce.

[TRANSLATED FROM: **A ARTE DE COMER BEM** BY ROSA MARIA (MME. H. LEONARDOS)]

Coconut Pudding No. 1
Pudim de Coco Nº 1

1 freshly-grated coconut • 1 cup sugar • 12 egg yolks • a few whole cloves

Mix coconut and sugar. Add egg yolks and the cloves. Mix but do not beat. Turn into a very well-buttered 1 1/2 quart pudding mould and bake in bain-marie in a 350° preheated oven for about 1 hour. Serve cold with an American-type cheese.

[MARIA DA SILVA ALVES, RIO DE JANEIRO]

Coconut Pudding No. 2
Pudim de Coco Nº 2

3 cups sugar • 1 cup water • 1 tablespoon butter • 6 egg yolks • 3 egg whites
thick milk of 1 coconut • 1 cup grated coconut • 1 tablespoon all-purpose flour

Cook sugar and water until it spins a thread when dropped from the tines of a fork. Add butter and cool, completely. Stir in the beaten egg yolks, coconut milk, grated coconut and flour, then fold in the stiffly-beaten egg whites. Pour into a caramelized (see p. 481) 1 1/2-quart mold and bake in bain-marie in a 325° preheated oven for about 1 hour or until a knife inserted in center of pudding can be removed clean.

Coconut Pudding No. 3
Pudim de Coco Nº 3

2 1/4 cups sugar • 3/4 cup water • 4 eggs, separated • 1 grated coconut
2 tablespoons butter • 1/2 cup all-purpose flour, sifted

Cook sugar and water until it spins a thread when dropped from tines of a fork. Cool, add stiffly-beaten egg whites, then beaten yolks. Beat well and add coconut. Cream butter and flour and add to the coconut mixture. Turn into a well-buttered pudding form and bake in a preheated 400° oven until a thick crust forms on top (about 30 to 40 minutes). Add whole cloves, if desired.

Coconut Pudding No. 4
Pudim de Coco Nº 4

1 1/2 cups sugar • 3/4 cup water • 5 cups freshly-grated coconut • 1/4 pound butter
8 egg yolks • 1/4 cup port wine • 1/4 teaspoon grated lemon rind
1/2 cup sifted all-purpose flour

Cook sugar and water until it spins a thread. Knead coconut with butter. Pour syrup over the coconut; return to low heat and simmer 10 minutes, stirring back and forth. Cool to room temperature. Slightly beat the egg yolks, add wine and lemon rind then stir into the coconut mixture. Add sifted flour. Turn into a well-buttered 1 1/2-quart pudding mould. Bake in bain-marie in a 400° preheated oven approximately 1 hour. When a knife inserted in center of pudding comes out clean, the pudding is done. Cool slightly, loosen edges and unmould on serving plate.

Coconut Blancmange
Manjar Branco de Coco

4 cups freshly-grated coconut • 1/2 cup hot water • 4 cups hot milk, with 1/2 teaspoon salt
8 tablespoons sugar • 8 tablespoons cornstarch • 2 tablespoons butter

Add the hot water to the coconut and squeeze out as much milk as possible and set aside. Add the hot milk to the residue and repeat the process. Combine the thick and thin milks. Mix the sugar and cornstarch and pour in some of the milk to make a smooth paste. Heat the rest of the milk and gradually stir in the cornstarch mixture, stirring constantly over low heat to prevent lumps from forming. When the blancmange is thick and satiny smooth, remove from heat and let cool. When cool, beat in the butter, and any flavoring. Turn into a 1 1/2-quart mold, refrigerate and unmould on a serving plate garnished with a compote of prunes or any other fruit.

Date Pudding
Pudim de Tâmaras

1/2 cup shelled, unsalted peanuts • 1/2 pound pitted dates • 3/4 cup sugar
6 eggs, separated • 1/2 cup milk

Grind peanuts and dates in meat grinder or in the blender. Add sugar, beaten egg yolks and milk and fold in the stiffly-beaten egg whites. Turn into a 2-quart caramelized pudding mould (p. 481) and bake in bain-marie in a preheated 350° oven for 40 to 50 minutes or until pudding responds to the custard test. If the pudding begins to brown on the top too quickly, reduce heat to 300. Let cool, loosen sides and turn onto serving dish. Refrigerate and serve with whipped cream garnished with strawberries or fruit.

[OTTILIA JANSEN DE MELLO, MINAS GERAIS]

Diamantina Blancmange
Manjar Diamantenense

5 tablespoons rice flour • 5 tablespoons sugar • 1/2 teaspoon salt • 2 cups milk
2 tablespoons butter • 1 tablespoon orange flower water

Sift rice flour with sugar and salt and add milk. Heat, stirring constantly until cooked and mixture thickens. Remove from heat, add butter and cool. Butter a pudding mould. Fill the mould by dipping a tablespoon into the orange flower water and then removing a tablespoon of the blanc mange to the mould. Remove each tablespoon of the mixture to the mould by first dipping the spoon into the orange flower water, until all the mixture is in the mould. Place the mould under the broiler to brown. Cool slightly, then unmould and refrigerate. Serve garnished with a fruit compote.

[LAURITA PIRES, MINAS GERAIS]

490

I - W a n t - M o r e   P u d d i n g
Pudim Quero Mais

2 cups sugar boiled with 1/2 cup water • 6 eggs • 1 tablespoon butter
1 cup grated cheddar cheese • thick milk from 1 grated coconut
2 teaspoons all-purpose flour • 1/4 teaspoon salt

Boil sugar and water until it spins a thread when dropped from the tines of a fork. Cool thoroughly. Beat eggs, add butter, cheese, coconut milk, flour and salt. Combine with the cold sugar syrup and pour into a 2-quart buttered mould. Bake in a preheated 350° oven for approximately 60 minutes. Allow to cool, then unmould.

[HILDA MADASI, BAHIA]

M a n g o   P u d d i n g
Pudim de Manga

3 well-ripened mangos • 1 teaspoon lemon juice • 1/4 teaspoon salt • 5 tablespoons sugar
3 eggs, separated • 2 tablespoons cornstarch

Peel mangos, slice and cut into small pieces. Scrape as much pulp from the seeds as possible. Mix with the lemon juice and salt, then sprinkle with sugar and let stand 10 minutes. Mash with a potato masher and add the egg yolks. Blend in the cornstarch and then add the stiffly-beaten egg whites. Turn into a well-buttered 1 1/2-quart mold and bake in a preheated 375° oven for 10 minutes. Reduce heat to 350° and bake 30 minutes more. Remove from oven and allow to cool in the mould then turn into a pudding dish. Refrigerate and serve with a crushed fruit sauce.

Snow Pudding
Pudim de Claras

12 egg whites (1 1/3 cups) • 1 1/2 cups sugar

Line a 2-quart mold with caramelized sugar (p. 481), which has been made from 2/3 cup of the sugar called for in this recipe. Beat egg whites until stiff and gradually add remaining sugar. Pour into the caramelized mold and bake in bain-marie in preheated 325° oven for approximately 60-70 minutes. Test for "doneness" and remove from oven when completely baked. Allow to cool at room temperature, loosen sides with a sharp knife and unmould. Serve with the following sauce:

1 quart milk • 12 egg yolks • sugar to taste • 1/4 teaspoon salt • vanilla or Crème de Cacao

Heat milk with slightly-beaten yolks and sweeten to taste. Add the salt. Cook until mixture coats a metal spoon, strain and cool. Add flavoring when the sauce is cold. Chill before serving.

[MARIA THEREZA SANCHEZ, RIO DE JANEIRO]

492

Orange Pudding
Pudim de Laranja

12 egg yolks • 8 egg whites • grated rind of 1 orange
1 1/4 cups orange juice • 1 1/2 cups sugar

Beat egg yolks and whites with a wire whisk and add grated rind and juice. Strain through a coarse strainer and mix in the sugar. Turn into a 1 1/2-quart caramelized ring mould (see p. 481). Bake in bain-marie in a preheated 375° oven about 20 minutes. Reduce heat to 350° and bake another 15 minutes, or until pudding responds to the custard test. Let stand 10 minutes, loosen edges with a sharp knife and turn onto serving plate.

[TRANSLATED FROM: **NOÇÕES DE ARTE CULINÁRIA** BY MARIA THEREZA A. COSTA, SÃO PAULO]

Velvet Pudding
Pudim de Veludo

1 1/2 cups sugar • 12 egg yolks • 1 quart milk • 3 egg whites
1 tablespoon all-purpose flour • 1 teaspoon vanilla

Remove 2/3 cup of sugar from the quantity called for in the recipe and caramelize it, (see p. 481) then line a 2-quart mould with the caramelized sugar. Beat egg yolks, add remaining sugar and beat until thick. Gradually add the milk, then the stiffly-beaten egg whites, flour and vanilla. Mix very well and turn into the caramelized mould. Bake in bain-marie in a preheated 325° oven for approximately 1 1/2 hours. Remove when pudding responds to the custard test for "doneness." Allow to cool to room temperature, loosen the sides with a sharp knife and invert onto serving dish. Serve chilled.

[TRANSLATED FROM: **NOÇÕES DE ARTE CULINÁRIA** BY MARIA THEREZA A. COSTA, SÃO PAULO]

Sweet Corn Pudding
Canjiquinha de Milho Verde

*7 ears fresh corn • 1 freshly-grated coconut • 1 cup milk • 1/4 teaspoon salt
5 tablespoons sugar • 1 tablespoon butter • 1/4 teaspoon anise seed (optional)
powdered cinnamon*

Shuck the corn and scrape off the kernels. Squeeze out thick milk from the coconut and reserve. Mix coconut residue, corn kernels and milk and grind very finely in food chopper or in electric blender. Strain through a coarse sieve, add salt, sugar, butter, 2/3 of the thick coconut milk (and aniseed, if desired). Cook over low heat, stirring constantly until the mixture thickens. When it is as thick as a cornstarch pudding, remove from heat and cool. Line a pudding dish with the other 1/3 of the thick coconut milk and pour in the pudding mixture. Refrigerate and serve with powdered cinnamon sprinkled on top.

[SARITA BRANT, MINAS GERAIS]

Pumpkin Custard
Pudim de Abóbora

1 cup canned or freshly-cooked puréed pumpkin • 3 eggs, slightly beaten
1/2 cup firmly packed brown sugar • 3/4 teaspoon salt • 1/4 teaspoon ginger
1/2 teaspoon cinnamon • 1 1/4 cups milk (or 1 cup evaporated milk)
1/4 teaspoon grated orange rind

Mix pumpkin and slightly beaten eggs, add sugar, salt and spices. Stir in the milk and orange rind. Pour into custard cups and bake in bain-marie in 350° preheated oven for 30-40 minutes or until it responds to the custard test. Yields 6 cups. If you bake the custard in a 1 quart mould, allow 1 to 1 1/2 hours to bake in a preheated 350° oven.

Tangerine Pudding
Pudim de Tangerina

3/4 cup sugar • 1/3 cup water • 1 teaspoon butter • 1 cup tangerine juice
6 egg yolks • 2 egg whites • 1 tablespoon all-purpose flour

Boil sugar and water until it spins a thread. Add butter and cool. When mixture is cold, add the tangerine juice and the beaten egg yolks. Add the stiffly-beaten egg whites and the flour, and pour into a caramelized mould (p. 481). Bake in a preheated 375° oven in bain-marie until pudding responds to custard test, about 35 to 40 minutes. When cool, turn onto a serving plate and refrigerate.

[OTTILIA JANSEN DE MELLO, MINAS GERAIS]

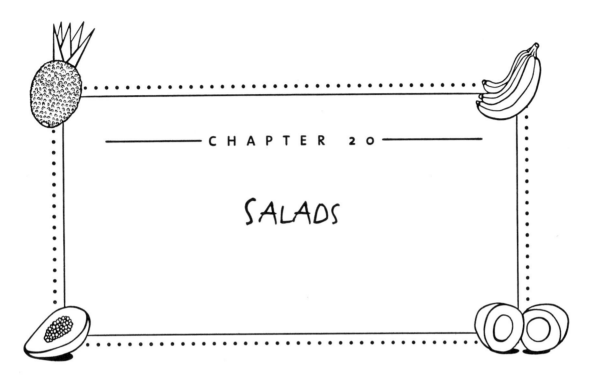

CHAPTER 20

SALADS

Oh, herbaceous treat!
Twould tempt the dying anchorite to eat;
Back to the world he'd turn his fleeting soul;
And plunge his fingers in the salad bowl.

SYDNEY SMITH, A RECIPE FOR A SALAD

Although modern educational material dealing with nutrition emphasizes the necessity of the daily consumption of a salad, the idea goes back four or five thousand years ago to the time when the Egyptians used cucumbers, onions and garlic to such an extent that, when the Hebrews were free from Egyptian slavery, they missed their daily allotment of these salad ingredients.

But it took a long time for the Brazilian to accept the idea that salads could not only be beneficial, but tasty as well. They are not the favorites in Brazil that they are with their Northern neighbors.

Salads have become so numerous in the United States that they have been classified in accordance with their temperature (chilled, frozen and hot) of the way they are served (bowl, decorative or individual.) Then there are entire meal salads, fruit salads, etc. But in Brazil, a "salad is a salad is a salad" as Gertrude Stein's "rose is a rose is a rose."

The Brazilian's indifference to *Saladas*, especially that of the *sertanejos* goes back hundreds of years. In 1809, Koster wrote of the *sertanejos*: "of green vegetables they know nothing, and they laugh at the idea of eating any kind of a salad."[1] This reluctance held true 45 years later when T. Lynn Smith went to Brazil.[2]

As an explanation, it should be pointed out in this respect that the habitat of the *sertanejo* in Northeastern Brazil, is an area of periodic drought. The economic system is based on sugar and cattle with only a small production of edible fruits and vegetables. It is not surprising, therefore, that salads are not part of the daily fare of this region, for the simple reason that the ingredients are not available.

---

[1] Henry Koster, *Travels in Brazil, 1809-1815* v. 1, p. 207.

[2] T. Lynn Smith, *Brazil, People and Institutions* (Baton Rouge: Louisiana State University Press, 1954), p. 290.

Today, due to the dissemination of more advanced ideas on nutrition, the Brazilian is becoming aware of the potentialities of salads and vegetables. He is looking upon the vegetable kingdom with more respect than the generation preceding him. At the same time, the Brazilian Government has set up specific agencies in the drought areas where, through better utilization of natural water resources and modern techniques, it will be possible to produce more edible crops. Thus, it is hoped that the Brazilians of the new generation will grow up with the habit of consuming more salads and vegetables than their parents.

Certain it is that the Brazilian housewife is turning more towards the salad course to lend beauty and interest to meal planning. In the areas where greens, and fruits, too, are plentiful, the homemaker has no problem in salad preparation, and with a little flare for combining foods that go well together and a little imagination, she is producing a variety of salad "symphonies."

A beautifully-presented salad, attractively served can be just as spectacular and decorative as any floral arrangement. Modern Brazilian housewives recognize this fact. They are leaning more and more to this chorus of fruits and vegetables to enliven their menus with gay songs of Spring.

Artichoke Salad
Salada de Alcachofras

1 cup diced apples • 1 cup grated carrots • 1 pound cleaned cooked shrimp
Russian dressing • 12 cooked artichoke hearts • hard-boiled egg slices and capers • lettuce

Mix apples, carrots and sliced shrimp with enough Russian dressing to hold. Season. Pile high on artichoke hearts and garnish with hard-boiled egg slices and capers. Place on lettuce leaves.

[TRANSLATED FROM: A ARTE DE COMER BEM BY ROSA MARIA (MME. H. LEONARDOS)]

Avocado Mousse
Mousse de Abacates

4 cups mashed avocado (5 or 6 small avocados) • 1 teaspoon salt
2 envelopes unflavored gelatin • 1/2 cup cold water • 1 tablespoon lemon juice
2 tablespoons grated onion • 3/4 cup mayonnaise • 1/2 cup whipped cream
shredded lettuce • cold, cooked shrimp marinated in lemon juice, salt and pepper

Peel and mash avocados. Add salt. Mix the gelatin in cold water and then heat over boiling water until it is dissolved thoroughly. Stir into avocado and add lemon juice and onion. Refrigerate until mixture begins to congeal, then fold in the mayonnaise and whipped cream. Correct seasoning. Turn into a 5-cup ring mould. Cover tightly with wax paper and chill in the refrigerator. Unmould on a bed of shredded lettuce or watercress and garnish with the shrimp. Serve with mayonnaise.

[OTTILIA JANSEN DE MELLO, MINAS GERAIS]

Stuffed Avocados No. 1
Abacates Recheados Nº 1

2 avocados • 3 chopped cooked carrots • 2 chopped apples • 2 hard-boiled eggs • salt
1/4 cup lemon juice • 1/4 cup cream • watercress • mayonnaise

Peel avocados, cut in halves crosswise and remove seeds. Cut each half into 2 round slices and chop the ends to mix with carrots and apples. Mash egg yolks, add salt, lemon juice and cream to make a dressing. Marinate the carrots and apples in the dressing and correct seasoning. Prepare individual salads on a large plate by placing rounds of avocado on the watercress and piling high with the marinated mixture. Garnish with leftover egg whites. Serve with mayonnaise. Yields 8 servings.

Stuffed Avocados No. 2
Abacates Recheados Nº 2

2 avocados marinated in lemon juice • 4 cooked prunes • 6 seeded black olives
2 tablespoons chopped celery • 1/2 cup chopped ham • mayonnaise to hold
lettuce • 1 peeled tomato

Peel avocados, cut in halves lengthwise and remove seeds. Marinate in lemon juice. Chop prunes and olives, mix with celery and ham and enough mayonnaise to hold. Season. Spoon some of this filling into the avocados, place each half on a bed of shredded lettuce and garnish with the quartered tomato and small mounds of mayonnaise. Yields 4 servings.

Beet and Potato Salad
Salada de Beterrabas e Batatas

1 pound potatoes, boiled in their skins • 1/2 teaspoon salt • 4 tablespoons hot milk
2 hard-boiled eggs, separated • french dressing • 2 sliced beets • salt and pepper
shredded lettuce

Cool potatoes, peel and slice. Dissolve salt in the milk, and pour over potatoes. Mash egg yolks into well-seasoned French dressing and spoon over the potatoes. Chop egg whites and sprinkle over potatoes. Marinate sliced beets in French dressing, then arrange in the center of a plate in overlapping slices. Surround with shredded lettuce, and lay potatoes also in overlapping slices. If necessary, season with salt and pepper. Serve with French dressing.

[MARIA BARBOZA NUNES, RIO DE JANEIRO]

Brasilia Salad
Salada de Brasília

1 cup slivered apples • 1 cubed orange • 1 sliced banana • 1/2 cup white seedless grapes
1/2 cup slivered Brazil nuts • 1/4 cup orange juice • salt and sugar to taste
mayonnaise and whipped cream mixed in equal proportions

Mix the fruits and add the nuts, saving a small amount for garnish. Stir in the orange juice, and add sugar and salt to taste. Mix mayonnaise with an equal amount of whipped cream and add enough to the salad to hold it together. Serve on watercress, with a little dressing on top and garnished with the nuts.

Broccoli Salad
Salada de Brócolis

1 package frozen broccoli • 4 medium-size potatoes • 2 tomatoes
1/2 cup hollandaise sauce • 1 hard-boiled egg

Cook frozen broccoli as directed on package. Drain and chill. Boil potatoes in their jackets in salted water and when cooked, drain, peel and allow to cool thoroughly. Slice and arrange on the outer edge of a round plate, interspersed with slices of tomatoes. The broccoli should be placed in the center. Pour sauce over the broccoli and sprinkle salt over the potatoes and tomatoes. Separate yolk from white of egg. Chop the white and sprinkle over the broccoli. Sieve yolk through a coarse strainer over the tomatoes and potatoes.

Cauliflower and Watercress Salad
Salada de Couve-flor e Agrião

2 packages frozen cauliflower • 1 bunch watercress • yolk of 1 hard-boiled egg
1 teaspoon salt • 1/8 cup lemon juice • 3/8 cup olive oil • piquant mayonnaise

Cook frozen cauliflower as directed on package. Drain, cool and chill. Wash watercress thoroughly. Place in a clean towel or napkin and, gathering the ends together, shake out all the moisture, then turn onto absorbent paper. Mash egg yolk with salt, add lemon juice and oil, and beat with a rotary beater. Arrange the cauliflower in the center of a round plate with the watercress surrounding. Spoon dressing over the salada and serve with a highly-seasoned mayonnaise.

Chick Pea Salad
Salada de Grão-de-bico

1 20-ounce can chick peas or garbanzas or 2 cups cooked chick peas • French dressing
2 tablespoons chopped spring onion • 1 tablespoon chopped parsley • salt and pepper

Drain chick peas and slightly warm with the French dressing. Add chopped onions, parsley, salt and pepper. Chill and serve.

N O T E : Chick peas may be purchased dry, soaked overnight and boiled the next day, like dry beans. Cover with clear, salted water and boil in a covered vessel. If it is necessary to add water, be sure it is hot, because if cold water is added, the chick peas will not cook. Allow about 1 1/2 hours to boil. The chick peas are done when you can crush one of them between the thumb and forefinger. They may be served as a vegetable by adding butter, salt and pepper.

Eggplant
Salada de Berinjela

1 eggplant • French dressing • salad greens • sliced tomatoes

Peel eggplant and slice in 1/4 inch slices. Cook in boiling salted water, but do not overcook. Drain on absorbent paper. Marinate in highly-seasoned French dressing and arrange on shredded salad greens. Garnish with sliced tomatoes.

Edward Salad
Salada Eduardo

2 small head lettuce • 1 bunch chicory • 2 cups shredded cooked fish • 2 ounces grated cheese
2 tablespoons vinegar • 1 tablespoon Worcestershire sauce • mayonnaise or French dressing
1/4 pound lean bacon, fried crisp • 3 hard-boiled eggs

Wash and dry lettuce and chicory and set aside a few tender leaves to garnish. Shred the rest of the greens, add fish, cheese, vinegar and Worcestershire sauce. Mix well. Combine with either mayonnaise or French dressing; taste and correct seasoning. Turn onto a bed made from the reserved salad greens and garnish with slices of hard-boiled egg and the crumbled pieces of crisp bacon.

[DAURA ALVES DA COSTA, RIO DE JANEIRO]

Fine Vegetable Salad
Boa Salada de Legumes

1 cup cauliflower flowerets • 2 sliced tomatoes • 1/2 cup green peas • 2 sliced potatoes
1 cup string beans • 1/2 cup French dressing • 2 sliced hard-boiled eggs • green mayonnaise

All the vegetables (except tomatoes) are precooked and chilled. In the center of a round serving plate, make a pyramid of the cauliflowerets and surround the base of the pyramid with sliced tomatoes standing upright. Spread the peas around the tomatoes and lay the sliced potatoes in a circle around the peas. Outline the potatoes with the string beans. Spoon the French dressing over the vegetables and garnish with the sliced eggs. Press small rosebuds of green mayonnaise on the cauliflower and around the edge of the plate. Serve accompanied by a small dish of the mayonnaise.

[MARIA BARBOZA NUNES, RIO DE JANEIRO]

Green Mayonnaise
Maionese de agrião e tomate

7 sprigs watercress • 10 leaves spinach • 1 teaspoon lemon juice • 3/4 cup mayonnaise

Wash greens thoroughly and simmer about 3 minutes. Drain, rinse in cold water and dry on absorbent paper. Chop the greens, add lemon juice and liquidize in the blender. Add mayonnaise. Yields approximately 1 cup.

Fruit Salad
Salada de Frutas

1 1/2 cups slivered apples • 4 slices cut pineapple • 1 cup seeded, peeled grapes
1 mango, peeled and slivered • 2 bananas, chopped • 2 ounces boiled ham, cut julienne
1/2 cup mayonnaise, mixed with • 1/2 cup whipped cream • salad greens • strawberries

Mix apples, pineapple, grapes, mango and bananas with the ham. Add the mayonnaise which has been mixed with the whipped cream. Taste and season. Serve on salad greens garnished with fresh strawberries.

Ham and Tomato Salad
Salada de Tomate com Presunto

Tomatoes filled with aspic • boiled ham • shredded lettuce • watercress • bananas
oranges • radish flowers • mayonnaise or salad dressing

Cut tops of the tomatoes and scoop out the insides. Make an aspic from the pulp and pour into tomato shells to set. Refrigerate. Cut the ham into slivers and place it in a mound in the center of a large plate. Surround the ham with shredded lettuce and cover the rest of the plate with watercress. Place tomatoes around the edge of the plate with sliced oranges and bananas. Garnish with radish flowers and serve with mayonnaise or a salad dressing.

[MARIA BARBOZA NUNES, RIO DE JANEIRO]

Leonora's Salad
Salada de Leonora

3 cups cooked leftover turkey, chicken or duck, diced • 2 tart apples, peeled and diced
1/2 cup chopped celery • 3 cooked carrots, cubed • 1/2 cup seeded grapes
1 cooked chayote, diced • 1/2 cup sliced beets • highly-seasoned French dressing
lettuce • mayonnaise • chopped peanuts

Mix ingredients in the order given and marinate in the French dressing. Taste and check seasoning. Let stand about 10 minutes to blend. Arrange on lettuce and serve dotted with mayonnaise and garnished with the peanuts.

Maria's Cold Plate
Prato Frio de Maria

Cooked shrimp marinated in lemon juice and salt
white asparagus tips rolled in cold, smoked tongue • artichoke hearts filled with chopped
hard-boiled eggs and capers • watercress • highly-seasoned mayonnaise
black olives • carrot curls

Place shrimp in the center of a large plate and surround with the asparagus tips. Line the rest of the plate with the watercress and artistically arrange the artichoke hearts, mayonnaise and black olives on the bed of watercress. Intersperse with carrot curls.

Melon and Ham Salad
Salada de Melão e Presunto

1 melon • 1/3 cup port wine • lettuce leaves • sliced ham • 1/4 cup fresh lime juice
1/4 cup honey • grated lime rind

Cut melon in half, remove seeds and peel. Slice in rounds. Pour the wine over melon slices and refrigerate, turning rounds over once in a while. Place melon slices on lettuce leaves. Roll sliced ham and place on lettuce leaves. Mix lime juice, honey and grated lime rind, and spoon over rounds of melon and the lettuce.

Okra Salad
Salada de Quiabo

1 package frozen okra • 1 tablespoon lemon juice • 1 tablespoon chopped onion
French dressing • salad greens • 2 hard-boiled eggs • capers

Cook frozen okra according to directions on package. Drain, cool and sprinkle with the lemon juice. Add onion and enough French dressing to moisten the okra. Taste and correct seasonings. Lift on to salad greens and garnish with sliced eggs with a caper in the center of each slice. Serve with extra French dressing.

Pineapple Salad
Salada de Abacaxi

Arrange wedges of canned pineapple on a bed of lettuce and watercress. Intersperse with canned asparagus and canned apricot halves filled with chopped bananas. Garnish with grated cooked beets and serve with a piquant mayonnaise.

Palm Heart Salad No. 1
Salada de Palmito Nº 1

1 small can drained palm hearts • 1 package frozen peas • 2 cups diced cooked beets
1 tablespoon minced onion • 1 cup diced cucumber • mayonnaise to hold
salt and pepper • lettuce • chopped black olives

Slice the palm hearts and mix with the peas, which have been cooked, drained and chilled. Add beets, onion and cucumber and enough mayonnaise to hold. Check seasoning. Pile onto lettuce leaves and garnish with the chopped olives.

Palm Heart Salad No. 2
Salada de Palmito Nº 2

1 small can drained palm hearts • mayonnaise seasoned with mustard
sliced tomatoes • sliced hard-boiled eggs • sliced boiled beets • stuffed olives

Slice the palm hearts and arrange in the center of a large round plate. Cover with mayonnaise. Surround palm hearts with a circle of sliced tomatoes and hard-boiled eggs on top of the tomatoes. Place a sliced stuffed olive on top of each slice of egg. Garnish the whole plate with thin slices of beets.

[TRANSLATED FROM: **AS RECEITAS PARA VOCÊ DA TIA EVELINA, 4**TH EDITION]

Rice Salad
Salada de Arroz

2 cups cold cooked rice • 1 cup canned peas, drained • 1 sour apple, cut julienne style
1 tablespoon chopped pimiento • 1/2 avocado, peeled and sliced • 1 tablespoon lemon juice
1 tablespoon vinegar • 2 tablespoons olive oil • 1 teaspoon prepared mustard
salt and pepper to taste • cooked beets, shrimp or hard-boiled eggs for garnish

Mix rice with the fruit and vegetables. Make a dressing of the lemon juice, vinegar, oil and mustard and add to rice and marinate. Season. Let refrigerate at least 30 minutes to set the flavor. Arrange rice in a pyramid on a bed of shredded lettuce or press into a mould and then unmould. Garnish with the cooked shrimp, eggs or beets. Serve with French dressing.

Rainbow Salad
Salada Arco-Íris

carrots • white squash • green peas • beets • vinegar • olive oil • lettuce • salt
chopped parsley • lemon juice • yolks of 2 hard-boiled eggs • olives

Arrange cooked vegetables on a bed of shredded lettuce in an artistic manner. Prepare a dressing with salt, parsley, lemon juice, vinegar and oil, and add the mashed egg yolks. Spoon the dressing over the vegetables. Chop the egg whites with olives and use for garnish.

[MARIA BARBOZA NUNES, RIO DE JANEIRO]

512

Prato Fino

Boil potatoes, peel and slice in round slices. Chill. Arrange in center of a plate and cover with well-seasoned mayonnaise. On top of the mayonnaise, sprinkle ground-up meat from cooked smoked sausages or frankfurters from which the casings have been removed. On the outer rim of the plate, overlay slices of apples, tomatoes and pineapple.

[IZAURA PINTO, MINAS GERAIS]

Salmon Salad
Salada de salmão

1 1-pound can salmon, drained • 1/4 cup croutons • 1 chopped hard-boiled egg
1/4 cup pickles, chopped (or relish) • 1/4 cup boiled, cubed potatoes
1 very thinly-sliced onion • 1/2 cup mayonnaise • seasoning
capers • watercress • sliced cucumbers

Remove skin and bones from salmon and mix ingredients in the order given, season to taste. Add the capers and mayonnaise and serve with watercress and sliced cucumbers. Serves 6.

Spinach Salad
Salada de Espinafre

1 cup raw shredded spinach • 1 hard-boiled egg • 1 peeled tomato • 1 minced onion
1 or 2 ounces boiled ham, cut julienne style or • leftover poultry • French dressing

Wash and drain the spinach, and crisp in the refrigerator. Dry, cut in fine shreds and measure 1 cup. Place in the salad bowl. Cut tomato in eighths and lay over spinach together with the sliced egg, onion and ham. Dot with French dressing and toss. Season to taste. Serve at once.

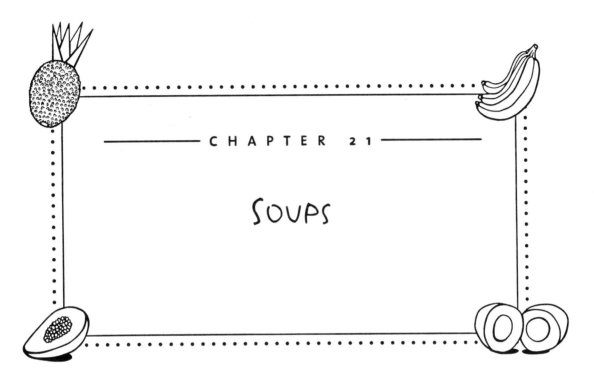

---— CHAPTER 21 ——---

Soups

Beautiful Soup! Who cares for fish,
Game or any other dish?

LEWIS CARROLL, ALICE'S ADVENTURES IN WONDERLAND, CHAP. 10

The mock turtle knew whereof he spoke, as a well-prepared soup, with plenty of meat, fish or vegetables can actually be served as a meal, and so, "who cares for fish, game or any other dish?" I remember reading an interview that a famous novelist gave to a reporter. She was telling of the lean years when she and her husband were striving for recognition in the literary world. The novelist would prepare a hearty soup, which she used to serve generously to her husband. Usually, after he had enjoyed it and probably had a second helping, he would decline the non-existent main course to which his wife had alluded when she served the pseudo first course.

"Beautiful Soup" goes back to the Bible when Esau sold his birthright for a "mess of pottage," which was said to be red lentil purée. Since Biblical times, soups have been one of the mainstays of popular nutrition and nearly every nation boasts of one soup that it calls its own. The Russians have BORSHT, the Italians have MINESTRONE, and the French BOUILLABAISSE and VICHISSOISE, while the American has devoted all his culinary skill to perfecting the many CHOWDERS, which are served as regional dishes in different areas of the country. It might be said in this respect that, until the present, no authority on American cookery has settled the question as to whether clam chowder should be made with tomatoes or milk: Manhattan or New England style.

Brazilians also have their favorite soups. One is *Canja* — a chicken rice soup — and the other is black bean soup. Split pea and lentil soups are also popular in Brazil while in some regions excellent soups are made from yams, corn, macaroni and in Minas Gerais State, kale.

There is a peanut soup served in Brazil, and the recipe is included below. This recipe, however, is not the same as the famous one used at the Williamsburg, Virginia Inn. Although both these soups are prepared from a chicken stock base, the Brazilian soup introduces the mashed peanuts mixed with rice and eggs, and baked like a cake. The cake is then cut into squares over which the hot broth is poured.

The Williamsburg peanut soup, on the other hand, adds peanut butter and cream directly to the stock.

Several ingredients are used by the Brazilian cook to thicken soups. Perhaps one of the best known is the pumpkin. I once had a cook who put pumpkin into any kind of soup she happened to be making and the results were always good. The truth is that Brazilians find the pumpkin a very versatile product and use it to a far greater extent than Americans, who are content to restrict its use to the Thanksgiving Day pie. In Brazil, the pumpkin comes to the table in soups and stews, as a vegetable, as well as in several desserts and candies.

Many flours and meals are also employed to thicken soups, especially rice, tapioca and potato flours and, sometimes, arrowroot. Cheese is another ingredient used to both thicken and flavor soups.

Brazilian soup recipes usually begin at the beginning, that is, by giving directions for preparing the stock. However, because such excellent prepared stocks are easily available to housewives in North America, it has been possible to take a legitimate short cut in presenting these soup recipes by deleting this preliminary step, which in no way affects the final product. Should one still wish to "begin at the beginning," it is suggested that any reliable cookbook be consulted for a beef or chicken stock recipe, which, with the exception of a few cream soups and the bean and turtle soups, form the basis for most of the recipes in this chapter. Otherwise, it is suggested that canned beef or chicken consommé be used as the stock or a good grade of bouillon cubes.

A Brazilian diplomat, Ambassador Leão Veloso, originated a kind of Brazilian bouillabaisse known as Leão Velloso Soup. This soup, which is actually more of a chowder, is very popular in Rio de Janeiro, where it is served in two well-known restaurants. Through the courtesy of Mr. João Machado, owner of the famous A Cabaça Grande Ltda., we are able to include the recipe for *Sopa Leão Velloso* as it is served in this famous restaurant.

Bean Purée with Coconut Milk
Feijão de Coco

1 pound pinto beans • 1 chopped onion • 1 peeled and chopped tomato
1 tablespoon chopped parsley • 1/2 cup olive oil • salt and black pepper
thick milk of 1 coconut

Pick and wash beans and soak overnight. Next day, drain and add enough clear water to cover beans. Cook in a covered saucepan until beans are tender, adding water as necessary to maintain a 2-quart quantity. Sauté the vegetables in 1 tablespoon of the oil (taken from the 1/2 cup) and, when brown, add to the cooked beans. Simmer 30 minutes, mash and press through a coarse sieve. The result should be a thin purée. Mix with the rest of the olive oil and cook over low heat. Season with salt and pepper to taste, add the coconut milk, heat thoroughly and serve.

N O T E : This purée is served in a soup plate as a first course, but it is not considered a soup in Brazil, even though it could pass as such. Traditionally, it should be followed by a dish made of some kind of fish. Usually, palm oil accompanies *Feijão de Coco* as many people prefer to add a few drops.

[LIA MAGRO, PERNAMBUCO]

519

Black Bean Soup
Sopa de Feijão Preto

1 cup dried black beans • 2 quarts beef stock • 1 cup canned puréed pumpkin
salt and pepper to taste • 1 thinly-sliced onion • 1/2 cup tomato sauce
3 teaspoons tapioca flour • 2 tablespoons butter
croutons or wedges of hard-boiled eggs or lemons

Pick over beans and wash. Soak overnight in 3 cups of water. Change the water and cover with 2 quarts of beef stock. Cook in covered saucepan over medium heat until beans are tender, adding small quantities of water as necessary. When beans are done, add pumpkin and cook, uncovered, with salt and pepper, sliced onion and tomato sauce until soup is of desired consistency. Strain and return to heat with tapioca flour and butter. Serve with croutons or wedges of hard-boiled eggs or lemons. Yields 7 cups.

Carrot Soup
Sopa de Cenouras

3 tablespoons tapioca or rice flour • 5 cups beef stock • 4 grated carrots
1/2 cup chopped parsley • 1/2 cup tomato sauce • grated Parmesan cheese

Mix the flour with 1/2 cup of the cold stock and gently heat the rest of the stock with the carrots, parsley and tomato sauce. When carrots are cooked, add the flour mixture and simmer until thick. Season to taste and serve with grated Parmesan cheese sprinkled on top. Yields 8 cups.

[REPRINTED FROM AUTHOUR'S ARTICLE IN JULY 1963 ISSUE OF **GOURMET MAGAZINE**]

Cheese Soup
Sopa de Queijo

2 tablespoons butter • 1/2 thinly-sliced onion • 2 tablespoons bread crumbs
1/2 cup grated Parmesan cheese • 1 1/2 quarts well-seasoned stock
3 egg yolks • 1 cup milk

Melt butter in a skillet and add the onion, then the bread crumbs. Gently fry until golden brown. Mix in the cheese. Add heated stock and bring to a boil. When ready to serve, add the egg yolks, which have been blended with the milk. Heat and check seasoning. Yields approximately 8 cups.

Chicken Soup
Sopa de Galinha

Chicken consommé • grated cheese • egg yolks

Heat chicken consommé. Thicken with 2 tablespoons of a mild grated cheese for each cup of soup. When ready to serve pour boiling hot over an egg yolk for each serving.

[TRANSLATED FROM: **A ARTE DE COMER BEM**, BY ROSA MARIE (MME. H. LEONARDOS)]

Chicken Soup with Rice
Canja

1 stewing chicken • 1 tablespoon butter • 4 chopped tomatoes • 3 quarts water
1 cut-up onion • 4 tablespoons parsley • 1 cup uncooked rice • 1 cup diced ham

Cut chicken in pieces and brown in butter with tomatoes over a low heat. Cover with water, season with salt and pepper, and add the onion and parsley, which have been tied in a cheesecloth bag. Cook chicken until tender, then remove from liquid and separate meal from bones and skin. Strain the broth and add enough water to make 3 quarts. Place chicken meat back in the broth together with the rice and ham and the bag containing onion and parsley. Simmer until rice is done. Remove bag of onion and parsley. Yields approximately 12 good-sized serving.

N O T E : Often, sliced carrots are cooked in the canja.

[REPRINTED FROM AUTHOR'S ARTICLE IN JULY 1963 ISSUE OF **GOURMET MAGAZINE**]

Coconut Soup No. 1
Sopa de Coco Nº 1

3 cups medium white sauce • 4 cups chicken broth • 1/2 cup grated coconut
1 cup thin coconut milk • 1/4 cup tapioca flour • salt and nutmeg • 1/4 cup heavy cream

Combine sauce with 3 cups of the broth and heat slowly. Add coconut and coconut milk. Cook in a double boiler for about 30 minutes. Mix flour with the other cup of broth until the mixture is smooth and free from lumps, then add to contents of double boiler. Simmer about 10 minutes. Season with salt and nutmeg to taste. Stir in the heavy cream. Yields approximately 6 1/2 cups.

Coconut Soup No. 2
Sopa de Coco Nº 2

2 10 1/2-ounce cans condensed cream of chicken soup • 1/2 cup grated coconut
3/4 cup thin coconut milk • 2 tablespoons rice flour • 1 cup milk
salt and nutmeg • 1/4 cup heavy cream

Prepare soup according to directions on can, using only 3/4 can of water for each can of soup (or milk, if a richer soup is desired). Add coconut and coconut milk. Simmer for about 15 minutes. Prepare a smooth mixture of rice flour and milk, then stir into hot soup. Cook over low heat, stirring constantly for 5 minutes. Season to taste with salt and a few grains of nutmeg, then stir in the heavy cream. Yields about 6 cups.

Corn Meal and Ham Soup
Sopa de Fubá com Presunto

1/2 pound raw smoked ham • 2 quarts beef stock
1/4 of a small head of cabbage in one piece • Seasoning
1/4 recipe for Corn Meal Mush, p. 53

Parboil ham in enough water to cover, for 15 minutes, or until it is not salty to the taste. Remove ham from the water and add it to the stock along with the cabbage. Simmer in stock until both ham and cabbage are done, then remove them from the stock and cut into fine slivers. Return to stock. Season to taste. Prepare separately a soup plate of corn meal mush, by following 1/2 the recipe on page 53. Pour into a shallow soup plate to cool. When cold, cut into strips, place in a soup tureen and cover with the hot soup. Yields approximately 8 cups.

[TRANSLATED FROM: **A ARTE DE COMER BEM** BY ROSA MARIA (MME. H. LEONARDOS)]

Corn and Shrimp Soup
Sopa de Milho com Camarão

1 pound fresh shrimp • garlic salt • black pepper • salt • 1 no. 2 can creamed corn (2 cups)
6 cups soup stock • 1/3 cup butter • 1 minced onion

Shell, devein and wash shrimp. Sprinkle with garlic salt, salt and black pepper. Let stand 15 minutes. Dry on absorbent paper and chop into small pieces leaving a few shrimp whole or in extra large pieces. Heat the corn with stock and cook over low heat for 10 minutes. Sauté the onion in 1/2 the butter, then add minced shrimp and cook over low heat until shrimp are done. Strain the corn and stock mixture into the shrimp, add the rest of the butter, check seasoning and serve.

N O T E : If a thicker soup is desired, it may be thickened by heating 2 tablespoons cornstarch or potato flour with the corn and stock.

Corn and Watercress Soup
Sopa de Milho e Agrião

4 cups clear, well-seasoned beef stock • 1/4 teaspoon marjoram
1/2 teaspoon chopped parsley • 2 cups canned cream-style corn, either white or yellow
1/2 cup chopped watercress • 2 tablespoons butter • salt and pepper
croutons • hard-boiled egg

Heat stock with marjoram and parsley, and simmer 5 minutes. Add corn, cover and continue to simmer another 25 minutes. Force through a coarse sieve. Add chopped watercress and butter. Correct seasoning and serve hot with croutons and garnished with very thin slices of hard-boiled egg. Yields 5 cups.

Cream of Artichoke Soup
Sopa de Creme de Alcachofras

4 large fresh artichokes • 2 cups water • 1 sliced onion • 4 cups medium white sauce
1 small can artichoke hearts • salt, pepper, nutmeg • 1/2 cup light cream • croutons

Clean and scrape artichokes and discard some of the outer leaves. Cut them up and place in a covered saucepan with the water, onion and the liquid from the canned artichoke hearts. Simmer until quite tender, then press through a coarse sieve, pressing as much of the pulp through as possible. Discard the residue and add liquid to the white sauce. Add drained artichoke hearts, season to taste and heat over low heat, stirring constantly, or use a double boiler. Just before serving, stir in the cream. Pour into a soup tureen, sprinkle with nutmeg, add a few croutons and serve.

Cream of Barley Soup
Creme de Cevadinha com Maçã

3/4 cup barley • 8 cups good beef stock • 2 bayleaves • 1 sliced tomato • 1 sliced carrot
salt and pepper • fried apple strips

Wash and pick over barley and soak 1 hour in cold water to cover. Add to the stock and cook slowly in a covered saucepan with the bayleaf, tomato and carrot for at least 1 hour or until well done. Press through a coarse sieve, season to taste with salt and pepper. Reheat and pour hot over strips of apple that have been fried in butter.

[TRANSLATED FROM: **A ARTE DE COMER BEM** BY ROSA MARIA (MME. H. LEONARDOS)]

Cream of Cucumber Soup

Sopa de Creme de Pepinos

*1/2 cup chopped onion • 4 tablespoons butter • 3 peeled and thinly-sliced cucumbers
1/4 cup chopped celery • 1 bayleaf • 5 cups beef or chicken stock • 1/2 cup cornstarch
2 lightly-beaten egg yolks • 1 cup milk • 1/2 cup chopped spinach*

Sauté onion in butter, then add cucumbers, celery and bayleaf. Cover the skillet and steam over low heat for about 1 hour or until cucumbers are very well cooked. Mix in the cornstarch and add the hot stock. Cook over medium heat, stirring for 10 minutes to thicken, then strain through a coarse strainer. Mix egg yolks with milk and add to the soup, together with the spinach. Heat and serve. Yields 7 to 7 1/2 cups.

Cream of Asparagus Soup

Sopa de Creme de Aspargo com Frango

1 cut-up chicken • salt, pepper and garlic salt • 2 10-ounce cans asparagus
4 tablespoons butter • 1 minced onion • 1/2 bayleaf • Bouquet garni[1]
3 tablespoons cornstarch • 4 cups milk • 3 egg yolks • seasoning

Wash and dry chicken and sprinkle with salt, pepper and garlic salt. Cut points from asparagus and reserve. Also save the liquid and the firmer ends of the asparagus. Melt 3 tablespoons of the butter in a large skillet and gently fry the chicken. When chicken is brown, add the onion, bayleaf, bouquet garni and the firm ends of the asparagus. Cook for 10 minutes. Pour 2 quarts of hot water over the chicken and cook until chicken is tender and the liquid has been reduced by half. Remove the chicken and save the best parts for a salad. Chop up broken parts to make 1 cupful. Strain the broth. Stir cornstarch into 1 cupful of the milk to form a smooth mixture. Add the other 3 cups of milk to the broth and heat. When mixture is hot, stir in the cornstarch-milk mixture and continue stirring until broth thickens. Add the asparagus tips, chopped chicken and the other tablespoon of butter. Mix the egg yolks with the liquid from the asparagus and stir into the hot soup. Taste to check seasoning. Yields 10-11 cups.

[TRANSLATED FROM: **A ARTE DE COMER BEM** BY ROSA MARIA (MME. H. LEONARDOS)]

---

[1] A tied bunch of parsley, onions, bayleaf and thyme, used in soups.

Cream of Lettuce Soup
Sopa de Creme de Alface

4 cups finely-chopped lettuce firmly packed • 2 tablespoons butter
2 1/2 cups chicken or veal stock • 1 tablespoon minced onion • 4 tablespoons rice flour
1 1/2 cups milk • seasoning

Wash and dry lettuce. Chop and measure 4 cups packed firmly. Heat lettuce in a covered saucepan with 1 tablespoon of the butter and 1/2 cup of the stock. Steam over medium heat for 10 minutes. Sauté onion in the other tablespoon of butter, add the remaining 2 cups of stock and pour over lettuce. Simmer the mixture in a covered saucepan for 30 minutes. Dissolve rice flour in milk, stir into lettuce mixture and cook slowly for about 5 or 10 minutes until mixture thickens. Strain through a coarse sieve. Season to taste. Serve garnished with a few strips of shredded lettuce and shredded boiled ham. Yields approximately 3 1/2 cups.

Farmer's Soup
Sopa Andaluza

1/2 pound pumpkin • 1/2 pound sweet potatoes • 1/2 pound tomatoes • 1/2 teaspoon salt
2 cups water • 6 cups good meat stock • 1/3 cup cooked rice • seasoning

Peel pumpkin and potatoes, cut small and add chopped tomatoes, salt and water. Cook in a covered saucepan until the vegetables are fork tender. Press through a sieve. Add to hot meat stock, simmer 30 minutes with the rice and season to taste with salt and pepper. Yields approximately 8 cups.

[TRANSLATED FROM: **AS RECEITAS PARA VOCÊ DA TIA EVELINA, 4TH EDITION**]

Palm Heart Soup
Sopa de Palmito

4 tablespoons rice flour • 1 cup milk • 6 cups good chicken or beef stock • seasoning
1 1/2 cups sliced cooked palm hearts (1 14-ounce can) • 3 egg yolks

Mix rice flour with a little of the milk to form a smooth paste and gradually add the rest of the milk, stirring to prevent lump formation. Pour into hot stock and cook at a low temperature until stock thickens. Strain and season. Add palm hearts, bring to boil, remove from heat and add slightly-beaten egg yolks, but do not reheat as the soup will curdle.

[IGNEZ CORREIA D'ARAUJO, PERNAMBUCO]

Peanut Soup
Sopa de Amendoim

1/4 cup raw rice • 2 ounces peanuts • 1/4 cup milk • 2 egg yolks • salt
1 quart good chicken stock • 1 1/2 cups cooked chicken meat, chopped

Boil rice in salted water and, when cooked, drain and wash in cold water. Drain again, place in blender with peanuts, milk, and purée. Remove and gently stir in egg yolks. Do not beat. Add salt to taste. Pour into buttered, square shallow baking tin and bake in 375° oven bain-marie until done (about 25 minutes). Remove to cake rack to cool and cut into squares. Place in soup tureen and then cover with the hot broth to which the chicken has been added. The batter may also be baked in very small cupcake tins for individual servings.

Potato and Watercress Soup
Sopa de Batatas com Agrião

3 cups grated raw potatoes • 1/2 teaspoon rosemary • 6 cups good stock
1/2 bunch of watercress • 2 egg yolks • 1/2 cup milk • seasoning

Cook potatoes and rosemary in the stock in a covered saucepan until potatoes are cooked. Drain potatoes, purée or sieve, and return to stock. Bring to boil, add the finely-chopped watercress and simmer while mixing the egg yolks and milk. Turn egg and milk mixture into a soup tureen and pour the boiling soup over the mixture. Stir and serve.

Lentil Soup
Sopa de Lentilhas

1 cup lentils • water (about 2 cups) • 3 cups well-seasoned beef stock
2 tablespoons grated Muenster or Parmesan cheese • 1 tablespoon butter
1 egg yolk • seasoning • croutons • thin slices of raw onion

Pick over the lentils, wash and cover with the 2 cups of water. Let soak overnight. Next day, add enough fresh, salted water to cover and cook in a covered saucepan over medium heat until lentils are done (about 1 hour). Purée the lentils and add to the hot stock. Check seasoning. Just before serving, add the cheese, butter and egg yolk by mixing with a small amount of the soup, and then stirring into the rest of the soup. Serve with croutons and thin slices of raw onion. Yields 5 1/2 to 6 cups.

Manioc or Cassava Soup
Sopa de Mandioca

1 pound manioc root (cassava root) • 2 tablespoons butter • 2 tablespoons grated onion
2 large peeled, chopped tomatoes • 1 tablespoon chopped celery • 8 cups soup stock
salt and pepper • 1 tablespoon finely-chopped parsley

Peel manioc root and grate it or cut very fine. Sauté in 1 tablespoon of the butter with onion, tomato and the celery. Cook over medium heat about 10 minutes, then add the hot stock. Cover and simmer until manioc is tender. This takes anywhere from 1 to 2 hours. Mash the manioc very well with a potato masher. Season well with salt and pepper and allow to simmer uncovered until soup thickens. Add the other tablespoon of butter and the parsley. Yields 10 cups.

Oxtail Soup
Sopa de Rabada

2 oxtails, wiped and cut in sections and dredged with flour • 3 tablespoons drippings
1/2 cup chopped onion • 1/2 cup minced parsley • salt, pepper, few grains cayenne
2 quarts hot water • 1 onion, cut in half • 3 quartered tomatoes, peeled
3 tablespoons washed barley • bouquet garni • 1/4 cup sherry wine (optional)

Fry oxtails in hot drippings with onion and parsley, salt, pepper and cayenne pepper. When the oxtails are good and brown, pour off excess drippings, add the hot water, halved onion, tomatoes, barley and bouquet garni. Cover and cook 3 hours, skimming occasionally to remove grease. When half cooked, correct seasoning and continue to cook. When thoroughly cooked, remove the bones and the bouquet garni. Wine may be added before serving. Yields 8 cups.

Pumpkin Soup
Sopa de Abóbora

4 cups strong chicken or beef consommé • 3/4 cup canned puréed pumpkin
1 tablespoon butter • salt and pepper

Boil consommé, add pumpkin and butter and reduce heat. Cook over low heat until pumpkin is well-blended with the consommé. Season well with salt and pepper. Yields about 4 cups.

VARIATION: Add cooked vermicelli or serve over croutons.

Rice Flour Soup
Sopa de Farinha de Arroz

1 quart good beef broth • 2 tablespoons rice flour • 2 egg yolks
1/2 cup cold milk • seasoning

Mix rice flour with a little of the cold broth and add to heated broth. Stir well while heating until the soup thickens. Remove from heat when it is thick and add the egg yolks that have been mixed with the milk. Stir well and season.

Sweet Potato Soup
Sopa de Batata-Doce

3 tablespoons butter • 1 minced onion • 1/4 cup chopped parsley • 3 chopped tomatoes
1/2 pound cooked sweet potatoes • 1 cup milk • 1 quart good beef stock • salt and pepper

Melt butter and sauté onion, parsley, tomatoes and potatoes. Mash with a potato masher, then add the milk and press through a sieve into the hot beef stock. Season with salt and pepper. Yields about 6 cups.

Tapioca Soup
Sopa de Tapioca

1 1/2 ounces tapioca soaked in enough water to cover for 4 hours • 1 quart stock
seasoning • 1/2 cup all-purpose flour • 1 egg • 1 cup milk • 1/4 teaspoon salt

Put soaked tapioca through a sieve and add to the hot stock. Cook 15 minutes over low heat and season to taste. Make a pancake batter of sifted flour mixed with egg, milk and salt, and drop by spoonfuls onto a buttered skillet. Fry on both sides, cut into strips and place in soup tureen. Pour hot soup over the strips and serve immediately.

[TRANSLATED FROM: **A ARTE DE COMER BEM** BY ROSA MARIA (MME. H. LEONARDOS)]

Turtle Soup No. 1
Sopa de Tartaruga Nº 1

3 tablespoons all-purpose flour • 2 tablespoons butter • 3 quarts turtle stock, p. 367
3/4 cup Madeira wine • 3 pounds cubed turtle meat, p. 367 • Seasoning

Brown the flour in butter and gradually add some of the turtle stock. Cook; adding rest of stock and bring to slow boil. Add the wine, meat and seasoning.

[TRANSLATED FROM: **A ARTE DE COMER BEM** BY ROSA MARIA (MME. H. LEONARDOS)]

Turtle Soup No. 2
Sopa de Tartaruga Nº 2

3 pounds raw turtle meat and bones • 2 quarts water • 1 quart chicken stock
2 chopped onions • 1/4 cup chopped parsley • 1/4 cup chopped celery • 2 bayleaves
6 cloves • 1 teaspoon sugar • 1 cup canned tomatoes • 6 peppercorns • 3 tablespoons butter
salt and pepper • 1/2 cup sherry wine

Wipe turtle meat, separate from bones and put meat, bones and gristle in a saucepan with the water and stock. Add remaining ingredients up through the peppercorns, bring to a boil, then cover and simmer for 1 1/2 hours. Strain and discard vegetables and bones. Dice the turtle meat into 1/4-inch cubes and sauté in the butter, turning so that cubes are lightly browned on all sides. Add turtle meat to the stock and also any drippings. Simmer the stock for 30 minutes until the turtle meat is tender. Season to taste with salt and pepper, add the sherry wine and serve.

Leão Velloso Soup
Sopa Leão Velloso

1 pound small fresh shrimp • 2 dozen mussels or clams
A 4- or 5-pound grouper, with the head • 4 peeled and chopped tomatoes
3 crushed garlic cloves • 1 teaspoon coriander seed • 1 tablespoon salt
3/4 cup chopped spring onions • 1 cup chopped parsley • cayenne pepper
1/4 cup olive oil or butter • 1 pound crabmeat • 1 pound lobster meat

1. Wash shrimp and mussels or clams very thoroughly to remove all the sand.

2. Cut the head from the fish, and slice fish into 1-inch steaks.

3. Make a stock by heating the fish head in 5 quarts salted water. When the water boils, add a *bouquet garni* of your favorite herbs and spices, cover the saucepan and simmer for 1 1/2 hours. Remove fish and the bouquet, discarding the latter and reserving the edible parts of the head.

4. Cook the shrimp in their shells in the same stock for 10 minutes, or until they change to a pink color. Remove them from the stock and remove their shells and the black veins; reserve.

5. Heat mussels or clams, in their shells, in the same stock for 5 minutes or until their shells open, and then take them from the stock. Separate mussels or clams from their shells and discard the shells.

6. Strain the stock, in case there are any particles of sand or shells.

7. Crush garlic cloves with coriander seed and the salt and add to the stock.

8. Add onions, parsley, tomatoes, and cayenne pepper to taste. Cover stock saucepan and bring to a slow boil, then simmer until all the vegetables are cooked.

9. Heat the oil or butter in a skillet and gently sauté the fish steaks with a little salt and pepper. When steaks are cooked, transfer to a platter and remove skin and bones.

10. Pull the fish apart and add to the fish stock together with crabmeat, lobster, shrimp, mussels or clams, and the edible parts of the head.

11. Add some of the stock to the fish drippings in the skillet, bring to a boil and pour into the stock.

12. Heat and check seasoning.

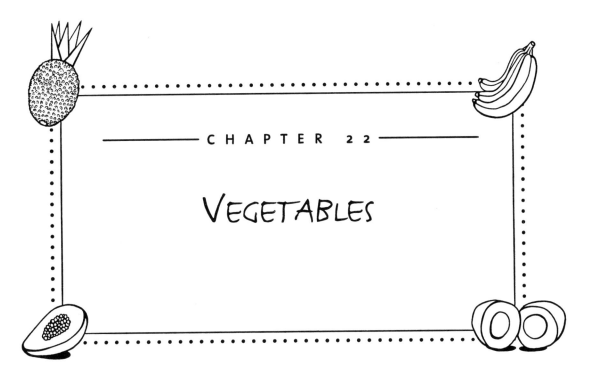

CHAPTER 22

VEGETABLES

The earth produces all things and receives all again.

THOMAS FULLER, **GNOMOLOGIA**, NO. 4493

As pointed out in the chapter on salads, the Brazilian is not overly fond of vegetables. This goes back to Colonial days when the slaves were better supplied with nutritional elements than their masters because they consumed large quantities of vegetable greens; to the time when "it was with the Europeanization of his table that the Brazilian became an abstainer from vegetables."[1] But at that time, it should be remembered, the colonizer did not have much of a variety from which he could select. There were the greens, so favored by the slaves and the maize and tuberous vegetables that constituted the diet of the Indians, and the white man had to make the best with what was at hand.

The Negroes ate great amounts of greens, such a *Taioba*, a leafy vegetable known as "elephant ears," and they liked cabbage and *Jerimum*, a plant of the gourd family *(cucurbitaceae)*. Okra, which is still an integral part of Afro-Brazilian cookery, was a great favorite. In fact, it is almost a certainty that the same slave source popularized okra in both Brazil and the Southern United States, where okra is used extensively as a vegetable and in gumbos.

Unlike the early colonists, modern city dwellers are more fortunate in having a greater variety of vegetables to choose from. City dwellers are mentioned specifically because not all regions of the vast country of Brazil are able to secure a plentiful supply of fresh vegetables. Thus, the apathetic attitude of the Brazilian towards vegetables is not only inherited, but, in certain areas may be attributed to the lack of supply. In addition, ingestion of raw vegetables subjected one to the danger of becoming infected. This, however, was eliminated years ago by the invention of the

---

[1] Gilberto Freyre, *The Masters and the Slaves* (New York: Alfred A. Knopf, Inc., 1956), p. 468.

salus, a container lined with a black germicidal substance, which is a common household item in Brazilian kitchens. All vegetables that are to be eaten raw are stored in the *salus* for at least one hour before being served.

Japanese immigrants have done much to increase fruit and vegetable production in Brazil, especially around the São Paulo area where they have established truck gardens. Through improvements in farming techniques, it is now possible to secure asparagus, artichokes, beets, broccoli, Brussels sprouts, cabbage, carrots, cauliflower, celery, chicory, collards, cucumbers, eggplant, garlic, lettuce, leek, okra, onions, red and green peppers, peas, parsley, parsnips, radishes and white turnips. If we add to these the familiar greens, roots, and cucurbits (squash, pumpkins, chayotes, gourds, etc.) and the beans, cará, manioc, maize, palm hearts, potatoes, yams and pear tomatoes, which the Indians used as food and medicine, it will be seen that there is a wide selection of vegetables to be had in the populated areas.

Besides the above, there are many vegetables in Brazil that are unknown in the Northern Hemisphere. *Bertalha* or vine spinach is one; another is *maxixe*.[2] This grows on a vine and resembles small cucumbers. *Jiló*, of the solanaceas family, is another, while *cará* and *inhame*, types of yams, are also used extensively.

The Brazilian cook who is fortunate enough to have so many vegetables at his/her disposal, has devised many ways of cooking them despite the fact that, as a foodstuff, they are not greatly appreciated. They are served with salt and melted butter or used in soufflés, puddings and cakes. Vegetables prepared with cheese are great favorites. In fact, many recipes in the following chapter depend on cheese for thickening purposes as well as flavor. Sometimes, the vegetable is prepared with a sauce or sautéed with onions, tomatoes and seasonings. They are often made into croquettes, and one of the best-liked ways of cooking vegetables is by mixing them with shrimp or meat. Two popular dishes made in this manner are Chayote with Shrimp (*Chuchu com Camarão*) and Chopped Meat with Okra (*Carne Picadinha com Quiabo*).

---

[2] Maxixe is also the name of a dance, a forerunner of the samba. It appeared during the latter half of the nineteenth century and attained great popularity. Like so many things that came to New York in the Prohibition Era, the *maxixe* was introduced to Broadway but it achieved little success.

The chayote, which is called *chuchu* or *xuxu*, is often served in Brazil. Pale green in color and pear-shaped, it is slightly astringent when peeled. It grows on a vine and although indigenous to the West Indies, chayote has long been a common vegetable in Brazil, and by importation, to several American cities. In taste, texture and water content (but not in shape) it resembles the flat, round green squash, and consequently this type of squash can be successfully substituted in many recipes calling for *chuchu*.

As in the case of salads, vegetables, although more numerous in Brazil, do not enjoy the same importance or popularity in menus as they do in the United States. The Brazilian eats them "with a grain of salt" and sometimes, reverting to colonial days of yore, he doesn't even taste them! But the enlightened Brazilian housewife continues to include vegetables in her meal-planning and brings home a good assortment from each *feira*,[3] trusting that part of her vitamin and mineral purchases will be consumed and enjoyed.

[3] This is a colorful open-air market where fruits, vegetables and manufactured goods are sold from push carts. In large cities the *feira* is set up in different parts of the city according to the day of the week. Feira in portuguese means "day."

Stuffed Artichoke Hearts
Fundos de Alcachofras Recheadas

Artichoke hearts, either canned or freshly cooked • sliced ham
deviled ham or chicken • grated Parmesan cheese

Cut the ham into small rounds to fit the artichoke hearts. Cover each with the deviled ham or chicken shaping into a small pyramid. Sprinkle the cheese on top. Arrange hearts in a buttered baking dish and bake in a preheated 400° oven for about 5 minutes. Remove carefully to a platter to serve with a roast or steak.

Bean Scramble
Fritada de Vagens

3 eggs, separated • salt and pepper • 1 cup cold cooked string beans

Beat egg whites until stiff, add beaten yolks and seasoning. Butter a casserole, place a layer of beans in it and cover with some of the egg mixture. Repeat with another layer of beans and spoon over the rest of egg mixture. Bake in a preheated 400° oven until puffed, and serve at once.

[LAURITA PIRES, MINAS GERAIS]

String Beans
Vagens

1 pound string beans • 1 tablespoon butter • 1/2 tablespoon all-purpose flour
1 cup milk • 1 egg yolk • 1 teaspoon lemon juice • seasoning

String the beans, wash, cut and boil them in salted water until they are half done. Drain. Melt butter and add beans, and heat gently for a few minutes. Mix flour with a little of the milk to make a smooth paste and add the rest of the milk. Pour over the beans. Cook, stirring once in a while and, when beans are tender and just before serving, add the egg yolk which has been mixed with the lemon juice. Add seasoning, mix well, heat for 1 minute and serve.

Creamed Beets
Beterrabas com Molho de Creme

4 cups cooked or canned sliced beets • 2 tablespoons butter • 1 tablespoon vinegar
1/4 teaspoon coriander powder • 1/4 cup light cream • seasoning
3 tablespoons bread crumbs • 3 tablespoons grated cheese

Sauté beets in butter and add the vinegar, coriander and cream. Steam over low heat 2 or 3 minutes. Season to taste with salt and pepper. Turn into a well-buttered casserole and top with the bread crumbs mixed with cheese. Brown under the broiler. Serve garnished with sliced hard-boiled eggs, or onion rings.

Stuffed Beets
Beterrabas Viroflay

10 medium-sized beets of equal size • salt • 1 cup milk • 1 tablespoon cornstarch
2 egg yolks • 1 tablespoon butter • 1/2 cup chopped cooked ham
2 tablespoons grated Parmesan cheese • 1 cup canned peas, drained

Boil beets in skins in salted water. When cooked, cool and peel. Make a good-sized cavity in each beet with a sharp knife and tablespoon. Reserve the removed portion of beets for salads or soups. Prepare a thick filling by mixing milk, cornstarch and egg yolks, then heating over a low heat, stirring constantly to prevent lumps from forming. Add the butter. When mixture is thickened, remove from heat then add the ham, cheese and peas. Mix, correct seasoning and spoon the mixture into the beets. Sprinkle with Parmesan cheese, dot with butter and bake in a preheated 400° oven for 5-8 minutes.

[TRANSLATED FROM: **AS RECEITAS PARA VOCÊ DA TIA EVELINA**, 4TH EDITION]

Broccoli Pudding
Pudim de Brócolis

10 to 12 broccoli flowers with tender stems, cooked in salted water • salt and pepper
1 tablespoon lemon juice • 2 tablespoons butter • 2 cups seasoned, mashed potatoes to which
2 raw eggs have been added • 3 hard-boiled eggs

When broccoli is cooked, drain of all the water and season with salt and pepper, lemon juice and butter. Butter a baking dish and line with 1/2 the potato mixture. Place broccoli flowers on top of the potato mixture and cover with slices of hard-boiled egg. Place rest of mashed potatoes over the eggs and bake in a hot oven until potatoes are brown. Serve plain or with a sauce.

Cabbage and Wine
Repolho com Vinho

1/2 medium head cabbage, shredded • 1 cup water • 3 tablespoons olive oil
1/2 cup minced onions • 1 small hot pepper, chopped • 1/2 cup chopped parsley
1/2 sliced green pepper • 1 cup tomato sauce • 1/2 cup white wine • 1 tablespoon vinegar

Shred cabbage, add water, cover and steam 5 minutes. Drain. Heat olive oil in a large skillet, add onions, hot pepper, parsley, green pepper, and sauté. When vegetables are done, add tomato sauce, white wine and vinegar that have been mixed together. Bring to boil and add the cabbage. Simmer in a covered skillet until cabbage is tender. Stir occasionally and add water by the spoonful, only if necessary, to keep cabbage from sticking. Correct seasoning.

[REPRINTED FROM AUTHOR'S ARTICLE IN JULY 1963 ISSUE OF **GOURMET MAGAZINE**]

Stewed Carrots
Cenouras Ensopadas

1 pound carrots • 2 tablespoons butter • 1 small minced onion • 1/4 teaspoon sugar
1/4 teaspoon salt • 1 cup soup stock • 1 tablespoon minced parsley

Pare and wash carrots, then slice thinly. Sauté in butter with onion, sugar and salt. When carrots are delicately brown, add stock. Cover and cook until fork tender. Mix in parsley before serving and correct seasoning.

Stuffed Carrots
Cenouras Recheadas

6 large scraped and boiled carrots • 1 tablespoon butter • 1 tablespoon all-purpose flour
1 cup milk • 2 egg yolks • 2 tablespoons grated cheese • salt and pepper
tomato sauce • grated cheese

Cool carrots. Scoop out centers with tines of a fork or a small spoon and save for soup stock or salads. Melt butter, add flour, stir, then add milk, continuing to stir over medium heat until mixture thickens, then add egg yolks. Stir well, remove from heat and add cheese, salt and pepper to taste. Allow to cool thoroughly. Arrange carrots in a baking dish, fill cavities with the mixture, dot with tomato sauce and sprinkle with grated cheese. Bake in a hot oven to a golden brown.

[TRANSLATED FROM: **AS RECEITAS PARA VOCÊ DA TIA EVELINA, 4TH EDITION**]

Carrot Croquettes
Croquetes de Cenouras

1/2 cup milk • 5 tablespoons all-purpose flour, sifted • 1 egg yolk • 1 tablespoon butter
salt and pepper • 4 carrots, cooked and mashed • 1 tablespoon chopped parsley
beaten egg • bread crumbs • oil for frying

Heat milk and flour and stir so as not to form lumps. Add egg yolk and continue stirring while you add butter, salt and pepper. Beat until smooth, then add carrots and parsley. Remove from heat, stir a few times to mix in the carrots and parsley, then turn out onto a platter and cool thoroughly. When mixture is cold, shape into desired size croquettes and let stand about 1 hour at room temperature. Roll in beaten egg, then in bread crumbs and fry in deep fat or oil heated to 375°. Remove to absorbent paper to drain off excess fat. Serve plain or with a sauce.

Carrots in Port Wine
Cenouras em Vinho do Porto

1 pound carrots • 2 ounces butter • salt and pepper • 1/2 cup port wine • 1 cup meat broth
• 2 egg yolks mixed with • 1 tablespoon butter

Peel carrots and cut in 1 inch slices. Brown the carrots in melted butter and, when nicely browned, salt and pepper them to taste. Add the wine and broth and bring to boil. Reduce heat to low and cook until tender. When ready to serve, add egg yolks mixed with butter. Stir, remove from heat and serve.

[TRANSLATED FROM: **AS RECEITAS PARA VOCÊ DA TIA EVELINA**, 4TH EDITION]

Baked Cauliflower
Couve-Flor Assada

2 cups cooked cauliflower buds

The flowers should be separated and cooked in slightly salted water until they are done. Do not overcook, as the buds should be firm. Drain, cool and place in a buttered baking dish. Cover with the following sauce:

1 tablespoon butter or bacon fat • 2 tablespoons chopped onions
1 tablespoon chopped parsley • 2 tablespoons chopped green pepper • 1/2 chopped tomato
1 tablespoon all-purpose flour • 1 cup meat broth, (bouillon cube or canned consommé)
sliced stuffed olives • bread crumbs • grated cheese • butter

Melt fat and sauté onions, parsley, green pepper and tomato until vegetables are cooked. Mix in the flour and then add the meat broth, and cook until thick. Season to taste and strain over the cauliflower. Add a few sliced stuffed olives. Sprinkle with bread crumbs and grated cheese (optional), dot with butter and bake in 375° oven until delicately browned.

Cauliflower and Ham
Couve-flor com Presunto

2 cups cauliflower buds • 2 eggs, separated • 1 tablespoon butter • 1 1/2 cups milk
2 tablespoons all-purpose flour • 1/4 pound chopped boiled ham • grated Parmesan cheese

Boil cauliflower in salted water until fork tender. Measure 2 cups of the flowers and reserve the stems for soups. Beat egg yolks with butter and add to the milk in which the flour has been thoroughly dissolved. Cook over medium heat, stirring constantly until thick. Remove from heat and add the ham and cauliflower. Cool to room temperature. Fold in the beaten egg whites. Turn into a preheated 375° oven for approximately 25 minutes.

[HILDA LEITE QUEIROGA, MINAS GERAIS]

Chayote Balls
Chuchu

4 large chayotes • 1/2 teaspoon salt • 1/2 teaspoon sugar • water to cover
2 tablespoons butter • black pepper

Peel chayotes and cut out small balls with a special utensil for this purpose. (Core the leftovers and discard the cores. Reserve the useful pieces of chayote for soup or chayote pudding). Add the salt and sugar to the balls and just enough water to cover. Cook until fork tender, drain and add the butter and black pepper.

Chayote Pudding
Pudim de Chuchu

6 chayotes • salted water to cover
1 cup bread moistened with milk and pressed through a sieve • 4 eggs, separated
4 tablespoons grated Parmesan cheese • 2 tablespoons butter • salt and pepper

Peel and quarter chayotes, then remove the cores. Cube, add salted water, cover and steam until fork tender. Drain, mash and let stand about 2 minutes until all the steam evaporates. Stir in the bread-milk mixture, the slightly beaten egg yolks, cheese, and butter, and then season to taste with salt and pepper. Fold in the stiffly-beaten egg whites. Turn into a well-buttered 2-quart plain mould and bake in bain-marie in a 400° preheated oven about 1 hour or until the pudding is firm. Loosen edges, unmould onto a serving plate and cover with tomato sauce.

N O T E : White squash may be substituted for the chayote, using 6 cups of the raw diced squash.

[MARIA DE LOURDES FURTADO, MINAS GERAIS]

Corn Cakes
Bolinhos de Milho

4 ears corn • 3 eggs • 1 tablespoon salt • 1/2 cup milk • 10 tablespoons all-purpose flour
Salt and pepper to taste • 3 teaspoons baking powder
1 tablespoon melted butter • 2 eggs, separated

Boil corn and eggs in salted water and, when cooked, grate the corn and peeled hard-boiled eggs to make 2 cups. Add milk, flour, salt and pepper, baking powder, butter and beaten egg yolks. Fold in stiffly-beaten egg whites. Drop by spoonfuls into hot fat and drain on absorbent paper.

[MARIA AMELIA AZEVEDO LEITE, MINAS GERAIS]

Corn Cups
Forminhas de Milho Verde

2 cups whole-kernel canned corn, drained • 1 cup milk • 1 tablespoon all-purpose flour
1 tablespoon butter • 3 eggs, separated • salt and pepper to taste • 1/2 teaspoon sugar
1/4 cup chopped ham • 1/4 cup seedless raisins

Put corn in blender with milk, flour, butter, egg yolks, sugar, salt and pepper. Fold in beaten egg whites, ham and raisins. Turn into well-buttered small muffin tins and bake in preheated 375° oven 20 minutes or until a knife inserted in center can be removed clean. Unmould into small paper cups and serve hot. Yields 12.

N O T E : To make a large mould, turn batter into a well-buttered 1 1/2 quart Pyrex baking dish. Bake in a preheated 375° oven 40 minutes or until a knife inserted in center can be removed clean.

[MARIA AMELIA AZEVEDO LEITE, MINAS GERAIS]

551

Eggplant
Berinjela

1 eggplant (about 1 1/2 pounds) • 2 tablespoons lemon juice • salt and pepper
1/4 cup olive oil • 1 minced onion • 1 tablespoon butter • 1 chopped scallion
2 tablespoons chopped parsley • 2 cups bread soaked in enough milk to make a mush
breadcrumbs • butter

Peel the eggplant and slice crosswise. Sprinkle with lemon juice, salt and pepper and let stand 1 hour. Fry in oil and arrange fried slices in a buttered casserole. Cover with a sauce made as follows: sauté onion in butter and add scallion, parsley and the bread mush, which has been passed through a coarse sieve. Cook over high heat 10 minutes, stirring continuosly, and then pour over eggplant. Sprinkle with bread crumbs, dot with butter and bake in a preheated 400° oven about 10 minutes to brown.

[TRANSLATED FROM: **AS RECEITAS PARA VOCÊ DA TIA EVELINA** 4TH ED.]

Eggplant with Shrimp
Berinjela com Camarão

1 medium eggplant (about 1 1/2 pounds) • 1/2 pound uncooked shrimp
2 tablespoons olive oil • 1 minced garlic clove • 3/4 cup chopped scallions
1 minced onion • 1/2 cup chopped parsley • 2 tablespoons tomato paste • 1 cup water
salt, pepper, Tabasco sauce • 1 cup croutons or toast cut into cubes • grated cheese (optional)

Peel and dice eggplant, and parboil in salted water. Drain and set aside. Clean and devein fresh shrimp and sauté in oil in large skillet with garlic, scallions, onion and parsley and cook until shrimp and vegetables are done. Add tomato paste and continue to cook for about 5 minutes. Add the eggplant and water, and cover. When eggplant is cooked, season well with salt, pepper and a few drops of Tabasco sauce, remove cover and let some of the liquid evaporate. Stir in the croutons, pour into a buttered casserole, sprinkle with grated cheese and bake 30 minutes in a preheated 375° oven. Serves 6.

Kale or Collards Mineira
Couve à Mineira

4 cups shredded kale or collards • 1/4 cup bacon fat

Wash and shred kale or collards by bunching leaves together and slicing very finely with a sharp knife. Plunge into boiling salted water and drain. Heat bacon fat in a skillet and gently fry kale or collards. Season to taste and serve.

VARIATIONS: Cabbage or chicory may be prepared the same way.

Lentil Pudding
Pudim de Lentilhas

1/2 pound lentils • 1/2 teaspoon salt • 1 stalk celery • 1/2 sliced onion • 2 sprigs parsley
2 eggs • 1/4 cup ketchup • 2 slices bread soaked in enough milk to make a mush
1 tablespoon butter • 2 tablespoons ground Brazil nuts • seasoning

Pick over lentils and soak in water 8 hours. Change the water replacing it with only enough to cover the lentils. Add salt, celery, onion and parsley and cook in a covered saucepan until lentils are tender. Mash and press through a coarse sieve. Add the eggs, ketchup, bread, butter and nuts. Check seasoning. Turn into a buttered 1 1/2 quart aluminum or tin mould and bake in preheated 375° oven from 30 to 35 minutes. Unmould and pour melted butter on top. Serve as an accompaniment for smoked meats.

Baked Lettuce
Alface Assada

2 medium-sized heads of iceberg lettuce • 3 quarts water with 1 tablespoon salt
1 cup plain yoghurt or sour cream • 1/2 teaspoon salt • a few grains black pepper
1 tablespoon butter • 2 tablespoons bread crumbs

Wash lettuce thoroughly and discard the thick, bitter stalks. Boil water with salt until it reaches a rolling boil and then add the lettuce. Cover and boil vigorously for about 10 minutes, then drain and plunge into a vessel of cold water. Remove after 3 or 4 minutes and drain again. Gather the leaves together and shred with a knife. Mix yoghurt with salt, pepper and butter (and 1/4 teaspoon of nutmeg, if desired). Place shredded lettuce in a buttered 9-inch Pyrex pie plate and spoon yoghurt mixture on top. Sprinkle with bread crumbs and bake in preheated 400° oven 10 or 15 minutes until it browns.

V A R I A T I O N : If you want to serve a really elegant (*grã-fino*) dish, arrange thin slices of peeled cucumber on top of the yoghurt. Brush with yolk of egg to which 1 teaspoonful of melted butter has been added and then bake.

M u l t i c o l o r e d   P u d d i n g
Pudim Multicolor

5 cups cold mashed potatoes seasoned with salt and pepper
1 cup chopped cooked spinach • 1/2 cup tomato paste • 3 egg yolks

Mix potatoes with seasoning and divide into 4 parts. To one part add the thoroughly-drained spinach (or chopped broccoli); add the tomato paste to another part and the egg yolks to the third part. The fourth part remains as is. Butter a mould or baking dish and start filling with layers of the 4 mixtures until all have been used. Dot with butter and bake in a preheated 400° oven until brown. Unmould and serve plain or with a sauce.

French Fried Palm Hearts
Palmito Frito

1 14-ounce can of palm hearts • 2 eggs • salt and pepper • bread crumbs • oil for frying

Drain palm hearts and cut each one in half. Mix eggs with seasoning. Roll palm hearts in the eggs, then in bread crumbs. Fry in deep fat at 375°.

VARIATION: Use same recipe substituing sliced cucumbers or thick slices of tomatoes for the palm hearts.

[TRANSLATED FROM: **AS RECEITAS PARA VOCÊ DA TIA EVELINA**, 4TH EDITION]

Palm Hearts No. 1
Palmito N° 1

1/4 cup olive oil • 1/2 pound chopped tomatoes • 1 chopped onion
1/4 cup chopped parsley • salt and black pepper • 1/2 cup white wine
1 tablespoon butter • 1 tablespoon all-purpose flour
1 30-ounce can palm hearts • sliced bread

Heat oil and sauté the vegetables and then add the salt and pepper. Remove from heat, add wine and strain. Melt butter and mix in flour, stirring so as to keep mixture smooth. Add strained liquid gradually and bring to boil. Slice the palm hearts, add to the sauce and keep warm. Meanwhile, sauté half slices of bread in butter, arrange on a platter and cover with palm hearts in sauce. Garnish with parsley.

[TRANSLATED FROM: **AS RECEITAS PARA VOCÊ DA TIA EVELINA**, 4TH EDITION]

Palm Hearts No. 2
Palmito N° 2

1 30-ounce can palm hearts • 4 tablespoons butter • 2 tablespoons cornstarch
1/2 teaspoon salt • 3 cups milk • 4 egg yolks
1 small can paté de foie gras • grated Parmesan cheese

Drain palm hearts (reserve the liquid for soup stock or gravy) and cut in 1-inch slices. Butter a Pyrex baking dish inside and place palm hearts. Mix cornstarch with salt and some of the milk to form a smooth paste and then add the rest of the milk. Beat with an egg beater and continue beating while you add the egg yolks. Heat over low heat until the sauce thickens. Taste to check seasoning. Pour over the palm hearts. Dot the top with pieces of the paté. Sprinkle the cheese over the top and bake in a preheated 375° oven about 30 to 35 minutes. Serves 6.

[TRANSLATED FROM: **RECEITAS CULINÁRIAS** BY MYRTHES PARANHOS]

Imperial Potato Crown
Coroa de Batatas Imperial

4 cups cold mashed potatoes • 1 thinly-sliced onion • 4 grated medium-size beets
2 large whole beets • 4 eggs • 1/2 cup grated Parmesan cheese
1 1/2 cups scalded milk • 4 tablespoons butter • salt and pepper

Mix potatoes, onion and grated beets. Slightly beat the eggs, add the cheese and combine with the potato mixture. Scald milk, add butter, salt and pepper and combine with the potato mixture. Turn into a 2-quart well-buttered ring mould and bake in a preheated 375° oven 45 to 50 minutes until firm. Unmould and garnish with the other sliced beets.

Potato Roly Poly
Rocambole de Batatas

5 medium potatoes • 2 tablespoons butter • 1 cup milk
4 tablespoons grated Parmesan cheese • 1 teaspoon baking powder
2 tablespoons all-purpose flour • 3 eggs, separated • salt and pepper

Peel potatoes, wash, quarter and boil in salted water. Drain and mash. You should have about 3 cups of mashed potatoes. Add butter, 3/4 cup of the milk, cheese and the baking powder sifted with the flour. Stir in the beaten egg yolks that have been mixed with the other 1/4 cup of milk. Season to taste with salt and pepper, and grated onion, if desired. Fold in stiffly beaten egg whites. Line an 18" x 12" x 1" baking tin with foil paper, then butter foil paper generously. Spread the potato mixture evenly on the foil paper, starting in the center. It is not necessary to have the mixture spread clear to the edges of the tin. Bake in a 400° preheated oven for about 25 minutes or until top is delicately brown. Remove from oven and invert tin onto a wet towel. After 5 minutes, loosen edges of the roly poly, peel off the foil paper and return the roly poly to the baking tin. Spread with a filling, roll up and secure with toothpicks. Reheat and serve plain or with a sauce.

N O T E : The Brazilian housewife uses this sort of dish as a very attractive first course or a light luncheon dish and also as an excellent way of using leftovers. It is delicious with a Creamed Shrimp Filling and Tomato Sauce (suggestion) on top.

S U G G E S T E D   F I L L I N G S : Chopped Beef, Brazilian Style; Cooked Spinach with Eggs; Heavy Cheese Sauce or any of the Fillings used in the chapter on Patties, Pies and Turnovers, p. 421.

S U G G E S T E D   S A U C E S : Mushroom; Cheese, Tomato, Onion, Meat, etc.

Potato Starch Soufflé
Soufflé de Fécula

2 tablespoons potato starch • 3 1/4 cups milk • 1 tablespoon butter
1/4 teaspoon salt • 3 tablespoons grated Parmesan cheese • 3 eggs, separated
1/2 cup seedless raisins

Mix the potato starch with 1/4 cup of the milk and heat the 3 cups with butter and salt. When the mixture boils, add potato starch and milk mixture and combine thoroughly, then remove from heat. Allow to cool completely. Add the cheese and egg yolks, then fold in the stiffly-beaten egg whites and the raisins. Turn into a buttered soufflé dish and bake 20 to 30 minutes in a preheated 325° oven.

[SARITA BRANT, MINAS GERAIS]

Pumpkin Soufflé
Soufflé de Abóbora

1 1/2 pounds canned puréed pumpkin • 1 teaspoon salt • 1 tablespoon butter
1 tablespoon cream • 3 tablespoons grated Swiss cheese • 3 eggs, separated

Mix pumpkin with salt, butter, cream, cheese and beaten egg yolks. Taste to check seasoning. Fold in the stiffly-beaten egg whites. Pour into a buttered baking dish. Sprinkle with grated cheese and bake in a preheated 375° oven until done.

Spinach
Espinafre

2 cups cold drained spinach • 1 tablespoon lemon juice • 2 tablespoons grated Parmesan cheese
4 tablespoons milk or 2 tablespoons light cream • salt and pepper • 2 hard-boiled eggs

Sprinkle lemon juice over spinach and heat with cheese, milk, salt and pepper. Add sliced hard-boiled eggs and serve hot over buttered toast.

Spinach Moulds
Forminhas de Espinafre

1 package chopped frozen spinach cooked and thoroughly drained, or
1 cup chopped cooked spinach, drained • 1 tablespoon butter • salt and pepper
2 eggs, separated • 1 tablespoon all-purpose flour • 3/4 cup milk • 1 tablespoon grated cheese

Be sure cooked spinach is well drained. Add butter, salt and pepper, beaten egg yolks, cheese, flour and milk, and heat until mixture thickens. Cool, fold in half the beaten egg whites and pour into small well-buttered individual moulds. Top with remaining egg whites and bake in a preheated 400° oven for 14 to 18 minutes.

[LAURITA PIRES, MINAS GERAIS]

Summer Squash and Sausages
Abobrinha e Salsichas

2 pounds summer squash • 2 tablespoons butter • 1 chopped onion
1 tablespoon chopped green pepper • 1/2 garlic clove pounded with
1/2 teaspoon salt • 4 peeled and chopped tomatoes • 1/4 teaspoon nutmeg
1/2 pound smoked pork sausages, fried • Black pepper

Wash and peel squash, remove any tough fibers, then cut into cubes. Melt butter and sauté onion, green pepper, garlic clove, salt and tomatoes. When vegetables are partially cooked, add the squash and nutmeg. Cover and steam until fork tender. Do not add water. Slice the sausages and fry gently, then add to the squash. Add the pepper, correct the seasoning, and cook about 5 minutes over medium heat. Serve with rice.

Sweet Potato Puffs
Bolinhos de Batata-Doce

3 cups cooked sweet potatoes • 1/4 cup chopped Brazil nuts • 2 lightly-beaten eggs
1/4 cup milk • 2 teaspoons baking powder • 1/4 teaspoon nutmeg • salt and pepper
beaten egg, bread crumbs • oil for frying

Mash potatoes thoroughly. Add Brazil nuts, eggs, milk and baking powder. Sprinkle in the nutmeg, salt and pepper to taste. Shape into balls or croquettes, roll in the beaten egg, then in bread crumbs and fry in 375° oil until delicately browned. Drain on absorbent paper. Yields 12 large puffs.

Stuffed Sweet Potatoes
Batata-doce Recheada

8 medium-size baked sweet potatoes • 2 tablespoons butter • 1/4 cup milk
1/4 cup light cream • 1/4 cup grated cheese • 1/2 cup chopped ham
seasoning, including nutmeg, if desired • beaten egg • grated cheese

Cut potatoes in halves lengthwise and scoop out the centers. Mash centers with next 5 ingredients. Season to taste. Pile mixture into potato shells, brush with the beaten egg, sprinkle with grated cheese and brown in a 400° preheated oven for about 15 minutes.

Golden Baby Turnips
Nabos Dourados

20 baby white turnips (or 5 large, quartered) • 4 tablespoons butter
4 tablespoons sugar • salt and pepper

Peel turnips and cook in boiling salted water for 15 minutes or until fork tender. Melt butter in a skillet, add sugar and burn, as for caramel. (It may be necessary to add a little water.) Place turnips in the syrup, heat and turn often so that turnips are evenly coated with the caramel. Sprinkle with salt and pepper and bake in a 375° preheated oven for 15 minutes.

[TRANSLATED FROM: **A ARTE DE COMER BEM** BY ROSA MARIA (MME. H. LEONARDOS)]

White Stuffed Turnips
Nabos Recheados

6 medium-sized white turnips • Grated cheese and butter

Peel and cook whole turnips in boiling salted water until they are fork tender. Drain and scoop out the center (use the centers for soups). Fill centers with Chopped Beef, Brazilian Style (p. 378) or Shrimp Cream (p. 358). Sprinkle with grated cheese, dot with butter and brown in the oven.

VARIATION: Onions may be stuffed in the same manner.

Vegetable Cake
Bolo de Legumes

4 eggs, separated • 3 slices bread, with crusts removed • milk
1 1/2 cups cooked peas • 1/2 cup chopped boiled ham • 1 cup cooked string beans
1 cup cooked sliced carrots • 3/4 cup cooked sliced cabbage • 2 tablespoons butter
Seasoning • Grated cheese

Beat egg whites until stiff, then add the beaten yolks. Soak bread in enough milk to make a mush. Mix peas and ham. Mix beans, carrots and cabbage with the butter. Butter a 2-quart mould and place in it one half the egg mixture and all the mush. Sprinkle with some of the grated cheese and add the peas and ham. Sprinkle again with cheese, cover with remaining vegetable mixture and top with the egg mixture. Sprinkle with grated cheese and bake in a preheated 400° oven from 25 to 30 minutes. Allow to cool slightly before removing from mould. Serve with your favorite sauce and garnish with sliced tomatoes.

[HILDA LEITE QUEIROGA, MINAS GERAIS]

EGG YOLK
EGG WHITE
RECIPES

The lavish use of eggs in Brazilian cookery, a heritage of the Moorish influence on Portuguese cooking, sometimes calls for the use of more or fewer egg yolks than whites. Following is a list of such recipes in this book, arranged to facilitate the use of leftover portions.

	TOTAL NEEDED		LEFTOVER		RECIPE PAGE
	Yolks	Whites	Yolks	Whites	number
Brazil Nut Cookies	0	1	1	0	265
Chocolate Balls	0	1	1	0	240
Coffee Batida	0	1	1	0	151
Peppermint Roses	0	1	1	0	254
Strawberry Frosting	0	1	1	0	189
Belgiums	0	2	2	0	264
Cheese Balls No. 1	0	2	2	0	99
Cheese Balls No. 2	0	2	2	0	100
Coconut Ice Cream	0	2	2	0	298
Fried Codfish	0	2	2	0	345
Mulatta's Eyes	0	2	2	0	251
Peanut Wafers	0	2	2	0	271
Shrimp Meringue	0	2	2	0	354
Nut Croquettes No. 2	0	3	3	0	252
Peanut Brittle	0	3	3	0	254
Peanut Creams	0	3	3	0	253

Cat's Tongue Cookies	0	4	4	0	267
My Friend's Cake	0	7	7	0	203
White Short Cake	0	7	7	0	210
Cybele Magro's Cake	0	9	9	0	223
Almond Balls	3	2	0	1	237
Brigadiers No. 1	1	0	0	1	238
Brigadiers No. 2	1	0	1	0	239
Carrot Croquettes	1	0	0	1	547
Coffee Egg Nog	1	0	0	1	144
Cornstarch Rusks	1	0	0	1	170
Crab Meat Filling	1	0	0	1	443
Fish Pudding	1	0	0	1	323
Fish with Coconut Milk Sauce	1	0	0	1	327
Lentil Soup	1	0	0	1	530
Little Apples No. 2	1	0	0	1	247
Liver and Ham Croquettes	1	0	0	1	413
Meat Balls No. 1	1	0	0	1	381
Milk Sweet Cookies	3	2	0	1	273
Pastry for Fried Turnovers	1	0	0	1	438
String Beans	1	0	0	1	543
Veal Cutlets No. 1	1	0	0	1	394
Wine Pastry	1	0	0	1	441
Anna Pereira's Shrimp Pudding	2	0	0	2	363
Bahian Shrimp Filling	2	0	0	2	443
Baked Fish No. 2	2	0	0	2	321
Baked Rice, Country Style	2	0	0	2	131
Bean Croquettes	2	0	0	2	120
Bom Bocados	5	3	0	2	212
Carrots in Port Wine	2	0	0	2	547
Cheese Filling	2	0	0	2	445
Cheese Patties	2	0	0	2	427
Cbeese Pie	2	0	0	2	430
Chicken with Palm Hearts	2	0	0	2	466
Coffee Drops	2	0	0	2	242
Corn Meal and Manioc Pastry	2	0	0	2	440
Cream Leticia	2	0	0	2	300
Cream of Cucumber Soup	2	0	0	2	526
Creamed Oysters with Palm Hearts	2	0	0	2	351
Don't Touch Me Cookies	2	0	0	2	271

Egg Sauce for Fish	2	0	0	2	57
Fine Corn Meal Cookies	2	0	0	2	272
Fish Stuffing No. 2	2	0	0	2	62
Florida Rice	2	0	0	2	135
High Society Candy	2	0	0	2	243
Hot Chocolate	2	0	0	2	145
Missy Cookies	2	0	0	2	275
Nut Croquetes No.1	2	0	0	2	251
Orange Coconut Kisses	2	0	0	2	246
Oyster Filling	2	0	0	2	444
Palm Heart Filling	2	0	0	2	447
Palm Heart Sauce	2	0	0	2	58
Papaya Bom Bocados	2	0	0	2	215
Peanut Soup	2	0	0	2	529
Pot Roast of Veal	2	0	0	2	399
Potato and Water Cress Soup	2	0	0	2	530
Potato Pastry	2	0	0	2	436
Rainbow Salad	2	0	0	2	512
Rice Flour Soup	2	0	0	2	532
Sardine Sauce No. 2	2	0	0	2	59
Shrimp Pie	2	0	0	2	432
Stuffed Beets	2	0	0	2	544
Stuffed Carrots	2	0	0	2	546
Three-Flour Biscuits	2	0	0	2	179
Ambrosia	3	0	0	3	290
Anna Pereira's Chicken	3	0	0	3	462
Boneles Stuffed Chicken	3	0	0	3	454
Cheese Soup	3	0	0	3	521
Chestnut and Sponge Cake Pudding	6	3	0	3	486
Chocolate Pave	3	0	0	3	292
Coconut Frosting	3	0	0	3	200
Coconut Pudding No. 2	6	3	0	3	488
Cream of Asparagus and Chicken Soup	3	0	0	3	527
Cream Pastry	3	0	0	3	439
Heaven's Bacon	6	3	0	3	217
Kisses	3	0	0	3	244
Little Apples No. 1	3	0	0	3	246
Manioc Pastry	3	0	0	3	435
Mock Chicken Legs	3	0	0	3	461

Mother Benta	3	0	0	3	219
Multicolored Pudding	3	0	0	3	555
Oyster Croquettes	3	0	0	3	352
Palm Heart Soup	3	0	0	3	529
Rich Pastry	3	0	0	3	436
Shrimp Pudding	3	0	0	3	361
Stewed Fish	3	0	0	3	334
Brazilians	4	0	0	4	267
Brigadiers No. 3	4	0	0	4	239
Orange Pudding	12	8	0	4	483
Palm Hearts	4	0	0	4	556
Peanuts Candies	4	0	0	4	253
Pernambuco Bom Bocados	4	0	0	4	213
Shrimp Pie	4	0	0	4	432
Siracaia No. 1	4	0	0	4	310
Tangerine Pudding	6	2	0	4	495
Apricot Delight	5	0	0	5	237
Burned Eggs	7	2	0	5	295
Chicken Patties	5	0	0	5	428
Little Hams	5	0	0	5	248
Mother-in-Law's Eyes	5	0	0	5	250
Brazilian Pudding	6	0	0	6	485
Cassava Pudding	12	6	0	6	485
Coconut Kisses	6	0	0	6	244
Sighs	6	0	0	6	270
Siracaia No. 2	6	0	0	6	311
Maiden's Delight	7	0	0	7	301
Angel's Double Chin	9	1	0	8	290
Coconut Pudding No. 4	8	0	0	8	489
Velvet Pudding	12	3	0	9	493
Coconut Pudding No.1	12	0	0	12	487
Quindins de Yayá	16	3	0	13	220
Egg Threads	36	3	0	33	48
Chicken Soup	?	0	0	?	521

HARD-BOILED EGGS

Egg White Sandwich Filling	0	8	8	0	106
Stuffed Crabs	4	0	0	4	350

PORTUGUESE INDEX

ENGLISH INDEX

Temperatures

FAHRENHEIT	CENTIGRADE	BRITISH	FRENCH
		11	
500			
	250	10	
475		9	7
450	225	8	
425		7	6
400	200	6	
375		5	
350	175	4	5
325		3	
300	150	2	4
275		1	
	125		

WEIGHTS

OUNCES	GRAMS	POUNDS	KILOS
36	1000	2¼	1.0
34			
32	900	2	0.9
30			
28	800	1¾	0.8
26			
24	700	1½	0.7
22			
20	600	1¼	0.6
18	500		0.5
16		1	
14	400		0.4
12		¾	
10	300		0.3
8		½	
6	200		0.2
4	100	¼	0.1
2			

Este livro foi composto na tipologia Perpetua
em corpo 12/16 e impresso em papel
off-white 90g/m² no Sistema Cameron
da Divisão Gráfica da Distribuidora Record.